UTAH AND THE GREAT WAR

UTAH AND THE GREAT WAR

The Beehive State and the World War I Experience

EDITED BY ALLAN KENT POWELL

Utah State Historical Society

The University of Utah Press
Salt Lake City

Copublished with the Utah State Historical Society.

Affiliated with the Utah Division of State History,
Utah Department of Heritage & Arts.

The Defiance House Man colophon is a registered trademark of the
University of Utah Press. It is based on a four-foot-tall Ancient Puebloan
pictograph (late PIII) near Glen Canyon, Utah.

20 19 18 17 16   1 2 3 4 5

Library of Congress Cataloging-in-Publication Data

Name: Powell, Allan Kent, editor.
Title: Utah and the Great War : the Beehive State and the World War I experience/
    edited by Allan Kent Powell.
Description: Salt Lake City : Utah State Historical Society and The University of
    Utah Press, 2016. | Includes bibliographical references and index.
Identifiers: LCCN 2016014220| ISBN 9781607815105 (pbk. : alk. paper) | ISBN
    9781607815112 (ebook)
Subjects: LCSH: World War, 1914-1918—Utah.
Classification: LCC D570.85.U8 U83 2016 | DDC 940.3/792—dc23
LC record available at http://lccn.loc.gov/2016014220

Printed and bound by Edwards Brothers Malloy, Ann Arbor, Michigan.

CONTENTS

ILLUSTRATIONS

ACKNOWLEDGMENTS

The authors of the seventeen articles that appear in this book deserve recognition and thanks for their years of research and commitment to writing about one of the most significant events in world history. The one hundredth anniversary of the United States' involvement in the Great War calls for a consideration of Utah's role in the conflict and an examination of how the world-changing event played out in the Beehive State. This collection of articles, hopefully, conveys the complexity, enthusiasm, patriotism, and sacrifices of an earlier generation.

All but one of the articles were first published in the *Utah Historical Quarterly* between 1978 and 2016, and as such represent nearly four decades of scholarship on Utah and World War I. It is appropriate that the volume appears as a joint publication of the Utah State Historical Society, established in 1897, and the University of Utah Press, founded in 1949.

In looking forward to the centennial of World War I, Reba Rauch, acquisitions editor for the University of Utah Press, contacted me about compiling and editing the volume. She and other staff at the press—Glenda Cotter, director; John Alley, editor in chief; Stephanie Warnick, managing editor; Hannah New, marketing manager; Dianne Van Dien, marketing assistant; and Sharon Day, business manager—have encouraged and facilitated the book in countless ways.

Brad Westwood, director of the Utah State Historical Society since 2013, has been an enthusiastic supporter of the book and has encouraged his staff to assist in every way possible. A special thanks to the dedicated staff: Holly George and Jedediah Rogers, editors of the *Utah Historical Quarterly*; Kristen Jensen, digitization project manager, who secured digital copies of the articles; Debbie Dahl and Lisa Buchmiller, on whom I could call for help at any time; and library staff members Doug Misner, Greg Walz, Michele Elnicky, Melissa Coy, and Heidi Tak, who operate the Utah History Research Center with their coworkers from the State Archives, Alan Barnett, Heidi Stringham, and Tony Castro.

Robert McPherson, member of the State Board of History and contributor to this volume, offered encouragement and support. Matt Heiss, an intern from Weber State University, rendered invaluable assistance with identifying articles for inclusion in the book. Stanford Layton, managing editor of the *Utah Historical Quarterly* from 1973 to 2002, and associate editors Miriam Murphy and Craig Fuller solicited, reviewed, and pushed to publication most of the articles in this volume.

Robert Voyles, director of the Fort Douglas Museum, and Walter Jones, recently retired from University of Utah Special Collections, read the initial manuscript and offered both helpful criticism and encouragement for the project. Finally, my deep appreciation to my wife Brenda for her unwavering and enthusiastic support.

INTRODUCTION

ALLEN KENT POWELL

As the Austrian archduke Franz Ferdinand and his wife Sophie, the duchess of Hohenberg, motored through the streets of the Bosnian city of Sarajevo on June 28, 1914, assassins waited to end their lives and set in motion a chain of events that would result in the deaths of more than ten million soldiers on the battlefields of Europe in what became known as the Great War, or World War I. In Utah, few took notice of the events in the obscure Balkan region of far away Europe and the circumstances that led to the assassination of the archduke and his wife. The front page headlines of the *Salt Lake Tribune* that fateful Sunday were devoted to such mundane topics as an appropriation to increase the number of tax collectors; a scandal over the dishonesty of members of the United States Senate Foreign Relations Committee; miners rioting in Butte, Montana; the poor health of former president Theodore Roosevelt; political affairs in Mexico; and an account and photo of Mrs. Charles H. Anthony and her trip from Muncie, Indiana, to dazzle Europe with fifteen trunks full of clothing and jewelry.

The next day, June 29, 1914, the news from Sarajevo took center stage in Utah's daily newspapers. Headlines from the *Ogden Standard* reported that condolences were pouring into the Austrian-Hungarian capitol of Vienna from all over the world, that martial law had been proclaimed in Bosnia, that bombs intended for the archduke had been planted along the railroad outside of Sarajevo, that well paid assassins and Serbian students had been arrested in the plot, and that these students had been aroused to action by the hate fomented by Serbian newspapers.

Six weeks later, when German troops crossed the border of neutral Belgium enroute to Paris, Utahns were still unsure as to what war more than five thousand miles away would mean for them. Headlines from the *Salt Lake Tribune* for the eight days following the assassination give a snapshot of the road to war: July 29, "Austria Declares War on Servia"; July 30, "All Europe is Mobilizing"; July 31, "Austria and Russia at War"; August 1, "Last Effort for Peace"; August 2, "Germany seizes Luxemburg, Kaiser Declares War on Russia, France Mobilizes"; August 3, "Great Armies Are Battling, France Ready This Time for Her Old Enemy"; August 4, "England For War, Germans Invade Holland, Great Britain to Keep Faith with Belgium"; and August 5, "War is Declared By England and Germany."

In subsequent months, the flood of newspaper accounts about the war deluged Utahns, who found it nearly impossible to follow the action in dozens of locations around the world: the western front in Belgium and France; the eastern front in Russia; the Balkans; the Austrian/Italian Alps; the Gallipoli campaign in Turkey and the Middle East; Africa; Asia; as well as the naval battles spread across the Atlantic, Pacific, Mediterranean, and North and Baltic Seas.

Utahns faced a number of war-related questions and issues: reports of German atrocities against the Belgian civilians; America's declaration of neutrality while providing loans and arms to England and France; and the German use of the submarine as a weapon of war, which led to the loss of 1,198 lives—including 128 Americans—when the British *Lusitania* went down off the southern coast of Ireland on May 7, 1915.

In the 1916 election, Utah voters chose the Democratic incumbent, Woodrow Wilson, as president, in large measure because of Wilson's appealing campaign slogan, "He kept us out of war." But only weeks after Wilson's reelection, war crept closer as German naval and military leaders persuaded the German Kaiser to resume unrestricted submarine warfare, which had halted after the 1915 *Lusitania* incident nearly brought the United States to a declaration of war against Germany. By early 1917, German leaders reasoned that the resumption of unrestricted submarine warfare could tip the scales toward a German victory before the United States could recruit, train, and transport across the Atlantic a force of sufficient size to engage the German army. On the diplomatic front, at the same time as Germany resumed unrestricted submarine warfare, word surfaced of a clandestine German initiative, known as the Zimmermann note, to secure Mexico's support against the United States. The Germans promised that the land comprising Texas, New Mexico, and Arizona—lost by Mexico to the United States in 1848—would be returned to Mexico after Germany's victory.

When the United States entered the Great War on April 6, 1917, Utah was still a young state, having gained statehood twenty-one years earlier and only after a half-century struggle. In 1917, what historians have called the Americanization of Utah was in full swing, as Utahns entered the mainstream of political, economic, and social life in the nation. Utah had sent its sons off in 1898 to fight in the Spanish-American War, and in the summer of 1916 Utah national guardsmen joined with those from other states along the U.S.-Mexican border. In 1916, Utah elected its first non-Mormon governor, Simon Bamberger, a German Jew, popular politician, and successful businessman. A year earlier, the state had executed the popular labor radical and IWW (Industrial Workers of the World) songwriter Joe Hill, reaping the wrath of many who saw the class conflict between labor and capital as the looming world struggle set to be ignited with the abdication and execution of Russian Tsar Nicholas II and the success of the Bolshevik Revolution. Economically and demographically, the state was prospering as mining, smelting, and the railroads brought a wave of immigrants from Italy, Greece, the Balkans, and other parts of Europe to Bingham Canyon, Murray, Midvale, Tooele, and the coal mines of Carbon County. German converts to the Church of Jesus Christ of Latter-day Saints had emigrated from their homeland and constituted a small but visible community within the state. Agriculture expanded with the wartime demand for food, especially as sugar beets and the accompanying sugar production became even more important elements in the Utah economy. The University of Utah gained regional, if not national, recognition as an important institution of higher education. Brigham Young Academy stood on the threshold of becoming a university. The Utah State Agricultural College, later Utah State University, served the state's agricultural community and enriched the cultural and intellectual life of northern Utah. In southern Utah, the Branch Agricultural College in Cedar City, later Southern Utah University, played a similar role in the educational and cultural life of the southern part of the state.

The selections that follow outline the war experience from a number of perspectives: the volunteer national guardsman recently returned from patrol duty along the U.S.-Mexico border; the drafted doughboy going over the top in the Meuse-Argonne offensive; women nurses and ambulance drivers who saw close up the terror of war; mothers and family members proud of their sons and brothers, yet fearful of the physical and moral dangers of war; German Americans whose loyalty to the fatherland clashed with their appreciation and love of their new homeland; opponents of the war who were incarcerated and forced to resign from prestigious positions for their beliefs and actions; citizens throughout the state who supported the war in a variety of ways—service on councils of defense, the purchase of liberty bonds, the growing of victory gardens, adhering to the call for meatless and wheatless days, etc.; politicians who addressed the long-term implications of the war; patriotic zealots who had no use for anything German, including language, books, music, food; the victims of a war-induced flu epidemic; proponents and opponents engaged in a bitter struggle over the question of U.S. participation in the League of Nations; and women who worked to establish a lasting legacy for their sons with the construction of Memory Grove, a peaceful and hallowed park along the historic City Creek on the east side of the newly completed Utah State Capitol.

On the eve of the centennial anniversary of the United States' entry into the Great War, these articles help us understand the nature and complexity of the conflict and its impact on Utah and its people.

1

THE NATIONAL GUARD ON THE MEXICAN BORDER IN 1916

RICHARD C. ROBERTS

On June 18, 1916, less than ten months before the United States declared war on Germany, President Woodrow Wilson activated all National Guard units from the forty-eight states, including eight hundred Utah guardsmen, for duty along the border with Mexico. The organization, transportation, and duty in southern Arizona proved to be, in the words of Utah historian Richard Roberts, "a preparatory and hardening period for the catastrophic fighting of World War I." While guardsmen kept watch along the border, regular army forces under the command of General Jack Pershing, soon to be named commander of the American Expeditionary Force in Europe, crossed into northern Mexico in a futile pursuit of Pancho Villa and his revolutionary forces who had carried out a deadly raid on the New Mexican border town of Columbus. Pershing and other regular army officers were appalled at the poorly equipped, ill-trained, and often poorly led and undermanned National Guard units, and instituted policies to strengthen their effectiveness. Utah guardsmen learned much during their nine-month tour of duty along the Mexican border. Ever present in their minds was the possibility of being sent to the battlefields of France. That possibility became a reality when the U.S. National Guard units were activated after the declaration of war against Germany on April 6, 1917.

As Americans followed the war reports from Verdun and Ypres and pondered their possible role in the European conflict, civil unrest in Mexico and guerrilla raids into U.S. territory in 1916 added another dimension to the war talk. The Mexican situation led President Woodrow Wilson to mobilize the National Guard to defend the border.

This call-up of the guard, including some eight hundred Utah men, did not lead to war with Mexico but served as a sort of dress rehearsal—exposing American military strengths and weaknesses—prior to the United States' entrance into World War I in 1917. A detailed look at the Utah National Guard experience on the Mexican border will help illuminate events of national and international consequence. To set the stage for the drama of 1916, a brief summary of events leading up to the border crisis will be helpful.[1]

The U.S.-Mexico border—more than eighteen hundred miles in length—had had a history of cattle raids, smuggling, Indian forays, and filibustering expeditions since the treaty of Guadalupe Hidalgo in 1848. But under President Porfirio Diaz the two countries were linked by railroads, American capital flowed south, and border troubles decreased. The Mexican Revolution of 1910 and Diaz's fall from power ushered in one of the stormiest periods in American-Mexican relations.

The short-lived presidency of Francisco I. Madero followed by Gen. Victoriano Huerta's seizure of power in February 1913 triggered internal discord and problems with the United States. President Wilson refused to recognize the Huerta government and revolutionaries led by Venustiano Carranza, Francisco ("Pancho") Villa, and Emiliano Zapata opposed Huerta from within. The Tampico incident of 1914 (in which the United States believed the flag was insulted), and the subsequent takeover of the port of Vera Cruz by American forces to cut off arms shipments to Huerta, precipitated his fall in July 1914. After a bloody struggle with his fellow revolutionaries, Carranza assumed the leadership of Mexico. The United States gave de facto recognition to the Carranza government, and the new leader gained support at home. However, Pancho Villa and others continued to oppose Carranza. Villa's fighting in northern Mexico and into U.S. territory led directly to the mobilization of the National Guard.

On January 10, 1916, a party of American mine officials and technicians returning to Mexico by train to reopen the mines at Santa Ysabel (near Chihuahua) were massacred and their Mexican assistants robbed by Villistas. Carranza promised to punish the insurgents, but the government's troops were spread thin guarding major cities and fighting both Zapatistas in the south and Yaqui Indians. Rumors of Villa's whereabouts and plans were rife.

Then, on March 9, Villa forces raided Columbus, New Mexico, killing eight soldiers and nine civilians. Almost immediately Brig. Gen. John J. Pershing was ordered to lead the punitive expedition into Mexico to capture or destroy the Villista bands. The presence of American soldiers in Mexico strained diplomatic relations between the two countries. Generals Hugh L. Scott and Frederick Funston, fearful of having to engage both Carranza's army and Villa's bands, recommended an immediate call of the National Guard of Texas, New Mexico, and Arizona following the May 5 Villista raids at Glen Springs, Texas, and nearby Boquillas, Mexico. The five thousand guardsmen from the border states were deemed inadequate to defend the long international boundary in the event of a full-scale war with Mexico. Therefore, on June 18, 1916, President Wilson called the entire National Guard into federal service.[2]

Utah received the mobilization call on June 18. By the following day all units within the state had been notified to report to their armories to prepare for entering federal service. The *Deseret News* reported that on the morning of June 19 Salt Lake City took on a martial air as militiamen dressed in "olive drab" with red or yellow cord trimming, indicating their artillery or cavalry affiliation, scurried about the city on their way to the Pierpont Avenue armory.[3] Other areas of Utah with units went through the same process as guardsmen rallied to the call. At the Ogden armory "almost every member of the troops was in high spirits and greatly pleased over the possible opportunity to see some real army service." Most militiamen were available, but the units of Ephraim, Manti, and Mount Pleasant had some men out of state on work assignments. A few men responded to the call from great distances. For example, Lt. A. R. Thomas of the 1st Battery telegraphed from California that he was giving up his business interests to return to his Utah unit; and Lt. F. A. Smith of Troop B in Ogden notified his commander that he was returning from Gary, Indiana, to take up his position in the troop. Two enlisted men, James H. Wolfe and Horace Hudson, returned from Pennsylvania to rejoin their units. Patriotism and morale were high as preparation for Mexican border service got underway.[4]

At the armories activity was intense: field equipment was issued, recruits were processed, physical examinations were given, and special gear was made ready for use. On the first day of duty the National Guard assigned special details to prepare Fort Douglas as a mobilization camp for the activated soldiers. The state opened a recruiting office at the David Keith Building on Main Street to bring the units to full complement. The battery moved its artillery weapons from the basement of the Capitol, where they had been stored for safekeeping at the insistance of the federal government, taking them to the fairgrounds to train the new recruits in the fundamentals of artillery duty and sharpen the efficiency of the veterans. Troops A and C of Salt Lake City drilled at the Pierpont Avenue armory for a few days before moving to Fort Douglas.[5]

While the National Guard prepared for the move to the border, men of the famous Black 10th Cavalry engaged Carranza forces at Carrizal, Mexico. A dozen officers and men lost their lives in the ill-advised encounter. Although the Mexicans suffered heavier losses, the battle was considered a tactical defeat for the Americans.[6] The United States demanded the immediate release of prisoners taken by the Mexicans, and the U.S. Department of War issued an order that all guard units should proceed to the border as soon as they could be mustered and that states should not delay troop movement with red tape or the preliminaries of mobilization. The situation appeared grave.

Many states responded to the War Department's imperative by sending to the border units that had not been mustered, equipped, or given physical examinations. These poorly prepared units were later subject to severe criticism from regular army officers. However, the Utah troops, under the command of Adj. Gen. Edgar A. Wedgwood, were held at Fort Douglas until they were fully uniformed, equipped (except for horses to be supplied at the border), examined, and mustered into federal service. Although the men were impatient to begin their border assignment, they avoided the problems and criticism other National Guard units faced by arriving at Nogales, Arizona, better prepared, and sooner, than most.

The call-up of June 18 had ordered Utah to provide one battery of field artillery and one squadron and two troops of cavalry. Following the fight at Carrizal, the War Department asked for one battery of field artillery, two squadrons of cavalry, and one field hospital unit, a total of about eight hundred men. As new men were recruited and units moved to the mobilization station at Fort Douglas, the main delay came in working out the muster roll and issuing the federal equipment. It took some time to prepare the exact information on each soldier, and state equipment could not be exchanged for federal equipment until the guardsmen were federalized. While the processing went on, the commanders devised training for the cavalrymen in tactics, map work, outpost duty, range firing with pistols and rifles, patrol duty, reconnaissance, and sanitation. The artillerymen drilled in formation, practiced with small arms, and maneuvered field pieces.[7]

The first unit ready for border service was Battery A, 1st Utah Field Artillery, commanded by Capt. William C. Webb. On June 26—just eight days after the president's call—the 142 enlisted men and 5 officers of the battery stood at Fort Douglas "with heads bared beneath Old Glory" while regular army officer Capt. W. B. Wallace "administered the oath of fealty and allegiance to the armed service of the United States." Reporting on the solemn occasion, the *Salt Lake Tribune* noted, "not a man was found wanting, not an article of equipment was found unfit." The battery was ready to do its duty in "defense of the flag." The next day the adjutant general ordered the battery to depart for the border, and the men entrained in the early hours of June 28.[8]

Colorful ceremonies attended the departure of Battery A. Thousands cheered as the artillerymen paraded to the depot, accompanied by John Held's Band, a high school band, local dignitaries, members of Elks Lodge, and veterans of the Grand Army of the Republic (GAR). In the square facing Harriman Station (Union Pacific Depot), the troops stood in ranks in front of a platform where speakers gave them words of encouragement. Salt Lake City mayor W. Mont Ferry urged the men to "uphold the reputation of this state" and return "crowned with honor." Gov. William Spry said the men, in answering the president's call, would "not only fulfill the traditions of the men who have gone forth before from this nation and state, but the traditions which have been made by that battery which preceded you into the rice fields of the Philippines." GAR leader N. D. Corser expressed gratitude that there were "some Americans left who are not too proud to fight." Captain Webb responded to these sentiments by stating the "Utah Battery will live up to all asked of it by the governor and mayor." With the ceremonies concluded, Battery A boarded the trains and departed for the Mexican border.[9]

The remaining Utah units left the state with little fanfare—the War Department had advised that troop movements and destinations be kept secret. On July 3, at an evening retreat, the 1st Squadron of the Utah cavalry—composed of Troops A, B, C, and D and led by Maj. W. G. Williams—formed on the Fort Douglas parade grounds and passed in review before Governor Spry and his staff and Lt. Eugene Santschi, U.S. Army mustering officer. Following a roll call of the 15 officers and 276 men of the squadron, the oath was administered and the muster rolls were signed, completing the federalizing process. The next day state equipment was exchanged for federal equipment, and in the predawn hours of July 7 the men moved quietly to Harriman Station to board a Southern Pacific train. Some of the soldiers sang songs like "Yankee Doodle" and "The Girl I Left Behind Me." When the bugles sounded departure time, families and friends made their tearful goodbyes. The 2nd Squadron of cavalry, commanded by Maj. W. B. Wallace, and the field hospital unit, under Maj. John F.

Sharp, left for the border on July 14. All that remained at Fort Douglas was Provisional Troop 1 consisting of twenty-four men under Capt. Thomas Braby, who hoped to organize a third cavalry squadron for border service, but this hope was never realized.[10]

Utah's response to the federal levy for men to defend the border was no less than enthusiastic. Additional men to fill out units were easily recruited, and veteran guardsmen made no effort to obtain discharges as they had a right to do.[11] Considering that the Utah National Guard was in the process of changing its infantry units over to cavalry when the mobilization order came and that an entirely new unit—a field hospital—was required, the dispatch with which the troops were mustered, equipped, and sent to Nogales was remarkable.

Local officials generally supported the call for troops. Governor Spry stated that enlistment was a personal matter and that the right of citizenship carried an "obligation of service." He called upon mayors to assist in the recruiting campaign. Important efforts in recruiting were carried out in Salt Lake City, Logan, Brigham City, Provo, and other cities where National Guard units were located. Mayor James E. Daniels of Provo was especially active in leading rallies for enlistment, and recruiting enthusiasm in Ephraim was demonstrated by several young women who marched as the Mountain Echo Band in the interest of enlistment for Troop C. In Salt Lake City the National Guard competed with the regular army for volunteers. Army recruiters distributed handbills that read, "Don't Let George Do It, Do It Yourself." A placard announced, "100,000 'Real Men' wanted for the United States Army at once. Come up and let us tell you about the Mexican trouble." The National Guard recruiter sent men out into the streets with a streamer that proclaimed, "200 men wanted at once for Mexican border duty. Good pay, clothing and board. Apply 242 South Main Street."[12]

The business community backed the National Guard by promising to keep the men's jobs open until they returned, and some even offered financial support to employees on military duty.[13] How many men this affected is not known, but the gesture was popular. Other businessmen, including George Auerbach, as well as the governor's staff raised $10,000 to support the men. They supplied three trucks, five motorcycles, and wire screening for the buildings on the border. Samuel Newhouse talked of donating a squad of armored vehicles to be used by the Utah troops, but nothing came of this offer. The Rotary Club gave $25,000 to help needy dependents of the military men, and the Salt Lake Baseball Club contributed baseball equipment to the servicemen. In addition to this private financial backing, the state paid $7,750.21 for the mustering of the troops, and the federal government paid an estimated half-million dollars for equipping and transporting the troops to the border. Adjutant General Wedgwood reported the Utah guardsmen were among the best supplied units there.[14]

All the Utah units were sent to Nogales, Arizona, where they were joined by National Guard troops from California, Connecticut, and Idaho. The Utah field artillery unit, which arrived at the border on June 29, 1916, claimed to be the first National Guard unit to arrive for border duty, although the official records give credit to the 1st Illinois Infantry Regiment that arrived on June 30.[15] The units were under the control of the regular army command in support of the 12th Infantry Regiment and the 11th Cavalry, which were stationed at the Nogales camp at different times. Eventually an estimated fifteen thousand men were camped at Nogales.

On arrival at Nogales the Utah field artillery positioned its camp a few hundred yards north on a hill overlooking the town with the artillery weapons emplaced to guard the border entrances from Mexico into Nogales. Batteries of the U.S. 6th Artillery were already camped there, but with the arrival of the Utah men all except Battery D moved to other areas along the border where they were needed. The Utah men soon cleared the knoll of rocks, prickly pear, and mesquite, and before long "the rows of tents, the parked artillery, and the picket lines of a modern military camp . . . supplanted the hot dry spot which had been the home of the reptile and tarantula since time immemorial." They designated this camp as Camp Stephen J. Little in honor of an American private who had been killed earlier by the Mexicans.[16]

The 1st Squadron of the Utah cavalry arrived at Nogales during a heavy desert rain to be greeted by a rousing cheer from the Utah battery, who helped them set up camp. Some critics thought it stupid to work in the rain, but to these soldiers it was evidence of their devotion to duty, esprit de corps, and feeling for their fellow Utahns. The commander of Nogales commended the Utah units for their attention to duty even under adverse weather conditions. The Utah cavalry camp was located four or five miles north of town, on the hillsides overlooking the Santa Cruz River, in order to protect the reservoir and water system of Nogales. The campsite surprised the cavalrymen, who had pictured the area as a barren waste. Instead, according to Corp. F. A. Timmerman of Troop A, they saw "mountains green with foliage and snow-capped on the highest points." From the hillside the men could see far south into Mexico, and the white posts marking the international border were clearly visible on the mountains and high hills to the east and in the valley to the west, "where the town of Nogales nestles." The 1st Squadron also had an excellent view of the other camps. Corporal Timmerman reported they could see a quarter-mile to the south "the tents of the California Guard, sheltering nearly 4,000 men" and "a half mile to the east . . . the Connecticut camp." Nearest to the border was the Utah battery. One visitor to the area, Rev. P. A. Simpkins of Utah, wrote that the camps were "splendidly" located with the cavalry and battery on the hilltops and the field hospital "in a fine and well-drained pocket back of the first range behind Nogales." The field hospital site was named Camp Lund, presumably after H. M. H. Lund, assistant adjutant general of Utah, who had been so cooperative and helpful in preparing the Utah units for the border.[17]

After the campsites had been cleared of rocks and brush, the men trenched around the tents to prevent flooding. More significant improvements included piping culinary and bath water to the camps and building screened mess halls, kitchens, and bathhouses. Reverend Simpkins noted the comfort and cleanliness of the camps, the good food, and the absence of "booze." So impressed was the congregational pastor that he could state, with little or no apparent irony, that there was not a "cooler or healthier summer resort in the country" than the Nogales camps. Capt. Wesley King, judge advocate of the Nogales district, echoed Simpkins's view of camp conditions, and the soldiers themselves seemed satisfied. Members of Troop H, 2nd Squadron, called theirs the "best camp on the border, ideal climate, beautiful, clean and interesting natural surroundings . . . comforts and conveniences that have only been made possible by great expenditures of money and a good deal of hard labor on the part of those who came first."[18]

The encampment of thousands of men from different parts of the country in the area surrounding the small town of Nogales caused few major problems for citizens or soldiers. The camps were well policed, according to Major Williams, and discipline was rigid. No arrests were made, and the few reprimands given were for minor infractions of camp rules. The men did not mix socially with the townspeople, although they did trade with local merchants and sometimes complained of the high prices they were charged. Busy with the routine of army life, the men made few other complaints except that the Arizona desert was the habitat of almost every kind of "lizard, centipede, tarantula, spiders, and creeping and crawling and flying bugs of every conceivable size, shape and color."[19]

The men quickly fell into the routine of drills, camp duties, border patrol, maneuvers, and long hikes. Occasional skirmishes kept the men alert and underscored the explosive potential of the situation. The artillery spent most of its time in position overlooking Nogales and the border. On one or two occasions there were exchanges of gunfire that made duty rather tense. After receiving horses and training with them, Captain Webb's battery made a practice march in August from Nogales to Tucson to Fort Huachuca, a distance of 150 miles, under full warfare preparations. In October the battery was invited to demonstrate artillery maneuvers at the Arizona State Fair in Tucson. The second march to Tucson was used as another training exercise. Participation in the fair brought favorable comment from the Arizona public and regular army personnel.[20]

Without horses during their first days of duty, the Utah cavalrymen were assigned to outpost duty along the international line and guard duty for strategic points in Nogales such as the water reservoir, railroad warehouses, ammunition depots, the ice plant, and other facilities essential to the community. After the men received their horses, the Utah cavalry was given a section of the border to patrol. This section, between 100 and 150 miles in length, extended both east and west from Nogales. About every 15 miles an outpost was established where a full-time guard was maintained. Cavalrymen patrolled the areas between outposts.

One important outpost was established at Buena Vista ranch, ten miles east of Nogales. There the Santa Cruz River crossed into Mexico, and through the river pass raiders had driven cattle from the United States into Mexico. The pass was also considered a likely point of entry for marauders. Another significant outpost lay thirty miles west at Arivaca, Arizona. In this vicinity were several ranches, near which troopers of the 2nd Squadron on border patrol had a skirmish with Mexican bandits. Among the cavalrymen this battle came to be known as the Battle of the Cow or, more correctly, the Battle of Casa Piedra, in reference to a stone ranch house along the international boundary.

The battle began on January 26, 1917, when a patrol of five cavalrymen from Troop E came upon approximately twenty-six Mexicans rustling cattle across the border near Ruby, ten miles east of Arivaca. As the patrol approached, the Mexicans took cover in and around the stone house and began firing at the Americans. Three troopers held them off while the other two went for reinforcements. Lt. William C. Stark returned with a part of Troop E from the nearby outpost, and gunfire continued through the night. The Mexicans remained in or near the house and the Americans took cover behind the surrounding rocks. The next day, Lt. Carl H. Arns arrived with the rest of Troop E from Arivaca, and after forty-eight hours of fighting Capt. Freeman Bassett brought more reinforcements from Nogales. By then the Mexicans had disappeared.

Major Wallace, commander of the 2nd Squadron, felt both men and horses had performed well under fire: "Now hostile fire is hostile fire and it doesn't much matter whether the shells are large or small. If they are coming at you good and fast, you are going to feel like ducking a few times and once in a while you are going to feel like getting out." The Utahns had stayed and fought. Major Wallace estimated that the Mexicans had fired "about 5,000 rounds of ball cartridges of various caliber and E Troop fired about 600 rounds." Mexican casualties were reported as three killed and seven wounded. The Americans had no losses.[21]

Another, less serious, incident occurred at the Nogales camp one August night when a sentry from Troop A noticed the horses moving away from the picket lines. On further investigation he discovered the horses were being led away by "Mexicans crawling along the road on their hands and knees." Troop A was called out to chase the thieves, but they escaped into the surrounding hills. The next night an attempt was made to stampede the horses by throwing rocks into the picket lines. A strengthening of the guard put an end to this kind of activity.[22]

On October 5 a provisional cavalry regiment made up of the two Utah squadrons and one squadron from California (an unhappy situation for the Californians, who did not like the resulting tendency to refer to the regiment as the Utah cavalry or, occasionally, as the "Mormon Rough Riders") made a training march of 250 miles from Nogales to Tucson to Fort Huachuca and back to Nogales. The 20-day maneuver took them through rough terrain covered with mesquite, chapparal, and cactus, and exposed them to every variety of Arizona weather. Each man carried a blanket roll, a shelter half, and extra clothing for rain or cold weather. For his horse he carried extra shoes, a curry comb and brush, and a feedbag with the day's grain ration. The regiment returned to Nogales hardened, tanned, and ready for action in the field if needed.[23]

The Utah field hospital unit experienced duty and training similar to the artillery and cavalry units. Their actual workload was light, since there were few battle casualties, but they did care for the sick and treat accident victims. They also maintained a useful watch on sanitary conditions in the camps. The field hospital made one training march to Sonora, Arizona, under simulated warfare conditions and ended up taking care of the patient overload from the newly constructed regular army base hospital at Nogales.[24]

The only other engagements of Utah troops came from unofficial encounters between the soldiers and civilian Mexicans in Nogales. Although the troops were reported as generally well behaved and the people of Nogales accepting of their presence, there was bound to be friction on occasion. The *Salt Lake Herald* reported that some soldiers returning from the border talked of street fights:

> Six of our company went out one evening not looking for a fight either, but we came upon about twenty-five natives. We had left our guns and ammunitions at camp, and not withstanding the fact the Mexicans were far greater in number we licked them with ease. One after another they went down with lefts to the jaw, and when they sneaked off, they were a sorry looking bunch.

The soldier continued:

> On another occasion we encountered a bunch of them [Mexicans] looking for trouble, and they got it. They were well armed with knives, and of the four or five men of our party only one had a revolver. To cut a long story short, we took the knives away from the "greasers" and we are now showing them as trophies.[25]

The men concluded from these encounters that the Mexicans were not very good fighters and could be defeated in almost any situation— braggadocio rather typical of young men testing their brawn.

Even as the National Guard units were rushed to the border in the summer of 1916, diplomatic measures were easing tensions between the United States and Mexico. On July 4, following the disastrous fight at Carrizal, President Carranza suggested mediation or direct negotiation between the two countries. Conferences were held at New London, Connecticut, during the ensuing months, and President Wilson ordered Pershing's forces to withdraw from Mexico on January 30, 1917.

Portions of the National Guard were withdrawn from the border much sooner. The Utah 1st Squadron and the one detachment of sanitary troops were sent home from Nogales following their practice march to Tucson and back. They arrived in Salt Lake City on October 30 and were released from federal service on November 10, 1916. The returning troops paraded in the city with a burro and fawn they had brought from the border and were hailed as heroes at a special turkey dinner in Fort Douglas. Mayor W. Mont Ferry declared that the state had "sent the best we had" and that the squadron had lived up to all expectations. Warm praise was also forthcoming from Col. John M. Jenkins of the 11th Cavalry, who commanded the men during the long march. It was reported that he "declared that the Utah troops were the best volunteer outfit he had ever seen or had in his command." The 1st Squadron commander, Major Williams, lamented the lack of action but reported that the men were in better condition and had profited greatly from their training on the border.[26]

On December 16, 1916, the Utah battery returned from Nogales with thirty-two horses (which each troop and battery brought back to their states for continued use in training) and guns and caissons, parading to Hotel Utah where the mayor and other officials hosted a dinner. Maj. Richard W. Young, former commander of the battery, read a letter from Brig. Gen. E. H. Plummer, commander of the Nogales area, that said, in part, "inspectors and instructors detailed from time to time with your organizations have in every case reported the battery efficient, well trained and well disciplined, and I can recall no instances of misconduct of members of your organization." After a few days of caring for the equipment and processing the men, the battery was mustered out of federal service on December 22, 1916. Two days later the field hospital men returned to Salt Lake City and went directly to their homes to enjoy the Christmas holidays, reporting back to Fort Douglas for release on December 29, 1916.[27]

The last Utah unit to return from Nogales was the 2nd Squadron, which had continued to patrol the border after the others had left. In March 1917 they were relieved of their duties by the U.S. 10th Cavalry and returned to Fort Douglas, where they were mustered out of federal service on March 8, 1917.[28]

For the most part, official reports on the border service of the National Guard were not as complimentary as the comments cited above. Maj. Gen. Hugh Scott, army chief of staff, thought the voluntary military system had "proved itself a failure" and "should be relegated to the past." The yearly training period of the guard was too short to produce effective units. He considered six months to a year necessary to make a well-trained soldier. General Scott also criticized the National Guard for not being able to recruit and maintain units at minimum strength. With 10 percent of the men failing to report and 29 percent unable to pass the physical requirements, 43 percent of the units sent to the border were "raw recruits." The National Guard sent 151,006 officers and men to the border—97,000 under wartime strength. The general concluded that "it is cause for very sober consideration on the part of every citizen of the country when the fact is fully understood . . . that the units of the national guard and regular army have not been recruited up to war strength in the crisis we have just passed through."[29]

Others also registered negative comments. Brig. Gen. William A. Mann, chief of the Militia Bureau, gave credit to the "high level of intelligence, enthusiasm, eagerness to learn and willingness of the Guardsmen," but he felt the "low levels of training and general know-how" of the citizen-soldiers were not satisfactory. Jim Dan Hill and Clarence C. Clendenen reference other critical comments made by officials and reporters against the National Guard. The chaos of mobilization, low level of training, and lack of plans and equipment were frequent targets for criticism. The War Department and the army had their share of criticism as well. The War Department had not adequately planned for the mobilization of the guard, nor for its use on the border. Some regular army officers resented the National Guard's new position as the second line of national defense—as provided in the National Defense Act—and opposed the continental army plan.[30]

There were also those who defended the National Guard and its service. Secretary of War Newton C. Baker praised the security and protection the presence of the guard gave to American residents along the border, as well as the "spirit with which the militia has met this call, and with which they are performing an important and necessary service to their country."[31] Even the irascible General Mann called "the mobilization of the National Guard and its dispatch to the border . . . a great accomplishment. . . . Undoubtedly the immediate purpose of the call was attained. It may not be too much to say that the knowledge and experience from the mobilization are incidental advantages worth the cost."[32]

In the case of the Utah units, the evidence indicates their service was efficient and performed in good spirit. Several reasons might account for this. The National Guard at that time was a voluntary service. The men were motivated by their own desire to belong and were not initially forced into duty by the government. They also had a tradition of service from the Spanish-American War and previous in-state emergencies, with some officers continuing on through the Mexican border period. Public sentiment in Utah was favorable toward their performance of duty, and the rather monolithic religious society from which they came gave them a unity and esprit de corps that was conducive to functioning in a disciplined organization. The Utah troops also had the advantage of being westerners not too far removed from their familiar environment. Adjustment to the border country was likely easier for them than for easterners. With these considerations taken into account, it seems possible that the praise given the Utah units might not have been far exaggerated.

Duty on the Mexican border ended, but threats of war persisted. The 2nd Squadron of the Utah cavalry returned home and was mustered out on March 8, 1917, but the Utah National Guard anticipated recall to active duty. Less than a month later, on April 6, 1917, Congress declared war on Germany. Without question the border crisis of 1916 had given the National Guard experience and training that would be vital in the months ahead.

NOTES

Originally published in the *Utah Historical Quarterly* 46 (Summer 1978): 262–81.

1. Many books have been written on this period in U.S. and Mexican history and on the military. See, for example, Ronald Atkin, *Revolution! Mexico 1910–20* (New York: The John Day Company, 1970); Robert D. Gregg, *The Influence of Border Troubles on Relations between the United States and Mexico, 1876–1910* (1937; reprint ed., New York: Da Capo Press, 1970); Haldeen Braddy, *Cock of the Walk: The Legend of Pancho Villa* (Albuquerque: University of New Mexico Press, 1955); Clarence C. Clendenen, *Blood on the Border: The United States Army and the Mexican Irregulars* (New York: The Macmillan Company, 1969); Samuel Flagg Bemis, *A Diplomatic History of the United States* (New York: Holt, Rinehart, and Winston, 1955); Jim Dan Hill, *The Minute Man in Peace and War: A History of the National Guard* (Harrisburg, PA: Stackpole Publishing Company, 1964); Maurice Matloff, ed., *American Military History* (Washington, D.C.: Office of the Chief of Military History United States Army, 1969); Russell F. Weigley, *History of the United States Army* (New York: The Macmillan Company, 1967).

2. The president's action was quickly supported by Congress. On June 23 the House approved by a vote of 332 to 2, and on the following day the Senate approved the Militia Act of 1916, signed by Wilson on June 3. The resolution authorized the president to draft into U.S. military service (under Section III of the National Defense Act) any or all members of the National Guard or organized state or territorial militias and militia reserves during the emergency but not to exceed three years. Another section of the resolution appropriated $1 million to support dependents of the guardsmen on active duty, up to $50 per month for families with no other source of income. This resolution placed the National Guard under direct federal control to be ordered wherever needed, including outside the United

States, without requiring another oath as a volunteer for overseas duty, as had been necessary during the Spanish-American War.

3. The Utah National Guard Armory was located then at 120–140 Pierpont Avenue in Salt Lake City. The building, designed by architect Carl M. Neuhausen, was recently accepted for listing on the National Register of Historic Places. Built for the Oregon Shortline Railroad, the structure housed at various times the Salt Lake High School, the National Guard, and several businesses.

4. *Deseret News*, June 19, June 20, 1916; *Salt Lake Tribune*, June 20, June 21, 1916.

5. See Richard C. Roberts, "History of the Utah National Guard, 1894–1954," PhD diss., University of Utah, 1973, 117.

6. Clendenen, *Blood on the Border*, 303–10. Of interest here is the fact that Pershing used Mormons from the exile colonies in northern Mexico as guides. One of these, Lemuel Spilsbury, was with the troops at Carrizal and advised against taking the cavalry through the town. Lt. Henry Rodney Adair believed, according to Spilsbury, that the Mexicans would flee at the cavalry approach. "'Well, you're just mistaken about that,' Spilsbury interjected. 'I know Mexicans that are just as brave as any Americans I have ever heard about, and they are not afraid to die.'" See Karl E. Young, *Ordeal in Mexico: Tales of Danger and Hardship Collected from Mormon Colonists* (Salt Lake City: Deseret Book Company, 1968), 222, and chap. 22.

7. For a detailed look at the state of the Utah National Guard immediately before the call and during the mobilization, see Roberts, "Utah National Guard," 115, 117–18; and "Report of the Adjutant General, 1915–1916," in State of Utah, Public Documents, 1915–16 (Salt Lake City, 1917), 5–6, 13.

8. *Salt Lake Tribune*, June 27, 1916. See also *Deseret News*, June 26, 1916.

9. *Salt Lake Herald*, June 28, 1916; *Salt Lake Tribune*, June 28, 1916.

10. *Salt Lake Herald*, July 4, July 8, July 10, July 11, July 12, July 14, 1916; *Salt Lake Tribune*, July 4, July 11, July 13, July 14, 1916; *Deseret News*, July 4, 1916; "Report of the Adjutant General, 1915–1916," 14.

11. *Salt Lake Herald*, July 7, July 8, July 9, 1916. The War Department ruled that guardsmen who had dependents with insufficient income could apply for release. Losses due to physical unfitness ran between 25 to 27 percent, mainly due to severe federal medical standards that eliminated men because of defective vision or because they exceeded maximum height and weight requirements for cavalrymen (5 feet 10 inches, 160 pounds). See *Deseret News*, June 20, December 16, 1916; *Salt Lake Tribune*, June 21, 1916.

12. *Deseret News*, June 22, 1916; *Salt Lake Tribune*, June 20, 1916.

13. Companies offering to keep jobs open included Union Pacific Railroad, Denver and Rio Grande Railroad, Utah Copper, Bingham-Garfield Railroad, and American Tobacco Company. Companies offering to pay full salaries or to make up the difference between a soldier's pay and his work salary included ZCMI, American Smelting and Refining, Utah Power and Light, American and National Express Company, and New York Life Insurance. See *Deseret News*, June 24, 1916; *Salt Lake Herald*, June 24, June 27, July 11, 1916; *Salt Lake Tribune*, June 1, July 13, 1916.

14. *Deseret News*, June 24, July 5, 1916; *Salt Lake Herald*, June 24, July 6, July 8, July 14, 1916; *Salt Lake Tribune*, July 7, July 8, July 14, 1916.

15. *Deseret News*, July 8, December 16, 1916; *Salt Lake Herald*, July 7, 1916; *Salt Lake Tribune*, December 18, 1916; Clendenen, *Blood on the Border*, 290.

16. *Deseret News*, July 8, October 30, 1916; *Salt Lake Tribune*, July 11, July 15, December 8, 1916.

17. *Deseret News*, December 16, 1916; *Salt Lake Tribune*, July 15, 1916; *Salt Lake Herald*, August 21, 1916.

18. *Salt Lake Tribune*, September 10, 1916.

19. *Salt Lake Tribune*, September 10, 1916; *Salt Lake Herald*, July 15, August 21, October 31, 1916; *Deseret News*, October 31, December 16, 1916; and interview with David A. Scott, former sergeant in Troop B, March 18, 1970, Ogden, Utah.

20. *Salt Lake Herald*, July 4, August 21, 1916; *Deseret News*, October 30, December 16, 1916.

21. *Deseret News*, March 5, 1917.

22. *Deseret News*, August 29, 1916.

23. *Deseret News*, October 30, 1916; *Salt Lake Tribune*, October 31, 1916; *Salt Lake Herald*, October 1, 1916; Scott, interview; interviews with Albert E. Wilfong, former lieutenant in Troop F, March 16 and April 5, 1970, Ogden, Utah.

24. *Deseret News*, December 16, 1916; *Salt Lake Tribune*, December 23, December 25, 1916.

25. *Salt Lake Herald*, October 31, 1916.

26. "Report of the Adjutant General, 1915–1916," 14; *Deseret News*, October 31, 1916; *Salt Lake Tribune*, October 31, 1916; *Salt Lake Herald*, October 31, 1916.

27. *Salt Lake Tribune*, December 17, December 23, December 25, 1916.

28. "Report of the Adjutant General, 1917–1918," in State of Utah, Public Documents, 1917–18 (Salt Lake City, 1919), 4; Wilfong, interview.

29. *Salt Lake Tribune*, December 8, 1916.
30. "Dry Run for Destiny," *The National Guardsman*, June 1966, 5; Hill, *Minute Man in Peace*, 207–43; Clendenen, *Blood on the Border*, 285–98.
31. *Deseret News*, August 22, 1916.
32. "Dry Run for Destiny," 9.

2

THE UTAH NATIONAL GUARD IN THE GREAT WAR, 1917–18

RICHARD C. ROBERTS

Drawing from his impressive study of the Utah National Guard from its nineteenth-century beginnings as the Nauvoo Legion and the Territorial Militia until the beginning of the twenty-first century, Richard Roberts provides a valuable overview of the Utah National Guard during World War I. He reminds us that the guard was made up of volunteers who took great pride in their contributions to the war effort. Building on a tradition of service in the Spanish-American War, in the Philippine insurrection, and on the Mexican border, a substantial recruiting campaign was launched in Utah to encourage its citizens to join the National Guard. Guardsmen served at home and abroad in Europe until the last were mustered out of active service in July 1919. State National Guards comprised one of three groups of soldiers who served during the war. The two other groups included the regular army, whose men were in active service before the declaration of war, and the National Army, comprised of volunteers and draftees who entered military service because of the war declaration.

Their duty on the Mexican border ended, the 2nd Squadron of the Utah cavalry returned home and was mustered out on March 8, 1917.

With the United States slowly becoming more involved in the Great War in Europe, however, the Utah National Guard (UNG) anticipated a new call to active duty. The guard's border experience appeared in retrospect to have been a preparatory and hardening period for the catastrophic fighting of World War I.[1]

Although Congress did not declare war until April 6, 1917, preparations for war moved steadily forward. At the suggestion of the federal government, Gov. Simon Bamberger issued a proclamation on March 24 calling for volunteers to enlist in the National Guard and thereby "discharge one of the obligations of citizenship." Recruiters hoped to enlist between five hundred and seven hundred men in the guard immediately to expand existing cavalry and artillery units to war strength and provide one more squadron of cavalry, a machine gun platoon, and a headquarters company—making a regiment of cavalry for Utah. In addition, a field hospital and sanitary troops were part of Utah's quota.[2]

Recruiting offices were opened in Salt Lake City on Main Street, at the Pierpont Avenue armory, and at the State Capitol; the armories in Logan, Ogden, Provo, Mount Pleasant, Ephraim, and Manti also served as enlistment stations. All postmasters, local officials, and religious leaders were asked to encourage enlistment in their areas.

Recruiting went slowly for a period, apparently because many men thought the National Guard would get border patrol duty or be designated as unmounted cavalry. Potential enlistees hoped instead to get into regular front-line fighting. Rumors that the Utah cavalry would be converted into artillery units gave some men a wait-and-see attitude.[3]

Renewed campaigning for recruits increased the ranks. The recruiting committee of the State Council of Defense, headed by Carl A. Badger, staged review parades in which the UNG, officials, and patriotic groups marched. A parade on May 5 included Governor Bamberger. Before a crowd of five thousand in front of the Salt Lake Tribune building on Main Street, Maj. B. H. Roberts, chaplain of the UNG, appealed to citizens to enlist. On Memorial Day the guard, state officials, troops from Fort Douglas, recruits, and Elks

Lodge members marched down crowd-lined Main Street. In the days immediately following the Memorial Day parade Rev. P. A. Simpkins; J. A. Reeves, chairman of the Training Camp Association of Utah; N. D. Corser, commander of the Grand Army of the Republic (GAR); and B. H. Roberts and other officers of the guard carried out a heavy speaking campaign throughout the state. Later, the artillery battery staged gunnery and maneuvering demonstrations at Liberty Park and West High School to draw crowds and encourage enlistments. These efforts produced results, and it was not necessary to resort to a draft as provided under Utah conscription law.[4]

On June 6, 1917, the state received orders from the War Department to reorganize the Utah forces into a regiment of light artillery. In compliance, the 1st Utah Field Artillery was organized. The new regiment consisted of six batteries with four 3-inch artillery pieces each, one headquarters company, one supply company, and a regimental headquarters.

Most of the personnel in the cavalry units converted over to the artillery and made up the major portion of the new regiment, but it was still necessary to recruit men in the areas of the home stations because the artillery batteries were larger than the cavalry units. The question of who would command the regiment was resolved when Governor Bamberger called Col. Richard W. Young, former commander of the Utah batteries during the Spanish-American War, to the post.[5]

With the change from cavalry to artillery the guard needed capable officers and NCOs (noncommissioned officers) to lead in the use of artillery weapons. Adj. Gen. W. G. Williams ordered all commissioned officers of the regiment and all NCOs of the former First Artillery Battery to assemble at the campsite west of the Jordan Narrows (present Camp Williams) for "intensive training in every duty that may be expected in an artillery regiment on active service against an enemy." In addition, all cooks, buglers, signal men, scouts, range finders, telephone and telegraph operators, horseshoers, and other enlisted specialists were ordered to attend.

During July 6–30 some 350 to 400 men encamped under Maj. E. LeRoy Bourne. Capt. William C. Webb, a veteran of the Spanish-American War and the Mexican border duty, served as senior instructor.[6] He planned and implemented a comprehensive training program that included instruction in all aspects of artillery use, from construction and concealment of gun pits to firing, as well as a range of subjects related to life on the battlefield.

Lt. Thomas Dewitt and his crew helped prepare the campsite by tapping a spring two miles up Beef Hollow, piping water to each company street in the camp and setting up water storage tanks. Grass and brush were removed from the company streets, tents were set up, screened kitchens were erected, long rows of white mess tables were constructed, and picket lines for 250 horses were built. The camp, even then, had some of the characteristics for which it has become famous, or infamous, over the years: rainstorms, windstorms, June grass fires, heat, dust, and mud.[7]

About two hundred troops arrived by railroad from the northern and southern areas, and some one hundred men from Salt Lake City brought four 3-inch guns, caissons, and a battery wagon pulled by horses along Redwood Road the twenty-one miles to camp.

After three weeks of strenuous training the men were tested for proficiency in the subjects studied. Following an inspection of the camp and a parade through Lehi on July 24, Col. John C. Waterman, 16th Army Division inspector-instructor assigned to Utah and Idaho, remarked that "these men have improved wonderfully during the encampment and their officers have every reason to be pleased with their showing. From these the Utah artillery has an excellent nucleus from which to build an efficient artillery regiment." On "Governor's Day," July 26, Bamberger made a final inspection of the men and witnessed their ability to maneuver the artillery wagons and horses.

During the final days of the camp the men were paid, and Adjutant General Williams issued mobilization orders stating that "under the proclamation of the president, the National Guard of Utah is drafted into federal service" and directing the men "to report to the armories of their units at 10:00 a.m. Sunday, August 5, 1917, to await orders from the department commander regarding their movement to a training site," presumably Camp Kearny at Linda Vista, California.[8]

On August 5 all units appeared at their armories with 100 percent attendance. The muster roll call was made as outlined by the National Defense Act of 1916, and the UNG members became regular army members in compliance with President Woodrow Wilson's proclamation, issued a few weeks earlier.[9]

Training continued at the local armories until August 14 when the men moved to the southwest section of Fort Douglas, where they began a mobilization encampment expected to last two or three weeks before moving to the California training camp—but, as is typical with the army, the wait became longer. Meanwhile the soldiers engaged in physical conditioning and artillery training in conjunction with the 42nd, 20th, and 43rd Infantry regiments stationed at Fort Douglas. During this time the final appointment and approval of officers were made and the regimental colors and guidons were presented by former senator Thomas Kearns and the Cleofan Society.[10]

On October 10, the day of departure for California, the Utah regiment broke camp and marched on foot through Fort Douglas "amid cheers of 500 infantrymen of the regular army who turned out and lined the roads through the reservation in honor of the departing regiment." That evening the soldiers were guests of the local Red Cross chapter at the Salt Lake City and County Building where a farewell supper was served. The men visited with relatives and friends until 9:00 p.m. when the regiment was reassembled and marched to the train depot. On Main Street the men began to sing "Tramp, Tramp, Tramp, the Boys Are Marching" and "cheering was taken up all along the line as the soldiers advanced, and it echoed and re-echoed from the buildings and cheer after cheer greeted the appearance of each successive battery organization as it moved along the line. Flags were in evidence here and there and they were waved fondly at the boys in Khaki." The *Salt Lake Tribune* noted that with "all the buoyancy of youth in their step, all the resolute determination of men ready to do or die, Utah's artillerymen went forth with smiles on their faces to do their duty for liberty, justice and humanity." At the depot relatives, friends, and well-wishers thronged to bid the soldiers goodbye.[11]

On October 13 the Utahns reached Camp Kearny, fourteen miles northeast of San Diego, the training camp of the 40th Division, which was made up of National Guard troops from California, Nevada, Arizona, Colorado, and Utah. The 40th Division became known as the Sunshine Division because of its insignia—a gold sunburst on a blue background worn on the upper sleeve of the uniform. It symbolized the sunny weather in the states from which the members originated. During World War I the men usually referred to themselves as "Sunshine Sammies." Maj. Gen. George H. Cameron of California commanded the division until December 1917 when Maj. Gen. Frederick S. Strong, a regular army officer, took over for the rest of the war.[12]

The camp was scheduled to receive and train more than thirty thousand men of the division for overseas duty. Divisions were organized at this time to have three infantry brigades, one artillery brigade, and other supporting troops such as engineers, cavalry, and air squadrons, but Gen. John J. Pershing had prevailed with the "square division"—two infantry brigades and one artillery brigade. Thus the 40th Division consisted of the 79th and 80th Infantry Brigades and the 65th Artillery Brigade. The 79th Infantry Brigade was made up of the 144th Machine Gun Battalion and the 157th and 158th Infantry Regiments. In the 80th Infantry Brigade were the 145th Machine Gun Battalion and the 159th and 160th Infantry Regiments. By the time the Utah artillery regiment reached Camp Kearny it had been designated as the 145th Field Artillery Regiment of the 64th Artillery Brigade. The other regiments of this brigade were the 143rd and 144th Artillery Regiments, made up for the most part of the California National Guard but with about one-third of the 143rd from Utah. Also included in the brigade were the 115th Trench Mortar Battery and the 115th Ammunitions Trains. Other units in the division included the 115th Engineers, which had about 25 Utah men, the 115th Signal Battalion, and the 40th Division Aero Squadron. The Utah field hospital, which trained at Camp Kearny, became the 159th Field Hospital of the division and later went into battle on the French front in 1918 apart from the 40th Division.[13]

The 65th Brigade was assigned a block of tenting area on the south end of the camp adjoining the artillery parade field. Platforms were built for the tents, which housed at first nine and then later five men per tent. Mess houses and kitchens with gas ranges and brick ovens were set up. The men hoped their training would be shortly accomplished and they would be sent to France and the battlefront. In this they would be sorely disappointed.[14]

The Utah regiment had entered the camp as a regiment of light artillery with 3-inch guns, but after a short period of training with these guns the 145th Field Artillery was converted to the bigger, motor-drawn 4.7-inch guns. Issued in January, the larger guns were soon dispatched to Fort Sill. Replacements were issued in March and April and drills and firing with them resumed. Most of the training consisted of maneuvering and firing the guns in target practice. Men fired over a trench area mock-up of the battlefront in Europe. The guns were placed in dugouts to conceal them from "enemy" positions and air observation. The 145th fired barrage, shrapnel, and smoke bomb exercises. The most technical of the firing, barrage, required that targets be taken up "a few yards in front of the line" and advanced "yard by yard into the enemy's territory," ahead of friendly troops. Shrapnel firing shot a metal-spewing shell to point targets along the front, and smoke bombing was a training technique in which the battery took sight on a target, aimed the piece, and "fired." Instead of real shells being fired, however, the range selected by the gun crew was telegraphed down the field, where crews set off special smoke bombs near the impact area to give the effect of an explosion to the observers near the weapon. In this way the gunners could practice making the adjustments and corrections needed to obtain a "hit" on their targets without using expensive live cannon shells.[15]

Since the Germans began to make use of gas on the front line, gas mask drills became necessary to provide protection against it.

Most soldiers were apprehensive about gas warfare. French and British officers who had had experience with it on the battlefront trained instructors in the 40th Division and then taught and supervised the gas training throughout the division. The men learned the characteristics of gases used by the Germans and the tactics employed. During the gas mask drills the men fit their masks to their faces as speedily as possible. The test required them to don a mask in six seconds. In February the brigade carried out a gas assault in which gassing took place at night while the men were firing in the trenches. About six men, none from Utah, did not react fast enough and received a slight gassing that required medical treatment.[16]

Other training included rifle and pistol practice. The battery men were trained to use the weapons in case of an attack on the battery area by the enemy. Training was done on range targets called *boches* (a derogatory French term for the Germans), which represented the European enemy.[17]

The regiment also carried out march maneuvers. In March and April of 1918 the three battalions of the 145th in turn made a two-day march with their equipment to Poway Valley, several miles to the east of Camp Kearny. This gave them experience in moving the batteries to different campsites and emplacements as in battlefield situations. In May and June the regiment made a "dismounted practice march" of 270 miles to Santa Ana, California, and back to Camp Kearny. In the last segment of the march, from Oceanside to Santa Ana, they made a record march of thirty-five hours elapsed time, with twenty-three hours of actual marching, which was highly praised by Maj. Gen. Frederick Strong, the division commander.[18]

In all this training the 145th Field Artillery Regiment claimed to be the best unit of the division, and they had the records to prove it! The 145th claimed to have the best health record in Camp Kearny, and Camp Kearny claimed to have less sickness and a lower death rate than most other training camps and even cities of similar population.[19] The *Vernal Express* printed a letter from Camp Kearny written by Laren Ross and dated February 15, 1918, that carried the health record further by saying:

> We haven't one venereal case in our whole regiment now. Pretty good for Utah isn't it. Best record made by any regiment. We also have less sickness than during any time we have been here. That was given out today by Colonel Young. We have had less arrests and acts of disorder while out of camp and in camp, also best artillerymen, to say it we have the best record in all things of any regiment. But we have got to work to keep our name. But Utah will keep it, you never fear.

The Utah regiment had a better than average record with the fewest AWOLs and deserters, with two notable exceptions. Capt. Richard F. King, commander of Battery B and coach of the regimental football team, apparently became embroiled in financial difficulties and love affair problems and deserted when these became too much for him. Pvt. Leo Fuhs of Battery A, a German alien who had joined the 145th, was arrested for criticizing the United States and declaring greater loyalty to Germany. These were the most glaring cases, but for the most part there was complete loyalty and a strong spirit of cooperation among the regiment.[20]

That spirit won recognition for the men. The 145th played football as they did everything else. They played to win and became the champion team of the 40th Division at Camp Kearny, but were beaten in competition in the Western Military Department. In a way that military disciplinarians claim to be a good indicator of morale and performance, the 145th won the "military courtesy contest," in which the Utah regiment had no marks against it. The accuracy of fire carried on at Camp Kearny by the 145th was praised by the American and foreign officers who observed it. In recognition of their skill the 145th was given first opportunity to fire at new targets and was awarded the place of honor in the marching review of the division before General

Strong and other dignitaries. The Utah group also claimed the fastest speed in firing a battery, although their record was not accepted as official. That this concern with records was not entirely satisfying to all the soldiers is evident from the anecdotes and the general tone of soldiers' stories compiled in their histories. Some stories are especially critical of Colonel Webb's mania for record-breaking and his demand that the regiment look at all times as if it had "stepped out of a band box." Some tactics of Colonel Webb, such as trying to make a record march from Camp Kearny to Santa Ana under strict water discipline that allowed no water to be consumed, were considered harassment. To many men the emphasis on high records and standards became annoying, but others considered them impressive.[21]

General Strong, for example, called "the regiment . . . one of the finest in the division" and said it was "bound to be a noted regiment abroad." Brig. Gen. LeRoy S. Lyons, commander of the 65th Brigade, paid tribute to the "expert marksmanship of the Utah gunners and officers who were responsible for the regiment winning the divisional championship in artillery fire, and their placing of the perfect barrage which won them fame throughout the western country." Inspector general reports also rated the performance of the 145th very highly.[22]

The behavior of the Utahns was recognized as outstanding too. Col. Richard W. Young, on a visit to Utah in March 1918, noted the "regiment has a record than which there is none better in camp" and said he "had been informed several times by others in San Diego that they were always glad to trade with the Utah men because they did not buy more than they could pay for and that their credit was good everywhere." Colonel Webb detailed in a speech "how high the regiment stood in the estimation of the people of southern California and army officers generally by their readiness to learn, their strictly correct habits, and gentlemanly demeanor." On another occasion he said:

> I want to say that a striking idea of what California people think of the Utah boys may be gained when I tell you that when we broke camp at Santa Ana [at the time the 145th made their

training march to Santa Ana] on Sunday morning at 5 o'clock, no less than 10,000 persons were on hand to say farewell to the troops. Peace authorities all along the route told one that the Utah boys were a "most decent bunch," and from other quarters I got Reports as to the high moral standards and gentlemanly conduct of the Utah boys.

The community of Santa Ana even gave a "loving cup" to the regiment that read, "To the 145th Officers and Men—you came to us as strangers. You won our hearts. You leave adopted sons." Finally, Chaplain B. H. Roberts, on tour in Utah with the 145th Band, which raised $15,000 for the incidental needs of the men of the regiment, claimed the reports that had reached Utah about the regiment "were no exaggeration." Since more than three-fourths of the men were Mormon church members, the conclusion might be drawn that a background of Mormon doctrine—which teaches hierarchy of authority, loyalty, responsibility of the individual, and high moral standards—contributed greatly to the performance of the 145th Field Artillery Regiment.[23]

By March 1918 the Sunshine Division was declared 100 percent efficient and ready for battle in Europe, but the call did not come. Considering all their claims to efficiency and their desire to see battle, one might question why they were not selected as one of the divisions to go on line against the Germans. Jim Dan Hill, in *The Minute Man in Peace and War*, states that certain divisions were designated under General Pershing's direction to be depot divisions—that is, divisions that were to send individual replacements to the front line. Hill says, "many officers and men of these replacement Divisions from the National Guard were resentful for decades because of the manner in which their units had been destroyed. This was particularly true of the proud and exceptionally well-trained 40th Division from California and the Mountain States." The main reason for the 40th being held out of combat seems to have stemmed from a "long-standing personal antipathy" between General Pershing and the 40th Division commander, Major General Strong: "Pershing had no intention of entrusting a high combat command to the 40th's commander." Thus the 40th Division had to be satisfied with training replacements for the war.[24]

In its role as a depot division the 40th provided replacement troops to other line units. In January the first of the "automatic replacement drafts" was drawn from the 40th Division, and 1,200 engineers of the division were transferred to Washington Barracks and became the 20th Engineers and the 534th Pontoon Train. On April 1, 500 infantrymen were transferred to the 42nd (Rainbow) Division fighting in Europe. In May and June another draft called for 5,000 infantry and 1,500 artillery troops from the 40th Division to be sent to various American units on the battlefront in Europe. These troops were assigned mainly to the 2nd Division, regular army, the 26th (Yankee) Division of the New England National Guard, the 32nd (Red Arrow) Division, the 89th (Middle West) Division, and the 77th (Metropolitan) Division of New York. Before the war was over the 40th Division had sent 27,000 replacement troops to the AEF (American Expeditionary Force) combat divisions.[25]

The June draft drew heavily from the Utah regiment, with 389 members of the 145th Field Artillery sent to various front-line units. In the 145th many volunteered to go to the front, but it appears others were inclined to stay with the regiment. Although the NCOs who volunteered with the replacement group had to take a reduction in rank to private in order to go, some did it anyway. E. W. Crocker, a lieutenant in the Headquarters Company, said most of the men in his unit volunteered and selections had to be made by the officers. In Battery B, however, Sylvan Ririe and Floyd Perry recalled that the policy generally was to select men who were not considered the best or the most cooperative of the soldiers. Ririe thought those who had special family backgrounds or the best positions in the battery were kept behind with the 145th and the rest were sent ahead as replacements. Some representative units this replacement group served in were the 16th Field Artillery of the 4th Division, the 17th Field Artillery of the 2nd Division, the 119th Field Artillery of the 32nd Division, and the 322nd Field Artillery of the 83rd Division.[26]

These units saw action all along the front of the Argonne Forest, Chateau Thierry, Champagne, Soissons, St. Mihiel, Verdun, and other lesser-known engagements. Casualties were heavy in all these battles, but of the 389 men sent in the June draft from the 145th, only 14 were wounded and only 5 were killed in battle or died of disease.[27]

Pvt. L. H. Deming told of his assignment to the 2nd Division in a published letter to his father that provides a rare glimpse of a Utahn in the war zone:

> We sailed from New York City the 28th of June and landed at Liverpool July 10. We had a submarine fight. I think it was sunk. Our ship had 6,000 men on board coming over but was sunk going back.
>
> We stayed in England a week and sailed from Southampton to Harve, France, and took the railroad to La Contine, a replacement camp in southern France. From there 150 men were sent to the Second Division. Many of them were since killed. We joined the Second Division at Chateau Thierry, where our division stopped the German drive and forced it back 50 kilometers across the Marne.
>
> The whole French Army was retreating when the Second went into action. We went to a reserve position in the Toul sector after that, while we moved back, traveling at night to Pont St. Vincent where we stayed a week. By that time we knew a drive was coming off somewhere. Then we moved up again more to the left and opened the drive in the St. Mihiel sector August 12.
>
> I worked for awhile on the gun crew. I'll never forget that barrage. The preparatory fire of big railroad guns started at 1 a.m. and the barrage opened at 5 o'clock. I forgot to tell you about our guns. We have 125 m. howitzers or about six-inch howitzers. The shells weigh about 96 pounds.
>
> After four days we were relieved and moved back. Our division took their objective in one day. They were given two and

it was the most important position of the drive—the capture of two towns in the center of the sector.

Two weeks later we were in the Champagne sector. The French tried to take a ridge for three weeks and couldn't take it. The Marines of our division took it, and forced the Germans to retreat 30 kilometers along the whole front. I'll never forget the dead I saw there. We were there from the 1st until the 28th of September and then relieved. Three days later the Second Division was put in the Verdun front between the Meuse and Argonne rivers, where the First Division had been fighting for a month and couldn't force the Germans back. For our barrage we carried 600 shells and opened up at 4 o'clock the next morning. At 8:30 we moved forward about 12 kilometers through the ground where the doughboys had passed two hours before. The fields were covered with dead. They were still warm and still dripping blood. I'll never forget those Marines. We stopped that night near a town and I went over the fields covered with dead and we found four German wounded. One could speak English. He laughed and said the war would be over in a week.

That night we dug little holes in the ground to sleep in. The Germans started to shell us and one shell fell 12 feet from my tent. In the morning I found a six-foot hole there. They shelled all night. One smashed the lieutenant's dugout and they fell all around. Several horses were killed. We moved out of there. The next night was worse than that. The shells came over four at a time but fell short. I had traveled half the night in the cold with mud to our shoetops, but once I hit my blankets I forgot all about it. We fired again in the morning. Then we moved farther to the right. By that time we had only half of our horses left and at times we moved our guns one at a time. We then moved into positions near the town of Beaumont, where we were shelled night and day. That was a nightmare. We were shelled several times with gas there and the battery had several escapes, and maybe you think we weren't glad when the armistice was signed while we were there! The Germans stopped about half their fire several hours before the time and after 11 o'clock there was no fire at all and I haven't heard any since.

But that wasn't the end. We were now following the Huns back to Germany. We passed through Belgium. Through Chenay, Montmedy and Arlon and are now resting somewhere in Luxemburg. The people of Belgium are sure grateful to the United States. They gave us anything we wanted. Several times I was grabbed and pulled into the houses to have a drink of "schnaps" or a cup of coffee. And at night many of the fellows slept in their homes. Of course I can't tell all that I have seen, but that will have to wait until I get home.[28]

After the replacements left, the 40th Division waited for the call to combat, but it was long in coming. New recruits were trained to bring the division back to full strength and efficiency, and finally in mid-July the division was ordered overseas. On August 2, 1918, the 145th entrained for Camp Mills, Long Island, New York, where they prepared for the move overseas. On August 14 the soldiers embarked on the *Scotian*, a former Canadian mail ship in poor condition, and the next day they sailed for England with a naval convoy. On August 28 the *Scotian* docked in Liverpool where the soldiers disembarked and marched to Knotty Ash Camp, a walled and secluded rest camp a few miles outside Liverpool. The camp was under the direction of W. G. Williams, former adjutant general of the state of Utah, who resigned his command of the Utah National Guard for the duration of the war in order to volunteer for active duty. The stay at Knotty Ash was short but eventful in that a rather serious incident occurred there. Apparently in reaction to the strict discipline and control Colonel Webb had maintained over the 145th, many of the men left camp to see the countryside against his orders. The following day, "August 30th, the entire Regiment marched out to an adjacent field. There they formed a hollow square and with the drums beating the Rogues March, the culprits were marched out and subjected to having both stripes and buttons ripped off—a punishment heretofore reserved only for traitors. It was a regrettable incident, detrimental to morale, and one which did little to enhance the Colonel's popularity."[29]

In France the 65th Field Artillery Brigade was separated from the 40th Division. The infantry brigades, trains, and medical units went to support the combat divisions of the U.S. 1st and 2nd Armies on the front line, and the artillery brigade was sent to southern France for further training.

On September 1 the 145th Field Artillery started its move to France by way of Southampton to Le Havre and on for a short stay at Veuille near Poitiers. Next the men went south to Gradianne near Bordeaux where they again stayed for almost two weeks before moving to Camp de Souge, a former French camp approximately twenty miles southwest of Bordeaux where old brick horse stables had been converted into barracks. There the 65th Brigade began intensive training in preparation for the front. The 145th trained with French 75 mm guns they had obtained after arriving in France. The artillery training consisted of a six-week course from about September 26 to November 9. While the training proceeded, Capt. Wesley King traveled to different areas of France trying to obtain 4.7-inch guns to equip the 145th for the move to the front. The 145th had received orders to take part in the assault on Metz and was being provided with guns and war materiel when the armistice was signed on November 11, 1918. The men of the 145th were disappointed that after all their training and preparation they had not gotten in on the action to defeat the enemy.[30]

Lt. Col. E. LeRoy Bourne, executive officer of the 145th Field Artillery, wrote of the disappointment in France in a letter to his wife that was published in the *Deseret News*:

> You cannot realize the disappointment we all feel in not participating in the war as combatant troops. It is inadequate consolation to know that we were ready to do so morally and technically. The regiment won new laurels in French artillery schools and was and is fit to function as a powerful fighting machine. It is

also inadequate consolation to know that there are hundreds of thousands of other American troops more fortunate than we. Someone has to be last, it is true, but the pity we bestow upon ourselves doesn't ameliorate our great disappointment But we are making the best of it and are ready for the next job, be that what it may.[31]

Pvt. Ralph Duvall expressed the men's frustration more bluntly in doggerel:

> At De Souge they made us like it
> We began to drill some more,
> But it wasn't any use at all,
> for soon they stopped the war.
> Now all we want to know is,
> what the Hell we soldiered for?[32]

With the fighting ended the prevailing mood was to get home as soon as possible. The 65th Field Artillery was scheduled to leave the latter part of December 1918. In the interim, while waiting for debarkation, the men of the 143rd (some of whom were Utahns and had earlier returned to the United States with Brig. Gen. Richard W. Young), the 144th, and the 145th worked as stevedores at Camp Genicart (Bassens) near Bordeaux, where they unloaded supplies from the United States and aided in the embarking process of the troops returning home.[33]

The 1,400 men of the 145th began their return home on December 24 from Bordeaux aboard the *Santa Teresa*, a newly constructed ship that had made its maiden voyage empty from the United States to France. The soldiers spent twelve days at sea, including both Christmas and New Year's Day. The *Salt Lake Tribune* reported it as a "pleasant voyage with plenty of facilities for their amusement." On Christmas and New Year's Day the troops were given a turkey dinner and special treats from the YMCA, the Knights of Columbus, and the Red

Cross, and the soldiers raced around the decks "playing the happy youngsters that they were." The only discomfort they suffered, the article said, was a little seasickness the first day out to sea on the Bay of Biscay. However, the men on the ship expressed ideas about the trip different from the *Tribune*'s. They said the *Santa Teresa* was so poorly constructed that the captain did not dare brave the rough seas of the North Atlantic and took the longer southern route home. They called the trip monotonous, except for the first day of seasickness, and thought the only excitement occurred on January 5 when the ship docked in New York Harbor.[34]

At Camp Merritt near Hoboken, New Jersey, the regiment went through the process of being re-Americanized, which included a delousing of the men and a steaming of their clothes to kill any germs from Europe. For some time it was uncertain where the 145th regiment would be mustered out of service. Several camps and posts considered were close to Utah, but finally the regiment was sent to the Utah State Agricultural College (USAC) in Logan, where the men would be apart from the city populations in order to prevent a possible spread of influenza and where adequate buildings were available to house them.[35]

On January 17, 1919, the 145th arrived in Ogden, Utah, on the troop train. At this time the regiment consisted of two battalions of men from Idaho and one battalion from California, Colorado, and New Mexico. Some of the latter were mustered out at posts closer to their homes, leaving 1,140 men and 45 officers to be mustered out in Utah. Another 65 enlisted men and 5 officers had remained in France as part of the occupation force with military police and mechanic assignments, and 13 men of the regiment had died in France from influenza.[36]

When the regiment arrived in Ogden officials expressed concern about the soldiers mixing with the crowds because of the threat of influenza. The troops were ordered to march from Ogden's Union Station up 25th Street to Washington Boulevard, then to 28th Street, back to 21st Street, and return down 25th Street to board the train. The orders stated that no crowds were to gather at the station and that "there would be no speaking nor will the soldiers be allowed to break ranks." The jubilation of the crowd in Ogden made it difficult to keep relatives and friends from meeting the soldiers at the depot, and touching homecoming scenes were left uninterrupted. The parade formed with Governor Bamberger and state officials preceding the regiment in automobiles and an escort of two hundred men made up of veterans of World War I from Ogden and Weber County. After the parade the men returned to the train and proceeded to Logan.[37]

Logan welcomed the soldiers even more enthusiastically than Ogden. At Center and Main Streets an "arch of welcome" had been erected with flags and electric lights decorating the structure and flashing "Welcome Home." Thousands greeted the men at the station and cheered as they marched to USAC on the hill, where the governor welcomed them back to Utah and praised their accomplishments, saying, "[you] left on a mission which you were prepared to fulfill at the cost of your very existence" and in which "you established a reputation for soldierly qualities in your state that had given you fame throughout the nation . . . made your people proud of you . . . and . . . brought victory to the nation." After Bamberger's speech the men were assigned quarters in the various college buildings, and "Utah's Own" settled down to the most favorable and comfortable condition they had enjoyed since leaving for the war.[38]

On January 18 the regiment staged a formal parade and review in downtown Logan for the governor, state legislators, and visitors. The crowd was impressed with their demonstration of marching, manual of arms, and the gas mask drill they performed several times during the course of the parade.

During the next few days the men completed the mustering out process under Col. Charles Ide and his staff of the U.S. Army Command from California. By January 21, 1919, the physical examinations and paperwork had been completed and the 145th Field Artillery was officially mustered out.[39]

Over the years the veterans of the regiment met with almost annual consistency in conventions that brought back the times they had served together in World War I. Some of the members of the 145th continued their service in the Utah National Guard and provided much of the important leadership during the 1920s, 1930s, and World War II.

As the men of the 145th Field Artillery disassembled, other Utah guardsmen continued in service—mainly those officers and men of the 145th Field Hospital who remained behind for occupation duty as the 159th Field Hospital. Inducted at Fort Douglas, Utah, on August 5, 1917, this unit had gone to Camp Kearny for further training and to provide medical support to the 40th Division. The field hospital was made up of five officers and forty-two NCOs and enlisted men—all from Utah. They left Camp Kearny in August 1918 with the 40th Division, arriving in France on September 2.

In France the 40th Division was split up and the 159th Field Hospital went to Grossouvre in the department of Cher to serve in a hospital in an old chateau. On October 27 the field hospital was moved to a place near Metz, approximately three kilometers from the front lines, where it was assigned duty as a gas resuscitation hospital. Here the men came under enemy shelling during the last few days of the war. Capt. George F. Roberts reported that they handled "more than 200 sick cases each day." After the armistice the bombings stopped, but casualties from the occupation were still coming to the hospital for treatment. The 159th Field Hospital returned to Utah on July 3, 1919, and was then mustered out of service.[40]

At a War Mothers service flag ceremony honoring the Utah men who had served in the war, Chaplain B. H. Roberts summarized the sacrifices of the Utah men. Referring specifically to the men of the 145th Field Artillery, he said:

> These men who have died [meaning the thirteen who had died of Spanish influenza in France] have made just as complete a sacrifice of their lives to their country as any who have fallen or shall fall in the battle line. They have faced a condition as deadly to them as charging through bursting shells, or the patter of machine guns or rifle bullets. The miasma of the dread disease

proved for them as deadly as the poisonous German gas, waves of shells and their restless suffering from fevered tortured bodies, and congested lungs, was as pitiful as any death from wounds of bayonet thrusts or shrapnel rents.

The heroism of the soldier consists in the fact that he offers his life to his country, with full interest to meet whatever fate may befall him. It is not his prerogative to choose his place in the line of battle, or to say when or how or where or in what manner he will fall, if fall he must. He does his part when in response to his country's call for service he says "Here I am, send me."[41]

In an earlier statement Col. William C. Webb concluded, "Our regiment would have done anything they would have required of us. No more soldierly, all-around decent bunch of men were ever gotten together than the 145th Field Artillery. There hasn't been a thing required of them, it doesn't make any difference how difficult the task was, that they didn't go to it with all the vim that it was possible for men to put into it."[42]

NOTES

Originally published in the *Utah Historical Quarterly* 58 (Fall 1990): 312–33.

1. See Richard C. Roberts, "The Utah National Guard on the Mexican Border in 1916," *Utah Historical Quarterly* 46 (1978): 262–81; Clarence C. Clendenen, *Blood on the Border: The United States Army and the Mexican Irregulars* (New York: Macmillan Co., 1969), 297–98; Jim Dan Hill, *The Minute Man in Peace and War: A History of the National Guard* (Harrisburg, PA: Stackpole Publishing Co., 1964), 261–63.
2. *Salt Lake Tribune*, March 25, 1917; *Salt Lake Telegram*, March 25, 1917; *Salt Lake Herald*, March 26, 1917.
3. *Deseret News*, March 29, May 23, May 29, 1917.
4. *Salt Lake Tribune*, April 17, May 31, June 2, June 22, 1917; *Salt Lake Telegram*, May 6, 1917; *Salt Lake Herald*, May 6, June 2, June 3, June 25, 1917; *Deseret News*, May 4, May 7, June 4, June 22, 1917.
5. An artillery battery required 190 enlisted men and officers; the cavalry unit was smaller with 105 enlisted men and 3 officers.

The headquarters company of artillery was made up of 92 men, and the supply company had 35 men. Including vacancies in the sanitary and field hospital units, over 500 new recruits were needed to bring the National Guard to war strength. Most of the artillery troops came from the cavalry, however, as cavalrymen were simply transferred as units to the artillery. Thus, Troop H of Logan and Troop L of Brigham City were consolidated into Battery A, field artillery. (This was shortly changed to Battery C, and Battery A went to Salt Lake City.) Troops B and K of Ogden were combined and became Battery B. One-half of the artillery battery in existence at the time was put with Troop A and became Battery C (later Battery A). The other part of the artillery battery was organized with Troop C and was known as Battery D. Troops F at Provo, E at Mount Pleasant, G at Ephraim, and D at Manti were made into Battery F. The machine gun troop of the cavalry was divided equally between Batteries C and D. The stations and commanders of the regiments were: Headquarters First Utah Field Artillery Regiment, Salt Lake City; Headquarters A Company stationed at Salt Lake City with Capt. Fred Jorgensen commanding; the supply company had its home station in Salt Lake City under Capt. Fred Kammerman. The First Battalion headquarters was in Salt Lake City with Maj. E. LeRoy Bourne in command. Under the First Battalion were Battery A, Salt Lake City; Battery B, Ogden; and Battery C, Logan. Leaders of these units were Capt. Curtis Y. Clawson, Capt. J. Ray Ward, and Capt. Edwin G Woolley Jr., respectively. The Second Battalion headquarters was also in Salt Lake City, led by Maj. William E. Kneass. Battery D, Salt Lake City, under Capt. Elmer Johnson; Battery E, Salt Lake City, under Capt. Alex R. Thomas; and Battery F, Provo, under Capt. Charles R. Mabey made up the units of the Second Battalion. Most of these men were recruited out of the areas of the home stations. See State of Utah, *Biennial Report of the Adjutant General for the Years 1917 and 1918* (Salt Lake City, 1919), 4–5. The listing of Troop M of Logan is a mistake in the report; it should be Troop H.

See also *Deseret News*, June 7, June 15, 1917; *Salt Lake Herald*, June 7, 1917; *Salt Lake Telegram*, June 7, 1917; *Salt Lake Tribune*, June 7, 1917.

The roster of the officers and men of the Utah Field Artillery, mustered into federal service on August 5, 1917, is found in Appendix IV of Roberts, "History of the Utah National Guard, 1894–1954" (PhD diss., University of Utah, 1973). See also E. W. Crocker, ed., *History of the 145th Field Artillery Regiment of World War I* (Provo, UT: J. Grant Stevenson, Publisher, 1968), 14–37.

6. Two days before the camp assembled Webb was promoted to lieutenant colonel and second-in-command of the regiment in recognition of his long and capable service in the National Guard.

7. *Salt Lake Telegram*, July 6, 1917; *Deseret News*, July 6, July 10, July 14, July 19, 1917; *Salt Lake Tribune*, July 8, 1917; *Salt Lake Herald*, July 19, 1917.

   As the camp got underway things became serious, as five men soon found out. Two sergeants of Battery F were charged with being AWOL (absent without leave) for overstaying a furlough at home, and three men were arrested and confined at the camp. A summary court-martial eliminated the three men from the National Guard and sent them home without pay. The two sergeants were sentenced to twenty days in the Salt Lake County jail, which after a few days was changed to a reduction in rank to private and confinement at the camp. After the first weekend leave five more men turned up missing, and it appeared to be more serious when three of them extended their stays to almost ten days, which made them deserters instead of AWOL. Two of the men had gone to the Presidio of San Francisco to an officers training course, which had been forgotten about, and the other three returned to camp and were court-martialed. See *Deseret News*, July 6, July 10, 1917; *Salt Lake Tribune*, July 6, July 11, July 12, July 17, July 22, 1917; *Salt Lake Telegram*, July 23, 1917.

8. *Salt Lake Tribune*, July 25, July 27, July 31, 1917; *Salt Lake Herald*, July 26, July 30, July 31, 1917; *Deseret News*, July 26, July 30, July 31, 1917. While awaiting orders Colonel Young nominated officers and NCOs for the regiment, and they were approved by Governor Bamberger. There was some shifting of assignments at this time, the most significant of which was the resignation of Capt. Fred Jorgensen as commander of the Quartermaster Corps because of defective vision. Jorgensen later served as adjutant general of Utah when Adjutant General Williams went into active service. Jorgensen filled this post until Williams's return in 1920.

9. State of Utah, *Biennial Report*, 4–5.

10. *Salt Lake Tribune*, August 13, 1917; *Salt Lake Herald*, August 14, 1917; *Deseret News*, August 14, September 4, September 7, 1917.

11. *Salt Lake Tribune*, October 11, 1917. See also *Deseret News*, October 11, 1917. In honor of the sacrifices these men were making, Lucy A. R. Clark and Evan Stephens wrote "The New Freedom Song" and dedicated it to Colonel Young.

12. *Salt Lake Tribune*, February 7, 1918; *Historical and Pictorial Review: 40th Infantry Division, U.S. Army, San Luis Obispo, California, 1941* (Baton

Rouge, LA: Army and Navy Publishing Co., 1941), 13–16; *Salt Lake Telegram*, December 6, 1917; *Deseret News*, December 6, 1917.

13. Hill, *The Minute Man*, 262–69; *Historical and Pictorial Review*, 54; *Deseret News*, October 26, October 30, 1917.

14. *Salt Lake Tribune*, October 22, 1917; *Deseret News*, October 15, 1917; *Salt Lake Herald*, October 14, 1917.

15. *Deseret News*, November 2, December 11, 1917; *Salt Lake Tribune*, November 6, November 13, November 19, December 11, 1917, January 29, January 30, 1918; *Salt Lake Telegram*, December 10, December 11, December 18, 1917, February 2, 1918; *Ogden Standard*, March 22, 1918.

16. *Historical and Pictorial Review*, 54; *Salt Lake Tribune*, January 18, January 19, January 27, February 4, February 18, February 24, 1918; *Salt Lake Telegram*, January 17, 1918.

17. *Deseret News*, December 13, 1917.

18. Ibid., March 28, March 29, 1918; *Salt Lake Tribune*, January 16, 1917, March 30, March 31, April 3, 1918; Crocker, *History of the 145th*, 42; *Historical and Pictorial Review*, 66.

19. *Salt Lake Tribune*, January 1, February 17, 1918; *Salt Lake Telegram*, February 9, 1918; *Salt Lake Herald*, February 9, 1918; *Deseret News*, February 11, July 1, 1918.

20. *Salt Lake Tribune*, February 23, 1918; *Salt Lake Herald*, January 3, February 25, 1918; *Deseret News*, January 3, February 25, 1918.

21. *Salt Lake Tribune*, January 28, January 29, January 30, February 3, 1918; *Deseret News*, January 30, February 14, 1918; *Salt Lake Telegram*, July 11, 1918; Crocker, *History of the 145th* 6–105 passim; interview with Ruel Eskelson, Brigham City, Utah, June 3, 1970.

22. *Salt Lake Herald*, February 9, 1918; *Salt Lake Tribune*, February 14, 1918; "Inspection of 65th F.A. Brigade, 40th Division," Alfred A. Stanbird, Inspector General, to Adjutant General, U.S. Army, December 19, 1917, 40th Division Records, National Archives, Washington, D.C. Subsequent reports in this record group are similar in their evaluation of the 145th.

23. *Deseret News*, March 25, June 15, July 1, July 9, July 10, 1918; *Salt Lake Tribune*, June 24, 1918.

24. Hill, *Minute Man*, 278–84.

25. *Historical and Pictorial Review*, 14, 15.

26. *Salt Lake Tribune*, July 12, 1918; *Deseret News*, July 13, 1918; interviews with E. W. Crocker, Salt Lake City, April 17, 1970; Sylvan Ririe, Ogden, June 17, 1970; Floyd Perry, Ogden, June 14, 1970; and Albert E. Wilfong, Ogden, March 16, 1970. For a list of the men sent in the June

replacement draft, see Roberts, "History of the Utah National Guard," Appendix V.

27. Noble Warrum, *Utah in the World War* (Salt Lake City, 1924), 71.

28. Deming's letter was published in the *Deseret News*, December 27, 1918.

29. Crocker, *History of the 145th*, 52, 53, 56–65; *Historical and Pictorial Review*, 66; *Deseret News*, January 23, 1919; Eskelson, interview.

30. *Deseret News*, December 26, 1918; interview with William Weiler, Salt Lake City, March 17, 1965; diary of Jefferson M. Haley, 1917–19, Bountiful, Utah, holograph in possession of family members.

31. *Deseret News*, December 3, 1918.

32. Ralph Duval, "And We Never Lost a _____ _____ Man: The Story of the 145th Field Artillery," typescript.

33. Crocker, *History of the 145th*, 65–75; *Historical and Pictorial Review*, 66; *Deseret News*, January 23, 1919; Weiler, interview; Haley, diary.

34. *Salt Lake Tribune*, January 5, 1919; Crocker, *History of the 145th*, 101–3.

35. Crocker, *History of the 145th*, 103, 104; *Salt Lake Tribune*, December 6, 1918; *Deseret News*, December 14, January 6, 1919. See Roberts, "History of the Utah National Guard," Appendix VI, for a list of regiment members who returned to Utah in 1919.

36. *Salt Lake Tribune*, January 3, January 19, 1919; *Deseret News*, January 6, 1919. For a list of those who died of influenza in France, see *Salt Lake Tribune*, November 30, 1918.

37. *Salt Lake Tribune*, January 17, January 18, 1919; *Salt Lake Herald*, January 18, 1919.

38. *Salt Lake Tribune*, January 18, 1919; *Salt Lake Herald*, January 18, 1919.

39. State of Utah, *Biennial Report of the Utah National Guard, 1919–1920* (Salt Lake City, 1921), 6; *Salt Lake Herald*, January 24, 1919.

40. Warrum, *Utah in the World War*, 65; *Biennial Report, 1919–1920*, 6; *Salt Lake Tribune*, January 3, 1919.

41. *Deseret News*, February 13, 1919.

42. *Salt Lake Herald*, January 18, 1919.

3

"A PERFECT HELL"

Utah Doughboys in the Meuse-Argonne Offensive, 1918

BRANDON JOHNSON

Soldiers from all nations most often compared the experience of war with Hell—that place where eternal torment and punishment reigned in full measure, all hope was lost, and the abandoned souls endured the unendurable. The following article looks at the experience of Utah soldiers during the Meuse-Argonne Offensive—named for the Meuse River and the Argonne Forest—in northeastern France, not far from the French-Belgian border. The campaign began on September 26, 1918, and concluded with the armistice that ended the war less than seven weeks later on November 11, 1918. Utahns were among the more than one million Americans who participated in the campaign, which left 29,277 dead and 95,786 wounded. Using contemporary letters published in local newspapers and other firsthand accounts by Utah servicemen, Brandon Johnson gives us a glimpse of the nature of combat and its long-lasting impact on those who served in the decisive campaign of "the war to end all wars."

The letter, dated January 14, 1919, brought unwelcome tidings from France. Mail was the tenuous thread that kept the Robert and Lucy

Moyes family of Ogden, Utah, tied to their son and brother Leroy since they sent him off to war in 1918. For Leroy, regular correspondence undoubtedly served as a happy reminder that he was not alone: he had a loving family back home that hoped one day soon he would return safe and sound from the battle-scarred fields of Europe. On the other side of the world, Leroy's family relied on his letters to track his (and his fellow soldiers') progress against the German army, which, back in 1914, had invaded Belgium and northern France, and then had dug in to wage a protracted war (now variously known as the First World War, the Great War, and World War I) against the French and their allies. But this newest letter from France was not from Leroy; it came from his commanding officer, Lieutenant Joseph P. Toole. "My Dear Mr. Moyes," the letter began. "Your son, Private Leroy Moyes, No. 2781852, company D, 364th Infantry, has been reported missing in action since Oct. 3rd, 1918, in the Meuse-Argonne operation, France. I have endeavored to obtain further information concerning his whereabouts but have not met with success. I sincerely hope nothing serious has happened to him and I will notify you if any news of him comes to the company."[1]

When Leroy Moyes left home at the age of thirty-one, he was far from the youngest draftee in the American Expeditionary Forces (AEF), then being cobbled together to fight in France, but evidence suggests he was still single, making him an ideal candidate for the job of waging war: if killed, he would not leave a widow or fatherless children behind. Following his physical examination and formal induction into the U.S. Army, the Utah "doughboy" (the era's popular nickname for American soldiers) eventually found himself attached to the 364th Infantry Regiment in the 91st "Wild West" Division, which saw heavy fighting near Gesnes and Eclisfontaine, German-occupied hamlets located near the eastern margins of the Argonne Forest. At some point late in the drawn-out battle now known as the Meuse-Argonne Offensive, Leroy was injured and admitted to a rear-area military hospital, where he wrote a single letter home, the last one his parents would get from him. In the long months that followed, the only word the Moyeses received from France was the letter from Lt. Toole.[2]

Perhaps Leroy's family gained some solace from the fact that he had not been killed on the battlefield, but making it to a base hospital certainly was no guarantee of survival in the Great War—large numbers of wounded men regrettably succumbed to injuries or disease while tucked snugly into hospital beds far behind the front lines. No doubt Robert and Lucy Moyes fretted over the possibility that their boy had cheated death in battle only to die, anxious and lonely, in some rear-area medical ward. Even Lt. Toole appears to have given up on the idea that the young soldier was still alive; in closing his note to the Moyeses, he referred ominously to Leroy in the past tense: the Utah doughboy, he wrote, "was a good soldier and always took a particular interest in his work. He always tried to do his very best and never complained no matter how hard the work."[3]

Imagine the Moyes family's surprise, then, when Leroy miraculously turned up in a New York hospital, alive and well, four months after Toole's missive arrived from France. Once the fighting men began trickling home to Ogden from the war zone back in 1918, the unfortunate Moyeses may have felt compelled to veil their deep sadness so as not to diminish the joy their neighbors felt at being reunited with their loved ones. But now the family surely felt only relief. According to the *Ogden Standard*, Leroy's father was eager to celebrate the "homecoming of his son who for months he mourned as lost."[4]

The story of Leroy Moyes is truly extraordinary; precious few similar tales ended so happily. The Meuse-Argonne Offensive, in which the young Ogdenite was wounded, was a bloody affair: the forty-seven-day-long battle, which lasted from September 26 to the last day of the war—November 11, 1918—ended with 26,277 American men killed and another 95,786 wounded, making it the deadliest battle in American history. (By comparison, in the costliest battle the U.S. Army fought in northwest Europe in the Second World War—what we now call the Battle of the Bulge—far fewer Americans were killed and wounded than were killed and wounded in the Meuse-Argonne Offensive in 1918, despite the fact that both battles were of more or less equal length. In the forty-four days of the Battle of the Bulge, 10,276 Americans were killed and 47,493 were wounded.[5]) For being the nation's most lethal battle, however, the fight for the Meuse River highlands and the Argonne Forest has attracted scant attention from historians, and even less notice from scholars of Utah history.[6] The story of Utahns' experiences in the Great War—especially in the Meuse-Argonne—remains effectively untold. Even the aging standard reference on World War I–era Utah, published in 1924, devotes only a handful of pages to the campaign.[7] The purpose of this chapter is to begin rectifying this historiographical lapse by recovering some of the stories of Utah men who fought or otherwise participated in the Meuse-Argonne campaign. This is not a comprehensive account of the offensive; rather, it is a collection of narrative snapshots that provide a soldier's-eye view of what it was like to undergo the process historian Peter S. Kindsvatter has dubbed "immersion in the environment of war"—a process that commences with being shipped to the war zone and culminates in actual combat experience and the frightening realization that tomorrow one's "number might be up." Firsthand accounts and other reports credited to Utah doughboys highlight the alienating and disorienting nature of the fighting in the Meuse-Argonne sector. Men witnessed nearly boundless destruction—both human and environmental—in the offensive, and endured terrifying brushes with death, physical wounds (sometimes severe ones), psychological distress, the loss of friends, and paralyzing fear. Even troops attached to rear-echelon support units were sometimes forced to witness and internalize the terrible consequences of war, while combat soldiers on the front lines saw and did things on the battlefield they ordinarily would not have seen or done. It does not take much imagination to deduce the impact wartime trauma had on them. And on top of such terrible individual consequences, Utah families also paid a heavy price, with more than a few losing fathers, sons, and brothers in the bloodshed that swept the Meuse-Argonne in 1918.[8]

The United States was a latecomer to World War I, only entering the fight on April 6, 1917, after nearly three years of increasingly tested neutrality. Not even the sinking of the ocean liner *Lusitania* by a German U-boat in 1915, with more than a hundred Americans aboard, was enough to get President Woodrow Wilson to break his resolve to stay out of the war. (He eventually won a second presidential term in 1916 on a peace platform.) Only a German offer to join forces with Mexico in a war against the United States and the resumption in 1917 of unrestricted submarine warfare finally brought America into the conflict. (The German high command reauthorized the nation's U-boats to attack and sink any ship approaching the British and French coastlines, regardless of the flag under which it sailed.)[9]

The United States, though, was woefully unprepared to fight a world war, even after watching the forces of rampant militarism and total war consume the European continent over the space of almost three years. America's peacetime army was unrealistically small, and its equipment and weapons were outdated and sparse.[10] But the United States did have the potential to supply enormous numbers of men to the cause of war through conscription. Indeed, by the end of 1918, the U.S. Army had marshaled over three million men for the war effort thanks to a draft set in motion by the passage of the Selective Service Act on May 18, 1917. The first draft lottery occurred on July 20, 1917, when Secretary of War Newton D. Baker drew the first number, thus calling up the men holding the same number in each local draft board's area. Of course, some of the men who found themselves in the AEF had joined the fight of their own volition as volunteers or had been nationalized as members of state National Guards, but the great majority (around two-thirds of the three million) were draftees.[11]

Men from across Utah found their way into the AEF through all three channels: volunteer enlistment, federalization of the National Guard, and conscription. One volunteer enlistee, Oscar Evans of Sunnyside in Carbon County, joined the army with a buddy hoping to avoid infantry service in the muddy, pest-infested trenches of France. Formal induction came on December 11, 1917, at Fort Douglas in Salt

Lake City, where doctors pushed and prodded Evans and his fellow inductees to the point of causing some of the young soldiers to faint. Without skipping a beat, the medical personnel used the time to inoculate the men. "They [the inductees] would fall," recalled Evans, "and the doctors would punch the needle in them and give them their shot." From Utah, Evans first went to Florida's Camp Johnson, where he was assigned to a transportation unit, then to Norfolk, Virginia, and finally to Brest, France, aboard a steamer manned by a green crew. For the duration of the war, Evans drove trucks.[12]

Like most new volunteers and draftees, Evans was mostly ignorant of army protocol. Shortly after he was issued his uniform, the young Utahn passed a lieutenant without saluting him, a military faux pas for which he received a strong dressing-down: "I told him [the lieutenant] that I had just got in," the innocent Evans remembered, "and I didn't know that I had to salute."[13]

Unlike many new volunteers, federalized national guardsmen were familiar with the military way of life. Guardsmen like Private Lamar H. Deming of Salt Lake City were prime candidates for deployment to the war zone. Not all guard units, however, were destined to see action in France. Deming, for example, was part of the 145th Artillery Regiment created from a federal order to reorganize the Utah National Guard. Originally called the First Artillery Regiment of the Utah National Guard, the unit was redesignated the 145th Artillery Regiment and given to the 40th "Sunshine" Division after shipping out to Camp Kearny, California. In the end, though, despite its evident preparedness for action in France, the 40th Division and its regiments became stateside "depot" units, providing replacement troops—including Deming—to front-line divisions in France. (Before the war was over, the Sunshine Division sent twenty-seven thousand replacements to AEF combat units.) Deming was detached from the 145th and left the United States in June 1918 bound first for the British port of Liverpool, and then for France, one of six thousand doughboys on a crowded ship. He arrived on the line just in time to join the 2nd "Indianhead" Division in stopping a march on Paris by the

German army.[14] (The regiment Deming left behind at Camp Kearny, the 145th Artillery, with its division, the 40th, eventually made it to Europe, but never saw combat duty.)[15]

For every volunteer enlistee and national guardsman like Lamar Deming there were many, many conscripts from Utah who ended up on the front lines. In the case of Kanarraville, a small Iron County town, of the sixteen townsmen who fought in the war, only one, Emery Pollock, volunteered. The rest, including young Leland Stapley, were draftees.[16] On the day of the draft lottery, Stapley's serial number—461—was the 110th number drawn; given that the War Department's quota for the entire county was only 46, he appeared safe from conscription. But authorities exempted too many of the men at the top of the list—men whose numbers had been drawn earlier in the lottery—or judged them to be physically or mentally unfit for military service, meaning that those further down the list would have to take their places. Only 20 of the first 125 draft registrants were conscripted into the army in the initial round of examinations, and Leland Stapley was one of them. (The county draft board eventually ruled that "all fathers, married before the passage of the law calling the draft, should be exempted," meaning that married men without children and unmarried men were forced to fill the county's quota.)[17]

Despite the apparent unfairness of the situation, Stapley took his licks and allowed himself to be inducted. The townspeople fêted him and his brothers-in-arms at a "rousing meeting" the afternoon before they were set to leave for basic training. Out came the "old martial band" and the food. "Fruit and melons were served to all present, followed by a dance," wrote the Kanarraville correspondent to the *Iron County Record*. The next day, the boys were on their way to Salt Lake City and then Camp Lewis, near Tacoma, Washington, where they were attached to the 346th Machine Gun Battalion of the 91st Division, the same division in which Leroy Moyes served.[18]

Many of the divisions that went into the Meuse-Argonne sector were initially organized regionally. As men were inducted, the army grouped them into units with men from the same area or section of the country. This, of course, was especially the case with federalized National Guard divisions, such as the 28th "Keystone" Division (Pennsylvania) and the 37th "Buckeye" Division (Ohio). But even some draftee divisions were organized along regional lines: men from West Virginia and the mountainous western counties of Virginia, Pennsylvania, and North Carolina filled the 80th "Blue Ridge" Division's ranks, while the 77th "Statue of Liberty" or "Melting Pot" Division originally contained a large number of recent European immigrants from New York, with names like Knifsund, Cepeglia, Karpinsky, Ziegenbalg, and Bejnarowicz. The shipping of replacement troops from stateside depot divisions to fill vacancies left by casualties, however, undercut the regional character of individual AEF divisions, and men from across America ultimately were thrown together in mixed units. While evidence shows that Utahns filled vacancies in a number of AEF divisions, the majority of the state's draftees ended up in the 91st Division, as its "Wild West" moniker suggests.[19]

Stapley estimated he and his companions spent a whole nine months in training, first at Camp Lewis and then at New Jersey's Camp Merritt (Stapley incorrectly assumed the cantonment was in New York). He and the rest of his battalion boarded the ship *Dano* at Hoboken on July 7, 1918, bound for France. Life on the *Dano* was "one continual jam," Stapley wrote in his diary (which was eventually excerpted in the *Iron County Record*). "We had daily inspections which are the curse of a soldier's life." The "main excitement" of the trip was a whale sighting, though the opening stampede for the canteen each day ran a close second. Upon reaching France, the young Utahn, like so many others before and after him, climbed aboard a freight car with "8 Horses or 40 Men" stenciled in French on its sides, bound for the country's interior and advanced training.[20]

Leland Stapley was only one of hundreds of young Utah men being swept into America's burgeoning war machine, and perhaps not unremarkably the experiences of those hundreds did not depart radically from his. Russell C. Wheeler of Slaterville registered for the draft in June 1917 and was in the first group of 120 men to appear before the Weber County draft board. If Wheeler hoped to escape the clutches of military conscription, the draft authorities disappointed him. As a single man without dependent children, he, like Stapley, was a prime candidate for the draft; married men with dependents were being exempted left and right. (Responding to the appeal of a married Ogden man with a dependent child whose local draft board had turned down his request for an exemption, the district draft board in Salt Lake City seemed to set a precedent in August 1917 that such men, as a matter of course, should be free from conscription.) The fact that Wheeler had received previous military training (at least if we choose to believe an *Ogden Standard* report to that effect) only made the Slaterville native even more attractive as a draftee.[21]

Like Stapley, Wheeler and his fellow Weber County draftees were assigned to basic training at Camp Lewis. Before they left for camp, citizens and dignitaries invited the newly minted soldiers to a party at a local café, where politicians were given the standard privilege of delivering long-winded speeches on the selflessness and patriotism of the departing men. The party's planners, however, also saved a little time for the soldiers themselves to speak to the café crowd; according to the *Standard*, they "express[ed] pride at being able to get out and fight for the cause of world liberty." Perhaps the oddest event of the night was an impromptu comedy show that "got everyone into a light-hearted spirit," and allegedly "did much to impress the boys with the fact that going to war is not so hard after all." One wonders how many of the draftees actually came to the same conclusion.[22]

Wheeler's judgments about training at Camp Lewis were highly positive. "You would probably like to hear how we are fairing [*sic*] in the army training camp," he wrote in a letter published in the *Standard*. "Well, to sum it all up, we are getting along first class." Military planners had assigned the Weber County men to the 91st Division's 362nd Infantry Regiment, Company M, where the officers, at least according to Wheeler, were quite solicitous. "These officers will do anything to add to our comfort," he declared. He also pointed out that Camp Lewis was "situated on one of the most picturesque spots in the west," and the "grub" the army served in camp was excellent, "although there is nothing fancy about it, and with not much of a variety." The meat, potatoes, unbuttered bread, and fruit went down "all right after a hard day's work." Wheeler's final verdict regarding training at Camp Lewis can be found in his advice to other draftees who might follow him into the 91st Division: "Tell all who are coming up here that they are coming to a fine place and will receive good treatment if they will do their part." As much as he liked Camp Lewis, however, Wheeler could not stay forever. Eventually he too had to bid the training depot goodbye and ship off to France.[23]

Men in the AEF—including doughboys from Utah—began and completed advanced training in France and entered combat or support units on a staggered schedule, though some like Lamar Deming went immediately into combat. America's full commitment to the cause of the First World War would not be made, however, until General John J. Pershing, commander of the American forces in France, launched his grand offensive between the Meuse River and the Argonne Forest in September 1918.[24]

Prior to the Americans' "big push," the Meuse-Argonne had been a French sector, one they had fought tooth and nail to keep. In 1916, in an effort to put France out of the war once and for all, the Germans launched an assault on the forts that ringed the ancient city of Verdun, one of the sector's key strong points; not surprisingly, the French army pushed back. The seesaw battle lasted for months, until both sides were exhausted. When the U.S. Army finally arrived on the scene, the tired French soldiers left to make room. Pershing put nine divisions on the line: the 77th, 28th, and 35th on the left; the 91st, 37th, and 79th in the middle; and the 4th, 80th, and 33rd on the right. A regiment from the 92nd Division, made up of African American draftees and white officers and put under the command of the French, served on the extreme left as a liaison between the American units and French troops to the west, while Pershing held the 1st, 3rd, 29th, 32nd, 82nd, and 92nd divisions in reserve. Most of the troops that jumped off on September 26, 1918, were green; only the 4th, 28th, and 77th had seen previous action. Across no-man's-land waited a hardened enemy dug into three very strong defensive lines.[25]

The American offensive began with a thunderous artillery barrage followed by the advance of the divisions General Pershing had chosen to lead the attack. AEF planners assigned the 91st Division, with its not inconsiderable number of Utahns, the task of driving up the middle of the American line. The "Wild West" men met only moderate resistance as they pushed over Chambronne Creek and past Véry toward Eclisfontaine near the Argonne Forest. On the battle's second day, however, elements of the 91st found themselves on the outskirts of the village of Epinonville, under heavy German artillery fire. Among the division's scattered units was Utahn Glenn Stewart. Stewart, a Millard County man, crouched patiently in a dugout, keeping his eyes peeled for enemy movement. (A real-life crack shot, he had made sergeant based on his expert rifleman classification and his ability to cut a pasteboard target in two with a machine gun at 1,700 yards.) Like so many other soldiers, Stewart witnessed some of the worst examples of war's bloody nature firsthand. In one case, while hunkered down in a hole, weapon in hand (probably a French-made Chauchat light automatic rifle), the Utah sergeant watched helplessly as a German plane dove on a forward aid station full of injured men and "deliberately drop[ped] two bombs." Placing the warheads with "fiendish cruelty," the aviator killed twelve "already maimed" men and injured forty more. Stewart also witnessed an enemy flyer down three Allied observation balloons with outlawed incendiary bullets designed to set the gas-filled balloons ablaze. According to an account published in the *Millard County Chronicle*, when the observer and his assistant saw the enemy plane, they jumped from the balloon trusting in their parachutes to save them. The assistant's parachute "met with a little wind and drifted off" to safety, but the observer was not as fortunate. His parachute was slow to deploy, giving the fiery balloon time to settle on top of him. The entire apparatus "enveloped him in flames." Stewart could only watch from his hole in the ground as the man burned to death above him.[26]

The fighting around Epinonville and other towns in the sector took a heavy toll on the 91st Division. On the battle's second day, Glenn Stewart saw "Hun artillery" nearly annihilate a retreating infantry unit, with an American soldier falling "at every shot." Stewart counted thirty-five men just around him that the Germans' effective fire had cut down (which included three men in his own squad). The barrage gutted the unit's leadership cadre, leaving some squads without any non-commissioned officers. It was, in the words of the *Millard Chronicle*, a "perfect hell."[27] The 362nd Infantry Regiment, made up mostly of Utahns, lost half of its men in a single afternoon of combat in the Meuse-Argonne campaign.[28]

On the battle's third day, while elements of the "Wild West" Division were still fighting around Epinonville, George Augustus "Gus" Faust of Fillmore found himself near the French village, looking across what in normal times must have been a lush, picturesque valley. Faust, a corporal in the division's 348th Machine Gun Battalion, wrote that the valley was now "checkered with machine gun nests, camouflaged, and in every possible way, cunningly concealed; there were trenches in well-defined rows; barbed wire entanglements aplenty." On the hill, the German artillery itched "to pour down on any part of our advance." The odds were stacked heavily against Faust and his comrades, but the machine gunners did not shirk the coming action. Forging across the bunker-studded dale, the Americans pushed the Germans out of their first line of defense, but the doughboys could not crack the second line, reinforced as it was by the first-line German evacuees. The defenders "certainly did pour it onto us," Faust recalled. "Not one of us had even time to eat a bit of hardtack or bully beef [a tinned meat product], nor was there time for any other thought than the work at hand."[29]

Unfortunately for us, Faust left no narrative clues concerning his emotional response to the violence he beheld at Epinonville. However, he did offer us a brief glimpse of the distress and even anger many soldiers, from Utah and elsewhere, must have felt at losing their friends in the intense bloodletting that marked the Meuse-Argonne battle. As Faust's machine gunners and their accompanying infantry slowly worked their way forward along the valley floor, they encountered a German machine gun emplacement. (The Germans' perfection of the art and science of defensive combat over the course of the war ultimately helped them build the world-class defensive frontier the Allies dubbed the Hindenburg Line, an amazing convergence of reinforced concrete, camouflage, and highly effective defense-in-depth tactics.) Faust watched in horror as a "squad of Huns" in the bunker "mow[ed] down our men until that nest was surrounded, and then to a man, after all that damage, when the game was up with them, up went their arms, with the full expectation of a peaceful walk back." The doughboys were livid, having just seen the Germans—now begging for mercy—coldly gun down their friends. No prisoners were taken that day, Faust declared tellingly.[30]

Clyde Bunker of Delta also personally witnessed the human violence and environmental devastation of the offensive's initial push. Before going "over the top" into no-man's-land, Bunker stripped to his olive drab uniform, a rain slicker, his cartridge belt, and his steel helmet, leaving behind his blankets and other equipment. He also carried his Chauchat automatic rifle and a light pack filled with a quarter loaf of bread, two cans of bully beef, and four hundred rounds of ammunition. Bunker had married his fiancée shortly before he landed in the army, so his desire to survive the war and return home, while no greater than anyone else's, surely ran high. Shortly before daylight on the first day of the offensive, he and his comrades filed into the American trenches—located about a hundred yards from the Germans—and when "zero hour" came, following a preparatory artillery barrage, they rushed over the parapet into the killing zone. The land resembled a moonscape. The Americans' heavy guns had mercilessly pounded the first and second lines of the enemy trenches, leaving overlapping craters and tangled masses of barbed wire strewn across no-man's-land. The once lushly forested terrain now lay denuded save for a few scattered, barkless stumps. All around the area lay the lifeless bodies of German and American soldiers, and neither side showed signs of wanting to curb the climbing corpse count. "One man put his head in a [German] dug out," Bunker reported, "and called to the enemy to surrender. He was almost completely severed in two by a burst of machine gun fire."[31]

Leland Stapley of Kanarraville witnessed much the same thing. "No farmer ever turned over the soil more thoroughly than the artillery had plowed up" the forest, Stapley wrote home. "There was not one tree but that was full of shrapnel." The doughboy only hinted at the human carnage he witnessed, perhaps because he was writing to his mother and did not want to upset her: "Some of the sights along the road would make a strong man weak," he wrote cryptically.[32]

Even support troops not directly assigned to combat roles could not avoid the startlingly gruesome sights and alienating terror of the Meuse-Argonne battlefield. Truck driver Oscar Evans recalled driving along the far eastern edge of the sector and seeing wild pigs rooting up buried corpses.[33] S. Clay Mills of Salt Lake City, on the other hand, experienced the terrors of combat on the western front in a far more immediate way. A clerk and occasional courier in an observation balloon company charged with spotting enemy targets for American artillery, Mills had crossed the Atlantic on an Italian ship, the SS *America*, and after less than a month in a French training camp he made his way to the front. In the Meuse-Argonne sector, German aviators and artillery regularly targeted the company's balloon, whether it was airborne or on the ground. But it was not just the balloon that found itself in the Germans' crosshairs. Near Mort Homme, a prominent hill just north of Verdun where the German and French armies nearly bled each other dry in 1916, the enemy incessantly shelled the area around Mills' makeshift clerk's office, which at the time was little more than a "tarpaulin thrown over a couple of sticks." The shelling finally forced him to move his workplace to a more secure dugout. (Mills discovered one of the grisly realities of war at Mort Homme: the physical remains of the dead rarely stay buried when their graves come under artillery fire. Following a bout of heavy German shelling, Mills noticed that "human bones & skeletons and skulls" now covered the hill.)[34]

In a letter to his father, written only a few days after the armistice was signed, Mills admitted that even he, a lowly company clerk, had come very close to, in his words, "getting it where the chicken got the AXE." On November 10, the day before the war ended, Mills and his company commander set out from Consenvoye, a town perched on the eastern bank of the Meuse River, to pick up the company's pay from the quartermaster. They crossed the Meuse and eventually caught up with the quartermaster in Romagne near the center of the sector, secured the money to pay their unit, and then turned back toward their bivouac at dusk. Deciding to take a shortcut back to Consenvoye, Mills and his commander crossed the Meuse on a bridge only recently built by AEF engineers. When they were only halfway across the bridge, a German artillery shell, seemingly out of nowhere, dropped out of the sky and detonated directly in front of their car. Before the "chauffeur could stop," Mills wrote home, "he ran into the big hole with his left front and hind wheel causing [the] car to tip to the left almost going over. It just did cling on to [the] edge by the other two wheels." If Mills saw his life flash before him in that second he did not let on in his letter, but he seems to have taken some time to reflect on his mortality following the experience, as evidenced by his next sentence: "If the driver had hit that hole square with both front wheels we would have plunged into the Meuse River, with about a 50 ft. fall."[35]

It turns out that even men of the cloth, who provided for the spiritual needs of men on the front line, occasionally experienced moments of pure dread in the war zone. Though they may have felt more prepared than most to deal with the twin realities of death and violence in war, military chaplains sometimes had "come-to-Jesus" moments when they were forced to ruminate on their own mortality. On one occasion, army chaplain Herbert Maw, destined to become Utah's eighth governor in 1941, visited a friend attached to an observation balloon unit. Maw was invited to accompany his associate in the balloon; the chaplain agreed and soon found himself in the air above the battlefield. "The balloon ascended to an altitude of around 2,000 feet," Maw later wrote in his memoir *Adventures With Life*, when "suddenly the anti-aircraft guns on the ground began blasting and the balloon began descending and we were ordered to jump. We were being attacked by a lone German airplane." The army equipped each balloon with parachutes, and since a balloonist could do very little to protect himself while in the air, he usually opted to bail out when attacked. Maw watched as his friend leaped over the edge of the observation platform that dangled below the sausage-shaped balloon, leaving him alone. "I was horrified," Maw recalled, "but finally climbed over the side of [the platform] and hung there for a moment before letting go. I felt the jerk of my parachute leaving the bag, but it seemed an eternity before I felt the tug of the chute opening." In what Maw may have counted as a small miracle, he and his companion floated to the ground unhurt.[36]

The slow progress of the green divisions he had sent into the Meuse-Argonne finally convinced General Pershing to take the worst performing units—including the 91st Division—off the front lines and replace them with seasoned ones such as the 1st and 2nd Divisions. For Lamar Deming of the 2nd, this meant another stint on the line. His division went forward on November 1, and by the end of the first day, under effective covering fire by the divisional artillery (of which Deming was a part), the unit gained a full nine kilometers of ground and had opened up a sixteen kilometer gap in the German defenses (though the enemy soon filled the hole).[37] The unfortunate product of the 2nd Division's success was a hefty number of casualties, which Deming described in a letter home, later published in the *Deseret News*. On the first day of the unit's push, wrote the young soldier, he and his comrades in the artillery moved forward "about 12 kilometers through the ground where the doughboys [in the infantry] had passed two hours before. The fields were covered with dead. They [the dead infantrymen] were still warm and still dripping blood." Later, when Deming and the other artillerymen stopped for the night, they dug holes for shelter and bedded down, only to be shelled heavily by the Germans. One projectile fell a scant twelve feet from Deming's dugout, leaving a six-foot-deep crater. "The next night was worse than that," Deming recalled. "The shells came over four at a time but fell short. I had traveled half the night in the cold with mud to [my] shoetops, but once I hit my blankets I forgot all about it." The German artillery fire had killed a good part of the 2nd Division's draft horses, forcing Deming and his fellow soldiers to move their guns "one at a time." When the division finally penetrated the outskirts of Beaumont, an impressive distance up the sector, the Germans again shelled them "night and day." Calling the experience "a nightmare," Deming wrote that he and his buddies "were shelled several times with gas there and the battery had sveral [*sic*] escapes."[38]

The ceasefire of November 11, 1918, produced spontaneous celebrations at the front as well as back home, and set in motion the negotiations that would ultimately lead to a peace treaty between the Allies and Germany. With the fighting at an end, Utah doughboys began to filter home. But of course not all the men who left in 1917 and 1918 came back. According to a state government report, a total of 535 Utah men died in the war, and a good number of those surely met their end in the highly lethal Meuse-Argonne campaign. One was Sheldon Axelson, a native of the small Emery County town of Cleveland. According to a report in the *Manti Messenger*, Axelson, who served in the 4th "Ivy" Division's 59th Infantry Regiment, had cheated death in earlier battles, but in the Meuse-Argonne a shell fragment finally ended his lucky streak. Wilford P. Ashton, a buddy of Axelson's from Blanding, wrote to his dead friend's family in 1921, perhaps hoping to provide them with some closure. "I did see him the night before they left for the front," wrote Ashton. Axelson's unit left its "position in reserve about 5:30 in the evening with full trust that most of them would stay with the organization." Ashton said he heard through the grapevine that his friend had joined some of his comrades for a quick meal when "a large shell" exploded nearby snuffing out his life. The Blanding man assured Sheldon's family that he mourned with them. "His life was nothing but exemplary," declared Ashton, "and I appreciate the happy days we have spent together." How the Axelson family mourned we do not know, but we can be sure the loss of young Sheldon hit them hard.[39]

66

Two other Utahns, close friends in civilian life, also left mourning families behind. Arthur Cahoon of Deseret and Orin Allen of Logan, along with Cahoon's wife, Vernell (or Vernal), and Allen's longtime fiancée, took a final camping trip into Utah's backcountry before the men had to report for induction. One can visualize the two civilians-turned-doughboys fixing this trip in their memories as a happy mental bulwark against the carnage and possible privation they were bound to experience in the war zone. But if they hoped to repeat that trip into Utah's mountainous wilderness, they were out of luck. Cahoon, a corporal, was leading a squad in the 363rd Infantry Regiment's Company M when a shell from one of the heavy guns exploded near him, killing him instantly. (The battalion major, who was standing only fifteen feet from the blast, remained unhurt.) Ironically, a fragment from the shell that killed Cahoon injured Allen. The burning metal mangled the young Utahn's legs and one of his shoulders, necessitating his removal to a rear area dressing station, where he lay out in the open all day. (This was likely due to the heavy casualties the division took around Epinonville.) That night, around eleven o'clock, an errant artillery shell fell on the aid station, killing thirteen men including Allen.[40]

Of course there were other Utah men who left the battlefields of Europe with their lives intact, but with their bodies broken. Men lost arms, legs, and other appendages to artillery blasts and suppurating wounds. Others suffered disfiguring damage to their faces. More than a few returned home with limps and other handicaps. Such was the case with Hugh Kelley, another Millard County man, who suffered from a gas attack in the Meuse-Argonne fighting. Weaponized poisonous gas—mustard, chlorine, and phosgene—killed or debilitated thousands of soldiers in the First World War, and belligerents on both sides used it freely. Despite the real danger the aerosolized poison posed, however, soldiers sometimes shrugged off putting on their protective masks when gas shells detonated nearby, as Kelley had chosen to do on one unfortunate occasion. In an instant, the gas leaking from the shell overtook him, and he began to cough violently. His ears and nose bled, and for two days, as he fought on, he wiped the trickles of blood away. At last, he gave up and went to an aid station. He returned home partly deaf and probably permanently injured from inhaling the gas.[41]

Kelley's brother, Jim, fared no better in the Meuse-Argonne. The Utah doughboy and his comrades had just routed a German strong-point on a hill when a shrapnel shell exploded over their heads, knocking him out cold and killing six men in his group. When he came to, reported the *Millard County Chronicle*, he noticed the explosion had torn his gas mask to shreds. He foggily looked himself over and discovered "a forefinger loose and wobbling, hanging on by only a strip of flesh." Amazingly, the wounded hand caused Jim no pain, but another injury, this one in his leg, did. In the hospital, doctors removed the finger and patched up his leg. Jim Kelley went home fingerless and no doubt limping, perhaps for the rest of his life.[42]

Then there were those who possessed invisible wounds—mental and psychological damage that even experts would have been hard pressed to spot. These injuries could fester for years undetected, while they slowly ravaged their victim's psyche.[43] This apparently was the case with Levi Taylor of Moab, who, according to the *Moab Times-Independent*, had been "on the line in France." The paper reported that Taylor suffered from shell shock, after surviving a German artillery barrage near the Argonne Forest, but he refused to let his parents apply for federal medical aid. According to his buddies, a dramatic change in his demeanor accompanied his brush with death.[44] Taylor's condition, reported the *Times-Independent*, remained "pitiful" as he struggled with the effects of the war on his psyche. The paper maintained that Taylor suffered from "delusions resulting from his experiences on the battle front"—presumably flashbacks and other symptoms of what we would now label post-traumatic stress disorder. A suicide attempt finally spurred Taylor's parents to action, and they took him to Salt Lake City where Veterans Bureau physicians could examine him. The doctors approved a claim for disability benefits, but Taylor did not want to stay at the hospital, so his physicians sent him home to recuperate under his parents' care.[45]

Things seemed to go back to normal after Taylor returned to Moab, though his family noticed his physical condition beginning to slip. Then one Friday in 1925, while talking to two of his sisters at his parents' home, Taylor calmly dismissed himself, went into a nearby room, and put a bullet in his head. What a tragic shift from the hopeful tenor of a letter young Levi wrote to his married sister, Ada Harris of Monticello, immediately following the war's end, talking about his eagerness to return to the United States and the anticipation he and his pals felt about marching in a big military parade down the boulevards of Paris![46]

And what of those uninjured Utah doughboys who seemed to adjust more readily to postwar life, despite having experienced directly the tremendous destructive power of modern warfare? How did they handle what they had seen and heard? Few shared their feelings publicly, either in spoken or written form. Some may have looked back fondly on their days in France as some of the best of their lives. Still, many former soldiers would have echoed the sentiment of one of their own: Sergeant Jack Francis of Salt Lake City. The Utahn had fought in the ranks of the much-vaunted 1st Division, otherwise known as the "Big Red One" (so named for the red "1" the unit's men wore on their sleeves). According to the *Salt Lake Telegram*, Francis "saw about as much service as happened to fall to the lot of any Utahn who went over." His declaration about what he wanted to do now that the fighting was over was short and unambiguous: "I don't even want to talk war again." It appears even those who seemed most prepared to reenter civilian life knew they were dealing with powerful demons. Once immersed in war, they would never be the same.[47]

NOTES

Originally published in the *Utah Historical Quarterly* 80 (Fall 2012): 334–53.

1. *Ogden Standard*, April 30, 1919; "United States Census, 1910"; index and images, FamilySearch.org, accessed March 29, 2012, entry for Leroy Moyes; Census records, Ogden, Utah, family number 124, page

number 6; United States Bureau of the Census, National Archives, Washington, D.C.

2. "United States Census, 1910"; "Veterans with Federal Service Buried in Utah, Territorial to 1966," index and images, FamilySearch.org, accessed March 29, 2012; Entry for Leroy Moyes, died September 2, 1954, veterans records, Family History Library microfilm, Utah State Historical Society, Salt Lake City, Utah. On the 91st Division, see *The Story of the 91st Division* (San Mateo, CA: 91st Division Publication Committee, 1919).

3. *Ogden Standard*, April 30, 1919.

4. Ibid.

5. Robert H. Ferrell, *America's Deadliest Battle: Meuse-Argonne, 1918* (Lawrence: University of Kansas Press, 2007), xi. Ferrell also claims the Meuse-Argonne battle was the largest in American history, with 1.2 million men actively involved at the front. For casualty figures in the Battle of the Bulge, see Max Hastings, *Armageddon: The Battle for Germany, 1944–45* (New York: Alfred A. Knopf, 2004), 235.

6. Immediately following the war, a handful of studies on the Meuse-Argonne Offensive were rushed into print. These included Frederick Palmer, *Our Greatest Battle (The Meuse-Argonne)* (New York: Dodd, Mead and Company, 1919); and Arthur D. Hartzell, *Meuse-Argonne Battle (Sept. 26–Nov. 11, 1918)* (Chaumont, France: General Headquarters, American Expeditionary Forces, 1919). Recent studies of the Meuse-Argonne, however, have been few and far between. See Paul F. Braim, *The Test of Battle: The American Expeditionary Forces in the Meuse-Argonne Campaign* (Newark: University of Delaware Press, 1987); Ferrell, *Deadliest Battle*; and Edward G. Lengel, *To Conquer Hell: The Meuse-Argonne, 1918* (New York: Henry Holt and Company, 2008).

7. Nobel Warrum, *Utah in the World War: The Men Behind the Guns and the Men and Women Behind the Men Behind the Guns* (Salt Lake City: Utah State Council of Defense, 1924), 39–55.

8. Peter S. Kindsvatter, *American Soldiers: Ground Combat in the World Wars, Korea and Vietnam* (Lawrence: University Press of Kansas, 2003), xx, 67–92.

9. David M. Kennedy, *Over Here: The First World War in American Society* (New York: Oxford University Press, 1980); Thomas Fleming, *The Illusion of Victory: America In World War I* (New York: Basic Books, 2003); and Justus D. Doenecke, *Nothing Less Than War: A New History of America's Entry into World War I* (Lexington: University Press of Kentucky, 2011).

10. Byron Farwell, *Over There: The United States in the Great War, 1917–1918* (New York: W. W. Norton, 1999), 56–57.
11. Ibid., 50–51.
12. Oral history interview with Oscar W. Evans, July 10, 1992, MSS A-5088, 5–6, Utah State Historical Society, Salt Lake City, Utah (Hereafter cited as Evans History). As a member of a support unit, Evans's ability to transport much needed supplies to men on the front lines quickly and efficiently was essential for victory.
13. Ibid., 6.
14. "United States Census, 1920"; index and images, FamilySearch.org, accessed March 29, 2012, entry for Lamar Deming; Census records, Salt Lake City, Utah, family number 277, page number 13A; United States Bureau of the Census, National Archives, Washington, D.C.; *Deseret News*, December 27, 1918; Richard Roberts, *Legacy: The History of the Utah National Guard from the Nauvoo Legion Era to Enduring Freedom* (Salt Lake City: National Guard Association of Utah, 2003), 102–25.
15. Roberts, *Legacy*, 117–19; *Deseret News*, December 3, 1918.
16. Kerry William Bate, "Kanarraville Fights World War I," *Utah Historical Quarterly* 63 (Winter 1995), 27.
17. *Iron County Record*, July 6, July 27, August 17, August 24, 1917.
18. Ibid., September 28, 1917.
19. L. Wardlaw Miles, *History of the 308th Infantry, 1917–1919* (New York: G. P. Putnam's Sons, 1927), 270–78; Lengel, *To Conquer Hell*, 35, 92–93, 121–22; Warrum, *Utah in the World War*, 47. According to Warrum, "all Utah men inducted into the service through selective enrollment [the draft] were sent" to Camp Lewis, the 91st Division's home base. Warrum also points out that more Utah men were assigned to the division's 362nd Infantry "than to any of the others, so it came to be regarded as a Utah regiment."
20. *Iron County Record*, April 18, 1919.
21. *Ogden Standard*, June 14, August 1, August 31, 1917. The appellant in the Ogden draft case, George Lowe Abbott, later enlisted in the army as a regular. See *Ogden Standard*, September 8, 1917.
22. Ibid., September 10, 1917.
23. Ibid.
24. *Deseret News*, December 3, 1918.
25. Lengel, *To Conquer Hell*, 58–62, 122.
26. *Millard County Chronicle*, June 26, 1919.
27. Ibid.
28. Lengel, *To Conquer Hell*, 172.

29. *Millard County Chronicle*, June 26, 1919. Gus Faust was the father of James E. Faust, second counselor in the First Presidency of the Church of Jesus Christ of Latter-day Saints. See Lynn Arave, "President James E. Faust Dies at Age 87," *Deseret Morning News*, August 10, 2007.

30. *Millard County Chronicle*, June 26, 1919.

31. Ibid., April 25, 1918; June 26, 1919.

32. *Iron County Record*, April 18, 1919.

33. Evans History, 11. Evans appears to have been so affected by what he saw in the war that he instructed his interviewer years later, "Now, I don't want to go into a lot of things I saw in France, the wicked things."

34. S. C. Mills, diary, December 16, 1917–November 26, 1918, MSS A-2032, Utah State Historical Society.

35. S. C. Mills to his father, November 24, 1918, MSS A-2032, Utah State Historical Society.

36. Herbert B. Maw, *Adventures With Life* (Salt Lake City: self published, 1978), 87–88.

37. Ferrell, *Deadliest Battle*, 112–29, 131–34; Lengel, *To Conquer Hell*, 387–99.

38. *Deseret News*, December 27, 1918.

39. *Manti Messenger*, April 18, 1919; November 12, 1920; May 17 and October 7, 1921.

40. *Millard County Chronicle*, November 14, 1918; June 26, 1919.

41. Ibid., June 26, 1919.

42. Ibid.

43. For more on the physical and psychological dimensions of combat in the First World War, see Alan Kramer, *Dynamic of Destruction: Culture and Mass Killing in the First World War* (New York: Oxford University Press, 2007), 211–67.

44. *Moab Times-Independent*, August 11 and August 21, 1924.

45. Ibid., June 18 and August 21, 1924. On the causes and consequences of shell shock and psychological trauma in combat, see Denis Winter, *Death's Men: Soldiers of the Great War* (New York: Penguin, 1978), 129–40.

46. *Moab Times-Independent*, January 3, 1919.

47. *Salt Lake Telegram*, September 9, 1919.

4

"IF ONLY I SHALL HAVE THE RIGHT STUFF"

Utah Women in World War I

MIRIAM B. MURPHY

Women were not subject to the draft nor were they allowed to volunteer for military service. However many women did volunteer for one or more of the thirty-five different kinds of work that were deemed appropriate for them. On a more informal basis, women also contributed to the war effort in whatever way they could, demonstrating a loyalty and patriotism equal to that of soldiers sent to the front lines. A few women did reach the battlefront as volunteers with private organizations, which secured for them the necessary documents to enter the battle zone as nurses, ambulance drivers, or canteen workers. Miriam B. Murphy, a prominent women's historian, examines the environment for women's service during the war, introduces the reader to a number of remarkable women whose stories offer important insights into Utahns and the war experience, and concludes with an assessment of the impact their service had on postwar Utah and the nation.

Old rivalries, competing national agendas, and a reckless arms race engulfed Europe in war in 1914, but America remained officially neutral until unrestricted German submarine warfare led the United States to cut diplomatic ties with Germany on February 3, 1917, and to declare war against her on April 6. National Guard units were mobilized, and volunteers and draftees swelled the regular armed service ranks. Civilians responded by organizing bond drives, running canteens, preparing surgical dressings, filling jobs vacated by servicemen, and performing countless other home-front assignments. Women, especially, devoted themselves to Red Cross work and other organizations such as the Salvation Army. But for many women that was not enough, and thousands volunteered to participate more directly in the war. Some risked their lives near the battlefront. Others served at military facilities in the United States. For some the war provided an unparalleled adventure that cast them in a heroine's role. Some died. Some won decorations. All contributed to the Allied victory.

Utah women participated in a wide range of war-related activities under the aegis of the State Council of Defense. Their efforts encompassed Americanization and citizenship classes, foreign and domestic relief, food production and preservation, conservation of limited clothing and food resources, health and recreation, and liberty loan drives. At the request of Gov. Simon Bamberger, Mrs. R. E. L. Collier chaired a committee to register women volunteers. Almost twenty-four thousand women throughout the state turned in cards pledging their support of the war effort by suggesting "thirty-five different lines of work" they felt both capable and willing to do if called upon. Their names were forwarded to local organizations such as the Red Cross. Another state committee, chaired by Mrs. F. E. Morris, "helped many patriotic girls and women to secure and hold places made vacant by the enlistment of men for military service."[1]

Although many women were mobilized statewide, their activities and accomplishments have received little historical scrutiny to date and are largely overshadowed by those of women during World War II. For Americans, World War I was a relatively short conflict, with the United States an official participant for only nineteen months. World War II, on the other hand, lasted more than twice as long for Americans, and, moreover, strained the nation's resources almost to the limit. Additionally, Rosie the Riveter and uniformed WACs (Women's Army Corps) and WAVES (Women Accepted for Voluntary Emergency Service) provided highly visible and enduring symbols of women at war. With the exception of the martyred British nurse Edith Cavell, most of the women directly involved in World War I had their "hour upon the stage and then [were] heard no more." Still, after almost three-quarters of a century one can state with confidence that their activities did "signify" something. This chapter examines those Utah women who opted during World War I for direct participation with the military or with civilian organizations that took them to the battlefront.

Two Utah women drove ambulances or other vehicles in France during the war. Elizabeth (Betty) McCune donned overalls in the summer of 1917 to learn auto mechanics and repair in the shop of Charles A. Quigley, 33 Exchange Place, Salt Lake City. She had mastered the workings of her new Chandler by mid-July and reportedly sailed with it for France on the *Rochambeau* on November 5. In addition to her vehicle, which she was required to provide and maintain, McCune was responsible for her living expenses and her own clothing. Her driving attire consisted of "a very soft leather suit of trousers and coat with high boots to the knees, . . . [a] waist with long sleeves, . . . heavy woolen underwear, . . . [a] driving coat . . . [of] rubber waterproof on the outside with leather on the inside, . . . a soft woolen inner coat, . . . long woolen stockings, . . . [and] a woolen knit helmet . . . to wear under her other caps."

Most women ambulance drivers in Europe worked through private organizations created by wealthy, socially prominent American and British women who wanted a more active and direct role in the war. These groups provided individual members with an umbrella organization and the documents necessary to enter the war zone and serve. Since each woman was required to be self-supporting (for the most part), participation was limited to those able to afford the cost. Additionally, some organizations required the women to supply their own vehicles. McCune reportedly signed up with "authorities" in such an organization in New York sometime in the spring of 1917.[2]

Maud Fitch of Eureka, Utah, wrote letters that present a very graphic and detailed account of her service as an ambulance driver in France.[3] Active in the Red Cross during 1917, she hungered for a chance to serve in Europe and joined the Woman's Motor Unit of Le Bien-Entre du Blesse, an organization directed by writer and book designer Grace Gallatin Seton.[4] Fitch arrived in New York in mid-February 1918. Intrigued at first by Grace and her author husband Ernest Thompson Seton, the thirty-five-year-old Utahn soon found Mrs. Seton "indefinite" and poorly organized. During almost three weeks in New York Fitch passed perfunctory examinations of her driving skill and knowledge of engine operation, bought her "truck" and paid in advance for a six-month supply of gas and oil,[5] was vaccinated, received her passport and visas, and was constantly entertained by friends. She sailed for France on the *Chicago* on March 7, the only woman in Seton's group able to depart on this ship.

By March 21 Fitch was settled in a Paris hotel. As disorganized as the New York operation, the Paris office of Le Bien-Entre du Blesse kept the eager Utahn in a holding pattern for almost two months. During that time she was fitted for a uniform she considered very impractical, took further tests of her driving ability from French officials, frequently attended mass, enjoyed the company of friends, and volunteered for work in canteens and with refugees. Impatient for action but aware of her contract with Seton's organization, Fitch tried to negotiate a temporary driving assignment with the Red Cross, which had no women among its ambulance drivers. She expressed hope on April 9, in a lengthy letter to her parents, that the Red Cross might indeed accept her:

> If they should . . . we will get into action AT ONCE—the magic of those two words! And to think at last I shall get into the very

vortex of the greatest conflict in the history of the world. I can't think what it will mean. If only I shall have the right stuff in me to benefit by it—to go into it and come out with one's soul and heart all fire tried!

That hope did not materialize, but Fitch kept busy, even consenting to do office work, she wryly told her father, for the Red Cross. On May 15, however, she could finally report:

I'm so thrilled I can hardly write, but at last really and certainly I am off for the front in a REAL Unit. We've all left the B.E.B. in a days time [and] joined the Hackett Lowther Unit. . . . It is the only Unit directly under the Military and we move with the [French Third] Army and under a French Lieutenant.[6]

Fitch and her companions headed to the front, north of Paris, advancing in their ambulances with a long convoy of troops toward the heart of the German army's spring offensive. The Hackett-Lowther women, replacing a section of men, found their first quarters in an abandoned chateau, probably near Compiegne, an area under steady shelling.

On the evening of May 30 Fitch was waiting several miles behind the lines when she was called to take "five assis"—wounded men who could sit up—to "a hospital back of this place." Accompanied by an interpreter who had messages for the French medical chief, she entered a scene of typical wartime confusion: "It got pitch black and the roads were filled—packed tight with sometimes three streams of advancing troops, cavalry and camions." Where the traffic was especially heavy with delays as long as an hour, she bribed those directing the flow with cigarettes to let her ambulance through. Occasionally her companion flashed a torch into the forest darkness to reveal a huge camion "lurch[ing] away . . . at the last minute." Stopping in a town square to get her bearings, she discovered that shelling had destroyed most of it, including directional signs, but she eventually reached the hospital. Returning over the bombarded roads was somewhat easier since the moon had come up and she was driving with the main flow of traffic. Home by 2:30 a.m., she fell instantly to sleep in the back of an ambulance, "and at 6 in the morning . . . breakfasted on nothing and washed some layers of dust off, then strolled about the hills with the guns at the front hammering in our ears." For a harrowing night rescue of wounded under heavy fire on June 9—an experience she downplayed in her letters home—she received the French Croix de Guerre. Later, a gold star was added to her medal.

By late spring Germany could not hold its advances on the western front. The Hackett-Lowther women moved with the French Third Army through territory previously held by the Germans and were often on the front itself. Fitch exulted in the first hint of victory and in the uniqueness of her opportunity to associate closely with French officers and men, whom she greatly admired. One time a French artillery crew invited her to fire their 75 mm field gun, and she was sure the shell had "killed some Boche[s]." On another occasion she piloted a surprised and ultimately delighted French colonel to his new advanced position at the front.

Fitch gave her parents a concise description of the work of the unit in a letter dated September 14:

> The "abris" you inquire about consist of any cellar or dugout . . .
> sandbagged against avion bombs. We only sleep in them at the
> "post des [sic] secours" . . . the first dressing stations near the
> lines, . . . to which the wounded are carried on stretchers. We . . .
> take the [wounded] from there back to a hospital where another
> car picks them up when they are rebandaged . . . and takes them
> further back. . . . The second work is . . . "back evacuation" work
> which of course one prefers not to do unless one's nerves have
> begun to get taut from frontwork. Often, as during the Compiegne attack, the first hospitals back were so crowded that we
> would be refused with our load by the first one and then another,
> thus necessitating a FEARFULLY long drive for the poor things.

And even now we have to take them from 40 to 50 kilometres as the hospitals were wary of moving up too quickly.

The women often worked twenty-four-hour shifts. When off duty they spent considerable time on the repair and maintenance of their ambulances, which is not surprising given the condition of the roads. Blowouts and breakdowns occurred so frequently they seemed routine. Practical jokes, pillow fights, and swimming in one of the many streams threading through northwest France eased the tension. In the lull between battles Fitch and the other women sometimes socialized with French officers or *poilus* (soldiers), sharing food, dancing, and just talking. Clearly, for Fitch it was the experience of a lifetime. Her letters home constitute one of the most remarkable firsthand accounts of World War I by an American.

Mary F. Starr of Salt Lake City, like Maud Fitch and Elizabeth McCune, had hoped to drive an ambulance during the war. Unable to realize that desire, perhaps because of the cost, she nevertheless embarked for France, where she worked in a canteen. A number of organizations, including the Red Cross, operated canteens in France during the war, but none was more admired by the soldiers than the Salvation Army's. One SA worker from Salt Lake City, Mae Morton, may have been the first Utah woman to reach the front. According to Noble Warrum, "She served for many months as near the firing line as a noncombatant was permitted to go, but the shifting tide of battle often placed her within the zone of danger, from which she never flinched so long as there was a chance to minister to the needs of the tired and hungry men of the trenches." Canteen work near the front was indeed dangerous. Decades after the war the efforts of people like Morton remained legendary.[7]

Other Utah women filled different wartime assignments with the military. Edith Walker of Magna, a business college graduate, had been in charge of Congressman William Kettner's California office staff until the fall of 1917 when she became the only female employee in the office of the constructing quartermaster at Camp Kearny, California. Another office worker, Joy DeCamp of Salt Lake City, served in the Paris headquarters of the American Expeditionary Forces. Four other women filled clerical positions in the U.S. Navy as yeomanettes: Norma Bessie Long, Edna Romney, and Beatrice Timmins, all of Salt Lake City; and Blanche Williams of Ogden.[8]

Most of the Utah women who served in the war were registered nurses. They signed up with the American Red Cross, which supplied the military with nursing personnel for its hospitals in the United States; field, evacuation, and convalescent hospitals in Europe; and mobile medical units, or dressing stations as they were often called, just behind the battle lines.

By the time the United States entered the war the Red Cross had already established twenty-five base hospitals for the army (with four more nearing completion), three for the navy, and three field units. More than seven thousand graduate nurses were enrolled nationally as a reserve, and "training for another regiment of nurses [was] underway." Since the War Department hoped to enlist twenty-five thousand nurses by the end of 1917, the Red Cross began an intense recruiting campaign nationwide. The Red Cross required enlisting nurses "to have had at least two years' training in a hospital that averaged fifty patients a day of both sexes," be registered to practice in their home states, provide evidence of good health, and be between ages twenty-five and forty. Utah had approximately 450 trained nurses when the United States entered the war. By the summer of 1917 a number of them had already volunteered and were serving at base hospitals in this country or were on their way to France.[9]

Julia O. Flikke described the mobilization of one American base hospital unit consisting of one hundred nurses and a staff of physicians. After "preliminary duty in southern training camps, where pneumonia was then prevalent," the nurses embarked from New York on an English freighter, ultimately arriving at a chateau outside Nantes on the French coast where Base Hospital No. 11 was established:

> The nurses' barracks were built in sections, with each division consisting of an entrance hall, four bedrooms and a washroom.

Electricity and cold running water were supplied, but all water had to be boiled before it could be used for drinking. As for hot water, that was a rarity to be had only at fixed hours.

Each nurse was assigned to a ward containing fifty patients and was assisted by two or three corpsmen as well as by many of the more active convalescents. The usual working day was twelve hours, with the exception of one time when an unusually large convoy of wounded arrived from the Argonne front and the entire staff was kept busy all night.

The operating room held four surgical teams "served by one nurse." Their primary tasks included removing shrapnel, closing machine gun wounds, and treating bayonet wounds. Some nurses from this hospital went into the field as part of a shock or trauma team helping the more seriously wounded closer to the front lines.[10] By April 1918 thirty-six Utah nurses were stationed "in the war zone" at similar facilities.[11]

In light of the 1918 German spring offensive, recruiting continued apace. More men and women needed was the message hidden behind optimistic headlines proclaiming victory to be at hand. Lettie B. Welsh, supervisor of nurses for the Mountain Division of the Red Cross, visited Salt Lake City on April 8 and 9 to enlist more nurses; five thousand were needed nationally. Because war demands something from everyone, she said, "those parents who give their boys gladly and willingly for their country need to give their daughters, that their sons may be rightly cared for."[12]

A few days before Welsh's visit, the State Board of Nurse Examiners had "enacted a war measure which, while it was not strictly in accordance with the provisions of our Act, seemed very necessary on account of the appeals of the Red Cross for nurses." The measure allowed a nurse within a few weeks of graduation to be registered by the state if the hospital would advance the date of graduation and if the nurse agreed to sign up immediately with the Red Cross. The board itself exemplified patriotism: two of its members resigned to serve overseas—Ella Wicklund on January 1 and Stella Sainsbury on April 18.[13]

Some eighty Utah registered nurses served in World War I, a figure that may represent one-fourth or more of all the RNs in the state.[14] Firsthand accounts of the experiences of these women are hard to find. A letter and other memorabilia of Mabel Bettilyon describe a dramatic scene in France. Mabel was "attached to Evacuation Hospital No. 1. In one night alone more than 800 wounded American soldiers were brought into this hospital, 136 of whom were assigned to [her] care for want of sufficient nurses." When the wounded arrived they had already had "first aid some place in the front lines." In the receiving ward the patients were "undressed and all their personal belongings such as money, letters, pictures . . . put in a Red Cross bag," she told her mother, "so if you have made any you can see how your little bit helps." Bettilyon praised the courage of her wounded countrymen, many who did not want to be sent home "until we get the Kaiser." Since this was an evacuation hospital, she cared for many German wounded as well, but was glad when they left. "So many people are anxious for German souvenirs," she wrote, "but . . . seeing our men wounded and dying is all I want that refers to Germany. I feel now as tho I wouldn't give the smallest place in my trunk for anything off a prisoner."[15]

Another nurse, Ruth Clayton, viewed her service in France as "the most important experience of her life because she was able to help." A 1915 graduate of St. Mark's Hospital School of Nursing, she joined the Army Nurse Corps in 1916 and may have served on the Texas border before going overseas. In France, working in a crowded hospital tent as part of a surgical team, she saw some of the worst gas cases—men with swollen, disfigured faces, some blinded. Doctors quickly decided which of the wounded had the best chance to survive and channeled their own and the nurses' efforts toward them. Facilities were primitive. Sometimes the only place to sit in the mess tent was on a wooden coffin. One doctor Clayton knew, overwhelmed by the magnitude of the job, worked around the clock, taking morphine—to which he became addicted—to keep himself going. Clayton "couldn't take hospital work" after the war and went into public health nursing, administering hearing and vision tests in Salt Lake City schools. Her patriotism never waned, however, and during World War II she volunteered as a nurse at Bushnell Hospital, a military facility in Brigham City, Utah.[16]

In England the work of women during World War I was to some extent tied to the suffrage movement; militant suffrage leaders supported the war effort and abandoned confrontations with the government in exchange for a promise of prompt action on suffrage after the war. Although women in the United States also achieved suffrage after the war, with the ratification of the 19th Amendment on August 26, 1920, the circumstances are not exactly parallel. The National American Woman Suffrage Association, under the leadership of Carrie Chapman Catt, realized that the success of their cause might hinge "on whether they . . . joined in the war effort." Not so for the National Woman's Party with its many Quaker members who picketed the White House, "took no steps toward organizing war work," and in response to the wartime slogan urging Americans to "make the world safe for democracy" displayed "Democracy Should Begin at Home" banners.

In Utah there was less of a connection between the war and the women's rights movement. Since Utah women had fought and won their suffrage battle during the State Constitutional Convention in 1895, they showed little inclination to tie their participation in the war to feminine political goals. Nevertheless, they continued to support national suffrage. For example, legislator/suffragist Elizabeth A. Hayward introduced a memorial to Congress urging immediate action on the suffrage amendment. It passed both houses of the Utah State Legislature and was signed by Governor Bamberger.[17]

The suffrage question aside, it is possible to see a thread other than patriotism connecting Utah's World War I nurses. This group included many leaders—women of skill, vision, and dedication who set new standards for the profession, developed new concepts in health care, and served their communities with distinction both before and after the war.

Ella M. Wicklund, Anna J. Hall, and Rose Karous, for example, were among those who successfully promoted passage by the 1917 legislature of an act requiring the registration of nurses, a measure of key importance in the development of professional nursing standards. Wicklund, a 1910 graduate of the Holy Cross School of Nursing, took charge of the hospital's new obstetrical department in 1916, served on the first State Board of Nurse Examiners, and served as secretary of the Red Cross in Salt Lake City before leaving for France early in 1918. Hall, who graduated from St. Mark's Hospital School of Nursing in 1912, is credited with raising the standards of nurses' training at Ogden's Dee Hospital by expanding the curriculum from two and a half to three years and opening an obstetrical section. She continued her pioneering role after the war by training as a nurse anesthetist in a Cleveland, Ohio, hospital and practicing in Utah until 1945. Karous was instrumental in introducing the visiting nurse concept locally. A 1906 graduate of St. Mark's Hospital, she chaired Utah's Red Cross Nursing Service for four years before she and her sister Frae joined the Navy Nurse Corps.[18]

Other nursing leaders who served in World War I include Anna Rosenkilde, a graduate of the LDS Hospital School of Nursing, who served in France with the Army Nurse Corps. She was the first nurse hired by the new Primary Children's Hospital in Salt Lake City in 1922 and was superintendent there until her retirement in the mid-1940s, a legendary caregiver whom the children called Mama Rose. Carrie Roberts, a 1911 graduate of St. Mark's, was one of the first public health nurses in Utah, appointed in 1913 to a position with the Salt Lake City Board of Health. Her duties included inspection and instruction in Salt Lake schools and "in private homes when such may be solicited or found necessary." Roberts, who enlisted in the spring of 1917, was assigned to hospital work at Fort Bliss, Texas, for fourteen months before being sent to Base Hospital No. 62 in Tours, France, for six months. Soon after her return home she spoke at a memorial service in the Amelia Palace in Salt Lake City honoring Jane A. Delano, who recruited thirty thousand nurses during the war and died during an inspection tour in France in April 1919. Another nursing leader, Agnes M. Hogan, a 1914 graduate of LDS Hospital who served overseas during the war, was a founder of the Utah Nurses Association.[19]

Although a majority of the nurses were single women in their twenties, Wicklund, Hall, the Karous sisters, Rosenkilde, Nancy V. Self, Anne E. Wiberg, and Luella Francy are known to have been in their thirties. Victoria Christensen, an LDS Hospital nurse therapist, may have been one of the oldest Utah nurses to serve. According to one report, she volunteered because her son was in the army and she wanted to help the soldiers. "Nursing is as important as the fighting, and it must be done. . . . Wonderful is the only way in which the work the women are doing over there can be described, and it will be even more brilliant before the war is over," she told a reporter.[20]

More than 270 American nurses lost their lives during the war. Many died from pneumonia or from the deadly influenza epidemic. It does not appear that any of the fatalities were Utahns. At least two Utah nurses did experience war-related health problems, however. Louise Owen, a 1916 graduate of the Dee Hospital School of Nursing in Ogden, "was released from military service due to pneumonia and complications which scarred her lungs and caused some problems all her life." Respiratory problems "didn't slow her down as she was very determined," according to her son. She worked as a private duty RN in both the Dee and St. Benedict's hospitals in Ogden until 1957 and was active in nursing professional organizations. She was a member of the Disabled American Veterans. Another woman, Ella H. Conover, was also reported as having "her health . . . impaired during her war service."[21]

At least two Utah nurses received special recognition for their service. Luella Francy, a 1907 graduate of St. Mark's and an emergency hospital nurse in Salt Lake City, began her wartime service at Fort Bliss. Later she was part of a medical unit "on detached service from the American army in France [sent] to help the American Red Cross in its relief work in the Balkans." This seven-member team, which included three doctors, established the only hospital in the area of Prizeren, Serbia. Francy received the Serbian Cross of Mercy for her work. Nancy V. Self, a prominent figure in nursing and health organizations in Ogden, served as a nurse with the American Expeditionary Forces in Europe and was "commended by the chief of staff of the host forces for her work in the field hospitals."[22]

Whether they were RNs, ambulance drivers, or canteen and clerical workers, Utah's women "veterans" obviously had "the right stuff." They did not consider themselves remarkable, however, nor did they view their wartime roles as masculine; rather, they saw a need and filled it with courage, dedication, and skill. Many of them witnessed the horrors of war—bombed villages and the dead, dying, and seriously wounded—firsthand. Their experiences should not be considered unique, inasmuch as women have served their country in every war since the American Revolution, but their many accomplishments in World War I undoubtedly foreshadowed expanding roles for women in the armed services in World War II and later conflicts.[23]

NOTES

Originally published in the *Utah Historical Quarterly* 58 (Fall 1990): 334–50.

1. Noble Warrum, *Utah in the World War* (Salt Lake City: Utah State Council of Defense, 1924), 107, 121–23. The role of working women in the war is beyond the scope of this chapter; clearly a detailed study of it is needed. Suffice it to say that women were the key workers in Utah's canning industry, for example, which boomed during the war as a result of government contracts. Women also continued to increase their roles as office workers during the 1910s, many of them taking over jobs previously held by men (stenographer, typist, bookkeeper, accountant, and clerk). That more mothers worked outside the home is indicated by a report that the day nursery at Neighborhood House in Salt Lake City was "strained to the utmost" during World War I. See issues of the *Payroll Builder*, a publication of

the Utah Manufacturers Association, for 1917–18; census occupational data for the years 1900, 1910, and 1920 that document the feminizing of many office jobs; and Lela Horn Richards, *The Growth of Neighborhood House* (Salt Lake City, 1929), 12.

2. *Salt Lake Tribune*, July 14, 1917; *Relief Society Magazine* 4 (1917): 690–91. The former account says McCune, a daughter of Elizabeth Claridge and mining millionaire Alfred W. McCune, signed up as "an automobile driver, carrying supplies to soldiers on the firing line," while the latter refers to her as an ambulance driver. I have been unable to find accounts of other service after her presumed arrival in Europe late in 1917. McCune (1891–1967) married Reginald G. Trower after the war.

3. Born on November 28, 1882, Maud was one of five children of Exilda Marcotte and Walter Fitch, Sr., a wealthy mine operator in the Tintic district of Utah. After the war Maud married and had a son. She died in Los Angeles at age 91. Her letters comprise 228 typewritten pages transcribed and compiled by her in a loose-leaf binder in the possession her son, Paul Hilsdale, in Los Angeles, to whom I am exceedingly grateful. All the quotations herein and data about her service in France derive from this source. I am also grateful to Max Garbette of Eureka, who generously shared information on Maud Fitch. Fitch's activities also received newspaper coverage. See *Eureka Reporter*, May 25, June 1, June 29, 1917; February 8, July 19, October 4, 1918; September 5, 1919; June 15, 1923 (the last article details the accidental death of her husband). See also *Salt Lake Telegram*, May 2, 1919, which announces her return from France.

4. For more on Seton, see *Who's Who of American Women*, volume 1 (Chicago: A. N. Marquis Co., 1958), 1156.

5. According to Fitch's letter on February 24, 1918, her father sent $792 to New York to pay for the "truck." On March 5, 1918, she told her father she was writing a check for $300 to the Eureka Bank to prepay for gasoline and oil. On June 18, 1918, Fitch advised her father to try to recover this money from Seton.

6. The Hackett-Lowther Unit was intended to be "all English" but accepted Fitch and some other Americans because "they couldn't get English girls across the Channel quickly enough" to satisfy the immediate need. Toupie Lowther, a well-known tennis player of the time, was a member of the Earl of Lonsdale's family. She worked in the field with the unit. Miss Hackett is mentioned as planning to visit the unit but is not further identified by Fitch. The women drivers were "rated as common, ordinary Poilus ('soldiers') in the army"

and received "3 sous a day. . . . We pay our chief, Miss Lowther, $30.00 a month for the upkeep of the Unit" (letter dated May 14 but probably written between May 15 and May 19, 1918). The Ford ambulance Fitch ultimately drove was donated by Scottish coal mine owners and workers (letter written in May 1918, no day given).

7. Warrum, *Utah in the World War*, 67–68, 62. See also, for example, an editorial in the June 16, 1946, *Salt Lake Tribune* that states, "Many soldiers of the First World War who had as youths gibed at the little bands of musicians standing on street corners were shocked into solemn respect for these Salvation Army men and women when they encountered them close behind the firing lines in France passing out coffee and doughnuts."

8. *Deseret News*, November 5, 1917; Warrum, *Utah in the World War*, 68, 204. There were undoubtedly other Utah women directly involved with the military in clerical or other positions at Fort Douglas in Salt Lake City or elsewhere, but I have been unable to find mention of them.

9. Henry P. Davidson, *The American Red Cross in the Great War* (New York: Macmillan Co., 1919), 6, 21, 79. The Red Cross served a recruiting function in cooperation with the American Nurses Assocation, funneling registered nurses into the Army Nurse Corps, established in February 1901, and the Navy Nurse Corps, established in May 1908.

   The 1910 U.S. Census lists 225 trained nurses in Utah, and the 1920 count lists 544. The 450 figure is my estimate of the number in 1917. Not all of the trained nurses were RNs, however; a Red Cross leader stated in 1918 that Utah had "some 300" registered nurses. See *Salt Lake Telegram–Herald Republican*, April 9, 1918.

10. Colonel Flikke, superintendent of the Army Nurse Corps, wrote a history of the corps published during World War II, *Nurses in Action: The Story of the Army Nurse Corps* (Philadelphia: J. B. Lippincott Co., 1943), 49–52.

11. *Salt Lake Telegram–Herald Republican*, April 9, 1918. Other Utah nurses were stationed at military hospitals in the United States.

12. *Salt Lake Tribune*, April 10, 1918. The name is spelled Welch in this account. See also *Salt Lake Telegram–Herald Republican*, April 9, 1918. Welsh, or Welch, spoke at the YWCA (Young Women's Christian Association) and to nurses at Salt Lake's three hospital nursing schools—Holy Cross, St. Mark's, and LDS.

13. State of Utah, "Utah State Board of Examination and Registration of Hospital Trained and Graduate Nurses," public documents, 1917–1918, vol. 2, report no. 18, 5–6.

14. See note 9. In addition to those listed in Warrum, *Utah in the World War*, 68–69, 204, other nurses in the war are mentioned in nursing school histories and contemporary newspapers. Also, 41 nurses were stationed at Hospital No. 27, at Fort Douglas. Some may have been Utahns. See Lyman Clarence Pedersen Jr., "History of Fort Douglas, Utah" (PhD diss., Brigham Young University, 1967), 316–18.

15. A daughter of Mary C. Bettilyon of Salt Lake City, Mabel was born in 1890 in Lower Augusta, Pennsylvania, and received her professional training at Reading Hospital. Married to Fred Crawford in 1924, she died in 1956. See undated newspaper clippings, including a printed letter to her mother, reproduced in Nadine B. Bettilyon et al., comps., *V. A. Bettilyon and Janet Winward Family History* (Salt Lake City, n.d.), 107–9, courtesy of Karen Bettilyon. See also Warrum, *Utah in the World War*, 68.

16. Born in 1893 in Salt Lake City to Alice Ellerbeck and Newell H. Clayton, Ruth married James S. Haws after the war and had one child, Ann. Widowed in 1933, she remained active throughout her life. She was a fifty-year member of Edith Cavell Post, American Legion, and a member of Our Lady of Lourdes parish. She died in 1985 at age 92. Telephone conversations with a niece, Wanda Clayton Thomas, and a granddaughter, Leslie Malone, on March 15, 1989; *Salt Lake Tribune*, September 28, 1985; Warrum, *Utah in the World War*, 69; Lottie Felkner and Mildred Larsen, *The St. Mark's Hospital School of Nursing Story* (Salt Lake City: St. Mark's Hospital Nurses' Alumni Association, 1970), 38.

17. See David Mitchell, *Monstrous Regiment: The Story of the Women of the First World War* (New York: Macmillan Co., 1965), xv–xvi; Arthur Marwick, *Women at War, 1914–1918* (London: Croom Helm, 1977); Eleanor Flexner, *Century of Struggle: The Woman's Rights Movement in the United States* (Cambridge, MA: Harvard University Press, 1959), chap. 21; *Relief Society Magazine*, May 1920, 274.

18. See *Laws of the State of Utah . . . 1917* (Salt Lake City, 1917), chap. 53, 182–85; *History of Holy Cross Hospital School of Nursing* (Salt Lake City, n.d.), 13, 23; Warrum, *Utah in the World War*, 26–69, 204; *Salt Lake Telegram–Herald Republican*, May 18, 1918; *Salt Lake Tribune*, June 24, 1960; Felkner and Larsen, *St. Marks' Hospital*, 38, 40; Sandra Hawkes Noall, "A History of Nursing Education in Utah" (Ed.D. diss. University of Utah, 1969), 39, 42; *Ogden Standard*, March 2, March 9, March 16, 1918; *Salt Lake Tribune*, August 13, 1965; *Deseret News*, August 13, 1965. In various sources Frae Karous's first name is listed as Fae, Frances, and Francis. The sisters' surname is spelled Korous in contemporary listings in *Polk's Salt Lake City Directory*.

19. Warrum, *Utah in the World War*, 69; *Deseret News*, February 25, 1956 (Church News section); undated *Deseret News* clipping, Utah State Historical Society Library, Salt Lake City; *Salt Lake Tribune*, June 17, 1951; June 3, 1956; Noall, "A History of Nursing Education," 41–42; Flekner and Larsen, *St. Mark's Hospital*, 49; *Salt Lake Tribune*, July 8, 1917; June 26, 1947; *Salt Lake Telegram*, April 28, 1919; *Deseret News*, June 25, 1947.

20. In addition to sources listed in notes 18 and 19, see Lilliebell Falck, *"Lest We Forget": Our World War Heroes* (Ogden, UT, 1927); *Deseret News*, October 1, 1923; World War I Service Questionnaire, microfilm, Utah State Archives, Salt Lake City; *Salt Lake Tribune*, July 2, July 8, July 9, 1917; *Salt Lake Telegram–Herald Republican*, May 28, 1918.

21. Flikke, *Nurses in Action*, 48; Raymond A. Swift, son of Louise Owen Swift, to author, November 6, 1989; *Ogden Standard Examiner*, March 30, 1984; State of Utah, "Biennial Report of the Utah State Board of Nurse Examiners," public documents, 1919–20, vol. 2, report no. 25.

22. *Salt Lake Herald*, September 26, 1919; *Deseret News*, October 1, 1923. Most of the Utah nurses would have received the Victory Medal and a sixty dollar bonus. See *Salt Lake Telegram*, April 22, April 23, 1919.

23. Interesting studies of women during the war not previously cited include: Margaret Randolph Higonnet, et al., eds., *Behind the Lines: Gender and the Two World Wars* (New Haven: Yale University Press, 1987); Diana Condell and Jean Liddiard, *Working for Victory? Images of Women in the First World War, 1914–1918* (London: Routledge & Kegan Paul, 1987); Susan C. Peterson and Beverly Jensen, "The Red Cross Call to Serve: The Western Response from North Dakota Nurses," *Western Historical Quarterly* 21 (August 1990): 321–40.

5

UTAH'S WAR MACHINE

The Utah Council of Defense, 1917–1919

ALLAN KENT POWELL

How does a nation mobilize for war at home and abroad, and how does it coordinate the resources, objectives, and needs of both? The answer for the United States between 1917 and 1919 was to utilize and coordinate a system of national, state, county, and local councils of defense. During World War I Utah's political, business, educational, and religious leaders worked with everyday citizens to make their councils of defense as effective as possible in order to demonstrate Utah's patriotism in the epic struggle. The councils of defense heeded the call for defeating the far-off enemy and controlling those at home whose loyalty and commitment did not measure up to the expectations and demands of a nation at war. The following chapter describes the structure of the Utah Council of Defense, highlights some of its leaders, examines four major areas of the council's activity, and offers an assessment of its effectiveness in the national wartime effort.

America's entry into the Great War in April 1917 called for not only the mobilization of men into military service but also the organization of the civilian home-front effort on a scale that was unprecedented in the nation's history and foreshadowed government expansion during the rest of the twentieth century. During the war, the primary vehicles for this expansion of government included the Council of National Defense, state councils of defense, and local councils of defense in the counties and communities throughout the country. This chapter will focus on the Utah Council of Defense during World War I: its organization, major activities, and relationship to the Council of National Defense; the opportunities and limitations that it brought for women; and its effectiveness as a means to involve Utahns in the war effort. Important in understanding the war effort in Utah is an examination of the role of the Church of Jesus Christ of Latter-day Saints (LDS) and how effectively Mormons and non-Mormons worked together in Utah in support of the war effort at both the state and local levels. All Utahns were concerned with how their patriotism would be judged by the rest of the country and especially the nation's wartime leaders.

The system of councils of defense represented an expanded experiment in federal, state, and local government mobilization, coordination, and cooperation that also involved most aspects of the diverse private sector.[1] The undertaking occurred in an environment where many individuals were wary of an expansion of the power of the federal government on one hand, yet, on the other, committed to cooperation and support of the federal government, especially during the war. The programs and activities of the state and county councils impacted thousands of Utah residents who gave their support and demonstrated that volunteerism and decentralization could be, and in fact were, strengths in a national effort. They tied Utah even more closely to the rest of the nation and allowed the state to demonstrate competence and commitment in working for greater efficiency and involvement of its citizens in a united cause.

The Council of National Defense was created by Congress on August 29, 1916, with the mandate to coordinate resources and industries for the nation's security and welfare. Six presidential cabinet members constituted the council—the secretaries of war, navy, interior, labor, agriculture, and commerce. The council was assisted by a volunteer advisory commission of experts and a small paid staff.

Following the United State's declaration of war on Germany, Newton D. Baker, chairman of the Council of National Defense, wrote to Governor Simon Bamberger of Utah and the other state governors requesting the organization of state councils of defense. Governor Bamberger moved quickly to call a meeting in his office on April 26, 1917, to establish the Utah State Council of Defense for the purpose "of bringing about the speedy and practical mobilization of every resource of the state."[2]

At the April 26th meeting L. H. Farnsworth, president of Walker Brothers Bank in Salt Lake City, was selected as chairman of the Utah Council of Defense and its executive committee.[3] Farnsworth oversaw the work of the council's twelve committees and pushed for the establishment of county councils, which included the same local organization as at the state level.[4] Service on the county councils and their committees was considered a patriotic obligation and opportunity. Typical of the resolve to carry out the service, those attending a meeting at the Piute County Courthouse to organize a council in one of Utah's smallest counties were told, "This is a call from the government. Every man must answer the call. Every man asked to serve as a committeeman should consider it a draft by the Government. There must be no refusals."[5] By and large, Utahns accepted the call. In Beaver County a heated confrontation occurred when residents from Milford and Minersville in the western part of the county traveled to the county seat in Beaver to protest their lack of representation on the county council of defense. As a consequence, two at-large members, one from Milford and one from Minersville, were added and two substitutions were made to give balance. J. F. Tolton wrote to state officials that the council's action "seems to have been the only solution of the affair to restore harmony between the two towns; and while Milford did not get all that she demanded, they seemed well satisfied and went home quite contented."[6]

The social impact of the war sometimes became evident in the local workings of the councils of defense. In Sevier County, for instance, county council member I. N. Parker requested that J. Arthur Christensen be removed from the council for failing to do his duty, denouncing his conduct and questioning his loyalty. Christensen was a member of the school board and an LDS bishop in Redmond but, according to Parker, had not become a member of the Red Cross, had not supported the Welfare Fund assessed for the town, and had only reluctantly subscribed $100 for a Liberty Bond. Parker concluded his letter, "The time . . . has now come when the pro-German sympathizers must be separated from the red blooded Americans, that their evil influences may not work to the injury of the people."[7]

While the national and state councils of defense were all male in leadership and would most certainly remain so, pressure mounted quickly, especially from voluntary women's organizations throughout the nation, to establish a women's counterpart to the councils of defense. The initiative for a separate women's organization during the war came at the height of female activism on several fronts: suffrage, temperance, child and women labor legislation, and other reforms associated with the Progressive movement. Many women cast involvement in the war effort as an expression of patriotism that men had to endorse without question and one that consequently might help win male toleration and recognition, if not outright support, for other causes championed by women.

As the Utah Council of Defense was being organized in late April 1917, the Woman's Committee of the Council of National Defense came into existence with Anna Howard Shaw, the honorary president of the National American Woman Suffrage Association, accepting the invitation to serve as chair of the national committee. She and her committee members moved quickly to develop a structure based on ten departments or subcommittees and to establish a woman's committee as part of each state council of defense. On August 3, 1917, Governor Simon Bamberger appointed eleven women to the Utah Committee on Woman's Work in the World War. Clarissa W. Smith

Williams, the first counselor in the Church of Jesus Christ of Latter-day Saints Women's Relief Society presidency, chaired the committee. The eleven women also joined forty-six men as members of the Utah Council of Defense. Membership leaned heavily toward business and industrial leaders but also included political, education, and religious leaders and women involved in philanthropic and social welfare activities.[8]

In effect, each state had two councils of defense—one male, one female, but with the inclusion of women members on the male-led state council. The duplication of some committees under the Utah Council of Defense and the Utah Committee on Woman's Work in the World War reflected this duality. Both groups had committees on finance and liberty loans, publicity, food supply, and conservation.[9] Utah followed the suggested model for committees from both the Council of National Defense and the Woman's Committee. The national and state organization reflected both a perceived reality of separate spheres of responsibility and a desire by women to have greater control over and independence for their own activities.[10] Yet there were limits, as overall leadership in the state and county councils of defense remained a male prerogative. This allowed Heber J. Grant, as chair of the State Central Liberty Loan Committee, to inform Mrs. W. Mont Ferry, state chair of the Women's Liberty Loan Committee, that the use of women speakers in the theaters to promote the sale of bonds was being discontinued and all speaking assignments would be filled by males "because it is believed that the men can be heard very much better in the theatres and there are many other activities that the women can carry on which they can do better than the men."[11]

In Utah, the involvement of women was facilitated by the Relief Society, the organization for Mormon women. The LDS Church organizations for girls, the Young Ladies Mutual Improvement Association, and children, the Primary Association, also became involved. In addition, nearly fifty statewide women's organizations and a host of local women's groups were recruited to work with the Utah Women's Committee.[12]

The United States Army and several federal agencies (including the Federal Food Commission, the Federal Fuel Administration, the U.S. Treasury Department, and the Committee on Public Information) only complicated the coordination efforts by setting up parallel administrative structures in the states for food, fuel, and liberty bonds. This threatened to duplicate, if not hinder, the work of the state council of defense committees. However, Utah was fortunate that W. W. Armstrong, the Federal Fuel and Food Administrator for Utah, also belonged to the state council and its executive committee. So too did Heber J. Grant, whom the Treasury Department had appointed to spearhead the Liberty Bond drive in Utah.

The overall mission of the Utah Council of Defense was to facilitate the nation's war effort in whatever ways it could but primarily through education, encouragement, and effective programs rather than enforcement and punishment. While information, suggestions, and direction were provided by the Council of National Defense and the National Women's Committee, no orders or funding came from Washington. State governors were responsible for establishing state councils and, ultimately, for the council's success or failure. Council members were unpaid volunteers, although a small number of employees were hired to handle the day-to-day operations. The state legislature provided limited funding and, in some cases, private businesses and organizations contributed to the operation of the council and specific programs under its direction.

While it is not possible to give a detailed account of all the undertakings for the war effort in Utah, the remainder of this article will examine four areas of primary activity—military affairs; food production and conservation; loans and fundraising; and the Americanization effort—before concluding with an assessment of the Utah Council of Defense.

The Utah Council of Defense had a varied and extensive involvement in military affairs. It assisted in the implementation of the Selective Service registration and conscription, including the determination of exemptions from the draft for essential industrial and agricultural workers; brought the Utah National Guard up to full strength through an active and ongoing recruitment program; and encouraged volunteers to join the army, navy, marine, and nurse corps. Further, the council provided for home defense and worked to maintain a good relationship with Fort Douglas and the military in Utah. For instance, the council issued calls for young women to register for training in local hospitals so they could take the place of nurses called into military service. It conducted a survey of military and naval resources throughout the state; this included identifying highways and railways that would help facilitate the mobilization of troops; supporting Utahns in the military service through soliciting donations to the Soldiers' Welfare Fund and encouraging citizens to write letters, send packages, and otherwise remind those in the military service that they were not forgotten and their sacrifice was appreciated. The council also assisted the wives and children of soldiers on active duty, looked for ways to help soldiers after the war, collected accounts of those in military service, and ensured the names of all those who served were recorded in an official history of Utah and the Great War. W. C. Ebaugh, secretary of the Utah Council of Defense, served as an intermediary between civilians and the military. In some cases he requested information from the army on behalf of family members about sons in the military. In another instance, responding to a request of the War Department, Ebaugh asked members of local councils to help locate photographs, maps, drawings, descriptions, and guide books from Belgium, Luxembourg, northern France, and western Germany that might be in the possession of Utah residents.[13]

After completion of a military census of each county, Governor Simon Bamberger, at the urging of the Utah Council of Defense, sent a letter to each man included in the census asking him to serve his county and state by enlisting in the Utah National Guard. If the National Guard did not reach full strength within thirty days, the governor would resort to a state conscription separate from that of the national Selective Service program. He closed his letter with the admonition, "It is the duty of such young men as you to prove to the country that you are not the degenerate sons of worthy sires."[14] By July 1917, Utah military units were at full strength and the threat of a state induction was no longer necessary.

With the completion of the military census, the War Department asked state councils of defense to complete military reconnaissance reports for their state. The Utah council identified a total of 155 quadrangles, averaging fifteen square miles in size. The reports provided detailed information for roads, trails, and bridges in each quadrangle. In addition, the reports included information on all industries, cities and towns, transportation facilities, water and fuel supplies, natural forage, the number of buildings and their dimensions, supplies on hand, and any other information that might be of value to the military. By war's end, 63 quadrangle reports for the most populated counties—Salt Lake, Davis, Utah, Weber, Cache, Box Elder, Tooele, Juab, and Millard—had been submitted.[15]

The Utah Council of Defense sought to help Utah's soldiers and their families in several ways. It solicited donations for the Soldiers' Welfare Work Fund, and Utah exceeded its $100,000 allocation by $10,000. When it was learned that the library at Fort Douglas was woefully inadequate, with only seven hundred mostly outdated books in its collection, the council found resources to build a library of twenty thousand books. Initiatives were also taken to meet the needs of the families of soldiers in the military. The finance committee recommended the establishment of a special committee to investigate the circumstances for each serviceman, identify his dependents, assess their needs, and take appropriate steps to alleviate the dependents' suffering. The council worked to end delays for wives and dependents to receive allowances and allotments to which they were entitled, and in emergencies worked with the American Red Cross to provide immediate relief. Attention was also given to securing meaningful employment for dependents of those serving in the military. In Salt Lake County, lawyers were organized to work in conjunction with the county clerk's office to provide needed legal advice to soldiers. To be sure, help for the soldiers and their families was often unavailable at the level envisioned by the Utah Council of Defense, and dependents found what assistance they could through extended family and community, church, and other institutions. In hindsight, had the Council of Defense not been disbanded immediately after the war, its work might have been extended to assist with the postwar transition that proved difficult to many soldiers. While some ex-soldiers returned to their old jobs or secured new places of employment, others who sought work immediately after their return "failed to find it, and began to question the sincerity of all those demonstrations which had marked their going and coming."[16]

But it was not the intent of the Utah Council of Defense to forget the soldiers or let their names and deeds go unrecorded. Funding was provided to produce three thousand feet of motion picture film of Utah servicemen and their training at Camps Kearny and Lewis. The films were premiered at a special showing on October 3, 1918, at the Paramount-Empress Theatre in Salt Lake City.[17] County councils of defense were directed to establish war history committees and appoint local historians to record the major activities within their communities, to compile a complete list of all who served in the armed forces, and to collect biographical information on those who served. The county histories were to be submitted to the Utah Council of Defense for inclusion in the records of Utah's war effort and use in writing a history authorized by Governor Simon Bamberger and the Utah State Legislature. In 1918, the state legislature appropriated five thousand dollars to the Utah State Historical Society for the writing of the history.[18] University of Utah history professor Andrew Neff was initially engaged to compile the history; when he was unable to complete the monumental task, Noble Warrum took on the project, which resulted in the 1924 publication of *Utah in the World War: The Men Behind the Guns and the Men and Women Behind the Men Behind the Guns.* Of the book's 456 pages, more than half include lists of Utahns who served, those who died during military service, and those who were recognized for their courage and distinguished service. Although the Utah Council of Defense was disbanded shortly after the war ended, the council was responsible for this history, which stands as a most important record of Utah's involvement in the Great War.

The council's activities to encourage and support food production and those directed at conserving valuable resources impacted all Utahns most directly. The wartime task was clear—produce more and consume less. A parallel objective was to secure the maximum use of what was produced. Farmers and ranchers, as well as citizens who had access to a plot of ground on which to grow a garden, shared the responsibility for food production. The first undertaking by the Utah Council of Defense was to conduct surveys with farmers and ranchers to determine their production capability and their specific needs for maximizing production. The surveys found that many farmers did not have the financial means to purchase seeds; accordingly, the council made $60,000 available under a loan program, payable when crops were harvested, for farmers to purchase nearly a million-and-a-quarter pounds of seeds. When grasshoppers threatened crops during the summer of 1917, the council provided more than nine tons of arsenic to farmers for use against the destructive insects. In the fall of 1917, when the shortage of apple boxes—essential for shipping Utah apples—threatened the loss of much of the crop, the council supplied two hundred thousand boxes. Efforts were undertaken to secure more storage facilities for the increase in potatoes harvested during the war. At the request of cattle and sheep ranchers, the council worked with the United States Forest Service to allow maximum capacity for sheep and cattle on public lands and to prevent the sale or slaughter of female livestock in order to increase the number of animals. When a controversy developed between an electrical power company and local farmers who depended on an increase in the power supply to pump necessary irrigation water to their crops, the council worked out an agreement with the two sides for the power to be paid for after the sale of crops.[19]

The council did not succeed in all of its endeavors related to conservation and food production. It could not reach a consensus on the proposed implementation of Daylight Savings Time in the state. The council polled its members, but the results were "so indefinite that it was not deemed wise by the officers of the Council to place ourselves upon record in this matter."[20] When the council sought to increase the number of farm workers by impressing the unemployed into an agricultural workforce, the police departments in Salt Lake City and Ogden reported an 85 percent decrease in vagrancy in the cities since the war began, noting "that the remaining men are not the type wanted by farmers."[21]

On the other hand, the council successfully urged individual families to grow "victory gardens" to produce fruits and vegetables for their own use. Council officials directed surveys, often through local Mormon wards, to identify lots available for gardens and requested that unused federal lands be made available for agricultural purposes.[22] While it was the usual practice for residents on farms and in towns to plant gardens, the practice was less common in cities. As a result of the 1918 victory garden campaign in Salt Lake City, 1,350 acres were utilized for 8,515 war gardens.[23] Classes and demonstrations were sponsored to teach the art of canning, and a railroad carload of pressure cookers was sold to the public at a nominal price, recognizing that "no Utah household is deemed ready for winter unless it has a cellar full of jellies, preserves and canned fruits."[24] Preserving homegrown produce was encouraged but hoarding was not. Saving and careful use of foodstuffs in anticipation of times of need, "which could be regarded as a virtue, or at least as an evidence of thrift in normal times, was a menace in times of war. Its logical result would be exorbitant prices, financial injury to consumers and eventual want or starvation for the poor."[25]

In the realm of conservation, the State Food Commission followed the lead of Herbert C. Hoover, head of the Federal Food Commission, in distributing to housewives and cooks a card with the title, "Win the War by Giving Your Own Daily Service." Directions followed for conserving such basic commodities as wheat and meat: "One wheatless meal a day. Use oatmeal, rye, or barley bread and non-wheat breakfast foods. Order bread twenty-four hours in advance so your baker will not bake beyond his needs. Cut the loaf on the table and only as required. Use stale bread for cooking, toast, etc. Eat less cake and pastry. . . . Beef, mutton, or pork not more than once daily. Use freely vegetables and fish. At the meat meal serve smaller portions and stew instead of steaks." If Americans followed these guidelines, the food administration promised, "there will be meat enough for every one at a reasonable price."[26]

To help secure women's participation in the conservation program, the State Food Administration organized a Utah Housewives Vigilance League. Women could join by signing a brief application with their name and address and mailing it to the Federal Food Administration offices in the Newhouse Building in Salt Lake City. The purpose of the organization was to provide women a voice in the local food administration by offering commendations or criticisms of the administration. However, no formal meetings were to be held. Members received an official emblem to wear and their names were added to the Federal Food Administration's mailing list to receive special food bulletins, recipes, and garden pamphlets.[27]

In an attempt to curb the consumption of sugar and unnecessary use of gasoline, the council instructed drug stores and soft drink parlors to close by ten o'clock at night. Hours for the purchase of gasoline were also restricted, with gasoline sales occurring no later than seven p.m. on weekdays, nine p.m. on Saturdays, and only between the hours of seven and ten a.m. on Sundays and holidays.[28] However, restaurant owners opposed attempts to limit the hours of Salt Lake City restaurants, and the Utah State Council wisely left it to county and local councils to set business hours in their areas.[29]

Other limitations on business activities followed. The Utah Commercial Economy Board, operating under the Utah Council of Defense, was charged with developing a plan for implementing the federal government's requests for economy measures with attention to specific needs and conditions within the state. W. F. Jensen was appointed commissioner for the board and, with his assistants W. E. Zuppann and E. S. Schmidt, moved quickly and decidedly to issues rules and regulations aimed at curtailing the use of gasoline and construction materials. The work in Utah attracted the attention of the Council of National Defense, and Jensen was invited to Washington, D.C., to instruct other states about Utah's program. According to Schmidt, "many of the rules which were issued met with a very considerable amount of opposition." With Jensen and his staff unwilling to change the regulations, the Utah Council of Defense stepped in to mollify the business community with the appointment of an advisory board that included B. F. Redan and Thomas Taylor, both members of the state council.[30] They worked to secure the support of Utah's business community, as the board had no enforcement authority but relied on voluntary compliance. While an estimated 95 percent of Utah's businessmen gave "instantaneous endorsement," the other 5 percent "were converted by patient effort and in a few instances by the exertion of some pressure."[31]

Commercial deliveries became a primary focus of the board, which asked merchants to restrict deliveries based on a city or town's population. Church leaders, newspaper editors, and special slides shown in movie theaters promoted the system. Merchants reported a total savings of nearly two million dollars a year; further, the number of deliverymen was reduced by 550, freeing men and boys for other work. The affected deliveries included not only groceries but also milk and cream, laundry, and ice. For milk deliveries, customers were required to provide one empty milk bottle for each full bottle of milk delivered. The measure was especially necessary as it was impossible to obtain new bottles from the manufacturers. Not all Utahns accepted the changes, and the restricted delivery of ice in Salt Lake City during the hot summer brought complaints. Ice deliveries were restricted to every other day, although ice companies did make concessions for emergencies. Authorities found that the ice shortages occurred not so much because of the delivery restrictions but because there was no one at home to receive the ice and because housewives were too extravagant in using the precious commodity for lemonade and ice water.[32]

In an effort to conserve essential construction materials, labor, capital, and transportation, the Utah Council of Defense represented the national War Industries Board in a nationwide conservation program whereby suppliers agreed not to furnish material for buildings unless the War Industries Board or the State Council of Defense had issued a permit certifying that the new building was essential to the war effort. In Utah, the state council asked the appropriate county council for its recommendation before reaching a final decision. Each case received a careful review. For example, construction of the new Pantages Theatre in Salt Lake City was approved because the workmen employed were not subject to military call and the building supplies had been secured in 1916, before the declaration of war. Nevertheless, the council vote was divided with seventeen for and seven against including Chairman L. H. Farnsworth, who defended his no vote by proclaiming he had "opposed the erection of the Pantages building from the beginning and still considered it as unnecessary."[33]

In another case, George M. Hess of Farmington petitioned E. P. Ellison, chairman of the Davis County Council of Defense, for authorization to build a new home in Davis County because Hess had to return to the county to run the family farm and the only available accommodation was a dark and damp basement.[34] Whether or not the construction of the Pantages, the George Hess house, or any number of new buildings in the state threatened the nation's war effort might be debated. But it is clear that the State Council of Defense and the appropriate county councils took seriously the request by the War Industries Board for a careful review of proposed new construction during the war.[35]

Utah was fortunate to have Heber J. Grant as the state chairman for the Liberty Bond campaign under the Department of the Treasury and, after January 1918, as chair of the Utah Council of Defense Finance Committee. In his leadership positions, Grant oversaw essentially all war-related fundraising efforts in the state. With experience in insurance, banking, and business ventures, and his leadership in stabilizing LDS Church finances before the war, Grant was connected to nearly all fields of finance in Utah. Furthermore, his ecclesiastical position as president of the LDS Church's Quorum of the Twelve Apostles gave him access to the state's predominant religious and cultural institution.

At least twelve separate fundraising campaigns were undertaken. Utahns were encouraged to invest as much as a quarter of their income for government securities.[36] Each state and county council of defense was given a specific quota for each campaign, which included five Liberty Loan campaigns and the War Savings Stamp campaigns, three Red Cross fund and membership drives, the Soldiers' Welfare Fund, the YMCA War Fund, and the United War Work Campaign. Utah women were very active in organizing and canvassing their communities and neighborhoods during the fundraising drives.

The county councils of defense were given responsibility for the Liberty Loan campaigns within their counties. The councils were instructed to set up an organization with seventeen separate committees and subcommittees under two major areas of activity—promotion and canvassing. Instructions were provided as to potential committee members and assignments, and suggestions for how the work might be done. The Committee on Capitalists, for instance, should consist of "very strong men of financial, church or state influence." The Committee on Clubs and Fraternal Organizations was "to go to each club and fraternal organization and endeavor to obtain their support. Have them organize soliciting committees within their own clubs." The Committee on Churches was to include "presidents of stakes, bishops, and ministers in the various churches . . . [who were] to discuss fully with their congregations and church members the necessity and importance of the Liberty Loan." The Committee on Women's Auxiliary should include representatives of "the relief societies, ladies' clubs, etc." who could provide speakers for club meetings, organize teas, and establish booths in department stores, hotels, and at county fairs to promote the purchase of Liberty Bonds. The Committee on Educational Institutions was to encourage school children to contribute twenty-five cents for a war bond that would be held by their school for use in the future.[37] However, local circumstances usually reflected a modification of the plan developed by Utah's Executive Committee. The councils of defense also assumed responsibility for warning those who purchased war bonds and stamps against schemers and swindlers who encouraged patriotic citizens to trade their government securities for worthless stock in unwarranted promotion schemes. The council urged citizens to keep the bonds they had purchased and invest in future Liberty Loan drives, as "Your government needs all the available money. It is, therefore, your patriotic duty to see that money which should go into government securities is not put into these questionable enterprises."[38]

Newspaper articles and advertisements accompanied announcements for each of the Liberty Bond and War Stamp drives. The headlines of one article asked "What Have You Given Up?" and then went on to query readers: "Have you given up your job and let your business future take care of itself? Have you said good bye to your family and friends and all you hold dear? Have you begun an entirely new career that may end, if you live, with health impaired, an arm off, a leg gone, an eye out? Have you given up your business future and said good-bye and taken a chance on coming back alive and well, and done it all with a cheerful heart and with a grim determination to do all you possibly can for your country?" With all the sacrifices being made by those in the military, the request for financial support seemed quite small, as the article concluded: "National War Savings Day is June 28, tomorrow. That day gives you the opportunity of showing in a practical way that you do appreciate what it means to the boys who . . . fight and die for you."[39] War Savings Stamps were offered for sale locally in various offices and businesses. Shoppers were encouraged to "ask for your change in Thrift Stamps. . . . Take a stamp instead of a quarter for change."[40]

Patriotic programs and rallies—with music, parades, speeches, visits by combat veterans, and even the exhibition of a mock trench on Salt Lake City's Main Street—fueled the drives.[41] Newspapers printed the

Table 5.1. World War I Fund Drives in Utah

Fund Drive	Dates	Quota	Subscribed
First Liberty Loan	April 17, 1917	$6,500,000	$9,400,000
Second Liberty Loan	October 1, 1917	$10,000,000	$16,200,000
Third Liberty Loan	April 5, 1918	$12,315,000	$12,531,300
Fourth Liberty Loan	September 28, 1918	$18,570,000	$19,878,000
Fifth Liberty Loan	April 21, 1919	$13,890,000	$15,500,000
First Red Cross Drive	June 18–June 25, 1917	$350,000	$520,000
Second Red Cross Drive	May 20–May 27, 1918	$500,000	$612,000
Red Cross Membership	August 1, 1917– February 28, 1919	$49,000	$67,000
Soldiers' Welfare		$100,000	$110,000
Y.M.C.A.		$10,000	$10,000
United War Work		$400,000	$412,000
War Savings Stamps			$5,614,540
Totals		$62,684,000	$80,854,840

names and amounts pledged—even when it was only twenty-five or fifty cents. Towns, counties, and states competed with each other to demonstrate their patriotism by the purchase of war bonds. When the initial attempt in Payson to raise money for the Fourth Liberty Loan fell far short of meeting the town's quota, headlines in the local newspaper lamented, "Payson Has Only 45% of Quota" and "Will Payson Fail?" Payson did not fail but met and exceeded its allotment of $125,700 by $8,500.[42]

But not all participated—at least to the extent expected. Some Utahns felt the quotas given to communities were unfair and that certain classes and individuals were not doing their share, while others grew weary of the constant demands for contributions. The Iron County Council of Defense explained the difficulty of the per capita assessment when nearly a thousand destitute victims of a homesteading scam were included in county's assessment: "These people were perhaps as loyal and patriotic as were the rest of the inhabitants of the county, but were in such destitute financial circumstances that the purchase of bonds by them was well nigh impossible."[43] Like Payson and other communities, Iron County found the fourth loan drive particularly difficult:

> The people of the county were beginning to feel the burden of financing the war. Money was not so plentiful, especially the bank accounts of the farmers who were not live stock owners, had been somewhat deflated. This is due to the failure of crops that year in this county. A novel method was introduced in the raising of the loans. The Council decided not only to apportion the communities as formerly, but also to apportion individuals. This met with great resentment by those so apportioned. Many refused to make the full apportioned contribution. Some became so disgruntled as to refuse to make any contribution whatsoever.[44]

The State Committee on Finances was asked to investigate charges "concerning difficulty in securing subscriptions to Liberty Loans from certain wealthy persons."[45] At the same time, intense social pressure demanded conformity: those who did not participate were threatened with having a yellow card submitted identifying them as a slacker who was "against the government and as such should go to Germany and live with those whom you endorse and in whom you believe."[46] Despite the challenges, the state, its counties, and its communities consistently met or exceeded the quotas set for the various fund drives. An estimated 90 percent of Utah's population contributed financially to the war effort, with a total contribution of $190 for every man, woman, and child in the state.[47]

Americanization, the fourth major area of involvement for the Utah Council of Defense, included publicity, education, preparation of the foreign born for citizenship, and measures to curb any pro-German sentiment among Utah citizens. Three committees took the lead in these areas: the Publicity Committee, chaired by A. N. McKay of the *Salt Lake Tribune*; the Americanization Committee, chaired by Harold M. Stephens, state superintendent of public instruction; and

the Women's Education Committee, chaired by Leah Dunford Widtsoe, a granddaughter of Brigham Young and the wife of University
of Utah president John A. Widtsoe. In a time before radio, television,
and computers, newspapers supplied the primary means for the distribution of information. McKay, with his connections to Utah's largest
newspaper and the network of other daily and weekly newspapers in
the state, was an effective leader, especially for the circulation of the
bulletins and circulars issued by the Council of National Defense.

The Women's Education Committee had two priorities directed
to both men and women. First, the committee disseminated information through Utah's universities, colleges, schools, churches, and
large businesses, directed primarily toward those "whose minds had
not grasped the significance of the war . . . who through ignorance
and indifference do not concern themselves with the great issues of
the war."[48] The second priority was among Utah's alien population,
who were encouraged to attend citizenship classes, night school, and
to learn English. The assimilation of the nation's foreign born was
deemed essential for several reasons: more effective military service
by those who enlisted or were drafted; greater participation in the
various measures to support the war; and a safeguard to ensure the
foreign born did not support the enemy as spies or become partakers
of anti-American propaganda.[49]

The Utah Defense Council chairman, L. H. Farnsworth, championed the Americanization effort and the anti-German campaign in
the state. In April 1918 he traveled to Washington, D.C., at the request
of Secretary of the Interior Franklin D. Lane, to attend a special meeting to discuss implementation of a national plan for Americanization
to be undertaken jointly by the Council of National Defense and the
Department of the Interior. At the Washington meeting, Farnsworth
supported the adoption of several resolutions: asking Congress for
an adequate appropriation for the Americanization effort, including
federal aid to the states for their Americanization work; requesting
industries employing large numbers of non-English men to cooperate in the national plan; and enlisting school boards throughout the

country to adopt rules requiring that elementary subjects be taught in the English language only.[50]

Upon his return to Utah, Farnsworth submitted a detailed report to the State Council of Defense. In the report Farnsworth reviewed the strength of the pro-German faction in the United States, which stood in opposition to Liberty Loan and Red Cross drives, and all campaigns to aid the army and navy. He sounded the anti-German alarm, reporting that New York City was the third largest German-speaking city in the world and the home of some thirty German-language newspapers. Farnsworth warned of the threat of German-language newspapers in the United States, whose circulation reached nearly 3.5 million readers. He noted that in some areas of the United States "considerable sums are expended yearly in teaching German—in some instances six times as much is being appropriated to teach German to Americans as is spent to teach Americanism to German immigrants." The state of Nebraska, he reported, was a hotbed of pro-German activity, with between two and three hundred parochial German schools. Repeating rumors gleaned from the national Americanization meeting, Farnsworth described alleged conditions in Nebraska, where "elementary subjects are taught in German. German patriotism is taught and the German national hymn is sung as part of the school routine. American national songs are never sung in one hundred of these schools and the American flag is never flown. It is said that in some of these schools the children are whipped for speaking English."[51]

Farnsworth ended his report with a stirring call to action: "A grave and critical condition now confronts our country and its Allies. We are called upon to make every sacrifice, our lives and our property, if need be, to forever crush the imperial government and military power of Germany, whose only standard is world dominion and the exercise of a brutal power. Ours is a righteous and just fight for humanity and victory, with the help of God, will be our reward."[52] After discussion of the Farnsworth report, the council appointed a special committee on Americanization and adopted a resolution urging "the superintendents of public instruction, the State University, the Agricultural

College, and all other institutions of learning within the State of Utah, that they forthwith discontinue, where they have not already done so, the teaching of the German language and the German ideals."[53] Subsequently, the University of Utah and the Utah Agricultural College in Logan reported to the council on their adherence to the directive, though "in . . . one instance . . . that problem was solving itself, because students were refusing to take the language, anyway."[54]

Farnsworth extended the anti-German and pro-Americanization initiative with a visit to the office of Anthon H. Lund, a native of Denmark and member of the LDS Church's Quorum of the Twelve Apostles, who oversaw the publication of Utah foreign-language newspapers, including the German-language paper, the *Salt Lake City Beobachter*. Farnsworth conceded that the non-English language newspapers could continue to be published, but that the church should do as the Council of Defense had advised and cease publication of the *Beobachter*. Lund took the matter to church president Joseph F. Smith, who decided to continue publication of all foreign-language newspapers, including the *Beobachter*.[55]

The Americanization Committee, under Harold M. Stephens, sought to coordinate Americanization activities throughout Utah. It surveyed the state to assess the number of immigrants who could not speak English or were illiterate, immigrant school attendance, and the educational facilities available for English and citizenship classes. The committee also worked to implement the federal Americanization program, as provided by the Division of Immigrant Education within the Bureau of Education and the Bureau of Naturalization. At the local level, the county councils of defense directed the Americanization program and appointed a committee for each school district, which would include the superintendent of schools as chairman, civic authorities, employers of foreign labor, labor unions, naturalized foreigners, and representatives of societies and organizations interested in Americanization work.[56] The goals of the Americanization effort were clear—to help immigrants learn English, understand American government, jettison the ideas and traditions from the Old

World that were not in harmony with American ideals, support the war effort in every way, and become United States citizens.

The work carried out by the Speakers' Bureau, which included the Division of Four-Minute Men, represented the most visible undertaking for publicity and education. The Speakers' Bureau cooperated with other organizations to schedule national and international speakers touring the country in behalf of the war effort. The bureau also handled the scheduling of the volunteer Four-Minute Men, who spoke in theaters, churches, and other venues to carry, "night after night . . . the official message of the Government and of the State Council of Defense to the audiences who assemble at these places of amusement and of worship."[57]

When James Scherer visited Salt Lake City in September 1917 at the request of the Council of National Defense to assess the status of the war effort in Utah, he was impressed, reporting that "without a doubt Salt Lake City is the most patriotic place I have visited, not even excepting New York or Washington." Scherer attributed the positive conditions in Utah primarily to the involvement of the Mormon Church in the war effort. Puzzled by why Mormons were "so zealously at war," Scherer determined it was because of the rough treatment of Mormon missionaries in Germany; now they "have an opportunity," he decided, "to get even." Scherer concluded his assessment of Utahns by stating, "That they are genuinely American I do not doubt; this added incitement to patriotism, however, seems to me to account quite logically for the extraordinary manifestations of loyal support of the Government that I found on every hand in Utah; while the superb organization of the church enables its authorities to give practical expression to their zeal."[58]

Mistreatment of Mormon missionaries in Germany might have been a minor reason for Utah's support of the war; however, Mormon missionaries had been mistreated in England as well. Utah and Mormon support for the war was a part of the "Americanization of Utah" that came after statehood in 1896. Support for the United States war effort was one of many ways Mormons could demonstrate their patriotism, Americanism, and the fact that Mormons were moving into the mainstream of the nation's political and economic life. B. H. Roberts, an LDS Church general authority and historian who served as a chaplain for the Utah National Guard during World War I, explained in his history of the LDS Church that "had Utah failed as a state in filling up the full measure of her duty, the people with the solidarity of church membership possessed by the Latter-day Saints considered, and being so largely in the majority, would have been held—and justly—responsible for any delinquency in duty of the state. If, on the other hand, the state reacts to duty faithfully and well, it reflects the patriotism of her people carrying such responsibility; but this without disparagement to the patriotism and full measure of credit due to the non-membership of that dominant church."[59]

The month after Scherer's visit to Utah, Franklin P. Lane, the secretary of interior and a member of the National Council of Defense, arrived in Utah as an honored guest and spoke to an overflow crowd of more than ten thousand at the Salt Lake Tabernacle on October 5, 1917. Lane reported that some along the eastern seaboard had stated that the level of patriotism in the far West was much less than in other parts of the country. But Lane had found that not to be true. Praising Utah specifically, Lane disclosed, "We have less complaints from the people of Utah back in Washington, than from any of the western states. You do not ask for gifts, but you are always willing to make gifts." Commenting on the patriotic military parade that preceded his address, Lane observed, "I have seen inspiring sights before, but never before has one so touched my heart as did your magnificent military parade which I witnessed in the streets of Salt Lake tonight. Oh, how I wish President Wilson himself could have seen it." Lane went on to talk about Utah's citizens, recalling, "We saw the streets of Salt Lake lined with the men and women who are giving their sons in response to the call of war and I saw no tears, only smiles, on the faces of those who are making the greatest sacrifice that can be made and seeking it gladly for the sake of liberty."[60] Utahns responded to Secretary Lane's visit and his praise by pledging ten million dollars to the Second Liberty Bond Drive.

In May 1918, another representative of the national council visited Utah. George B. Chandler, chair of the highly successful Publicity Committee of the Connecticut State Council of Defense, toured the western states to review the status of the state councils and offer ideas for more effective ways to carry out publicity measures in the West. Like others, Chandler gave a glowing report of Utah: "There exists here an organization which, in my opinion, has no superior, and possibly few equals in this country. It is to all intents and purposes the organization of the Mormon Church converted into a war machine. It reaches each individual searchingly and unerringly."[61]

The Church of Jesus Christ of Latter-day Saints, its leaders, and its members deserved the recognition offered by representatives of the Council of National Defense. Church members were encouraged to volunteer for military service, purchase war bonds, grow victory gardens, serve on county and local councils of defense, canvass their wards and neighborhoods in behalf of the war effort, write to the servicemen, and pray for a quick and decisive victory. Church leaders such as Heber J. Grant and Clarissa Smith Williams volunteered their services on the Utah State Council of Defense and mobilized the church network of stakes, wards, and women's relief societies. Mormon leaders made church buildings such as the Salt Lake Tabernacle available for patriotic rallies and purchased Liberty Bonds in the name of the church. The LDS Women's Relief Society made available to the federal food program its precious grain, stored over the years in anticipation of a return of food shortages and famine.[62] As the Council of National Defense representatives found, there was no shortage of loyalty, patriotism, or commitment to the war effort on the part of Utah's Mormons. But the "Mormon war machine," as identified by George B. Chandler, was not the complete answer to questions about the character and nature of Utah's World War I experience.

As the war ended, some hoped that the system of state, county, and community councils would continue. In a bulletin dated January 17, 1919, the Council of National Defense urged state and local leaders to work with their state legislatures and take other steps for their organizations to become permanent, to include all individuals and groups in the community, to be "truly democratic in character, and . . . bring . . . its forces to bear now upon local and permanent community problems as well as upon the problems arising out of the war."[63] Nevertheless, most saw the war emergency as over, were weary of the public and private intensity of the past two years, and were anxious to return to their prewar normality. The Utah Council of Defense ceased operations on July 1, 1919.

To be sure, not all efforts by the State Council were completely successful, and some were of questionable value. Disagreements, personality conflicts, and rivalries among state and local leaders arose from time to time. But these were of little consequence compared to the unity of purpose that propelled Utahns and their fellow Americans forward in their quest to defeat German militarism, prevent future wars, and preserve and spread democracy. The strength of Utah's war effort, in addition to the role of the LDS Church, can be found in a number of factors. Foremost was the leadership of Governor Simon Bamberger. A German-born Jew and successful Utah businessman, Bamberger gave the Utah Council of Defense high priority. He ensured that the council was politically bipartisan. He, a Democrat, appointed a Republican, L. H. Farnsworth, as chair. Bamberger made sure the council membership was religiously diverse with the appointment of Catholics, Jews, Protestants, and Mormons. He included the leading representatives of businesses, industry, and communities as members and was quick to appoint women to the council and to encourage their participation in all aspects of the war effort. Once the council began to function, the governor moved to a behind-the-scenes, supportive role.

Continuing their prominent role in the national suffrage movement, Utah women accepted the opportunity to demonstrate their importance to the economic and social life of the state, justifying, if such was necessary, their qualifications for greater involvement in the political activities of the state. With such motivation and a deep sense of patriotism coupled with the desire to do whatever they could to make a difference, Utah women of all faiths stepped into the spotlight of public activity. Ruth May Fox expressed their expectations in a declaration to the LDS Young Ladies' Mutual Improvement Association: "A woman's world will rise from this war." Other speakers echoed this assertion, claiming "that women are playing as important a part in the war as men and that after the war women's part will increase."[64]

The statewide network of county and local councils was particularly effective in Utah. As a part of that network, small and remote counties were included as equal partners. Local people had a role to play on county committees, just like their fellow citizens throughout the state. Furthermore, the degree of their patriotism could be quantified in their subscriptions to the Liberty Loan drives, in the number of articles they made for the Red Cross, and the number of their young men sent off for military service. Towns and counties competed with each other, especially in the Liberty Loan drives. Closely related to the intrastate competition was the interstate competition, as Utahns were determined to defend their place in the galaxy of states after a nearly half-century struggle for statehood that had only ended two decades prior to the United States' entry into the war. Linked to this outlook was the perception that Mormons were disloyal and anti-American. Indeed, Mormon misgivings about the federal government ran deep. The government had been unresponsive to the persecution of Mormons and the martyrdom of their prophet Joseph Smith. Even worse, the oppressive federal government had sent a substantial occupation army, along with a host of antagonistic territorial appointees, to administer the government in 1850s Utah. It had delayed granting statehood for nearly a half century and only after forcing the LDS Church to abandon the practice of polygamy. After statehood, government representatives had challenged the seating of duly elected Mormons to Congress. With the exception of the southern secession and the long aftermath of Reconstruction, no other geographical region in the United States seemed as disloyal and ripe for rebellion as the Mormon West, particularly Utah.

What better opportunity to demonstrate once and for all that Mormons and Utahns were now one hundred percent American and loyal to the federal government than by complete dedication to the war effort? The statements by Scherer, Lane, and Chandler during their visits validated the idea that Mormons were, in fact and in deed, loyal Americans. The opportunity for Mormons and non-Mormons to work together in the noble crusade was a refreshing change from the bickering that preceded and, to a lesser extent, followed the war.

The councils of defense were intended to be politically nonpartisan so that a large group of patriotic citizens seeking to play an active, voluntary role in the war effort could make a meaningful contribution. As such they brought an intimacy, intensity, and fervor to the mission that government officials and bureaucrats could not match. As Andrew Love Neff, a history professor at the University of Utah, observed, the councils were "something new, something fresh, corresponding to the spirit of the hour for strange and extraordinary developments. The well-established agencies could not begin to command the attention and secure the publicity or the response that was accorded the brand new devices." From the beginning of the war in April 1917 until their disbandment in July 1919, "the Councils of Defense brought about a merger of the forces that were seeking to advance the war program into an organized and useful agency which became a chief and effective agent of the government."[65]

Finally, the relationship between the federal, state, and local governments served to foster goodwill, respect, and cooperation. All aspects of the war effort—from the Selective Service and such things as the Americanization effort to food, fuel, and Liberty Bond work—were carried out at the grass roots level by local Selective Service boards, defense councils, and committees. While the federal government, through the Council of National Defense and other agencies, provided guidelines and suggestions, there was little enforcement by federal agencies that, for the most part, cooperated and coordinated with each other. In Utah, the federal government was no longer the enemy

nor the object of distrust or fear but the keystone in a partnership
with carefully defined objectives that all should embrace. No other
undertaking demonstrates this partnership more clearly than the war
time effort in which the federal, state, and local councils of defense
worked to secure victory.

NOTES

Originally published in the Utah Historical Quarterly 84 (Winter 2016):
48–49.

1. William J. Breen, *Uncle Sam at Home: Civilian Mobilization, Wartime
   Federalism, and the Council of National Defense, 1917–1919* (Westport,
   CT: Greenwood, 1984), xiii–xvii.
2. "Council of Defense Planned for Utah," *Salt Lake Tribune*, April 9,
   1917.
3. Louis Henry Farnsworth served as chairman of the Utah Council
   of Defense from its establishment in 1917 until it was disbanded
   in 1919. A prominent banker and Utah businessman, Farnsworth
   was at the head of many organizations and a member of important
   social groups. One of his children, Louis D. Farnsworth, served six
   months as an officer with the American Expeditionary Force in
   France. Noble Warrum, *Utah Since Statehood, Historical and Biographical* (Salt Lake City: S. J. Clarke, 1910), 2:200–3; J. Cecil Alter, *Utah,
   the Storied Domain: A Documentary History of Utah's Eventful Career*
   (Chicago and New York: American Historical Society, 1932) 2:579.
   Historical records show that Farnsworth carried out his assignment
   as chairman of the Utah Council of Defense with efficiency and
   effectiveness, a point that Andrew Love Neff made in correspondence, referring to him as "unquestionably a splendid executive . . .
   as the documents prove." However, Neff expressed dismay at the lack
   of documents available for writing a history of Utah and the Great
   War, which Farnsworth saw as a criticism of his administration of the
   Utah Council of Defense. To this, Neff responded, "you have a poor
   comprehension of historical values and historical material. The truth
   is that you and your associates were so busy making history that
   you had little time to record it. Naturally and properly you were so
   absorbed in winning the war, and solving the paramount problems
   of the hour, that the minutes speak all too briefly and modestly of

the accomplishment." See correspondence in box 12, fd. 12, Andrew Love Neff Papers, 1851–1940, MS 135, Special Collections, J. Willard Marriott Library, University of Utah, Salt Lake City, Utah (hereafter Neff Papers, JWML).

4. All counties, except the remote Daggett County with its scattered population of less than four hundred individuals, established county councils of defense. Later, under a request from the National Council, the organization was expanded to include local councils in communities and areas within Utah. For a list of the individuals serving on the county and local councils of defense, see Noble Warrum, *Utah in the World War: The Men Behind the Guns and the Men and Women Behind the Men Behind the Guns* (Salt Lake City: Utah State Council of Defense, 1924), 97–102. Two weeks before the armistice, M. Larsen, a member of the Daggett County Liberty Loan Committee, requested information about how to establish a Daggett County Council of Defense. M. Larsen to Heber J. Grant, October 28, 1918, box 2, fd. 11, Utah Council of Defense Records, 1917–1919, MS 107, JWML (hereafter Council Records, JWML).

5. *Piute Chieftan (Marysville, UT)*, September 20, 1917, copy in Utah State Council of Defense Miscellaneous Correspondence, Utah State Councils of Defense, Administrative Records, Series 10335, Utah State Archives and Records Service, Salt Lake City, Utah (hereafter Council Administrative Records, USARS).

6. J. F. Tolton to W. W. Armstrong and W. C. Ebaugh, July 27, 1918, box 3, fd. 1, Council Records, JWML.

7. I. N. Parker to Parley Magelby, January 18, 1918, box 3, fd. 23, Council Records, JWML. Parker resigned from the Sevier County Council of Defense on May 16, 1918.

8. For a list of members of the Utah Council of Defense and their committee assignments, see Warrum, *Utah in the World War*, 94–96.

9. Other committees under the Utah Council of Defense included legal, sanitation and medicine, coordination of societies, industrial survey, man power survey, military affairs, state protection, and transportation. The other committees for women included home and foreign relief, health and recreation, general economies, welfare of women in industry, social service agencies, child welfare, education, and registration of services.

10. For a discussion of women's involvement in the war, see Christopher Capozzola, *Uncle Sam Wants You: World War I and the Making of the Modern American Citizen* (New York: Oxford University Press, 2008), 83–116.

11. Undated copy of a letter from Heber J. Grant to Mrs. W. Mont Ferry, box 2, fd. 10, Council Records, JWML.

12. These statewide women's organizations included the United Daughters of the Confederacy; National American Woman Suffrage Association; National Woman's Party; Woman's Republican Club; Woman's Democratic Club; National Federation of Musical Clubs; Young Woman's Christian Association; Order of the Eastern Star; Daughters of the American Revolution; Utah State Nurses' Association; Woman's Christian Temperance Union; Pythian Sisters; Association of Collegiate Alumnae; Woman's Relief Corps; Red Cross; Federation of Labor; Federation of Women's Clubs; National Council of Woman Voters; Jewish Relief Society; Girls' Friendly Societies; War Relief Work; Relief Work for Allies; National Society Daughters of Revolution; Ladies of the Grand Army of the Republic; Florence Crittendon Mission; National Kindergarten Association; Utah State and Parent Teachers Association; Neighborhood House; Orphans Home; Women Trustees of State Universities; Congress of Mothers; Soldier's Club Room Committee; Ladies of the Maccabees; Catholic Women's League; Women of Woodcraft; Rebecca Lodge; Utah Daughters of Pioneers; and aid societies of the Presbyterian, Methodist, Baptist, Congregational, Christian, Christian Scientist, Unitarian, and Episcopalian churches. This list is included as part of a Report of Organizations to the Woman's Committee of the Council of National Defense, Andrew Love Neff Papers, 1919–1923, MSS B 41, box 1, fd. 11, Utah State Historical Society, Salt Lake City, Utah (hereafter Neff Papers, USHS).

13. "Hendrickson Not Killed," *Gunnison (UT) Gazette*, June 7, 1918; "Council of Defense," *Davis County Clipper*, August 2, 1918; "Uncle Sam's Men Need Pictures of Places in Germany," *Mt. Pleasant (UT) Pyramid*, May 31, 1918.

14. Undated letter from Governor Simon Bamberger, in Miscellaneous Correspondence, Council Administrative Records, USARS. In a companion document, "Why Join the National Guard," prospective volunteers were encouraged to join, as "The National Guard is the only organization which will carry the name of the State of Utah throughout the great world war." Furthermore, it would be to the volunteer's great advantage: "In the National Guard you will be a Utah man among Utah men—friends and acquaintances on every hand—surrounded by comrades in whom you will be interested and who will be interested in you. Your officers will be men who know your homefolks. They will feel it their duty to see that you

get a square deal at every stage of the game. All the officers and men will be pulling together for the fame of the Utah team. Your officers will know that in your home town you amount to something, and so will your comrades. Your parents will know that you are among friends that you are being well treated and their worry over your welfare will be reduced to a minimum."

15. Warrum, *Utah in the World War*, 112–13.
16. Ibid., 153.
17. Executive Committee Minutes, October 2, 1918, box 1, fd. 2, Executive Committee Meetings, Council Records, JWML.
18. *Report of the Utah State Historical Society*, Public Documents of the State of Utah, 1919–1920, Part 2, 5; see also, L. H. Farnsworth and Arch M. Thurman, *Report of the Council of Defense of the State of Utah*, (Salt Lake City: F. W. Gardiner, 1919), 50–51. Andrew Neff did leave behind drafts of the history, which are included in box 1 of the Neff Papers, USHS, and box 11 of the Neff Papers, JWML. For a summary of the war history project, see Gary Topping, "One Hundred Years at the Utah State Historical Society," *Utah Historical Quarterly* 65, no. 3 (1997): 219–23.
19. Warrum, *Utah in the World War*, 103, 125, 126, 128, 129, 130.
20. Minutes, Utah State Council of Defense, July 20, 1917, box 1, fd. 1, Council Records, JWML.
21. Executive Committee Minutes, January 19, 1918, box 1, fd. 2, Council Records, JWML.
22. "Agricultural Committee," microfilm, miscellaneous correspondence, Council Administrative Records, USARS.
23. "War Gardens," *Deseret News*, August 13, 1918. In Logan, Old Main Hill at the Utah Agricultural College was plowed and used for victory gardens. At the University of Utah, vacant land was offered to faculty and employees at no charge for growing gardens. Nearby Fort Douglas provided more than enough free manure for the gardens. John A. Widstoe to Joseph F. Merrill, November 23, 1917, box 2, fd. 14, Council Records, JWML.
24. Warrum, *Utah in the World War*, 138; see also, Minutes of the Conservation and Emergency Committee, July 11, 1917, Council Administrative Records, USARS.
25. Warrum, *Utah in the World War*, 137.
26. Ibid., 133.
27. "Loyal Women of Utah Organize Housewives Vigilance League," *Parowan (UT) Times*, May 1, 1918.
28. Warrum, *Utah in the World War*, 132.

29. The decision came down at a July 26, 1918, meeting of the Utah
State Council of Defense Executive Committee. Utah officials sent
a questionnaire to the other forty-seven states and found that some
had restrictions, some did not, some were considering implementing
restrictions, and others had implemented then rescinded the restrictions. After reviewing the results of the survey, the Utah Council
of Defense passed a resolution "request[ing] each County and City
Council of Defense to take up the question of early and uniform
closing in their respective communities and place in operation such
regulations as in their opinion will best fit their own communities."
Executive Committee Minutes, July 26, 1918, box 1, fd. 2, Council
Records, JWML.

30. E. S. Schmidt to A. L. Neff, October 5, 1920, box 12, fd. 14, Neff Papers,
JWML.

31. Farnsworth and Thurman, *Report of the Council of Defense*, 24.

32. Ibid., 25.

33. Ibid., 26; Warrum, *Utah in the World War*, III, 132. Nevertheless,
groundbreaking for the Pantages Theatre did not take place until
December 1918.

34. Geo. M. Hess to E. P. Ellison, October 11, 1918, Council Administrative
Records, USARS.

35. After the national War Industries Board program was implemented, the Executive Committee of the Utah Council of Defense
reviewed more than fifty applications in October and November
1918. Most were private residences, and most were approved. Other
projects included schoolhouses in Kanarra, New Harmony, and
Sego; a library in Salt Lake City; a bank in Woods Cross; a garage
and machine shop in Monroe; and a rooming house and store in
Bingham. The construction of shops in North Salt Lake for the
State Road Commission was initially disapproved, but after officials
met with the Executive Committee, approval was finally secured
on November 6, 1918. The review at the local and state levels took
considerable time, as directions from the National War Industries
Board were vague and unclear. Finally, in a lengthy letter dated
November 12, 1918, from R. D. McLennan, chief of Non War Construction Section, War Industries Board, twelve kinds of construction
were identified that did not need approval. The exemptions included
farm and ranch buildings; railroad-related facilities; federal, state,
and municipal roads and bridges; parks and playgrounds; public
utility buildings and facilities; irrigation projects; mines; oil, natural gas, and food production facilities; schoolhouses, churches, and

hospitals; and federal, state, and municipal buildings not costing over $25,000. Executive Committee, Utah State Council of Defense, Minutes for October 9, 16, 23, and 30, November 6 and 13, 1918, box 1, fd. 2, Council Records, JWML.

36. Executive Committee Minutes, June 29, 1918, box 1, fd. 2, Council Records, JWML.

37. "To County Councils of Defense and Liberty Loan Committeemen, Second United States Liberty Loan, 1917," included as Appendix 6 in James Scherer, "Confidential Report on Utah," P 1–2, entry 364 (old entry 14-D1), box 784, fd. RG 62, Confidential Report on Utah, Records of the Council of National Defense, National Archives and Records Administration, College Park, Maryland (hereafter Records of the Council of National Defense).

38. Secretary of the Utah Council of Defense to Dear Sir, August 16, 1918, box 2, fd. 3, General Correspondence, June 10, 1918–September 30, 1918, Council Records, JWML.

39. "What Have You Given Up?" *Paysonian*, June 27, 1917, Council Administrative Records, USARS.

40. "City Council of Defense Notes," *Logan (UT) Republican*, March 23, 1918.

41. Farnsworth and Thurman, *Report of the Council of Defense*, 33. Patriotic singing committees were established by the state and county councils of defense. Edward P. Kimball was appointed chairman of the state committee and under his direction a pamphlet of patriotic songs was printed and distributed throughout the state. Letter signed by Arch M. Thurman, August 30, 1918, with a copy of the pamphlet, box 2, fd. 3, Council Records, JWML.

42. "Payson Goes Over with Big Margin: Districts Oversubscribes by $8,500 for Fourth Liberty Bond," *Paysonian*, October 24, 1918, Council Administrative Records, USARS.

43. Iron County Council of Defense, handwritten report, 12, Council Administrative Records, USARS.

44. Ibid., 21. Nevertheless, all of the Iron County communities met their quotas except for Kanarraville, where citizens subscribed $6,000 of their $7,900 allotment.

45. Undated letter from W. D. Sutton, Council Administrative Records, USARS. In a letter dated November 25, 1918, from J. W. Hanson, chairman of the San Juan County War Work Campaign, to Heber J. Grant, Hanson reported "that the rich do not respond like the poor" and went on to cite the example of a poor, crippled person who willingly donated twenty-five dollars for the United War Work

Campaign, the same amount given reluctantly by the richest man in the county. Utah State Council of Defense Correspondence, box 12, fd. 18, Neff Papers, JWML. There were wealthy men who did use their wealth to purchase Liberty Bonds. The *Salt Lake Mining Review* noted that Colonel Enos A. Wall had subscribed $500,000; Matthew Cullen, $125,000; and J. E. Bamberger, $100,000. Copies of articles that appeared in the May 30 and June 15, 1917, issues of the *Salt Lake Mining Review* in "Utah and World War I—Councils of Defense," box 11, fd. 26, Neff Papers, JWML.

46. "No Yellow Cards for Utah," *Piute Chieftain*, June 27, 1918. Millard County residents were told that "The cards go to the Council of Defense and what will be done regarding them no one knows." "War Savings Certificate Drive Now Under Way," *Millard County Chronicle*, June 6, 1918.

47. Warrum, *Utah and the World War*, 34.

48. Ibid., 121–22; Farnsworth and Thurman, *Report of the Council of Defense*, 29.

49. Farnsworth and Thurman, *Report of the Council of Defense*, 44.

50. Warrum, *Utah in the World War*, 105.

51. Ibid., 106.

52. Ibid., 107.

53. Ibid.

54. "Schools Adhere to Ruling on German," *Salt Lake Tribune*, June 4, 1918.

55. John P. Hatch, ed., *Danish Apostle: The Diaries of Anthon H. Lund, 1890–1921* (Salt Lake City: Signature Books, 2006), 708, entries for October 21 and 22, 1918. For an account of other pressures to stop publication of the *Salt Lake City Beobachter* during World War I, see Thomas L. Broadbent, "The *Salt Lake City Beobachter*: Mirror of Immigration," *Utah Historical Quarterly* 26 (October 1958): 340–46; and Allan Kent Powell, "Our Cradles Were in Germany: Utah's German American Community and World War I," *Utah Historical Quarterly* 58 (Fall 1990): 370–87.

56. Farnsworth and Thurman, *Report of the Council of Defense*, 45–46.

57. Ibid., 48–49. The National Committee on Public Information sent out nearly fifty bulletins for dissemination to the thousands of Four Minute Men in the nation. These bulletins covered such topics as food production, liberty loans, the Red Cross, dangers to the nation, the meaning of America, and whether or not the income tax was a tool in a capitalist's war. Each bulletin insisted that speakers adhere strictly to the four-minute time limit and assisted speakers

with various outlines for handling the topic, along with a couple of sample speeches. Other sections designed to help the speakers included "Drive Home One Thought," "Points for Every Speech" "Suggestions for Opening Words and Other Phrases," and "Important Points for All Speakers." Copies of some of the bulletins are in box 5, fd. 9, Council Records, JWML.

58. Scherer, "Confidential Report on Utah," Records of the Council of National Defense.

59. B. H. Roberts, *A Comprehensive History of the Church of Jesus Christ of Latter-day Saints, Century One*, vol. 6 (Provo: Brigham Young University Press, 1965), 455. The six-volume comprehensive history was first published in 1930.

60. "Lane Pays Tribute to Patriotism of Utahns," *Salt Lake Tribune*, October 6, 1917.

61. G. B. Chandler, "Report of George B. Chandler: Impressions of Western Tour" (June 1918), 11–12, box 25, file E. 39, Council of Defense, 1917–1919, RG 30, Connecticut State Archives, Hartford, Connecticut. Breen, *Uncle Sam at Home*, 71, identifies the Utah Council, along with those in Washington, Colorado, and New Mexico, as the four best state councils in the western United States. One state that did not make Chandler's list and whose wartime history contrasted sharply with Utah was Montana, where Governor Sam Stewart assumed chairmanship of the nine-member Montana Council of Defense. In late February the state legislature passed the Montana Council of Defense Act, giving the council broad-ranging power "to create orders and rules that would have the same legal force as acts of the duly elected legislature. All state government offices and officials were placed at the council's disposal. . . . Any person violating an order or rule of the council was subject to fine and imprisonment." Michael Punke, *Fire and Brimstone: The North Butte Mining Disaster of 1917* (New York: Hyperion, 2006), 236. In his chapter, "Some Little Body of Men," 235–52, Punke summarizes the Montana experience by explaining that the council voted to conduct its business in private and throughout the remainder of 1918 issued seventeen "orders" that had the force of law. These orders required council permission for all parades and other public demonstrations, restricted newspapers, banned certain books, prohibited the use of the German language in schools and churches, and assumed inquisitional authority to subpoena witnesses and documents for its investigations. The state council's power extended to county and local councils of defense, whose decisions were subject to being overruled by the state council.

62. The Relief Society made available 6,165 tons of wheat or 205,518 bushels, for which the federal government paid $1.20 a bushel. The income was used to assist the poor. The LDS Church and its auxiliaries also purchased nearly $1.5 million worth of bonds and thrift stamps. Roberts, *Comprehensive History*, 6: 467–70.

63. National Council of Defense, Bulletin No. 20, Circular No. 49, January 17, 1919, copy in box 2, fd. 5, General Correspondence, 1919, Council Records, JWML.

64. "Patriotism Feature of Mutuals Meeting," *Salt Lake Tribune*, June 9, 1918. One important area of activity for Utah women was the prohibition of alcohol. In a resolution to the executive committee of the Utah Council of Defense, the Women's Committee requested the Utah Council ask Governor Bamberger to urge President Wilson to utilize the power given him by Congress to immediately enact a nationwide "war prohibition" on the manufacture and sale of beer and wines. The resolution summarized how prohibition would contribute to the war effort by saving grain, sugar, and working days; increasing efficiency; reducing crime; and freeing up money. In addition, it would "release the labor of about 600,000 men now employed in the production and sale of beer, and will release hundreds of thousands of railroad cars now needed for the transportation of coal and necessities." Minutes, Utah State Council of Defense, June 15, 1918, box 1, fd. 1, Council Records, JWML.

65. "Utah and World War I—Councils of Defense in Utah," typescript, box 11, fd. 6, Neff Papers, JWML.

World War I soldiers from Utah at Fort Lewis, Washington, prior to being shipped overseas. Used by permission, Utah State Historical Society, all rights reserved.

Maud Fitch of Eureka, Utah, served as an ambulance driver on the western front in France. Used by permission, Utah State Historical Society, all rights reserved.

Simon Bamberger served as Utah governor during the pre-war, war, and post-war years from 1916 until 1920, when he declined to seek reelection. Bamberger was born in Germany to Jewish parents and was Utah's first Democratic governor. A successful businessman, he died in 1926.

Members of the Utah Council of Defense meet in the board room of the Utah State Capitol Building. The council, appointed by Governor Simon Bamberger, was responsible for coordinating Utah's war effort from 1917 to 1919. Governor Bamberger is seated at the end of the table to the right. Next to Bamberger is A. L. Farnsworth, chairman of the council.

Members of the Washington County Council of Defense. County Councils of Defense were organized along the same lines as the State Council of Defense, with council members responsible for specific areas of the war effort. Pictured from left to right: *front row*—Thomas Judd, Industrial Survey; Edward Snow, Food Supply; John R. Wallis, Publicity; Arthur A. Paxman, State Prosecution; W. O. Bentley, Jr., War Savings; David H. Morris, Legal; *second row*—John T. Woodbury, Manpower; Joseph T. Atkin, Transportation; D. C. Watson, Sanitation; Warren Cox, Finance; *third row*—Chas. R. Worthen, Military; C. G.Y. Higgins, Secretary; and Albert E. Miller, Labor. Used by permission, Utah State Historical Society, all rights reserved.

A man and three plow horses prepare for the planting of Victory Gardens on Old Main Hill at the Utah State Agricultural College in Logan. Special Collections & Archives, Merrill-Cazier Library, Utah State University.

The D. R. Allen family Victory Garden, June 21, 1918. The garden was located at Elizabeth Street between 200 and 300 South in Salt Lake City. Used by permission, Utah State Historical Society, all rights reserved.

School children were recruited to work on Utah farms. Used by permission, Utah State Historical Society, all rights reserved.

William Riley Hurst—shown here in 1918 with his sisters Nedra, Dora, and Gwen—obtained this copy of an American officer's uniform from Montgomery Ward. He became the envy of other Blanding boys as he proudly wore the uniform until he outgrew it. Used by permission, Utah State Historical Society, all rights reserved.

Mechanical arts students at Brigham Young University prepare posters in support of the 1917 Third Liberty Loan campaign. The posters read: "Thank God We Are Americans; Now Is the Time to Fight Make Your Dollars Win; We Don't Want to Be Ruled by the Kaiser We Are Americans; Training School 100% in Liberty Loan; 3rd Liberty Loan Mass Meeting Tabernacle Tonight; and Make the World a Better Place to Live." L. Tom Perry Special Collections, Harold B. Lee Library, Brigham Young University.

A crowd gathers on December 1, 1917, at the Salt Lake City Red Cross headquarters in the Gardo House on South Temple Street. Used by permission, Utah State Historical Society, all rights reserved.

University of Utah students and faculty knitting for the war effort. Used by permission, Utah State Historical Society, all rights reserved.

Members of the University of Utah Red Cross unit knit sweaters, scarves, socks, and other items for American soldiers as part of the civilian contribution to the war effort. Used by permission, Utah State Historical Society, all rights reserved.

Soldiers of the Students' Army Training Corps gather in front of the Park Building at the University of Utah. Beginning in the late summer of 1918, virtually all able-bodied male students were enlisted as privates in the army. Members of the Students' Army Training Corps wore army uniforms, were given military instruction, and lived under army discipline. Used by permission, Utah State Historical Society, all rights reserved.

Carpenters and other construction workers were recruited for work in the shipyards on the Pacific coast. Special train cars transported Utahns to California. Used by permission, Utah State Historical Society, all rights reserved.

Brigham Young University students wear hygienic masks as a precaution during the 1918 influenza epidemic while attending an assembly in College Hall. The school was forced to close for the last three months of 1918 because of the flu epidemic. L. Tom Perry Special Collections, Harold B. Lee Library, Brigham Young University.

6

SOLDIERS, SAVERS, SLACKERS, AND SPIES

Southeastern Utah's Response to World War I

MARCIA BLACK AND ROBERT S. MCPHERSON

What happens when the shots fired at Sarajevo in 1914 reverberate into the isolated villages of a region in transition from the pioneer days of the past couple of decades to the modern era? The sparsely populated southeastern Utah's reaction to the outbreak and course of the war was, in many ways, similar to other parts of rural Utah. War brought a patriotic fervor that sent some young men as volunteers. Others waited for the selective service draft to call them to the colors. Of those found eligible for the draft, some sought deferments as the care of wives, children, and other dependents held sway. Those not eligible for military service contributed to the war effort in different ways—the purchase of liberty bonds and other wartime contributions, adhering to meatless and wheatless days, growing victory gardens, collecting scrap and other reusable items, writing letters to servicemen, and producing and donating socks and sweaters. Alert to the possibility of enemy spies and saboteurs active in the vicinity, wary observers sometimes found what they thought to be evidence of their presence even in a most unlikely place as southeastern Utah.

On April 6, 1917, President Woodrow Wilson signed a joint resolution of Congress that launched the United States into World War I, a conflict the nation had watched unfold in Europe for three years. The general population favored such an act, although some felt diplomacy still offered a better solution. Once the country was committed, however, most people locked arms, dug in for the fray, and looked for the best way to succeed in a war that had already exacted a terrible price in men, money, and equipment from America's allies.

Rural southeastern Utah appeared to be one of the least likely areas in the United States to be affected by these events, since the combined white populations of Grand and San Juan counties numbered fewer than 10,000 and were spread over approximately 11,500 square miles.[1] A back-to-the-land homesteading movement had been underway for the previous seven years, as the great sage plain east of Blue Mountain yielded to the plow of the dry farmer. Yet vast stretches of slickrock and canyon country remained just as vacant as the day they were formed.

Towns like Blanding, Monticello, and Moab served as the centers of activity for this huge geographic area that supported a population primarily employed in agrarian and livestock industries. Each of these towns offered the amenities of civilization, including two newspapers—the *San Juan Blade* in Blanding and the *Grand Valley Times*, later *The Independent*, in Moab. As with most newspapers in a rural setting, the life of the community pumped through their pages, providing a fine record, albeit for public consumption, of births and deaths, comings and goings, successes and failures, as well as prevalent attitudes of those who read its columns. Often a week-by-week description of events ensued.

Not surprisingly, when America committed itself to World War I the newspapers of southeastern Utah provided the clarion call to arms. Patriotic sentiments ran high, but filling the draft quotas established by the government required more than just enthusiasm. For instance, the induction board screened seventy-four men from Grand County and eighty men from San Juan County to fill their respective quotas of twenty-three and twenty-seven. The military fully expected only

50 percent of the men between the ages of eighteen and forty-five to be eligible for service because of physical disabilities, marriage exemptions, or alien status. What the review board encountered was surprising. Every inductee was required to pass a physical examination, but a large portion of the unmarried men were "rejected on some minor defect" while the married men "went through with flying colors."[2] Twenty-four of the eighty men from San Juan passed the physical examination; nineteen of them filed for exemption because of dependent relatives. A similar figure of 30 percent eligibility held true in Moab. The final summary of the first draft notice in San Juan eventually listed sixteen eligible, fifty-six discharged, five already enlisted, and three unaccounted. A second call for eighty-five men netted thirty-one eligible.[3]

The U.S. provost marshal, Gen. E. H. Crowder, facing similar problems nationwide, believed the ten million men needed to fight in the war could only be obtained through a draft system since "The volunteer system for raising an army is gone. It will never return. The principle of selection has been tried and proved by our people."[4] Yet, obviously, a better means was needed to determine eligibility, so he repealed existing regulations and instituted a new system of classification. The draft boards of Grand and San Juan started by mailing questionnaires to registrants concerning former occupations, physical fitness, official positions, religious responsibilities, citizenship, dependents, and attitudes toward the war. Based on the responses, the government placed the potential inductee in one of five categories. Class 1 included single and a few married men whose enlistment would not disrupt adequate support of their dependents or stifle agricultural and industrial pursuits. Class 2 consisted of those who could join the service without disrupting the support of any dependents and who worked in agriculture but did not hold a key position. Class 3 comprised both supporting dependents and those who held a prominent agricultural position but were not married. Class 4 were men taken as a last resort, without regard to dependents or position. Class 5 were those absolutely exempt. A year after this law went into effect, Grand County either had registered or had serving almost three hundred men.[5]

Although the draft cast the largest net of procurement, many volunteered, especially as the spirit of national service took hold in the communities. Omni Porter, foreman at the Grayson Cooperative Company's sawmill in Blanding, could attest to that. His crew of five men attended a farewell dance for some enlistees. Early the next morning they also set off to enlist, leaving their foreman with 150,000 feet of logs waiting to be cut. Porter complained that he lost his engineer, his ratchet setter, two off-bearers, and the planning machine man. His proposed solution: hire women.[6] Two other boys from Blanding wanting to enlist caught a ride to Thompson to board the train but were captured by their girlfriends and, as the story goes, were married on their way home. They never made it to the war.[7]

W. W. Barrett was the first of many to leave San Juan County to serve his country. Although his name was not at the top of the draft list, he volunteered to be the first to go. Many others followed his example. One man sold his plumbing outfit and car to enlist. The army welcomed his knowledge of mechanics and gasoline machinery, making it improbable he would ever enter combat. Riley Hurst, a young boy during the war, told of his seventeen-year-old brother who wanted to sign up with the others so badly that he was willing to lie about his age. His father, reluctant to let him enlist, said if he told his true age he could go. The army accepted him. Eventually fifty-four men from Blanding would join the service; only three would not return.[8]

Those not fortunate enough to don a uniform found other ways of promoting the cause. Donations to Soldier's Welfare, war stamps, liberty loans, the Red Cross, and food rationing provided important symbolic as well as real means for every individual and community to express support for the war. Newspapers equated financial assistance to military service, pointing out that "Somewhere in France today, your boy is fighting to save the world from tyranny . . . they are giving their lives freely for you [so] you should therefore lend your money just as freely. . . . Be ready to go the limit."[9]

Federal, state, and local governments established quotas and expected them to be filled. A good example of this trickle-down approach is seen in the federal government's attempt to raise $10 million for Soldier's Welfare. Of this amount, Utah had to raise $100,000 and San Juan County $190. The Council of Defense for San Juan, a local organization tasked with coordinating a variety of war-related activities, decided to raise the sum by splitting the amount as follows: Bluff $30, Blanding $70, Monticello $70, and La Sal $20. To create a fund of $20 for contingent expenses, the council added an additional $5 to each community's assessment.[10]

The people of San Juan were more than willing to support this and other programs. In predominantly Mormon communities the church became intimately linked with the process. On one occasion LDS (Latter-day Saint) leaders devoted a Sunday afternoon meeting to the purchase of liberty bonds, as patriotic speeches centered on the importance of their sale. Monday morning found ready buyers. By Tuesday night, $37,000 worth of bonds had exchanged hands, while several outlying districts still had not reported. Newspapers listed the amounts individuals pledged, with highs ranging from $1,500 to $5,000 and a low of $50. Within a week, San Juan County reached its goal of $50,000 with the help of "231 patriotic citizens." Six months later San Juan again went "over the top," the headline using trench warfare terminology, as the county met its $30,000 assessment.[11]

Grand County's spirited sales pushed it to the top of counties in the state for per capita war savings and thrift stamp sales. Unfortunately, it sank to fifth place when other counties such as Piute and Carbon edged it out; San Juan advanced from the twenty-seventh to the twenty-first position among the twenty-nine counties. Later, Grand again assumed the lead, working hard all the while to maintain its edge on patriotism.[12]

Many of these monetary accomplishments required great sacrifice in a region where poverty abounded. Alice Black provides a good example of the price of patriotism. She had been saving money for a year or more to visit some friends. The anticipated cost of the trip was fifty dollars, which she had saved penny by penny. When Alice attended the previously mentioned Sunday meeting, the ringing patriotic speeches convinced her to abandon the trip and buy a liberty bond instead. Expressing no disappointment or regret, she was proud of her purchase and more than ever supported the war effort.[13]

Parents encouraged children to save their change and invest in liberty bonds. National estimates claimed that if 20 million children in the United States each saved a quarter a week to buy a thrift stamp, then $260 million would be earned to help feed, clothe, and arm the men in the trenches.[14] Community groups used different approaches to make this a reality. *The Independent* offered a free thrift stamp for every new subscription brought in. The paper reasoned that this would give the young people business experience as well as help them do their bit for Uncle Sam. Students in Monticello earned sufficient money to pay for $300 worth of liberty bonds. The school board paid the boys to chop and haul wood while the girls sewed and knitted.[15]

Youths also raised agricultural products for the war. When it became apparent that the United States would have to double its food production in order to meet demands, the secretary of agriculture sent out the distress cry—"S.O.S."—which he translated as "Soldiers of the Soil." He challenged boys and girls to raise more crops, thus "rendering as great a service to their country as the soldiers in uniform." Southeastern Utah established its own soldiers of the soil program; in Moab and surrounding areas twenty-four boys enlisted in the "greater crops" campaign to raise beans and corn. The adult LDS sunday school class organized a contest with prizes for the aspiring farm hands. In San Juan, the "M. I. A. [youth group] [was] to Help Win the War" by pledging its financial support and "work, work, work."[16]

The metaphorical joining of soldiers with agriculture did not occur by chance. As many young men volunteered or were drafted, a labor shortage arose in the fields. San Juan county commissioner George A. Adams talked to Gov. Simon Bamberger and federal officials about keeping the young men, soon to be drawn into the service, at home on the farm. Adams believed that "a soldier in the agricultural field— a soldier of the commissary, as President Wilson calls him—is at present of as much service to his country as a soldier on the battlefield."

He hoped to arrange for those who volunteered to count toward filling the quota of soldiers, reducing the number of men drawn from the county.[17]

The shortage did not turn out to be as serious as initially expected. Relief came from a number of areas, such as the machinery brought in to help, imported Mexican laborers, a working reserve comprised of hundreds of boys representing every county in the state, and men skilled in farm work who volunteered to help.[18]

The government also did what it could to encourage farmers. Homesteaders who left for the service had their time in uniform counted as part of the required residence on the land. In 1917 the government asked those who remained on the farm to increase their production of wheat by 12 percent, translating in San Juan County into an additional ten thousand planted acres. This was facilitated by plowing new land or old pastures and by exchanging labor and machinery. By 1918 wheat was so desperately needed that the federal government asked Utah to produce one million bushels more than the five and a half million produced in 1917. Nineteen San Juan dry farmers rose to the call, enjoyed the government-regulated price of two dollars a bushel, and did their best to support the established goals, never thinking much about the long-term effects these programs would have on the soil. That debt would be paid later, in the 1930s, with the establishment of the Soil Conservation Service.

The other side of the food production program called for decreased consumption. The government instituted regulations to ensure sufficient food for the soldiers. In 1918 the people of southeastern Utah, living in an area of significant agricultural production, followed the same rationing cycle established throughout the nation. Mondays and Wednesdays were wheatless with an additional wheatless meal every day throughout the week. Tuesdays were beefless and porkless. Customers could purchase white flour only if the same amount of substitutes—such as bran, cornmeal, and barley flour—were also obtained. One "war bread" recipe called for 33 percent potatoes. Hoarding of any foodstuffs was labeled not only unpatriotic but also "direct assistance to the enemy."[20] Thus, everyone was encouraged to buy less, serve less, and waste less.

One of the greatest bulwarks against waste and inaction came through the response of women to the war. Although they did not leave home to fight, their contributions to the war effort stood shoulder to shoulder with those of the men. Many positions usually occupied by males were now thrown open for women. One widow in Blanding, whose son was in the army, decided to learn to drive four horses on a sulky plow. The newspaper reported, "There may be stumps and stones, as is often the case in new land, but this American mother is as game for all the bumps and possible tip-overs, as she would ask her sons to be when they meet the enemy."[21] Many other women helped keep their family farms afloat as male labor became scarce.

Governor Bamberger visited San Juan County several times during the war, and on one occasion voiced his appreciation for women's contributions to the war effort. Red Cross work in Utah was an honor to all, he said, and the state was second to none in reaching its quota of men for the army and navy. Bamberger believed mothers should feel proud and honored for the opportunity to furnish their government with that most dear to them—their sons.[22]

Like their male counterparts, women also readily enlisted for local war service. Each female registrant received a card with different activities from which to choose. In Blanding, seventy married and single women appeared at the registrar's door, filled out the fifty available registration cards, and indicated their willingness to sew, knit, and do work that would not take them from home. Thirteen of the seventy offered to join the Red Cross nurse program, requiring them to be ready to leave with only twenty-four hours' notice.[23]

Local newspapers ran advertisements for women's work on the Wasatch Front—stenographers, typists, telegraph operators, laboratory assistants, inspectors of small arms ammunition, statistical clerks, and a variety of other positions opened to lure them into the job market.[24]

How many women responded to these opportunities is difficult to determine, but in southeastern Utah nursing became a well-respected wartime occupation that removed women from their homes. Grand County furnished one student nurse for the Red Cross, with several more willing to serve. Eventually, others joined their ranks. Their course of training covered a three-month period, after which they were assigned to war hospitals to provide "the best that the woman-hood of America can offer in courage, devotion, and resourcefulness."[25]

However, not all of women's traditional qualities were desirable. Using the stereotype of a gossip, local newspapers listed ten "patriotic don'ts" for females. The article began, "Until the world is stricken dumb, women will talk," then went on to place as a top priority, "Do not chatter. Keep to yourself the news you hear, your own impressions, and your apprehensions."[26] The column then warned that women should not listen to alarmists or complain about hardships but instead be moderate in their spending, encourage the departure of soldiers to the front, and radiate confidence.

The fervor shown by women in accepting these various roles was summarized by a bit of doggerel appearing in the *San Juan Blade* a week before Christmas 1917. The unknown author wrote:

> The old hen merrily cackled her lay
> As she flew from her nest in the new-mown hay.
> And she sang the chorus from day to day—
> "Hurrah! hurrah! hurrah!
> I'm working for the U.S.A.
> Hurrah for the U.S.A.!"
> She roamed through the meadows with willing feet
> And caught bugs and grasshoppers, juicy and sweet
> And she sang as she worked: "Our soldiers must eat.
> Hurrah! hurrah! hurrah!
> I'm glad to work for the U.S.A.
> Hurrah for the U.S.A.!"[27]

In the spirit of the old hen, each community formed its own Red Cross chapter through which to funnel goods and services to soldiers. For instance, Grand County received a request for 305 pairs of socks and 51 sweaters to be delivered in two months. Sizes were given and only the best was expected. At Christmas the Red Cross workers, in cooperation with the LDS Primary organization, shipped 100 homemade fabric articles to soldiers at the front.[28]

The Red Cross also held auctions in every community in southeastern Utah. Citizens of Bluff raised $95 for their local chapter, a substantial payment considering the small population and their involvement in other fundraising activities. In Monticello one such auction epitomized the wartime fervor. Everything from quilts to hair tonic and watches to chickens brought in cash. Several items were purchased then donated and resold two or three times. But no one surpassed six-year-old Pearl Mortensen when she removed her beaded bracelet from her arm and said, "Sell this for the Red Cross."[29] Other children gave rings and nickels, fetching five dollars and one dollar respectively. Total sales for the evening brought in $235.

Grand County stamped its own brand on money raising. Local cattlemen donated heifer calves to be labeled with the mark of humanity—ARC for American Red Cross. Two or three calves from each rancher accumulated into a herd of sixty animals that were shipped to the National Western Stock Show in Denver. There the Red Cross entered the cows in a competition with the prize money and sales credited to the appropriate county chapter. The people of Grand County counted their war chest as $2,500 richer.[30]

Underlying all of these physical sacrifices was an unrelenting conviction that defeat of the Germans was a righteous, justified undertaking. By demeaning the enemy and painting their actions as despicable, the United States prepared itself psychologically to destroy the Germans with a clear conscience. Southeastern Utah arose from its generally peaceful pose and started a vitriolic campaign that mirrored national sentiments. Fueled by reports from the front lines that Americans had found Belgian girls and women chained to German machine guns, that torture and other forms of cruelty were the order of the day, and that submarines were sinking cargo vessels on the open seas, anti-German sentiment skyrocketed.[31] One article from Philadelphia, reprinted in local papers, took well-known phrases and added some "German" twists such as "Blessed are the child-murderers, for they shall inherit the earth"; "Be sure you are right handy with firearms, then go ahead"; "Dishonesty is the best policy"; "Hell on earth and hatred for all men"; and "Do unto others as you suspect they might do unto you if they ever get to be as disreputable as you are."[32]

The religious tinge to many of these quotations was not by chance. The LDS Church and its membership took a very strong position against German aggression by placing the war in an eternal perspective. One church speaker came to Blanding from the Agricultural College of Utah (present Utah State University) and insisted that the U.S. Constitution was an inspired document, that the "government [was] destined to complete victory," and that "Mormonism stands right squarely and without reserve for the right in this war." The speaker's "words met the perfect response of silence, not free from tears, for the nineteen soldier boys from Blanding who have aroused a keen sympathy in the hearts of all who know them."[33]

Three weeks later the *San Juan Blade* reprinted a speech given by Secretary of Commerce William C. Redfield in which he claimed, "The things we saw and see are but the outward and visible signs of an inward and dominant evil . . . [fostered by] the presence of the malign power that gave them birth."[34] Redfield rooted himself firmly in the New Testament's Paulinian duality, where the forces of good and evil wage a continual war for domination of the earth. Hearkening back to Puritan New England, he warned, "We fight not the people called the Germans, not even the political entities known as the central powers, so much as evil enthroned among them using them for its purposes, possessing them as devils are said to have done mankind of old."

One wonders just how accepted a tongue-in-cheek letter, purportedly written by Kaiser Wilhelm II to Lucifer, was by the residents of southeastern Utah. In it the kaiser complained that Satan had compared him to Nero, the Roman emperor, and that really the German was far worse and should not be slighted. After all, Nero could not bomb schools to kill children, drop poisoned candy on them, or sink ships transporting women and babies. At the end of a fairly lengthy admission of sins, the kaiser made Lucifer this offer: "Let us have a dual throne. With your experience coupled with my nature, we should be able to make a hell that would surpass all previous efforts."[35] Some writers used poetry to express their sentiments about the kaiser. Albert R. Lyman, a local historian and editor of the *Blade*, penned a few lines entitled "The Kaiser's Goat" that captured the down-home spirit against the Germans, as personified by their leader:

> Bill had a little submarine
> Built by Von Peter Krupp,
> And everywhere his playmates sailed
> He tried to blow them up.
> They begged that he would cut it out
> And though he said he would,
> He got some more torpedoes
> And torpedoed all he could.
> These playmates met one afternoon
> To talk about Bill's boat,
> And climbing boldly o'er the fence,
> They got his little goat.
> They hung it by its little neck,
> And there it's hanging still,
> And on the fence is written
> "The goat of Kaiser Bill."[36]

On the positive side, the LDS Church armed its members with a very clear picture of the enemy and what should be done about him. Although its young men serving missions were draft exempt, one soldier from Blanding wrote home saying there were about two thousand Mormons attending church with him at Camp Lewis, Washington.[37] Recruiters appealed to Mormon values. Utah's 145th Field Artillery ran an article in the *San Juan Blade* asking, "Why not go with your own brothers, cousins, and relatives? Why not lend your strength and talent by the side of your brother Utahn, that autocracy may be forever drowned?" After all, "highly trained, efficient, and lovable" officers led the "flower of Utah among the enlisted men."[38] The real, however, could be very different from the ideal.

The opposite faction from those serving their country included "slackers" and "spies." While very little evidence exists concerning the activities of either of these groups, the papers cried for vigilance against both. When Grand County announced its fourth liberty loan campaign, it also specified that every property owner in the county would invest in government securities, stated the amount and rate at which this would be done, and generated a list of people and incomes within the county to ensure that it was. People were told that after the war, when all the accounts were in, there would be only two groups to which everyone would belong—those who did and those who did not do their duty.

To ensure those who did not do their duty were properly recorded, the committee supervising the collection of money had twenty "slacker" cards to be sent into the Treasury Department with the names of the recalcitrants. *The Independent* reported problems in Davis County with slackers who were not paying their share toward the "people's war." Records checks and retribution would follow.[39] In San Juan, Sheriff Frank Barnes hunted down Ernest Spencer at his trading post twenty-five miles south of Bluff because he had reportedly failed to register for the draft. The trader claimed he had taken care of that business in Mancos, Colorado, and that he was innocent. The newspapers did not report the final outcome of this incident, but Lyman recorded in his history at the time that "There is not a yellow streak nor a slacker in the entire county. Its Council of Defense is as firm for democracy as the old Blue Mountains itself."[40] Spencer was probably innocent.

The animosity against those who did not participate in the war effort became intense, as neighbor watched neighbor to ensure each was doing his or her job. The more dramatic the displays of patriotism became, the better it was to avoid the slightest hint of being a laggard. The following verse, though not the best example of controlled rhyme, illustrates the fever pitch felt by some against slackers:

> If you can hold your tongue when German backers
>   Are loosing theirs and damning Uncle Sam;
> If you can keep from cussing out the slackers
>   And flaying smug hypocrisy and sham;
> If you can wait and not be tired of waiting,
>   While reptile papers keep us on the rack;
> If you can stand the pacifistic prating,
>   And never have a yearning to strike back-
>
> If you can see your country's cities plastered
>   With sycophantic warnings against war;
> If you can watch a yellow-livered dastard
>   Refusing to confront things as they are;
> If you can see a swarm of crawling lizards,
>   Squirming through the marriage license door-
> Men with atom souls and smaller gizzards,
>   Disgracing those who honored names they bore-
>
> If you can hear an orator denouncing
>   The liberty for which our nation bled;
> If you can let him go without a trouncing
>   Or punching in the bally traitor's head;
> If you can smile when lying propaganda
>   Seduces men who ought to know the truth;
> If you can tolerate their rotten slander
>   And bear it with an idle fist, forsooth-
> If you can sneer at men who wear the khaki,
>   Or jeer at those who wear the navy blue;
> If you can whisper like a skulking lackey,
>   About the men who have the nerve to do;

If vanquishment of brutal foes appalls you,
    If you can't prove your right to be a man-
You may be everything your mother calls you,
    But believe me, you are not American.[41]

Spies, on the other hand, were not as easy to detect or as easily proven guilty. Today, the thought of spies ranging through the isolated countryside of southeastern Utah is ludicrous, but during the war years it was serious business. Indeed, the reasoning followed that because it was such an unlikely place it was ideal for the enemy to observe the war movements within the country. People considered it better to "apprehend a dozen men who later prove themselves to be beyond reproach, than to allow a single guilty person to get away."[42]

Official sources outside of the counties gave credence to the reality of spies. Sheriff Barnes, for instance, received a letter from the governor's office saying that a widespread conspiracy existed targeting the destruction of livestock, grain, and food storage facilities. The message encouraged Barnes to take immediate steps to protect these things. The sheriff told all cattlemen to arm themselves when they rode the range and to bring in anyone looking suspicious. A week and a half later the Council of Defense organized a company of fifty men armed with high-powered rifles and appointed four men to furnish a "military map" of San Juan County. To enhance self-defense and improve marksmanship the sheriff inaugurated a rifle and revolver club.[43]

Approximately two months later Mormon apostle James E. Talmage was quoted from the pulpit as saying, "There is no place in this church for traitors, whether they be native or foreign born"; they must be "dealt with." The war, he believed, was "a necessary preliminary to the coming of Christ."[44] On the same page an article warned, "everyone should look out for spies." People were advised to write letters that contained no military information, to "look with suspicion on strangers," and to "ferret out the spies who walk abroad throughout the land . . . [in order to] run the enemy aliens to earth and nip their treacherous, murderous and destructive activities in the bud." Not surprisingly, the local government ordered all female German aliens in southeastern Utah to register on June 17, 1918.[45]

With a theoretical German hiding behind every rock and sagebrush, it was not long before reports of them started to surface. "Enemy planes" flew over La Sal until, eventually, the government identified them as American aircraft flying out of the aerial school in Columbus, New Mexico. Young Riley Hurst, who suffered with nightmares generated by terrifying propaganda, recalled riding with a friend from Monticello one evening and looking at a star. Soon the star was "moving," and by the time he got to Blanding it was a German plane spraying the wheat crops with poison. His friend's dad confirmed the observation, rooted in a common belief of the wheat farmers in the area.[46]

Perhaps the most insidious German "plot" was the smallpox epidemic that erupted in the winter of 1918. The first person to contract the disease, David Black Jr., stated unequivocally that he had gotten it from a person on the Navajo reservation. Six or eight other cases appeared, causing Blanding to go into quarantine. Rumors as to its origin spread, crediting the Germans with infecting the mail. When the state sent vaccines to treat the disease, rumors again spread that the enemy had contaminated the serum. Wiser heads prevailed, insisting the only way to prevent a full-scale epidemic was for people to avail themselves of proper medical treatment.[47]

The experience of the men who left southeastern Utah to serve in the armed forces varied with each individual and circumstance. Yet a general pattern flowed through what many of them encountered, or at least what was reported in the newspapers. The first in a series of events—the sendoff—was one of the most indelible. The initial step was a banquet and dance hosted by the soldier's town. Patriotic decorations, a live band, and a number of tables prominently placed for those departing and their families all accentuated the importance of national service. A respected individual, after the meal, gave a rousing speech, followed by the new enlistees sharing their thoughts. In some instances citizens circulated a purse to defray the expense of travel to the recruiting stations in Green River, Price, or Salt Lake City. Finally, the dance went well into the night.[48]

The following day, townspeople escorted the men by car (relatively new to this area) on a long journey over bumpy dirt roads that wound through hills and over slickrock. One group added cars as they traveled so that by the time they departed Moab forty vehicles lined the way.[49] Most enlistees entrained in Thompson for Salt Lake City. After an initial introduction to the military they went to their branch specialty school, where they learned a trade in artillery, infantry, or some other skill. Training sites included Fort Riley, Kansas; Camp Kearny, California; Camp Lewis, Washington; and Camp Mills, Long Island.

Life at these facilities was rigorous but surprisingly pleasant for the Utahns. One artilleryman enthusiastically described his impression of Camp Kearny near San Diego. Where six months before only brush had existed, there now were miles of paved streets, sewage and water systems, electric lights, many "modern conveniences," and "cantonments and tents almost as far as the eye can see."[50] Conditions in camp were more advanced than in the soldier's hometown of Blanding, where electricity, water, and sewage disposal systems were nascent and paved roads nonexistent. No wonder he penned, "We have plenty to eat and to wear, and worked but a small portion of the time. . . . We soldiers have an easier time of it than the ones left behind." Other men offered similar sentiments: "This is the life for me"; "We have good eats and good beds. The cars are the best they have in the East. . . . I am having the time of my life"; and "we are enjoying good health and everything else that falls to the lot of the soldier . . . good quarters, good food, good clothing, and best of all, we are in with a good lot of men."[51]

This last point is instructive, since most of the recruits from southeastern Utah came from a homogeneous background. Though not all were Mormons, a large enough percentage from Utah were that they could congregate in fairly significant numbers on Sundays. One man wrote, "We have one of the best batteries [artillery units] in camp. It is made up of men from Utah and Montana, the majority of us are Mormons and there are a few returned missionaries among us and they are doing a splendid church work here. . . . We always hold Mutual meetings once a week."[52]

Aside from the religious aspect, many of the men called upon skills acquired from their rural lifestyle at home. Letters attest to the benefits of obtaining proficiency in marksmanship, packing horses and mules, mechanical ingenuity, and living out of doors.[53] One thing that many held in common was a desire to ship out to France. The men's letters frequently mention that if they missed the fighting it would be the "disappointment of [their] life." One soldier wrote that inasmuch as "the United States is fighting for the democracy of the world . . . I want to do my part."[54] Another said when an officer canvassed his company for volunteers to go to France "the entire company stepped forward at once and the question as to who should go, had to be settled another way."[55]

Once the soldiers arrived in Europe their likelihood of survival was fairly good. Ratios based on statistics from the Allied forces showed a 29:1 chance of being killed; 49:1 chance of recovering from wounds; 500:1 chance of losing a limb; and that for every ten men killed by bullets another would die from disease.[56] The previously quoted figures from Blanding of fifty-four men serving, three of whom died, seem to support these statistics.

On November 11, 1918, the Germans signed an armistice ending the war. News of the surrender tore through the towns of southeastern Utah like unexpected lightning in the crisp fall air. Rapid demobilization allowed many of the servicemen to be home within three months. The towns held official welcome-back and thank-you-for-serving celebrations that rivaled the occasions of their departure. Festivities in Monticello started at 3 p.m. and lasted into the early morning hours. The obligatory banquet, speeches and responses, and dance received a new wrinkle when the returning soldiers and a lieutenant staged a drill exhibition during intermission.[57] Following the conclusion of this display of patriotic fervor, the uniforms were hung in the closet or consigned to mothballs, to be resurrected for annual

Fourth of July or Pioneer Day celebrations in the future. The war was finally over for southeastern Utah.

In summarizing the attitudes and actions of the people of Grand and San Juan counties during World War I, it is easy to relegate them to a naive, quaint period of American history, when the idealism of the progressive movement, the emphasis on patriotic history, and an our-nation-right-or-wrong attitude blinded people to the stark realities of financing and waging a war partway around the world. Certainly not everyone bought into the plan. Yet enough people subscribed to these beliefs to establish a pattern of fervent love of country and its causes. When Studs Terkel referred to the activities of World War II as fighting "the good war," he could have just as easily turned the clock back twenty-three years and applied his phrase to World War I. Along with tremendous death, destruction, and hatred, there surfaced strong feelings of love, devotion, patriotism, and sacrifice not found to the same degree in most of the recent U.S. wars. Southeastern Utah, like much of the nation, rose to the occasion and offered its services unstintingly, reflecting involvement, not isolation and disillusionment. That would come later, with time.

NOTES

Originally published in the *Utah Historical Quarterly* 63 (Winter 1995): 4–23.

1. Deon C Greer et al., *Atlas of Utah* (Provo, UT: Brigham Young University Press, 1981), 114, 119.
2. *Grand Valley Times* [hereafter cited as *GVT*], July 27, 1917; *San Juan Blade* [hereafter cited as *SJB*], August 11, 1917; Justin A. Black, interview by Louise Lyne, July 11, 1972, Utah State Historical Society and California State University–Fullerton, Southeastern Utah Project, 9.
3. *SJB*, August 24, 1917; August 31, 1917.
4. Ibid.
5. *SJB*, December 28, 1917; December 7, 1917; *GVT*, September 20, 1918.
6. *SJB*, August 10, 1917.
7. Riley Hurst, interview by Robert S. McPherson, April 2, 1992, Blanding, Utah, manuscript in possession of author.

8. *SJB*, September 7, 1917; February 22, 1918; Albert R. Lyman, *History of Blanding, 1905–1955* (Blanding, UT: Author, 1955); Hurst, interview.
9. *SJB*, June 20, 1918.
10. *SJB*, November 6, 1917.
11. *SJB*, October 26, 1917; November 2, 1917; *The Independent* [hereafter cited as *TI*], April 18, 1918.
12. *TI*, May 2, 1918; August 1, 1918; *GVT*, September 20, 1918.
13. *SJB*, November 2, 1917.
14. Karl Lyman, interview by Carolyn Black, March 19, 1992, San Juan County Historical Commission, 1; *SJB*, February 1, 1918.
15. *TI*, June 13, 1918; *SJB*, December 21, 1917.
16. *GVT*, May 18, 1917; *SJB*, January 18, 1918.
17. *SJB*, August 18, 1917.
18. *TI*, June 27, 1918.
19. *SJB*, September 4, 1917; September 21, 1917; February 22, 1918.
20. George Arthur Hurst, "Journal," 172, Utah State Historical Society Library; *SJB*, February 1, 1918; March 22, 1918; February 8, 1918.
21. *SJB*, March 8, 1918; March 22, 1918.
22. *SJB*, October 19, 1917.
23. Catherine Moore, interview by Jessie Embry, April 23, 1979, Southeastern Utah Oral History Project, Charles Redd Center, Brigham Young University, Provo, Utah, 13; *SJB*, November 9, 1917; November 16, 1917.
24. *TI*, May 9, 1918.
25. *TI*, August 1, 191; August 8, 1918.
26. *SJB*, February 1, 1918.
27. *SJB*, December 14, 1917.
28. *TI*, July 4, 1918; *SJB*, December 21, 1917.
29. *TI*, April 18, 1918; June 6, 1918.
30. *TI*, August 8, 1918.
31. *GVT*, September 6, 1918.
32. *GVT*, June 21, 1918.
33. *SJB*, December 21, 1917.
34. *SJB*, January 4, 1918.
35. *SJB*, March 8, 1918.
36. *SJB*, September 4, 1917.
37. *SJB*, August 10, 1917; December 14, 1917.
38. *SJB*, March 22, 1918.
39. *GVT*, September 20, 1918; June 13, 1918.
40. *SJB*, October 11, 1917; Albert R. Lyman, "History of San Juan County, 1879–1917," Special Collections, Harold B. Lee Library, Brigham Young University, 116.

41. E. C. Ranuck, "Straight Talk," *SJB*, September 7, 1917.
42. *GVT*, October 19, 1917.
43. *SJB*, November 16, 1917.
44. *SJB*, February 1, 1918.
45. *TI*, June 13, 1918.
46. *GVT*, July 27, 1917; August 17, 1917; Hurst, interview.
47. *SJB*, January 18, 1918; January 25, 1918; February 8, 1918.
48. *SJB*, November 9, 1917; August 10, 1917.
49. *SJB*, September 21, 1917; *GVT*, September 21, 1917.
50. *SJB*, November 2, 1917.
51. *GVT*, September 20, 1918; *SJB*, December 7, 1917; February 15, 1918.
52. *SJB*, February 15, 1918.
53. *SJB*, August 17, 1917; February 22, 1918.
54. *SJB*, November 2, 1917.
55. *SJB*, March 22, 1918.
56. *TI*, August 1, 1918.
57. *SJB*, February 26, 1919.

7

KANARRAVILLE FIGHTS WORLD WAR I

KERRY WILLIAM BATE

There was no town or city in Utah not impacted by World War I. It might be suggested that the consequences of war were more pronounced and real in small towns like Kanarraville, a village of about three hundred residents located between Cedar City and Saint George. Sixteen young men from Kanarraville saw military service during the war. Their absence was felt on the farms and ranches where they had labored and in the social circle of young people in the community. Yet their departure was celebrated and their mission validated through the purchase of liberty bonds and other manifestations of support for the war effort. Using a valuable collection of oral histories with local residents conducted in the 1980s, along with contemporary letters and newspaper articles, Kerry Bate gives us a revealing glimpse of one town's experience during the war.

Kanarraville, about twenty miles south of Cedar City in Iron County, boasted a population of around three hundred in 1918. The town's reactions to—and participation in—World War I are available in diaries, contemporary newspaper accounts, church records, and oral history interviews conducted in the 1980s. Because of these rich sources we know that town members, though torn between patriotism and isolationism, grumblingly did what they saw as their duty but questioned the basic premises of the "Great War." Kanarraville's experiences may speak to the general reactions to the war in rural Utah.

A January 3, 1915,[1] letter from Maryanne Campbell Wilson— a Belfast, Ireland, cousin of Kanarraville's midwife young Elizabeth Stapley—anticipated a question:

> I'm sure you are anxious to hear how we get along these war times. Well, we have much to be thankful for. We have food to eat (tho much dearer than usual) and at any rate we only eat to live, but some people live to eat. It will be harder on them than us. . . . Ireland is not so badly off as England or Scotland. She has peace as far as the war is concerned, save for the men she has sent to the front. . . . The Government thinks she should send more men, and *so do we all.* So that this dreadful war might be brought to an end. Yes there has been talk about peace, but I am afraid it will not come yet.

Maryanne added, "People are afraid to cross the ocean. Now so many ships have been sunk by the cruel Germans, who seem to have no pity for women or children." She wrote again in mid-1916 saying, "We are praying that God may bring an end to the war. He could stop it on a moment if it was His Will. . . . Peace is beautiful. God grant we may have it soon again." And she added, "Did you hear of the Rebellion In Ireland at Easter?"[2]

Despite this sort of subtle proselytizing for the war, most Utahns were far from enthusiastic. Woodrow Wilson, campaigning in 1916 that he had kept the United States out of war, received such a landslide in this state that he helped elect Utah's first Jewish governor, Simon Bamberger, despite a Republican-sponsored, anti-Semitic parody of the Utah state anthem published in the *Iron County Record*: "Democracy's latest star/Jew-tah, we love thee./Thy Lucre shines afar,/Jew-tah, we love thee."

But even before Wilson's second inaugural the public realized American involvement in the war was almost inevitable because of the continued sinking of neutral ships, which Maryanne Wilson had complained of in 1915. On January 31, 1917, Germany announced unrestricted submarine warfare, and three days later the United States severed diplomatic relations. Calling it an "irony of fate" after the recent election, the *Iron County Record* editorialized on February 9, 1917, that war would "be somewhat of a disappointment to those fond but hysterical wives and mothers who cast their votes for Wilson for the sole reason that he had 'kept us out of war.'"

On April 6 the county newspaper's predictions were realized as war was declared, followed by proclamations from the governor of Utah and the president of the Utah Agricultural College calling upon the people to organize and cooperate in increasing productivity for the war effort.[3] Iron County school superintendent L. John Nuttall lectured to "a good sized audience" in Kanarraville "on the subject of war and the need of more and better cultivation of our farms."[4] Elizabeth Stapley's Irish cousin was predictably happy: "I see America has Joined 'The Allies.' What have you to say to that? We are all pleased to have America help us to stay the Giant. Never was such a war, and never was such a wicked Leader. The Kaiser's name will go down to posterity with a black Mark against it Like the Bible Kings . . . he feared not God nor man."[5] Mormon missionaries wrote the midwife's Australian nephew that "Our people in America are now greatly excited over the war and are making rapid preparations to assist the Allies. . . . The world is in a dreadful condition."[6]

The jingoistic *Record* was as enthusiastic as its European cousins, endorsing the recently passed Conscription Act on May 4, 1917. But a note of caution was sounded by the Kanarraville correspondent to the *Iron County Record* on June 1, 1917: "Registration Day June 5th seems to worry some of the young men," commented the reporter, "also some of the women don't feel any too well about it. They feel that if the men could do their scrapping on their own land it wouldn't be so bad."

But with typical obedience Kanarraville people turned registration into a patriotic celebration and registered all 32 men of draft age.[7] When the first conscription list of 202 was drawn for the county's quota of 46 men, only 3 were from Kanarra.[8] Even those who escaped were hardly comforted: "Owing to the fact that so many of the men examined last week were found deficient," reported the *Record* on August 17, "and to the further fact that a heavy percentage filed affidavits of exemption, it was found necessary to call for some 62 additional men to take the examination." Among the first 125 men examined in the first group and "found physically fit and did not claim exemption" were Kanarra's Jesse C. Roundy and Leland C. Stapley. William A. Olds, originally rejected for not meeting the weight guidelines, was found fit when that requirement was adjusted.

The August 17, 1917, issue of the *Record* carried an article about eager Iron County volunteer Gene Woodbury, who was turned down by the army, navy, National Guard, and even something called the "aviation corps." "He is all broken up over it and practically discouraged with living," noted the newspaper.[9] Significantly, few from Kanarra were eager to volunteer. Of the sixteen Kanarraites who eventually served, only Emery Pollock was a volunteer. "Nobody wanted their family [members] to go," Arvilla Woodbury explained, "but [if] they were drafted in, they had to go. . . . [T]hey were afraid they'd git killed."[10]

The first six Kanarra draftees were announced in the *Record* on August 24, 1917. One, Victor L. Sylvester, never served, probably because he had a wife and small child. Four men left Kanarraville on September 19: town athlete Jesse Roundy, good-natured sheepherder Wells Williams, nearly illiterate George E. Roundy (he described his race as "whight" in his war service questionnaire[11]), and mischievous Leland C. Stapley[12] ("I'm gonna grease yer head an' swaller ya whole!" Leland used to growl at his little cousin, Leola Stapley Anderson[13]). "A banquet was given the departing soldier boys the day before their entrainment at Lund," the Kanarraville correspondent reported on September 28, adding, "The old martial band was out in full force and a rousing meeting was held in the afternoon. Fruit and melons were served to all present, followed by a dance. The boys all expressed their appreciation of the honor shown them."

Actually having men in service may have prompted townsfolk to participate in the second liberty loan subscription: only nine

Kanarraites had subscribed $800 to the first liberty loan drive, despite preaching in church in favor of it.[14] But forty-seven townsfolk subscribed $4,750[15] to the second. In addition, the Kanarra school district subscribed $100. Draftee Leland Stapley's sister Lenna remembered that the townsfolk "were patriotic, I've never seen more patriotic people than they were then. We bought war bonds, even the school went out, I can remember I was only a fifth grader or something, we went out and gleaned beans, sold em, and bought a war bond."[16] The bond was eventually cashed in to buy the school a Victrola.

While the local newspaper was touting "one of the greatest film attractions yet produced"—*The Birth of a Nation*—a new list of registrants was published with men in first through fifth classes. Leon (pronounced "Lee-own" in Iron County) Davis and his hard-drinking cousin Wallace were the only Kanarraville men in the first class, which, the *Record* reported, was "arranged in classes according to the order in which they will be drafted."[17] On January 25 the *Record* reported, "Rens Davis goes this week to Hurricane Valley to take the place of one of his boys who will have to take the physical examination for military service. About ten of our boys have been placed in class one, and with four already in the training camps and three on missions, we will feel the scarcity of help." Seven Kanarra men were examined "and found fit for service."[18]

So on February 1 the town held "an entertainment in honor of the ten boys who successfully passed the examination for the U.S. Army. A short program preceded a dinner, which never in the history of Kanarra was a better one given. At night a dance was given. The Parowan orchestra furnishing music."[19] Town storekeeper Riley G. Williams furnished all the boys' meals, and two baseball games were organized between "the soldiers" and "the rest of the town." It was not a good omen that the "town" beat the soldiers twice.[20]

The third liberty loan drive began in earnest in early April 1918, with the *Record* predicting that "with the stirring events on in Europe, it should not be hard to obtain subscriptions . . . this time."[21] "We had in attendance at our afternoon services last Sunday . . . U.T. Jones and

Emily C. Watson in the interest of the third Liberty Loan," the Kanarraville correspondent reported on April 19. Iron County was responsible for coming up with $94,000 of Utah's $10 million allotment. Kanarraville was dunned $5,000 and expected to raise it by April 18. However, only $4,750 had been raised by April 26, according to the *Record.*[22]

James Lorenzo "Rens" Davis returned home from the sheep herd in late February thinking that two of his boys were shortly to be drafted. That proved erroneous, and he complained that "he was misled,"[23] but not for long. A subheadline in the county newspaper on May 10, 1918, announced, "TWO KANARRA BOYS TO ENTRAIN TODAY," and the story explained that Iron County's quota "for the present month will be 32. Of this number two, Leon and Wallace Davis of Kanarra, will leave this afternoon for Camp McDowell, California." The newspaper went on to explain that "Oline Parker, of Kanarra, will leave either the 12th or 13th for Boulder, Colorado." (However, Kanarraville seems to have had no Oline Parker, and no such person can be found in published lists of Utah's World War I soldiers.) These draftees were followed on May 26 by handsome William B. Williams, town sprinter Jewett Wood, and sheepherder Kumen ("Que-man") B. Williams. (Kumen's mother was not ready for this and mournfully referred to her soldier-sons as "the two little boys."[24]) William's shy brother Ervin soon joined these men, but not all of them stayed to serve. Athletic Jewett Wood came home on June 5, allegedly discharged for defective teeth, but townsfolk suspected it was for a certain mental vacancy (when a 35-mile-per-hour speed limit was posted in town, he commented solemnly that "I couldn't make that dorn thing git up to 35!").[25] Perhaps their conviction that Jewett was not quite bright was reinforced by the county newspaper report that he "has nothing but good words for the camp and the military training he has been receiving."[26]

Still, the manpower shortage continued and the federal government served notice that men without useful occupations would be drafted. These included not only gamblers, fortune tellers, and racetrack and bucket shop attendants, but also waiters, bartenders, passenger elevator operators, domestics, store clerks, theater attendants, and ushers.[27]

Recently returned missionary William B. Stapley followed his brother Leland into the service, reporting to the local board on June 14. "That upset my dad, my mother," recalled William's sister, Lenna Stapley Williams. "It was hard to get communication at that time, World War I. Telephone, newspaper. We didn't have TVs or radio then. I know it was a big worry."[28] But there were some payoffs: William Stapley used his first army paycheck to buy the elegant Sophia Parker an engagement ring.[29]

William was followed two weeks later by Lorenzo Wendell "Wennie" Davis, the snare drum player in the martial band, who had been out herding sheep in Panguitch; Wennie was sent to Camp Lewis in Washington.[30] By July anxious parents got word that Leland Stapley and Wells Williams were to be sent overseas, and in late August more Kanarra boys were called up: fiery Will Roundy's common-sense son Marion, who had received his induction notice on April 13,[31] and a dour young German farmer, Gustave H. Pingle. On August 23, 1918, the *Record* published the names of thirty-four draftees, including five from Kanarra. However, Pingle was turned down at Camp Lewis. The Kanarra correspondent to the newspaper reported a week later that "Five of our boys answered the call to go to the colors. This call has taken all of the first draft men in class 1 from this place and all but one in the registration of June 5, 1918." The fall registration showed twenty-nine Kanarra men on this list.[32]

Perhaps typical of Woodrow Wilson's 1916 Utah voters was Kanarraville's Phebe Reeves Davies, a staunch Republican who was so worried about her son Elmer being drafted that she voted Democratic. She lived to be 102, but she never made the mistake of marking the Democratic ticket again.[33] Elmer, the catcher on the town baseball team, was drafted in July and sent to Camp Lewis. "I don't believe in wars," he explained later. "I don't think they settle anything. . . . I didn't want to fight anybody, but I did want to stick up fer our rights. Now, that's the way I feel about it. I figger you got to stick up fer your rights, an' I think that was the attitude, mostly. But I don't know, it don't seem like you git very for in a lotta these squabbles, they jest makes a few more enemies! I'm not very quarrelsome myself; I think it's better to have a friend than an enemy."[34] Elmer's sister Bessie's response to the draft was even more pointed: "we all hated it like everthing."[35]

Brothers Leo and Claud Balser presented quite a contrast: Leo was handsome, well built, and six-foot-tall, weighing in at 180 pounds; Claud was small, sickly, and hard of hearing.[36] But both were called up at the same time as Davies.

Reports of some Iron County deaths were not long in following these drafts. Henry M. Jones of Enoch and Elmer Jesperson of Cedar City were the first reported fatalities. But even with such a modern thing as an aviation corps, in some areas military science had made little progress. In 1777 Dr. Benjamin Rush issued a circular to officers of the Revolutionary army of the new "United American States" and warned, "A greater proportion of men perish with sickness in all armies than fall by the sword." As it was in 1777, so it was in 1918: half of Cedar City's soldiers died from influenza,[37] though no one from Kanarraville lost his life in this war.

Leland Stapley, the 91st Division bugler, sent his diary to his mother, Harriet "Hattie" Berry Stapley. She proudly turned it over to the *Record*, which published it on April 18, 1919, as "WAR EXPERIENCES FROM IRON COUNTY SOLDIER'S DIARY." Stapley had been sent to Camp Lewis, Washington, and from there across the country to Camp Merritt, New York. "People at every station gave us candy, cigarettes and wished us good luck," he noted with satisfaction. After nine months in New York he sailed on the ship *Dano* to Halifax to join a twenty-two-ship convoy. "Life on board was one continual jam," he wrote. "We had daily inspections which are the curse of a soldier's life. The trip across was one hard knock with another. The main excitement was the sighting of a whale now and then, and the rush for the canteen when it opened."

Stapley landed in France on July 22, 1918, and shipped from there to Le Havre. "We traveled on an English ship, being fed on fish which nearly made us all sick from the smell," he wrote, "but after living on tea and dried fish in this rest camp for two days, we would have welcomed the grub that was thrown through the porthole of the ship." From there he was shipped out in a boxcar, which did not impress him when he noticed it was labeled "8 Horses or 40 Men." When he finally got to Lou Vere, he said, "The first thing we did was to 'police' up the town and taste some of the French wine. And the next thing was trying to learn the French language. But we found it much easier for the French to learn ours." On September 3 he "hiked to Bonnett. There we got our first instructions in air bombing. One was not allowed to smoke after dusk in the open."

Things began to heat up on September 21 when he wrote, "Another red-letter day. While here we had our first taste of Fritz. One afternoon we were all engaged in a little card game, we heard a whiz through the air that made us duck our heads and chilled our blood. The shell landed about 150 yards from our quarters and sounded like it was in the house." Five days later he experienced a real battle:

Sept. 26th. 3:00 p.m.—zero hour. It is impossible to describe the noise made by the cannon. Hundreds of them firing at the same time with huge shells bursting all around. The lights of Broadway are mere glimmers when compared with the lights of the battle. The flashes of the guns, star shell lights and signal rockets lighted up the horizon in one continuous stream of fire. Daybreak found us moving through the forest DeHesse and every tree and bush screened a light of heavy guns. We traveled in trucks to the edge of no man's land. From there we made our way on foot carrying machine guns and equipment and rations in a light pack. In marching over no-man's land, which had been in the hands of the Germans for four years, we had to cross one large shell hole after another. We saw the effect of artillery fire. No farmer ever turned over the soil more thoroughly than the artillery had plowed up the forest of Cheppie. There was not one tree but that was full of shrapnel. Kilo after kilo—it was one shell hole after another. Some of the sights along the road would make a strong man weak. We halted at sundown on the outskirts of Very to eat. Some of us didn't have time to eat. I had three boxes of A.M. and with a slice of bacon hanging from my mouth I made my way through Very which was being shelled by heavy Hun guns. That march was the hardest part of the fight for it looked just like a death trap to me, as men were falling here and there, with shells on all sides of us, but we marched right through. We spent the second night in the rain with only a rain coat.

Then the diary entries get very brief: "dodging H.E.'s and shrapnel and air raiders"; "A Hun plane came over and dropped two large bombs, the first striking near to us and the last one came down on a group of engineers killing forty men and fourteen horses. Such was the excitement each day"; "Two runners were killed"; "One's nerves sure go to pieces in time under shell fire"; "One could see now and then a skull of some brave warrior who had been dug up by a high explosive shell"; "thirty-two Boch[e] prisoners killed"; "had some sneezing gas which is nothing very nice. One cannot keep his mask on when he gets in touch of that gas."

The diary abruptly ends on November 11, Armistice Day, with Leland concluding, "This is only part of what happened, yet it will do you till I get home. . . . The boys from Iron county who were along with me are Wells Williams of Kanarra, Stanley Benson, Thomas H. Myers, John Mitchell, Claud Harris and Oscar Thornton of Parowan. All are feeling fine and looking for the day for for [*sic*] them to sail for home." He signed off, "Your Loving Son, Bugler LELAND STAPLEY."

Probably Leon Davis had the most adventurous life overseas because he was sent to Siberia to fight the Red Army. Leon, who found it hard to leave home, complained that the mail was undependable and that the cooks "had big sores on em." Moreover, he was convinced that "he had the meanest sergeant ever lived."[38] He also kept a diary as wonderfully readable as Leland Stapley's. It begins on June 23, 1919, with a train ride from Shkotova to Kangow in company with "a million bed bugs to an inch in the train car our squad stayed in."[39] The next day, with an eighty- or ninety-pound pack, he hiked to a mountain top, writing that "The Bolschivicks had blown up three power houses in about ten miles so we road when we could and walked when we had to." The "Bolschivicks" had also blown up or burned out bridges all along the way. The following day, "the Bolschivicks opened up on us. I had just moved and a big slug hit where I was standing just a second before. . . . We shot three or four guys on the hill. By this time our Corp[or]al had came back, and we turned around and saw three Bolschivicks right behind us. We all shot and got them and we thought there were more behind so we retreated back to the bridge. . . . There were 156 Bolschivicks killed and 2 Americans wounded." He disarmed two of the dead Russians and found they had "two packs, two guns and ammunition. One of the packs contained a can of powder, under clothes, a cup, bread and a pocket book that had about 41 rubles in. The other about the same." This day ended with the complaint, "We had supper about 6 p.m. no dinner and a darn little breakfast."

They were near a town called Kazunba when they "came on a Bolschivick out post. They had to leave in such a hurry they left one shoe and all their clothes. They also left a can of dynamite. We got within about 1 mile from town and they opened fire on us. We fought for about an hour, one man in my squad got hit in the foot and bled to death—Peter Bernell." The next day, "We buried Pete. Our squad were pale-bearers, a squad to fire the volley. Our squad went first with the body and then the squad to fire the volley and then the rest of our Company and a company of Japs there were four graves and Pete's made the fifth one within two or three days. We buried him then went back to camp. That was our Fourth of July."

The mail was unreliable: Leon recorded one day, "Got 15 letters from Ma and one from Kitty." The food was too reliable: "We got up and had reverly [sic] then breakfast which consisted of bacon, cornmeal mush and molasses no sugar or milk. We have had this for about one month straight and most of the time hard tack so damn hard you couldn't break it with an 'ax.'" Next day: "we had the same thing for breakfast."

August 9 was a special day: "The regemental band came up last night and played a few pieces. . . . The band sure sounded fine. The Y.M.C.A. man came up and gave us all a bar of chocolate and some cigarettes." On August 10 "fourteen of the class 'A' boys turned in their equipment today to return to the states and they sure are a tickled bunch. I wish I was with them." KP was no more welcome in Russia than anywhere else: "Got up and went on K.P. it was hell we had to scrape spuds as big as marbles for three meals for 250 men we never got through until 7:30 p.m." That night "No 3 outpost fired 2 shots and some of the boys got out of bed and put on their clothes, but it didn't bother me much I turned over and went back to sleep. Next morning we found out they were shooting at a porky pine and thought it was some Bolschivick." The diary ends on September 11, although Leon was not discharged until November 4, 1919.

The last U.S. "crusade" to have had a dramatic impact on townsfolk was the abolition of polygamy. Unlike the resistance generated by the "raids" of the 1880s, the drafts and loan drives of the war years enjoyed the unwavering support of the Mormon church hierarchy. Church leaders preached from the Kanarraville pulpit the importance of subscribing to the bond drives. Bishop's counselor Joel J. "Dode" Roundy was an optimist, explaining in church that "he looked for good to come out of the war," and later arguing that "the Mormon soldier boys are preaching the gospel by example."[40] Perhaps Dode Roundy was not thinking of his nephew, Leland Stapley, sampling French wines and complaining that he could not smoke after dark. It was more comforting to think of his son Jesse Roundy serving a mission like his son Ren than to imagine Jesse killing people.

There was also the pleasant side benefit of this war that some of Kanarra's wildest young men began to more soberly contemplate their prospects for eternity. "Sister Harriet Balser told of Leo and Claud writing home and saying they believed in the gospel and they wanted a book of Mormon," Kanarraville church minutes noted on October 6, 1918. And Wells Williams won a headline ("Wells Williams Sees Religious Awakening") in the *Iron County Record* on November 30, 1917, with his comments in a letter to his brother R.J. that "You know I believe that I am a better boy since coming to training. At least I attend church more often, and now that I am out here I can see a greater need of taking a deeper interest in the study of Mormonism; and there is no question but that the Mormon boys are gaining distinction here in camp." Wells was to become a Kanarraville bishop.

National press reports of Utah's enthusiasm for the war effort seemed to have a positive effect elsewhere: Kanarraville's William Grant Piatt wrote appreciatively from the Alabama mission field that Utah's oversubscription to the liberty loan drives and enthusiastic patriotism made his job easier. Even a letter from Kanarraville's gentle missionary James Lorenzo Roundy took on military metaphors as he spoke of putting "on the whole armor of God . . . tak[ing] the shield of faith, the helmet of salvation and the sword of the Spirit."[41] A reputation for obedience to authority, personal cleanliness, and a reticence about patronizing prostitutes made Mormons attractive military recruits. One gentile major stationed at Camp Lewis, Washington, was quoted in the local newspaper on November 30, 1917, as saying, "I wish that all the boys were Mormons, as they are the boys looked to for good, clean moral bodies, and they are the ones that are capable of doing things efficiently." However, rural Mormon boys also took their prejudices with them: volunteer Pratt Tollestrup of Cedar City wrote the *Record* casually that "The other day a couple of Nigger soldiers broke out with the smallpox," and his only worry seemed to be that the disease would spread to the white troops.[42]

Given the Mormons' conviction that they had higher moral standards and a better form of religious organization than others, townsfolk worried most about the effects degenerate gentile values would have on their rambunctious young men. "Brother Bently here in the rest of the Sunday School spoke a time on the morality of the world and the footfalls [*sic*] for the soldier boys from among us, also of the snares which will be laid for our young people at home," the ward minutes reported on February 10, 1918.

If military-aged men were the biggest contribution Kanarraville could make to the front lines, it was the efforts of townswomen that accounted for the most significant home contribution. The Rocky Mountain Division of the Red Cross organized chapters throughout the state and asked members to canvass door-to-door for contributions. An *Iron County Record* headline on November 30, 1917, stated that "Red Cross Work Begins Here Soon" and called for the immediate collection of linen. The Mormon Relief Societies in the various communities accepted most of the responsibility for this work.

The Kanarraville Relief Society, once moribund, had been completely reorganized in November 1911 when new—mostly younger—officers were installed. The new president was Sarah Catherine "Kate" Roundy, a homebody who "wasn't out in the public." The minutes reported that Kate "Said She felt weak in trying to fill her position She was called to," but she was undoubtedly strengthened by the capable women assigned to be her coworkers. Frances Rebecca Pollock Williams, Kate's niece, was appointed as first counselor. Frances was described by Thelma Berry Lovell as "very energetic" and "a pusher,"[43] a judgment shared by Arvilla Woodbury, who described Williams as "one of the main ones . . . always up an' comin' an' doin' things." Williams also ran the post office, supervised the telephone switchboard, and revived the town drama club.

By 1918 the second counselor was Kate's regal sister-in-law, Harriet "Hattie" Berry Stapley, a religious woman who loved to read but did not share the Stapley talent for music. She told a story about herself and her sister-in-law sitting under the awning of the house singing church hymns as their men came in from the field with a load of hay. "What's that noise?" asked one of the men. "Oh," came the answer, "that's the damned old grindstone!"[44] Because Hattie's father had been killed by a mob in what became known as the "Tennessee Martyrdom," the Berrys were treated—and thought of themselves—as Iron County gentry.

Then there was the Relief Society secretary, Betsy Jane Parker Smith. "She was old, old, old," recalled eighty-seven-year-old Arvilla Woodbury: "Aunt Betsy come across the plains."[45] Betsy had an excellent voice and used to team up with Kate's brother John Alma Stapley to sing "For the Mormons Shall Be Happy" at Fourth and Twenty-Fourth of July celebrations, and she was described by Lynn Reeves as "quite a public-spirited woman."[46]

At first even this November 1911 reorganization seemed halfhearted: the new officers were not formally set apart for their new positions until March 1912, at which time Kate, encouraged by twelve attendees, said "she was pleased to see so many out."

When Kate first began attending meetings the older women would reminisce about Nauvoo and pioneer Utah. But under her stewardship they increased their teaching efforts by visiting the homes of townswomen, studied current events and disease prevention, and completed their own Relief Society building in the town square across the street from the Roundy home. Though the hall was used as a school during the week, some of the war work took place in it. Heated with a pot-bellied stove that burned coal from Will Reeves's coal mine, it was as warm and comfortable as a home. But it was hardly an architectural attraction: a half-basement structure locked with a huge bar over the front door, it was so solid and serviceable that when townsfolk got too rowdy with Dixie wine on the Twenty-Fourth of July, the Relief Society hall doubled as a jail.[47]

Unfortunately, recordkeeping was not a strength of the newly reorganized group. Kanarraville Relief Society minutes apparently were not kept from 1915 to 1920, the war years. Other records, however, fill us in. Allie Knell of Cedar City was responsible for "Women's Work" in Iron County during World War I,[48] and enough information can be picked up from the Iron County Record to feel certain she was successful. Kate Roundy, as the local Relief Society president, supervised Kanarraville efforts. A description in the newspaper of the busy scenes in Relief Society halls throughout the area is informative: "White-haired grandmothers, whose fingers have not forgotten their skill, are using all their spare moments to knit warm socks and sweaters for the soldier boys; busy mothers are leaving their home duties undone to go to work rooms and sew on hospital supplies; school girls are turning out surprising quantities of Red Cross garments; even the tiny tots are begging to be allowed to clip rags or make wash clothes, or do something to help win the war."[49]

The Red Cross needed crutch pads, washcloths, ambulance pillows, comfort pillows, pillowcases, socks, sweaters, pajamas, bed shirts, bandages, napkins, tray clothes, ice bags, and hot water bottle covers. Kanarra's Relief Society sisters did "all that," Reba Roundy LeFevre remembered. "They knit their sweaters an' they knit their socks an' they done all this other stuff," spurred on because so many of them had relatives in military training camps. "My mother used to make a lotta that stuff," Lynn Reeves recalled. "I can remember her making those knitted sweaters, you know, sleeveless sweaters . . . an' she was a good seamstress . . . all the women in town here jest buckled right in an really done whatever they could to help." Lenna Stapley Williams agreed: "I got so I could even knit," she laughed, "but I can't now."[50]

March 1918 stands as a month of special accomplishment. At the first of the month, Kanarraville women contributed ten pajama suits and were hard at work on socks, napkins, and handkerchiefs. By the middle of the month they had completed forty napkins, thirty-two ice bags, twenty-eight tray cloths, eleven pairs of bed socks, nine handkerchiefs, and twelve washcloths. By the end of the month the Relief Society had contributed an additional ten suits of pajamas, four sweaters, and many more socks. They were even instructed to contribute to the war effort by saving candy and gum wrappings made of tinfoil and worth sixty cents a pound. Meanwhile, the drama club staged a fundraising minstrel show—"In Dixie"—to a packed house on a night of drenching rain and planned another play.[51]

When it was time to choose people to serve on the official Red Cross fundraising committee, Kate's husband Dode was listed instead of the shy Kate.[52] But it was the women who did most of the work. "The Red Cross made another call on us for funds," the Kanarraville correspondent reported in the *Iron County Record* on June 7, 1918. "The ladies from the Relief Society who are Red Cross members, took up the canvass, carrying Kanarra 'over the top.'" And then, in the querulous tone this correspondent adopted during the war, the article continued, "We feel that we are called on pretty heavy to keep up the war activities. With only a population of 300 we have 11 men in service now and expecting more to go this month."

Another cause of complaint was rationing. The espionage law of June 5, 1917, was used as the basis for a July 15 proclamation restricting exportation of a large number of products; this was followed by the organization of the U.S. Food Administration under Herbert C. Hoover. He called for one wheatless meal a day, meat only once a day, and restrictions on other products like milk, fats, sugar, and fuel. "'General Rules' called on Americans to Buy less, serve smaller portions. Preach the 'Gospel of the Clean Plate.' Don't eat a fourth meal. . . . Full garbage pails in America mean empty dinner pails in America and Europe."[53] Or, as the U.S. Food Administration put it more bluntly in a later comment, "BLOOD or BREAD." It was your patriotic duty to eat less because "You will shorten the war—save life if you eat only what you need and waste nothing."[54] With Mormon stake president Wilford Day as the Iron County food administrator,[55] the Kanarraville Relief Society sisters tried to obey the government-mandated meatless, wheatless, and sugarless days. At first the *Iron County Record* pitched in with good cheer, publishing recipes for rice bread, potato cake, and oatmeal waffles.[56] But even this pro-war newspaper was pressed to complain that "wheat substitutes are hard to find" and attacked Hoover's food administration efforts as "more of a detriment than a help."[57] The *Record* was left lamely arguing that carrots could be substituted for flour in cookies, pudding, conserves, and soup.[58] Lucky for Kanarra folk the potato crop of 1917 was so successful that by the fall of 1918 they still had two thousand bushels on hand and were wantonly using them for pig feed.[59]

Kate Roundy presided at a special sacrament meeting on March 17, 1918. "Sister Sarah C. Roundy gave a report of the Relief work and conservation," the minutes reported, and the rest of the time was taken up by Rees James Williams talking about war gardens and Rosa Webster Berry preaching on "Red Cross Work" and the "Red Cross Story—Life of Clara Barton." A few months later this was again the main subject of a Kanarraville LDS sacrament meeting: "Sister E. Watson of Cedar City here in the int[e]rest of the Red Cross spoke about the necessity of our doing all we can to help in the Red Cross drive. Brother John Nuttall County Supt. of Schools spoke of the purpose of the Red Cross and what it means to the wounded and starving. Brother Wallace Williams being a member of the Committee to gather Red Cross funds spoke a few minutes."[60]

How much appreciation all of this work by the Relief Society sisters received is unknown: Elizabeth Davies Parker used to threaten her daughters that if they did not get the dishes done she would "call in the Relief Society ladies" to make their dresses, a chilling threat that prompted the girls' immediate attention and obedience.[61]

With their sons in training camps or overseas and their savings subscribed to liberty loan drives, the women busy collecting materials for bandages and pillows, and the county newspaper representing the Germans as barbaric Huns bayoneting the wounded, it was to be expected that there would be some inattention to civil liberties. This lapse was promoted by such groups as the Committee on State Protection: "Propagandists and other disturbing or disloyal elements were kept in check by the constant vigilance" of this committee, reported the official history of Utah's World War I activities, which added, "The work of this organization, while it could not be made public, was nevertheless effective and deserving of commendation."[62] These efforts were aided by the *Iron County Record*, which on November 30, 1917, felt compelled to reprint an Iowa editorial headlined "Satan Abdicates in Favor of Kaiser." The paper also worried about sabotage, urging the organization of "Vigilance Committees, [and] Defense Committees" that would be "especially entrusted with the work of looking up any suspicious characters that may drift into or through our part of the country. . . . [The] feeling on the part of pro-Germans is bound to grow more bitter and acute, and we can expect more and more of these acts of treachery at home."

Not having any real local enemies, Iron County residents were quite content to manufacture them, as Clare McCoy of Salt Lake City learned to her discomfort. She went to Cedar City as a representative of the University Society Publishing Company in 1918. Hoping to sell children's books to anxious parents, McCoy spoke in hushed tones, lodged at a private home, seemed secretive, and asked too many questions about the local war effort. The snoopy Cedar City librarian, Mrs. Watson, knew intuitively that McCoy whispered to hide a German accent, that she was ferreting out information to assist the Central powers, and that her long-range plans probably included sabotage. Watson sent a letter to McCoy, forcing the issue to a head. The suspect promptly submitted a long list of credentials, including references to some of the most distinguished citizens in the state, and wrote testily to the county newspaper that "If Cedar City is still insat[i]able" for proof of her good character, "I can have Judge Strump of the Walker Bldg., of Salt Lake, and Lawyer Waldo, both friends of long standing, having known me all my life, produce the necessary legal documents to prove my identity." She concluded, "I have visited about seventy-five towns in Utah since we have been at war, including smelter and mining towns. My experience in Cedar City was the first of its kind."[63]

America's participation in the war was surprisingly short-lived, given the length of time the Central powers and the Allies had been fighting. The armistice was signed November 11, 1918, just as Elmer Davies got orders sending him to Siberia. While the headlines were blaring in giant type in the *Iron County Record*, there was other rejoicing: "I was damned glad the war ended," Elmer said later. "I was a little scared of the prospect of being shipped out."[64]

But after the celebrations there was a change. A nationwide epidemic of influenza just as the war ended did nothing to lift community spirits; there was cynicism and bitterness in response to the Treaty of Versailles; the sacrifices to "make the world safe for democracy" seemed a mockery as the world became safer for British imperialism; and a national mood of restlessness swept the country. This disillusionment was echoed in the words of Rulon Berry Piatt:

(Q) What was it like down there [in Kanarraville] during World War I?

(A) Well I can tell you, it was pretty tough going. You know how many boys?—there was twelve boys out of Kanarra went in that one bunch into the old Utah National Guard, they went to France, all the bunch, Utah Division, and there were twelve of the Utah boys right out of there, there was Ervin Williams, Kumen Williams, Will Williams, I believe Jesse [Roundy] was in it—they don't all come to me right now, but there was a big bunch strolling out of Kanarra in that bunch.[65]

(Q) Were people pretty upset about the Germans and all that?

(A) Yes. They didn't accept that war at all. We Kanarraites never accepted it.

(Q) Didn't like the war?

(A) Yes, didn't think there was any sense in it.

(Q) Why was that?

(A) Well, they just weren't that temperament of people. They just didn't like it.

(Q) Was it too far away?

(A) No, not particularly that, they just felt like it was too much of a money grabbing proposition—monopoly—like Great Britain: Own the world! Germany wanted to own the world! That's what they felt.

(Q) So people down there were not very sympathetic?

(A) They were not sympathetic! At any time![66]

Kanarraville townsfolk may have shared Rulon Piatt's disillusionment and suspicion, but they still celebrated the return of the "soldier boys" with dances and parties and listened avidly to their war stories.[67] "Elder William B. Stapley took up a portion of the time telling about life in the camp where he trained," reported the Kanarraville ward minutes of January 26, 1919: "Said the discipline was very strict but was allright when he got used to it. Said he enjoyed most of the time. Said he believed the gospel had been spread more by soldier boys than by Elders in the same length of time." But privately he told family members that his fellow soldiers were just "a waitin' for the sergeant to get up front and get on the battle line so they could all shoot at him."[68]

Kate's son Jesse Roundy ended up in a logging camp in the state of Washington. "Elder Jesse C. Roundy told about some of his experiences in the lumber camp," the minutes explained on January 26: "Said it was a pretty rough life but not so bad as it might have been. Said he was not sorry of the time he had been in the training camp."

Reba LeFevre said her parents, Kate and Dode Roundy, believed World War I "was something that shouldn't be done. And they didn't think our folks should have been over there. But they would have kept on warring until maybe we'd of been worse than ever, so we just went over and ended it right there. . . . [T]hey were horrified to think that France and England and all of them would send over here for soldiers to come over there and fight them." Midwife Elizabeth Stapley had definite opinions as well, despite the enthusiasm of her Belfast cousin. "She thought it was jest put on. Thought they was no use of having that war," explained her granddaughter: "Lotta people in Kanarra said it wasn't called for. Jest somebody wanted to gain an' they jest stuck the war on." Elizabeth's granddaughter Sarah, who had posed for a photograph in a uniform, came to agree with her grandmother: "it was uncalled for."[69]

Even church officials had trouble deciding what it all meant. Brother William H. Lyman of the Iron County Stake spoke in the Kanarraville Ward on May 18, 1919, "of the effect of the War and the speculation as to what is going to take place now the war is over. Said he wondered what would happen if Germany refused to sign the peace terms." Then, in typical Mormon fashion, he put an intelligible gloss on the madness of men at war: the "first great conflict took place in heaven, and the war here is satan and his hosts trying to destroy the souls of men."

The pointlessness of it all is exemplified in another letter—this time from Dublin, again written by Elizabeth Stapley's cousin (April 8, 1919): "I am sorry to say 'Old Ireland' is not quite a comfortable place to live in just now. The *'Sinn Feiners'* want the British Government to give them a present of it. . . . Your boys ought to soon get home though some of them don't want to leave the army and I fear they will be wanted to settled the disturbed countries, who are all behaving so wickedly." And Maryanne Campbell Wilson prattled on about an army captain cousin who "doesn't want to go home he wants to go to Russia to punish the Bolshevicks."

But Kanarraville had not fought the war to keep Ireland under the thumb of Great Britain, nor to punish the wicked Bolsheviks. Perhaps it is fitting that with this letter the family correspondence ends.

NOTES

Originally published in the *Utah Historical Quarterly* 63 (Winter 1995): 24–49.

1. Misdated 1914, typescript in my possession.
2. Probably late June 1916, typescript in my possession.
3. The *Iron County Record*, April 20, 1917, 1, carried Governor Bamberger's April 11 "Proclamation" as well as a statement by E. G. Peterson, president of the Utah Agricultural College.
4. *Iron County Record*, April 20, 1917.
5. June 26, 1917, typescript in my possession.
6. Arthur D. Taylor and William C. Heckmann to Mr. D. S. Todd, Esq., Essington, New South Wales, May 29, 1918, typsecript in my posses-sion; Interview with Reba Roundy LeFevre, January 15, 1988, 31–32.
7. According to the *Iron County Record*, Kanarraville men registered in the first registration were Leo S. Balser, Ellis Christensen, Lorenzo Wendell Davis, Wallace Davis, Leon Davis, David [Elmer] Davi[e]s, Wain [sic] Davis, William Andrew [sic, Albert] Olds, Gustave Henry Pingle, William Grant Piatt, John D. Parker, George E. Roundy, Jesse C. Roundy, Horace M. Roundy, Marion A. Roundy, William B. Stapley, Leland C. Stapley, Carlos E. Smith, Victor L. Sylvester, William Bazel Williams, Kumen D. Williams, Wells A. Williams, Joseph E. Williams, Daniel R. Webster, George Berry Williams,

Junius F. Williams, Lorenzo J. Williams, Jewett Wood, Raymond A. Williams, John Layron Williams, and Noel B. Williams. On July 6 the *Record* added Joseph Victor Ford to this list.

8. *Iron County Record*, July 13, 1917, 4; July 27, 1917, 1. The *Record* on August 17, 1917, says the quota was forty-eight men.

9. *Iron County Record*, August 17, 1917, 8. Somehow Woodbury finagled himself into Company D, 2nd Balloon Squadron (see the *Record*, November 23, 1917, 1, 5, for a letter he wrote to his father from Omaha).

10. Interview with Harriet Arvilla Ford Woodbury, January 31, 1988, 13. This and subsequent interviews cited in this article are in the Utah State Historical Society Library, Salt Lake City.

11. World War I Service Questionnaires (hereafter WSQ) 1914–1918, series 85298, reel 19 box 9, Utah State Archives, Salt Lake City.

12. *Iron County Record*, June 1, 1917, 5, shows George Roundy was herding sheep at the time he was drafted; the *Record* on July 6, 1917, says "Leland Stapley and Kumen and Wells Williams came in from the sheep camps to spend the Fourth." Also see *Record*, September 28, 1917. Leon Davis was listed as one of the six, but for some reason he was not drafted at this time.

13. Interviews with Leola Amelia Stapley Anderson, November 21, 1987, and November 24, 1979, 36.

14. "Brother S. J. Foster was here and spoke in the interest of the Liberty Bonds . . . ; Brother Frank Wood also spoke in the same cause," Kanarraville general minutes, Book D 1914–1922, January 4, 1914, to March 19, 1922, 86 (at June 10, 1917, sacrament meeting).

15. *Iron County Record*, June 8 and June 15, 1917, lists hundred-dollar Kanarraville subscribers of the first drive as John W. Berry, Hyrum C. Ford, Rees J. Williams, John H. Williams, J. W. Williams, Joseph S. Williams, and William A. Berry, and fifty-dollar subscribers as John W. Piatt and William Spendlove. Subscribers to the second drive are listed in the *Record*, November 10, 1917, but are not identified by place of residence. Therefore my calculations are based on the names of persons I know lived in Kanarraville at the time, assisted by the fact that they are mostly listed together.

16. Interview with Rebecca Alenna Stapley Williams, February 1, 1988, 14–15.

17. LeFevre, interview, January 15, 1988, 29; *Iron County Record*, January 4, 1918, 1. Only one person was in second class, seven in the third class, and five in the fourth class with Kanarra associations: #13 William Albert Olds, #66 Joseph Ammon Ingram, #182 Victor L. Sylvester,

#218 Joseph Victor Ford, and #225 Percy Newton Wilkinson. This list was revised and published in the *Record* on January 11, 1918, with the following names added to first class: Jos. E. Williams, Marion A. Roundy, Jos. F. Williams, Leo S. Balser, David E. Davis, Jewett Wood, William B. Stapley, Wm. V. Williams, Lorenzo Wendell Davis; third class: Horace M. Roundy; and fourth class: John Layron Williams, Wm. Melbourn Williams, Wayne Davis, Raymond A. Williams, Junius F. Williams, Lorenzo J. Williams, and Noel B. Williams. On *Birth of a Nation* also see "Special with Clansman Group," *Iron County Record*, January 11, 1918, 4.

18. *Iron County Record*, February 1, 1918, 1.
19. *Iron County Record*, February 8, 1918, 1.
20. *Iron County Record*, February 8, 1918, 1. The February 15, 1918, issue carries a letter by David Elmer Davies correcting the initial story, which says James S. Berry—not Riley G. Williams—gave the soldiers a dinner.
21. *Iron County Record*, April 5, 1918, 1.
22. "Third Liberty Loan Drive On," *Iron County Record*, April 12, 1918, 1; "Liberty Loan Roll of Honor," April 26, 1918, 8. Only $3,300 was raised from people who are identified as Kanarraville residents; however, I have identified as Kanarra residents the following individuals whose residence was not listed in the article: J. W. Berry ($200), W. A. Berry ($100), George Berry ($900), Claude Balser ($50), and Leo Balser ($50).
23. *Iron County Record*, March 1, 1918, 4.
24. Woodbury, interview, January 31, 1988, 15; "Recruits Will Leave May 26th," *Iron County Record*, May 17, 1918, 1.
25. *Iron County Record*, May 24, 1918, 4; Anderson, interview, 43–45; Woodbury, interview, 11–12.
26. *Iron County Record*, June 14, 1918, 4.
27. "Men Without Useful Occupations to be Drafted into Army," *Iron County Record*, May 24, 1918, 1; "Registrants Must Work or Fight," June 21, 1918, 1.
28. Rebecca Williams, interview, 14.
29. Sophia Parker Stapley, *Together Again: An Autobiographical History* (Oakland, CA: Third Party Associates, 1976), 220.
30. Interview with Lynn Reeves and Ella Batty Reeves, January 16, 1988, 18; *Iron County Record*, June 28, 1918, 4.
31. LeFevre, interview, January 15, 1988, 28; *Iron County Record*, April 19, 1918, 4. The *Iron County Record*, July 5, 1918, reported, "News has been received from Camp Lewis that Leland Stapley and Wells Williams have, or would shortly, leave the camp for over-seas."

32. *Iron County Record*, September 20, 1918, 1; November 1, 1918, 1; November 8, 1918, 5; November 29, 1918, 5.

33. Interview with Sylva Mae Davies Williams, June 27, 1988, 5.

34. Interview with David Elmer Davies, January 16, 1988, 1–2.

35. Interview with Bessie Elizabeth Davies, February 1, 1988, 1.

36. Interview with Fredrick Wilford Balser, May 28, 1988, 10, 22.

37. "Memorial Services for our Gold Stars," *Iron County Record*, February 21, 1919, 1; L. H. Butterfield, ed., *Letters of Benjamin Rush* (Princeton, NJ: Princeton University Press, 1951) 1: 140 (and see also 1: 130 and 1: 146).

38. Interview with Donna Davis Munford, March 2, 1992. Munford reported that Davis crossed the ocean in "a really creaky old battleship and they had a storm and the old sergeant had them come on deck and asked if there were any Mormons on board; so he stepped out and he [the sergeant] said, 'dismissed; this boat will never sink.'"

39. Typescript of "Diary of Leon Davis While in Russia," furnished to the author by Mr. Davis's son Raymond Davis on July 14, 1993.

40. Kanarraville general minutes, Book D 1914–1922, 90 (sacrament meeting September 23, 1917). At this meeting "Brother John W. Piatt bore testimony. He advised the boys to go [to] the temple of the Lord before going to the war"; General minutes, 105 (sacrament meeting July 7, 1918).

41. "News From the Alabama Mission," *Iron County Record*, May 17, 1918, 4; July 6, 1917, 1, 4; November 23, 1917, 4. Piatt also congratulated the South on its patriotism: "The states which once ceceded [*sic*] from the Union are now the first in obedience to their country's call." See Roundy's letter—where the headline mistakenly says "Elder J. A. Roundy Writes Interestingly" instead of Elder J. L.—in the *Record*, January 4, 1918, 5.

42. *Iron County Record*, December 28, 1917, 1; Noble Warrum, *Utah in the World War: The Men Behind the Guns and the Men and Women Behind the Men Behind the Guns* (Salt Lake City: Arrow Press, 1924), 288.

43. Interview with Thelma Berry Lovell, June 27, 1988, 7.

44. Rebecca Williams, interview, 9.

45. Woodbury, interview, 8.

46. Reeves and Reeves, interview, 13–14.

47. Balser, interview, 11.

48. Warrum, *Utah in the World War*, 99.

49. "Red Cross is in Financial Straits," *Iron County Record*, March 15, 1918, 1. See also "Cedar Ladies Do Red Cross Work," January 11, 1918, 1; "Work of Iron Co. Red Cross Chapter," February 22, 1918, 1; "Work

of Iron County Red Cross Chapter," February 22, 1918, 8; "Red Cross Ladies Are Still Active," March 1, 1918, 1; "Ladies, Attention!" June 14, 1918, 1.

50. Rebecca Williams, interview, 15.

51. "Red Cross Ladies Are Still Active," *Iron County Record*, March 1, 1918, 1, 4; "Red Cross is in Financial Straits," March 15, 1918, 1, 4; March 29, 1918, 4; "Save the Tin Foil and Assist the Red Cross," June 28, 1918, 1.

52. "Red Cross Drive On Next Week," *Iron County Record*, May 17, 1918, 1. Also see May 24, 1918, 4: "The Red Cross committee has completed their canvas and the money sent to Cedar yesterday. Kanarra is another town in Iron County that raised her full quota."

53. Warrum, *Utah in the World War*, 133–34.

54. *Iron County Record*, May 17, 1918, 1. Also see "Wheat and Meat Rations Reduced," January 11, 1918, 1.

55. Warrum, *Utah in the World War*, 136; *Iron County Record*, June 15, 1917, 1.

56. "Wheat Substitutes in Wartime Cooking," *Iron County Record*, February 22, 1918, 1.

57. "Wheat Substitutes Are Hard to Find," *Iron County Record*, April 5, 1918, 1.

58. "Carrot to the Rescue," *Iron County Record*, April 5, 1918, 3.

59. *Iron County Record*, May 3, 1918, 4.

60. Kanarraville general minutes, Book D 1914–1922, 102–3 (May 19, 1918).

61. Esther Parker Robb, "Stories and Early Memories," in Stapley, *Together Again*, 99.

62. Warrum, *Utah in the World War*, 114.

63. "Apparently No Cause for Suspicion as Spy," *Iron County Record*, April 5, 1918, 4.

64. Kristina Messerly Loosley, "Veteran Reflects on Change," *Daily Spectrum* (Cedar City), Veterans Day 1987, quoted in Davies, interview, 3–4 (his surname is misspelled "Davis" in this article).

65. Kanarraville men in World War I:
BALSER, Claud, inducted, 8-27-18 to 2-24-19, Inf. (Warrum, 310; Williams, 30).
BALSER, Leo S., inducted, 8-27-18 to 6-12-19, MG Bn (Warrum, 310; Williams, 30).
DAVI[E]S, David E., inducted, 8-27-18 to 2-4-19, D Brig (Warrum, 335; Williams, 30); WSQ reel 1 box 3.
*DAVIS, Leon, inducted, 5-10-18 to 11-4-19, Inf. (Warrum, 335; Williams, 30); WSQ reel 7 box 3.
DAVIS, Wallace, inducted, 6-10-18 to 1-11-19, Inf. (Warrum, 336; Williams, 30); WSQ reel 7 box 3.

GRAFF, A. LeMar, inducted, 10-6-18 to 12-7-18, SATC (Warrum, 351; Williams, 30).

*POLLOCK, Emery L., enlisted, 2-11-18 to 7-9-19, BS (Warrum, 275; Williams, 30).

ROUNDY, George E., inducted, 9-19-17 to 1-24-19, D Brig (Warrum, 412; Williams, 30; *Record*, Sept 28, 1917); WSQ reel 19 box 9.

ROUNDY, Jesse C., inducted, 9-19-17 to 12-30-18, D Brig (Warrum, 412; Williams, 30; *Record*, Sept 28, 1917); WSQ reel 9 box 9.

ROUNDY, Marion A., inducted, 8-27-18 to 10-24-19, D Brig (Warrum, 412; Williams, 30).

*STAPLEY, Leland C., inducted, 9-19-17 to 4-28-19, MG Bn (Warrum, 423; Williams, 30; *Record*, Sept 28, 1917); WSQ reel 21 box 10.

STAPLEY, William B., inducted, 6-15-18 to 12-17-18, FA (Warrum, 423; Williams, 30); WSQ reel 21 box 10.

WILLIAM[S], Joseph E., inducted, 5-26-18 to 1-24-19, 145 FA (Warrum, 438; Williams, 30); WSQ reel 24 box 11.

*WILLIAMS, Kumen D., inducted, 5-25-18 to 1-24-19, D Brig (Warrum, 438, says Iron County; Williams, 30).

*WILLIAMS, Wells A., inducted, 9-19-17 to 4-28-19, MG Bn (Warrum, 438; Williams, 30; *Record*, Sept 28, 1917).

*WILLIAMS, William B., inducted, 5-26-18 to 1-24-19, 145 FA (Warrum, 438; Williams, 30); WSQ reel 24 box 11.

*Overseas duty.

Sources: Warrum, *Utah in the World War*; Opal Pollock Williams, *Kanarra is a Pretty Little Town* (Kanarraville: Author, 1984), 30. The latter source lists Kanarraville's World War I veterans and shows a plaque erected in their honor by Bruce F. Parker. Williams and the plaque both list Arthur Hartley Woodbury, but according to Warrum, 294, he enlisted from LaVerkin, 6-23-16 to 7-2-19. He moved to Kanarraville after the war.

66. Interview with Rulon Berry Piatt, May 19, 1982, 11.

67. *Iron County Record*, February 14, 1919, 5: "Another soldier boy has returned home. He is Elmer Davi[e]s and arrived last Friday. He looks and feels fine and is proud of his experiences while in Camp Lewis. Also, another of our missionaries is back—Elder Lorenzo Roundy. He came in on the passenger car last Thursday. He has only the highest of praise for the missionary labors, but of course is glad to be home again after 27 months in the mission field. . . .

"Last Monday there was a 'welcome home' party for our returned missionaries and soldier boys, which was crowded, both at the meeting and the dance. The meeting commenced with singing 'The Star-Spangled Banner.' Prayer was offered by Bp. Berry. A duet was sung by the Misses Taylor and Bateman. The address of welcome was delivered by R.G. Williams. Then there was a short talk by Kumen Williams, on behalf of the Sammies. A short talk by Lorenzo Roundy, returned missionary. Refreshments were served and the meeting was dismissed until the time for the dance. During the dance Otto Reeves gave a short talk and the soldier boys gave a drill, but the house was too crowded to do justice to them or to permit of the maneuvers they would like to have executed."

Also see *Iron County Record*, March 7, 1919, 3: "Last Saturday evening, commencing at 4 p.m. a welcome home party was given in honor of two more of our returned soldier boys—Leo Balser and Marion Roundy, who recently arrived from Camp Lewis. The party consisted of a program, which commenced by the singing of The Star-Spangled Banner. Prayer was offered by Otto Reeves. The address of welcome was given by Bishop Berry. A solo was nicely sung by Miss Taylor, and a Chorus by the soldier boys. At the close of the meeting a bounteous repast was served by the committee and aids, with a dance in the evening. The whole affair was a perfect success."

68. LeFevre, interview, October 12, 1984, 14.
69. LeFevre, interview, January 15, 1988, 31–32.

8

IMMIGRANTS, MINORITIES, AND THE GREAT WAR

HELEN Z. PAPANIKOLAS

Helen Papanikolas pioneered the study of Utah's ethnic groups among a generation of historians beginning in 1970 with her publication of Toil and Rage in a New Land: A History of Greek Immigrants to Utah, *and her work as editor of* The Peoples of Utah *and its fourteen chapters on Utah's ethnic groups (published in 1976 by the Utah State Historical Society) as a contribution to the celebration of America's bicentennial. Helen Papanikolas continued her celebration of Utah's ethnic heritage with the publication of several novels about the immigrant generation's experience in Utah as well as other historical articles, including the following article, which looks at the impact of World War I on Utah's immigrants and minorities: Italians, Greeks, Bosnians, Montenegrins, Herzegovinians, Serbians, Croatians, Japanese, Jews, African Americans, and Native Americans. What is clear is that for many Utah immigrants the war in Europe was not only relevant, but was an event that shaped the course of their lives, whether they volunteered for military service, took advantage of the expanding employment opportunities the war brought, or saw families and friends in their homeland devastated by war.*

The assassination of Archduke Franz Ferdinand of Austria by a Serbian student, Gavrilo Princip, on June 28, 1914, in Sarajevo, Bosnia, was duly noted on the front pages of Salt Lake City newspapers. Most Utahns, however, showed no special interest in the affairs of an obscure, hardly known people.

To the South Slav immigrants in Utah—Slovenes, Croats, Serbs, and the few Bosnians, Montenegrins, and Herzegovinians—the news was momentous.[1] Foreign-language newspapers printed in the East and Midwest arrived in Utah and created a furor in Salt Lake City; the Carbon County coal mining camps; the Magna mill; the Murray, Midvale, and Tooele smelters; and the Bingham Canyon copper mines, in all of which immigrants made up the greater part of the workforce.

The Greeks had immediate access to news with the Greek-language *O Ergatis* ("The Worker") and the Japanese with the *Utah Nippo*, both published in Salt Lake City. The nationalistic concerns expressed in Serbian, Croatian, Slovenian, Greek, and Italian newspapers were fueled by visiting editors, national leaders, lodge officials, and native country speakers who inflamed their compatriots over the consequences of the Austro-Hungarian war on the Serbs. Frenzied talk and fistfights exploded in coffeehouses, lodges, boardinghouses, and mines.[2]

The warring countries were all represented in the United States and in Utah by small to significant numbers of immigrants.[3] To Americans the brawling of immigrant groups over European events was the ultimate evidence that these newest arrivals could never be Americanized; their concerns were totally with their native countries. Also, the immigrants openly professed their expectation to return to their homelands after trading their needed brawn for American money. This was not the aim of immigrants from northern Europe, Britain, and Scandinavia. Mormon missionary activity continually drew them, most often in family groups, to Utah, where they intended to live permanently. Their attitudes toward their adopted country were closer to those of Americans.

The immigrants who were not Mormons were beset both from within and outside their ethnic neighborhoods—called Greek towns, Bohunk towns, Jap towns, Wop towns, and Little Italys by a rancorous American public. Their volatile nationalism, born of historic struggles for freedom, had affronted the Americans from the beginning of their entry into the country. They faced the same discrimination as the Irish in their mass migration of the 1840s but had not the advantage of knowing the English language.

American labor resented them because they would work for less than the native born. Especially galling to Americans was the immigrant practice of sending money back to their countries to pay for sisters' dowries and help impoverished parents. Money made in America should stay in the United States, demagogues railed, and the Americans took up the tirade. Further, the immigrants—or the "unassimilable," as journalists called them—were leaving the ranks of labor with their savings, becoming businessmen, and competing with Americans. A few also married American women, an anathema to the nation's mores.

When Germany entered the war to bolster Austria-Hungary against Serbia, the status of German immigrants in the United States changed. Once looked upon as sober, industrious people who would be an asset to the country, they became Huns and *Boches* ("thick-headed persons"). So great was the pressure on them that they began calling themselves Dutch, Russian, and Swiss.[4] The virulence directed toward the Germans spread to all southern and eastern Europeans.

The South Slavs were most affected by the war. The Serbs were Eastern Orthodox, used the Cyrillic alphabet, had earned their freedom from the Turks, and had established the Kingdom of Serbia in 1882; the Croats and Slovenes were Roman Catholic, used the Latin alphabet, and were still subjects of the Austria-Hungary Empire.[5] Ancient political and religious animosities were further deepened in Utah by the practices of Serbian labor agents, who, although hiring some Croats, gave preference to their own countrymen.

The Croats and Slovenes were at first exempted from war service because they could well be fighting relatives in the Austro-Hungarian army. The "Serbs . . . looked upon the war as a veritable crusade and as the concluding episode in the five-hundred-year struggle for national liberation," according to one historian.[6] When Serbs, however, saw their sons and brothers leaving for the army while Croats and Slovenes were granted exemption because of their country's alignment with the Central powers, turmoil erupted. As more young Serbs left to serve in the French and Serbian armies, their volatile energies went with them. In Bingham Canyon more than two hundred Serbs volunteered, and with their absence the South Slav community settled back into the historic undercurrent of hostility among its factions.[7]

Immigrant Greeks from the mainland were divided between support for King Constantine, who insisted on the country's neutrality—his wife was the kaiser's sister—and Premier Eleftherios Venizelos, who pushed for Greece's entrance on the side of the Allies and who was vociferously upheld by Cretan Greeks.[8] Like the Serbs, the Greeks had been Ottoman subjects for centuries. They were hostile to the Turks, who were allied with Bulgaria and the Central powers.

Immigrant Italians were involved with the war and its effect on their homeland earlier than the Greeks. In 1914 Italy had declared neutrality, but in April 1915 the secret Treaty of London committed the country to the side of England and France and against its former allies, Germany and Austria. Italy had been at war for almost two years when Greece joined the Allies on July 2, 1917, three months after the United States joined on April 6, 1917.

The Balkan and Mediterranean immigrants and the fewer Asians in the state were wary, fearful that they would be taken into the army, where they did not understand the language and where they could be killed with all hope of fulfilling traditional duties to their families dying with them. They did not rush to volunteer. Everywhere they were bombarded by the patriotic fervor of the Americans. Gala communal affairs were held, not only in cities and farming areas but also in industrial centers where immigrants lived clustered in their ethnic neighborhoods. Typical was an account in the *Tooele Transcript*. After a parade the onlookers walked to the opera house, where "patriotic exercises were held." A banquet followed with soldiers, former soldiers, and their parents as guests of honor. A male chorus sang "The Star-Spangled Banner"; dignitaries gave speeches; and the California infantry and Tooele baseball teams played a game. The festivities ended with an evening dance in the opera house.[9]

Along with this kind of exhilarating patriotism a dark propaganda swirled immigrants and labor radicals together. Always attacking radicals, the *Utah Mining Review*, for example, could now link them with hampering the war effort: "Hanging is too good for the I. W. W., the pro-German, the pacifist and the anarchist who is attempting to thwart the government in its prosecution of our righteous war against the brutal foe that is at war with nearly all mankind."[10]

Those immigrants who had come to America as boys or adolescents were buoyed by the wartime fervor and were eager to show they were not radicals but loyal to the United States. They spoke English with some facility, although accented, and had made acquaintances among their American peers. Some began to volunteer, but others felt ambivalent. Methods used by some to avoid service have become folklore: a recruit's continuous false coughing led to a suspicion that he was infected with tuberculosis and brought his desired discharge; others learned that a pretense of stupidity became an effective means to avoid the front lines and be assigned to care for cavalry horses. Others, balking at first, decided "the food [in the army] was pretty good." For some the war solved their inability to find work.[11]

A year after war was declared the Price *News-Advocate* printed an article entitled "Greek Boys Hold Big Celebration." Special trains took the Greek miners from coal camps to Price, where the Sunnyside band led them in a march to the Greek church. In high spirits the men sang, danced, listened to the familiar, stirring patriotic speeches about the historic struggle of the Greeks against the Turks, and expressed their loyalty to the United States.[12]

In late July, however, when the Carbon Country draft call was issued, the Greeks questioned its fairness. The draft call was sent to 801 men, 221 of whom were Greeks. Of these, 40 were naturalized or had taken out first citizenship papers.[13] Although the next two issues of the newspaper carried the names of 5 to 10 Greeks who were entering the army, a large number asked for exemption because of their alien status. Spurred by the outcry in Greek newspapers, the men wanted to know before joining the army what would become of Greek provinces now under the yoke of the Turks, English, and Italians after the war: "Will the Greeks take part in the war to help big nations steal Greek lands? The allies must make themselves clear first. Greeks hate Kaiser but can't fight him for national reasons."[14]

Several disreputable labor agents and interpreters added to the confusion of Greek immigrants who did not speak English. They took advantage of the men, often with the connivance of American railroad officials and mine foremen, also known as the "straw bosses." In Carbon County, Greeks were told they must pay an illegal five-dollar fee to the lawyers who processed draftees. The men paid the fee in the belief that it absolved them from any association with the U.S. Army.[15]

Young immigrants of all nationalities continued to volunteer or were drafted into the army. Several newspapers, mainly in Carbon County and Bingham, printed weekly news of the soldiers and quoted from letters written by immigrants in the service. The Price *News-Advocate* printed an entire letter from T. H. Jouflas with the caption: "He Shows the Greeks in U.S. What They Ought To Be Doing." The newspaper said it had "always been more than ready to give credit to loyal Greeks for doing their part as adopted sons of Uncle Sam." Jouflas's letter read in part:

> All we want, and what we are going to get is the Kaiser's goat. . . .
> Believe me the people over here are thinking the world of Uncle
> Sam's boys. I had more than 50 Greeks around here telling me
> that they would like to join the U. S. army only they wished

they could talk the American language . . . they told me that [if] I could fix it so they could join they said they didn't want salary. Can you beat it.[16]

Another such story, "Bingham Oriental Enlists in Uncle Sam's Army," appeared in the *Press Bulletin*:

Kil Seurk Kim, native of Hawaii, born of Korean parentage and who has been a resident of Bingham for sometime . . . is a real American and he is the first Binghamite of Oriental ancestry to fall in line. He is well known in Bingham and has many friends in camp. He is a young man of intelligence . . . and is an authority on Oriental customs and racial traits. Furthermore, he is an interesting conversationalist and furnishes much entertainment and dispenses much information on various topics to Bingham people.[17]

Bingham immigrants responded to induction with more alacrity than those in Carbon County. The Utah Copper Company reported 284 of its workers were serving in the army with all nationalities represented.[18] The copper company employed the greatest number of men: 1,800, of whom 1,200 were immigrants. An article in the *Utah Copper Enterprise* acknowledged the workers' patriotism:

From the railway station one could see, through the smoke made by trains and steam shovels, a mountain deeply scarred—the edge of the great mine—and from it, above the haze, a glorious flag flew assertively. That flag, 20 by 40 ft., cost $156 and was bought with contributions, of 25 cents to a $1 apiece, made by the workers on the occasion of the campaign for the Third Liberty Loan.[19]

The induction of immigrants into the army, however, did not alter American hostility toward them as a whole. To counter this dangerous threat and to show their allegiance to the United States, the immigrants held patriotic rallies. In Bingham's Commercial Club, Italians heard local Americans review Italian history and exhort those who were not citizens to become so without delay. The editor of the Salt Lake City *Italian Gazette* and a San Francisco Italian (whose importance was not explained) were prevented from delivering speeches at this event because their car was stuck in the mud outside of town. The program was, nevertheless, full:

> Miss Contralto rendered the Italian anthem in a most effective manner. . . . Dominick Pezzapane speaking in the Italian tongue, delivered an address which held the closest attention of the Italians and appeared to make a deep impression on them. He spoke especially on Liberty bonds. . . . Mrs. John Contralto spoke in Italian to the women about the Red Cross work in Italy, France and Belgium.[20]

"Patriotic Greek Pageant Takes Camp by Storm," the Bingham newspaper reported on the front page. The Greeks "spared no expense." They paid the railroad fares for the 20th Infantry and 24th Infantry Band to lead a parade to the IOOF (Independent Order of Odd Fellows) hall. The band's music was "mighty fine." Many floats followed, decorated with American and Greek flags and emblems of the Allies. A large, "handsome portrait of George Washington" was carried by young Greeks. In the hall the Greek consul gave a "rousing" address in both English and Greek on behalf of the Red Cross. "Pretty girls and ladies" carrying flags then took up a collection that netted $700.28. At the conclusion of the "most impressive feature of the kind ever seen in Bingham . . . Thea Sweitzer gave the soldiers a free meal."[21]

In the Commercial Club, Serbians gave farewells in the spring to their young men—already ninety were at the front; and the Japanese, who were "right up the mark on Red Cross and Liberty Bonds," held a liberty mass meeting in the fall. In Winter Quarters, Carbon County, Greek miners bought $9,000 worth of bonds; four of them subscribed to $1,000 each. In Bingham a Greek immigrant invested his entire

$2,000 savings in bonds. Throughout the coal camps Greeks held "Get out the Coal" rallies, and immigrant miners ignored the Industrial Workers of the World's attempts in Bingham to call strikes.[22]

Despite these patriotic endeavors, inflammatory pronouncements were printed in local newspapers, especially in Carbon County because of its large immigrant population:

> Fathers and mothers who are sending their American boys to fight in Italy if need be and for the safety of both Greeks and Italians and all other races are getting more and more incensed at the whelps who think [of] nothing but getting American dollars under the American flag but who would not turn a hand over to save that flag from being dragged in the dirt by the Kaiser's bloody cutthroats. Some of the worst specimens of this sort are going to get some early day western treatment if they do not wake up to their duty soon.[23]

The *Bingham Press Bulletin* on May 10, 1918, reported on a mass meeting held in the Swedish temperance hall to protest an article in the *Salt Lake Tribune* that alleged:

> 125 Finns as I.W.W.'s [had] been discharged from Bingham mines. [It] was branded a falsehood . . . believed caused by animosity towards their temperance movement and trying to clean up the camp, improving moral conditions. Denied Finns were pro-German . . . and since America entered the war they were unanimous in their opposition to strikes.

Ethnic prejudice appeared in many guises. The September 6, 1918, issue of the *Bingham Press Bulletin* carried the heading: "Isolation of Huns Favored by Speaker." The nationality of a person suspected of a crime began to be stressed. Two lynchings of Greeks were thwarted in Utah by their armed countrymen.[24] Immigrants also learned it was expedient to carry liberty bonds at all times. An eighteen-year-old

Greek traveling through Idaho was almost lynched by farmers. On his way to Montana he had stopped overnight and attended a movie. When the Pathé News showed war atrocities, he was pulled out of the theater and taken to a tree to be hanged. He begged the men to look into his pocket for bonds. The liberty bonds saved him, but he was told to get out of town immediately.[25] Foreigners, the newspapers and politicians increasingly proclaimed, were incapable of being good American citizens. Immigrants suspected of being radicals were deported. Bombings were traced to immigrants with sympathies for Germany and Austria-Hungary. At the same time great numbers of immigrants were volunteering for the armed services or were being inducted.

The immigrants in the U.S. Army shared the miseries of *all* soldiers, but their incomprehension of English added to their fears when given orders of which they were unsure. Besides the Serbs who left for Serbia, a number of Greeks preferred to return to their homeland to fight in the Greek army. The few with special skills fared better there than their compatriots in the American army, particularly those who knew French, then the language taught in Greek schools of higher education. Several of Utah's Greek immigrants, including one from Nestani in Peloponnesus and another from Crete, saw no action in France; because of their knowledge of French, they were put in charge of guarding German prisoners. The better-educated immigrants were often given translating duty. A native of Melfi, Italy, Ben Colobella also knew French, Russian, Spanish, and English and was sent to Siberia with the American army. There he developed rheumatism, which would limit his postwar work opportunities. After the war the government sent him to school to learn shoe repairing.[26]

Hatsuto Hakata, a Utah Japanese man born in Hawaii, remembered his war experience as frightening even though he saw no action. At the time of induction he was in his early twenties. He had an eighth grade education, spoke English fluently, and was the only soldier in his group guarding German prisoners who was not Caucasian. Later, he would recall humorous stories of army life and "how good the French were to the American soldiers."[27]

Knowing sufficient English, however, was of little help in technical matters. James Galanis had seen the rioting and burning of South Omaha's Greek town by Americans in 1909. He fled to Utah and worked in the Carbon County mines until he and the writer of the article "Why the Greeks Don't Fight" established the Helper Golden Rule Store. He and his partner, Tom Avgikos, volunteered and became sergeants in France. As his son later recalled:

> He was made a sergeant in France and because he could speak some French, he was occasionally used as an interpreter. His discharge certificate cited him for his campaigns in Chateau Thierry and the Second Battle of the Marne and for his "excellent horse-manship." (To my knowledge my father was never on a horse.) He was a gas mask instructor and afraid to have the masks removed prematurely, he had the men keep them on long after they should have been removed.[28]

The Black experience was entirely different from that of the immigrants. During the war years the black population in Utah increased; the 1910 census showed 1,144 blacks in the state, while the 1920 census listed 1,446. Railroads had brought more blacks to Utah to meet wartime demands. Black women actively worked for the war effort and formed an organization to sell bonds. African Americans were swayed by leaders, especially by W. E. B. Du Bois, who encouraged war service as an opportunity to earn equality. Others, however, pointed out that it had not done so in previous wars, and the military actively discouraged blacks from enlisting. An army report later said: "Had the response to the call for volunteers been so ardent among all classes of people, especially the foreign born, as it was from the American Negro, it is fair to say that selective draft would not necessarily have been so extensive."[29]

African Americans have a history of military service: 186,000 served in the segregated Union army and 27,000 in the integrated Union navy, primarily as messmen. In the Spanish-American War sixteen regiments of black volunteers were in combat and were noted for their heroism on San Juan Hill with Teddy Roosevelt's dismounted rough riders. Black soldiers of the 24th Infantry from Fort Douglas, Utah, were involved in combat duty in both Cuba and the Philippines. The infantry of almost 450 soldiers arrived at Fort Douglas in October 1896.[30] Two decades later, as the United States was being pulled closer to the Allied cause, four black regiments were serving in the West.[31]

During World War I recruiters were unwilling to accept blacks in the regular army because of their distaste for integration, their racist view that blacks could not handle artillery, and, especially, the Houston riot of 1917. Three race riots occurred in 1917: in East St Louis, Illinois, nine whites and forty blacks were murdered by mobs; three blacks and three whites died in Chester, Pennsylvania, riots; and the black 24th Infantry stationed in Houston went on a rampage.[32] The troops had complained of intense discrimination in buses and eating places and of brutal treatment by police officers. The agitation grew and weapons were taken from the soldiers in fear they would retaliate. On August 26 two white policemen arrested a black woman for ostensibly using abusive language. An African American military policeman asked the white men to explain the arrest. One officer, witnesses later testified, said, "I don't report to any Negro," hit the soldier over the head with his pistol, and as he ran fired at him. The rumor that the black man had been killed sent the soldiers running to the ammunition tent, where they took guns, marched to the city, and killed seventeen whites. In the battle four blacks died. Nineteen black soldiers were later hanged.[33] The Houston riot was uppermost in recruiters' assessment of blacks arriving to volunteer; yet, the service of blacks was crucial to the war effort.

It was soon apparent that the war would not be won in the two or three months initially predicted. As defense plants geared up they drew workers by the thousands, among them southern blacks: 500,000 moved north and competed for jobs and housing. The army needed a great pool of men, and blacks were then inducted in large number—370,000 or 11 percent of American combat forces. The established ratio for the army was one black for every ten whites. The recruitment of blacks was a scandal in many parts of the country, particularly in the South and blatantly in Fulton County, Georgia. Young, unmarried whites were regularly exempted at the same time that married blacks with many children were being inducted.[34]

Unprepared, the army did not have enough uniforms. The first black volunteers were given, to their humiliation, old Union blue Civil War uniforms.[35] White officers feared guns in the hands of the African Americans and drilled the men with hoes, shovels, and picks over their shoulders.[36] Many white officers resisted command of black troops. Black officers were then commissioned, almost all college graduates, but too few—only one for every 2,600 men. The Wilson administration insisted on rigid segregation in the military. Jack Duncan, a ninety-three-year-old black veteran living in Salt Lake City, smiled in reminiscence on being asked about black officers: "Oh, yes, we had black officers. Everyone in my regiment was black. We had a colonel who was black."[37] A colonel was as high as a black could advance; no matter how qualified, he could not go beyond the "deadline."[38] At first black officers were believed to lack the mathematical ability to qualify as artillery officers. This was refuted by the record of the 349th, 350th, and 351st artillery regiments and the machine gun units of the 92nd Division.[39]

Jack Duncan was more fortunate than most African-American soldiers. He was twenty-one years old and farming in Hiawatha, Missouri, when he was inducted into the army. His older brother was already an army cook. After basic training at Camp Funston, Kansas, with the all-black 92nd Division, he was sent overseas where he spent nineteen months as a chauffeur for officers, but his main duty was driving ammunition trucks to the front. Three-fourths of all black soldiers were used in noncombat operations as messmen, stewards, latrine orderlies, and stevedores on French docks for the American Expeditionary Forces. A separate regiment of the 92nd served, unsegregated, with French troops.

In comparison with blacks far fewer Asians in proportion to their numbers enlisted or were inducted in Utah; the greater number of those who served came from the West Coast. Only one Utah Native American (a Ute) has been positively identified in state war records. Navajos, Gosiutes, Utes, and other Native Americans considered the conflict in Europe to be a white man's war and for the most part were determined not to serve in the army. Moreover, prior to 1924, when all Indians were given U.S. citizenship, most of those living on tribal lands in the West were not U.S. citizens and could not be drafted, although the Selective Service Act required all U.S. resident males of draft age to register. Very few Navajos felt motivated to volunteer for the army, but some contributed to the war effort by buying bonds or donating fleeces to the Red Cross. Utah's Gosiutes, angry over unresolved grievances with the government, influenced by Idaho Shoshones, and bullied by their unsympathetic agent, actively resisted attempts to register them. After numerous confrontations 163 Gosiutes did register. A few are believed to have crossed the state line and enlisted in Nevada.[40]

The World War I service records for Utah may have omissions.[41] The records were transferred several times before being permanently placed in the Utah State Archives.[42] The war services questionnaires from which the information was taken were poorly filled out, often in pencil. Many prospective recruits, both American and immigrant, were illiterate and others filled out their forms. Religion was not listed, which precludes knowing how many Jews served in the armed forces. Almost all born in Russia have Jewish surnames, as do many giving their birth country as Germany, Poland, and Czechoslovakia. The mother of a registrant was often listed with only her given name, providing no clue to mixed parentage.

The registrants gave their birthplace and date; frequently their residence was listed as a boardinghouse or hotel. A picture emerges of many young men roaming the country looking for work. Place of last employment was often answered with the name of the employer, such as "Mr. Jenkins." Was Mr. Jenkins a farmer or cattleman? Often pictures of the registrants in army uniforms were included, showing the young men—called "boys" by officials—standing stiffly, wearing

Table 8.1. Birthplace of Utah Immigrants/Minorities Serving in the Military during World War I

Italy 385	Scotland 65	U.S. Hispanics 38	Syria 8(h)
Greece 349	Canada 63	Turkey 24(e)	Philippines 7
England 282	Russia 61(b)	Australia 15	Poland 7
Sweden 135	Norway 54	Belgium 13	South America 5
Denmark 132	France 51(c)	Wales 12	India 4(i)
Mexico 92(a)	Switzerland 49	Hawaii 11(f)	Albania 3
Holland 85	U.S. Blacks 45	Serbia 10(g)	South Africa 3
Germany 75	Austria 43(d)	China 9	Hungary 3

Two each from New Zealand, Romania, and Algeria (French surnames); one each from Persia, Virgin Islands, Jerusalem, North Korea, Hong Kong, Samoa, Nicaragua, Guatemala, Portugal, Puerto Rico, Luxembourg, Afghanistan, and U.S. Native American (Ute). (a) 50 with Anglo surnames; (b) most Jewish, but several Armenian surnames; (c) includes Basque surnames; (d) includes Serbs, Croats, and Slovenes; (e) 11 Armenians, 6 Greeks, 4 Turks, 2 Americans, and 1 Syrian; (f) 5 Caucasians, 3 Japanese, 3 Hawaiians (1 born in Iosepa, Utah); (g) Kingdom of Serbia (see also Austria); (h) Lebanese surnames; (i) 2 Anglo surnames. (Extracted From War Services Records)

ill-fitting uniforms, legs wrapped in puttees, and feet turned outward. The interviewers could have given future researchers a wealth of material if they had monitored the registrants' answers.

More than 21,000 Utahns served in the armed forces; of these 2,156 were of foreign birth or were U.S. ethnic/racial minorities. The 1910 census listed Utah's population at 373,351. In that year the four numerically highest immigrant groups listed in the service records had the following total numbers: Greeks, 4,039; Italians, 3,172; English, 18,083; and Swedes, 7,227. Immigrant women and men were not counted separately until 1920, when the figures for males were: Greeks, 2,731; Italians, 2,253; English, 7,189; and Swedes, 2,887.

The figures from the census and the service records appear to substantiate the Greeks' and Italians' assertion that more of them were inducted into the armed forces in proportion to their numbers in Utah than were the American born and the immigrants from Britain and Scandinavia. More information would be needed to verify this complaint. The large numbers of English and Swedish males listed in the 1920 census, however, included underage boys. By 1917 a small second generation of Italian Americans was approaching war induction age; the Greeks, who came to the United States later, had an even smaller number of children by the time of the war.

The statistics also mirror continued, although diminished, Mormon immigration from Britain, Scandinavia, and northern Europe, as well as colonization in Mexico when polygamy was disavowed. Some Canadians may also reflect polygamous roots. Non-reservation Indians and those being assimilated into the community through conversion to the LDS Church frequently anglicized their names, making it difficult to differentiate them from other registrants. Further, the army had only two designations for race: white and "colored."

Of Utah's 21,000 servicemen, 665 were war casualties. Of these, 74 were of foreign birth or were U.S. ethnic/racial minorities.[43] Those who survived returned to an America bent on forcing immigrants to become Americanized immediately. Under the "Red Scare," massive arrests and deportations of purported radical immigrants began, the Palmer raids in Chicago being the most significant. In the "Red Summer of 1919" lynchings of blacks increased: in 1917 there were forty-eight; in 1918, sixty-three; and in 1919, seventy-eight—ten were veterans, several in uniform when they were burned alive.[44]

Immigrant veterans were granted citizenship, except for the Japanese. Immigrants who had asked for exemption were denied citizenship applications for five years. Although foreign-born veterans became members of the American Legion, established in March 1919, the organization led the Americanization fight with stinging attacks on all immigrants."[45] A capricious attitude toward the immigrant serviceman characterized the American Legion. On one hand a visiting national commander reviled immigrants, oblivious to the ethnic veterans listening to him, and on the other hand American and immigrant veterans formed lifelong friendships.[46]

In Salt Lake City Greek veterans established their own American Legion Post No. 4 and wore their uniforms while carrying the flower-decorated tomb of Christ around the Holy Trinity Greek Orthodox church on Good Friday.[47] Often immigrants wore their uniforms on visits to their native countries, conferring instant prestige on themselves. Other immigrants bitterly denounced the war on their return from France, convinced that munitions manufacturers had worked clandestinely to promote hostilities for monetary gain.

The American Legion spearheaded the doomed, compulsory education program. The Japanese were the most faithful in paying the ten-dollar registration fee and attending classes. Of the thirty-five immigrants in Carbon County who registered for the program, almost all were Japanese.[48] Catholic nuns taught a class mainly for Greeks and Italians in the Arthur Utah Copper Club.[49] The majority of immigrants refused to attend the classes, saying they were too tired in the evening. These men had rudimentary reading and writing skills in their own languages and feared they would be humiliated in trying to learn English.

The American Legion stridently continued its campaign against the immigrants. When Carbon County coal miners joined the unsuccessful national coal strike in 1922, the legion unleashed its most formidable propaganda weapon: striking was un-American. The immigrants were called "Bolsheviks" and "I-Won't-Work slackers," and cries grew that they be deported to their native countries. Considerable attention was also given to immigrant bootleggers; however, this could not be taken seriously because a greater number of Americans found it lucrative to make and sell illicit liquor.[50]

Two years later the Ku Klux Klan, many of them members of the American Legion, harassed the immigrants by marching in Salt Lake City and Magna and burning crosses on Salt Lake City's Ensign Peak, in the Bingham foothills, and in the Helper rail yards and on its mountain slopes.[51] In 1921 and 1924 quotas were placed on immigration to the United States, and the numbers from southern and eastern Europe were dramatically curtailed.

The Japanese were severely affected by the war: they were no longer allowed entrance into the United States. *Issei*, or first-generation Japanese, became—like the Chinese earlier—ineligible for citizenship, and *Nisei*, (second-generation) women, married to *Issei* had their citizenship revoked by the Cable Act of 1922. In 1931 a new organization, the Japanese American Citizens League, successfully lobbied to have two legislative acts passed. Nisei women regained their citizenship and seven hundred Japanese World War I veterans were granted citizenship.[52]

Reminders of the war are seen in unexpected places. In the Greek mountain village of the author's father stands a monument, erected by a Chicago immigrant, to the Greek Americans of the village who died alongside their countrymen in both world wars. And in Grimaldi, Italy, is another, achieved through the efforts of two immigrant Italian brothers—one from Columbia, Carbon County, and the other from Pueblo, Colorado—honoring the immigrant Italians and the native Grimaldians who died in the war.[53]

The Great War was a catalyst that intensified nativist feelings against immigrants and minorities. The Ku Klux Klan was the most visible expression of it. The immigrant experience during the war years settled for most foreign born the question of repatriation. Because many immigrants made visits to their homelands and returned to the United States, where they were counted, not as returnees, but as new immigrants, the actual number who remained in their native countries can only be conjectured; it is commonly believed to have been small.

Immigrants were advised to become American citizens immediately to enable them "to travel anywhere in the United States safely." The immigrants flocked to apply for citizenship, and overt prejudice against them lessened into covert forms. The grandchildren of immigrants have faced little discrimination. African Americans, though, have not yet reached their expectations of true equality through military service.

NOTES

Originally published in the *Utah Historical Quarterly* 58 (Fall 1990): 358–70.

1. The Balkan wars of 1912–13 had returned to the Serbs 17,241 square miles of land annexed by the Austro-Hungarian Empire in 1908, but many villages were still within Austrian borders. Militant Serbian university students were at the forefront of those demanding the

Serbs be united. Archduke Ferdinand had devised the coup that extended Austrian territory into Serbia and was a hated symbol to the Serbs. At the news of the assassination Serbs pulled down Austrian flags and replaced them with their own throughout Sarajevo. Ancient hostilities flared up and the Croats, although a subject people to Austria, retaliated by ransacking Serbian shops, schools, clubs, and houses.

2. The author grew up in Carbon County in the 1920s when such incidents were often recalled.
3. The Allies comprised Russia, France, Great Britain, Italy, United States, Japan, Romania, Belgium, Serbia, Greece, Portugal, and Montenegro; the Central powers included Germany, Austria-Hungary, Turkey, and Bulgaria.
4. Those representing themselves as Russians had some basis for credibility: they were descendants of Baltic Germans whose land had been taken in the expansion of Russia's borders during Catherine the Great's reign.
5. L. S. Stavrianos, *The Balkans Since 1453* (New York: Holt, Rinehart and Winston, 1966), chap. 14.
6. Joseph Stipanovich, "Falcons in Flight: The Yugoslavs," in *The Peoples of Utah*, ed. Helen Z. Papanikolas (Salt Lake City: Utah State Historical Society, 1976), 380.
7. Ibid., 380–81. The two hundred figure for Serbian soldiers does not correspond with the War Services Records; an explanation could be that most Serbs left to serve with the Serbian army or that the number was mere surmising.
8. Stavrianos, *The Balkans Since 1453*, 556–58.
9. *Tooele Transcript*, August 3, 1917.
10. *Utah Mining Review*, August 15, 1917.
11. Interview with Paul Borovilos, November 12, 1989; interview with John Naccarato's stepdaughter, Vera Cuglietta, July 1, 1990.
12. *Price News Advocate*, April 12, 1917.
13. Ibid., July 26, 1917.
14. Ibid., January 3, 1918. The writer, Tom Avgikos, a well-educated Greek businessman, was co-owner of the Golden Rule Store in Helper. He served in France and was scheduled to enter officers' training in London when the war ended. World War I Questionnaire, War Services Records, microfilm, Utah State Archives, Salt Lake City.
15. Told to the author by her father, George Zeese.
16. *News Advocate*, May 19, 1918.
17. *Bingham Press Bulletin*, February 15, 1918.

18. Ibid., September 20, 1918.
19. T. A. Rickard, "The Mine," *Utah Copper Enterprise*, spring 1917, 36.
20. *Bingham Press Bulletin*, April 5, 1918.
21. Ibid., May 24, 1918.
22. Ibid., March 22, October 4, 1918; *News Advocate*, April 22, 1918; Rickard, *Utah Copper Enterprise*, spring 1917, 45.
23. *News Advocate*, January 3, 1918.
24. See Helen Z. Papanikolas, *Toil and Rage in a New Land: The Greek Immigrants in Utah, 1974*, 2nd revised edition, reprinted from *Utah Historical Quarterly* 38 (1970): 155–56.
25. Nick Zeese, second cousin of the writer's father.
26. Interview of Gust Kouris by the author; Ethnic Archives, G30, Marriott Library, University of Utah; interview of Anast Chipian's son John, November 13, 1989; Cuglietta interview.
27. Interview of May Hakata Horiuchi, his daughter, Salt Lake City, November 19, 1989.
28. Louis Galanis to the author, April 19, 1990. Galanis and his partner left their business to be run by employees. When they returned from France, they found their business had declined. They built it up again and added another store in Payson, Utah, and one in Delta, Colorado.
29. W. Allison Sweeney, *History of the American Negro in the Great World War: His Splendid Record in the Battle Zones of Europe* (New York: 1919), 74.
30. See Ronald G. Coleman, "Blacks in Utah History," in Papanikolas, *The Peoples of Utah*, 130–32.
31. Ibid.; Sweeney, *History of the American Negro*, 74.
32. Bernard C. Nolty, *Strength for the Eight: A History of Black Americans in the Military* (New York: The Free Press, MacMillan, 1986), chap. 7; W. Augustus Low and Virgil A. Clift, eds., *Encyclopedia of Black America* (New York: McGraw Hill, 1981), 232.
33. Low and Clift, *Encyclopedia of Black America*, 836.
34. Charles S. Williams, *Negro Soldiers in World War I: The Human Side* (New York: A. M. S. Press, 1923), 21. Of 815 white men called, 526 were exempted; of 202 blacks, 6 were exempted.
35. Sweeney, *History of the American Negro*, 133.
36. Ibid., 27.
37. Interview with Jack Duncan, November 20, 1989, Salt Lake City. On his return to the United States, Duncan heard blacks were being recruited in Salt Lake City for work on the railroads. He spent the rest of his working life in the city as a porter in the airport and as a waiter in several hotels, mostly in the Hotel Utah.

38. Sweeney, *History of the American Negro*, 75.

39. Ibid., 80.

40. The 1910 census shows 2,110 Japanese males and 371 Chinese males; in 1920 there were 2,936 Japanese males and 342 Chinese males. See also Garrick Bailev and Roberta Glemi Bailey, *A History of the Navajos: The Reservation Years* (Santa Fe: School of American Research Press, 1986), 118; David L. Wood, "Gosiute-Shoshone Draft Resistance, 1917–18," *Utah Historical Quarterly* 49 (1981); Joseph H. Peck, *What Next Doctor Peck?* (Englewood Cliffs, NJ: Prentice Hall, 1959), 190–91.

41. To compute the number of each immigrant group serving in the armed forces, the author examined the twenty-one thousand Utah veterans' records and tallied the immigrants by their country of birth.

42. The peripatetic journey of Utah war records is recorded by Steve Wood in the Utah State Archives. A fire, believed to be arson, destroyed the national war records in St. Louis, Missouri. See Walter W. Stender and Evans Walker, "The National Personnel Records Center Fire: A Study in Disaster," *The American Archivist* (October 1974): 521–49.

43. Immigrant casualties: Italy, 17; Greece, 13; England, 10; Sweden, 4; Mexico, 4 (3 Anglo surnames); Denmark, 4; Finland, 3; 2 each from Ireland, Scotland, Serbia, and Russia; U.S. Hispanics, 2; 1 each from Hawaii, Canada, France, Philippines, Japan, Holland, Poland, China, and Switzerland. Compiled from War Services Records and Noble Warrum's *Utah in the World War* (Salt Lake City: Utah State Council of Defense, 1924).

44. Low and Clift, *Encyclopedia of Black America*, 232.

45. *News Advocate*, November 30, 1922.

46. See story of Last Squad Club in *Salt Lake Tribune*, March 2, 1986.

47. The minutes book, 1926–33, in the Greek language, is in Special Collections, Marriott Library, University of Utah; Borovilos interview.

48. *News Advocate*, November 30, 1922.

49. Borovilos interview.

50. See Papanikolas, *Toil and Rage*, 166–75; Papanikolas, "Bootlegging in Zion: Making and Selling the 'Good Stuff,'" *Utah Historical Quarterly* 53 (1985): 268–91.

51. Papanikolas, *Toil and Rage*, 176–81.

52. See Julia E. Johnsen, *Japanese Exclusion* (New York, 1925).

53. Personal communication from Philip F. Notarianni, Magna, Utah.

9

OUR CRADLES WERE IN GERMANY

Utah's German-American Community and World War I

ALLAN KENT POWELL

With the outbreak of war in 1914, many German Americans in Utah demonstrated a fervent patriotic loyalty to the land of their birth. Monetary contributions were made, a few motivated by a deep sense of duty volunteered for service in the German army, and those with friends and relatives in the homeland worried about their fate. In 1917, when the United States declared war on Germany, the situation was much different as Utah's German-American community faced both the collective and the individual question of loyalty. Did their allegiance lie with their new adopted land, or were their ties to the fatherland so strong that they demanded the highest measure of loyalty? In the super-charged era of war, neighbors, friends, and even family members were keen in looking for signs or actions of less than 100 percent Americanism. How this story played out in Utah is the subject of the following chapter.

As World War I broke across Europe in August 1914, Utah's nearly ten thousand German-born residents followed the faraway events with keen interest.[1] Most pondered the impact of the war on family and friends in the homeland. Some speculated on the political and economic implications for Germany. Few considered that the war would bring a crisis of collective and individual loyalty to the mountains and valleys of Utah some five thousand miles away from the battlefields of western Europe.

Over the course of three years the United States moved away from a position of uninvolvement and neutrality and became an active ally of France and Great Britain against Germany and Austria. Between August 1914 and 1917, Utah's German-born community demonstrated a dual loyalty to both their former homeland and their adopted country. Although often uncomfortable, this dual loyalty was possible in democratic America until the declaration of war, even though Germany's swaggering militarism piqued most Americans who also sided with Britain and France because of historical and geographical ties. When war came it impinged directly on traditional American habits and ideas of tolerance and pluralism. As historian John Higham observed, "The struggle with Germany suddenly imposed enormous tasks upon a loose built, peaceful society, calling for an unusual output of manpower and materiel." Consequently, he concluded, "The war seemed so encompassing, so arduous, that the slightest division of purpose or lack of enthusiasm appeared an intolerable handicap to it."[2]

Utahns joined willingly in the national war effort. They oversubscribed to the liberty bond drives, sent brothers and sons off to fight, and demanded unequivocal loyalty from their German-born neighbors.[3] In the eyes of the nation these actions reflected positively on Utah and in particular on the Mormon Church, whose own loyalty had been under attack for nearly three-quarters of a century.[4] This *gleichshaltung* was not without agony for Utah's German community, and its manifestation can be followed through the pages of Utah's only German-language newspaper, the *Salt Lake City Beobachter.* The purpose of this chapter is to describe how German Americans in Utah, as reported in the *Salt Lake City Beobachter*, responded to World War I before and after America's official entry into the conflict.

Established in 1890, the *Beobachter* ("The Observer") was the principal news source for most of Utah, Wyoming, and Idaho's German-speaking population. It was also sent to Europe, where it circulated among members of the Church of Jesus Christ of Latter-day Saints (LDS). The newspaper was founded by Joseph Harvey Ward, an American-born member of the LDS Church who had served as a missionary in Germany. Ward owned, edited, and published the newspaper from 1890 until his death in 1905, when the Beobachter Publishing Company was established with the LDS Church holding controlling interest. A board of directors was elected, which appointed Arnold H. Schulthess as editor and business manager. Schulthess was born in Neukirch, Switzerland, in 1865, baptized into the LDS Church in Salt Lake City in 1882, and served as president of the German mission from early 1899 until August 1901.[5]

On New Year's Eve 1913, Arnold Schulthess offered his readers best wishes for a new year and his hope that the paper would continue "to bring a message of peace to every house—near and far—that it entered."[6] Although the *Beobachter* called for peace as 1914 dawned, within four months the newspaper began carrying articles reflecting the tense situation between Russia and Germany. A front-page article on April 1, 1914, observed that Russia appeared to have something against Germany and was stirring up the Poles against Germany and the Slavs against the Austro-Hungarian Empire. Later that month another article reported the mistreatment of a German pilot and two crewmembers being held in a Russian prison on charges of spying.[7]

Speculation about a forthcoming war ended when the August 5 issue of the *Beobachter* announced, "The War Has Become Reality." Salt Lake City Germans demonstrated a great measure of patriotism toward their homeland at the outbreak of World War I. More than five hundred attended a mass meeting held on August 5, 1914, in the German hall at 323 State Street. The meeting began with an opening song, "Deutschland, Deutschland Uber Alles." Charles Peters, temporary chairman of the meeting, gave a brief review of the events leading up to the war. Thunderous applause exploded at his concluding statement: "With our

Kaiser only one condition existed in the present conflict—victory or death." Dr. F. Moormeister followed with a speech that expressed the sentiments of most in attendance: "We stand at the eve of a world war and can only wait to see what the future will bring. Our cradles were in Germany and there is where our hearts are now." Those assembled also drafted and adopted a dispatch to the German ambassador in Washington, Count Johann Von Bernsdorff, indicating that Salt Lake City's Germans had long prayed that peace might be preserved but now would pray for victory for their homeland. The leaders of the August 5 meeting also discussed the establishment of a permanent organization, the German American Relief League, to support the German cause. Before concluding the business of the meeting, Peters offered a toast to President Woodrow Wilson and the United States of America, after which all joined in singing "The Star-Spangled Banner."[8]

In the following days other expressions of loyalty to Germany emerged. Kaiser Wilhelm II was shown great respect. The *Beobachter* published the text of his August 4 speech to the Reichstag justifying the declaration of war. Persons who recruited six new full-paying subscribers to the *Beobachter* earned a canvas painting of the kaiser with a gold frame. The Liberty Theater showed the film *The Fighting Germans* from June 18 through 25, 1916. Kaiser Wilhelm II appeared in the film, and his picture was used to advertise it. News of the heroism of German soldiers related to German immigrants in Utah appeared regularly in the *Beobachter*.[9]

German patriotism found nourishment in the poems appearing periodically in the *Beobachter* during the early months of the war. Readers were urged to take pride in being German and recognize virtue in Germany's conduct of the war. Representative of this spirit is the poem penned by Friedrich G. Fischer of Sandy, Utah, titled "Zum Trost for Mein Vaterland" ("For the Comfort of My Fatherland"):

> My Fatherland, My Fatherland
> What law have you broken
> That from the Alps to the ocean shore

hate is spoken against you.
You beautiful mighty realm of peace,
In the entire world nothing is your equal
When dark nights come
God protect you. We deny you not.

My Germany, O Germania,
You are not defeated.
How united and majestic you stand
in these troubled days.

For freedom, yes, the greatest good,
We willingly offer our blood.
While victory and illusion now must pass,
You, the land of the true will survive.

My Homeland, My Fatherland,
Who has the right to judge you?
To bring complete destruction?
With your arts and learning,
With your music and your strength,
With God's help alone,
You must and will be the victor.[10]

Nevertheless, some readers complained that the editors of the *Beo-bachter* were not patriotic enough. These critics wanted bigger headlines about Germany's victories, more "noise" about the war effort, and stronger attacks against Germany's enemies. Still, the editor charged, when the German government asked for five or ten dollars to help Germany there was little to be seen or heard of these "firework patriots."[11] During the first few months of the war the *Beobachter* listed four hundred contributions—ranging from twenty-five cents to one hundred dollars—to the German Red Cross for a total of twenty-six hundred dollars.

War brought the immediate removal of all American LDS mission-aries from Germany and Switzerland. Hyrum W. Valentine, president of the Swiss-German mission, secreted 20,000 marks into Germany, visited all of the American elders, gave them enough money to pay their obligations and for passage to Liverpool, and arranged for local members to continue church activities. A number of German and Swiss saints questioned the wisdom and need to remove the American elders at the beginning of the war. They argued the elders were in no danger and could not understand how a shepherd could leave his flock. Instead of leaving Germany, some suggested, it would have been better if the American missionaries had volunteered their service for the Red Cross. Church leaders responded that they acted to remove the American elders under the order of Secretary of State William Jen-nings Bryan for all Americans in the warring nations to return home as quickly as possible. Although the American missionaries had been well treated by the German government and people, and although the Americans left with nothing but praise for the Germans, church leaders could not predict what the future would bring and feared that if the missionaries stayed they might land in prison or suffer other mistreatment. Furthermore, the German saints were not without shepherds, and if problems arose that local leaders could not handle they could turn to President Valentine for counsel. Acknowledging that service in the Red Cross was noble, church authorities reminded members that these elders had been called to preach the gospel of Christ. The time was short, the field ripe, and the workers few.[12]

With the removal of Mormon missionaries, increasing difficulties in maintaining contact with Europe, and growing anti-German senti-ment throughout America, Utah's Germans took great comfort in an address by Anthon H. Lund to the German-speaking saints in the Salt Lake Assembly Hall on September 11, 1915. As an LDS general author-ity born in Denmark and an immigrant who knew firsthand many of the trials of the German saints in Utah, Lund's sympathetic and sooth-ing words supplied a much-needed balm for the beleaguered Utah Germans. He reminded the congregation that God was no respecter of nations. God loved all his children. Lund continued: "We have gathered in a land where we have become citizens of another nation. But that does not mean that we should lose our love for our fatherland or the great leaders. We should continually remember the land where we were born and the people to which we belong." Speaking of his experiences as a young immigrant in Utah, Lund recalled a feeling against foreigners then and noted that although people looked down upon them he was never ashamed of his homeland. He always remembered the good things and great people of his native land and urged the assembled immigrants to do the same and pass that knowledge on to their children. He concluded, "love for our Fatherland does not detract from our love for the country which has taken us in. The person who forgets and criticizes his own Fatherland will not be a good citizen of this land."[13]

News of the first wartime casualties to reach friends and relatives in Utah was chronicled on the front page of the *Beobachter*. Many attended a memorial service held in the Salt Lake Assembly Hall on July 30, 1916, for one fallen German soldier, Wilhelm Kessler. Born July 23, 1887, in Neukirchen, Rheinland Pfalz, Kessler joined the LDS Church in 1907 shortly before his twentieth birthday. Three years later he immigrated to Utah where he stayed with his sister, Helene Kuehn, and her family. In October 1912 he returned to Germany as a missionary. After stays in Berlin and Hannover, his next assignment took him to Basel in March 1913 to become the editor of *Der Stern*. When war broke out he left his mission to volunteer for the German army.

In a letter to the *Beobachter* written on July 30, 1914, at the time Kessler made his decision to leave his mission for the army, the German patriot wrote:

> I am compelled to take this step by the guiding voice of my deepest conscience. It may be that some of my dear friends will not approve. . . . I understand their point of view, but no one can rob me of my high regard for the homeland, the future of this just endeavor, and my decision to keep unsoiled my honor as a loyal

son of Germany. Let me keep my belief that all authority is from
God and that we must give the Kaiser his due. Let me keep my
confidence in God that he can protect his children even in the
most dangerous of circumstances. I know that many of you share
my opinion and can justify my action. To you goes my heartfelt
thanks. The sins of the Slavs are great and the blood shed by
their crimes cries to heaven. God will punish them. The dark
clouds must be lightened with force so that the gospel rays can
be received in unrestricted freedom, which is not now the case in
the Slavic countries. I am of no use to my church now, but I can
enlist in the service of my fatherland and thereby further God's
intentions. Not until peace is restored will the harvest finally
be ripe. Then we, the patriots, can be of greatest support to the
mission. But everything is in God's hands. His will be done.[14]

In his last communication from France to friends in Utah, Kessler
observed that already reports of England's efforts to turn American
opinion against Germany had reached the western front. "We have
learned that the English are spreading great lies about us. Don't
believe them. We are keeping Germany's honor high and are successful. Right is on the side of Germany."[15]

A grenade splinter tore a deep gash in his lower leg during the
fighting near Fricourt on September 29, 1914, and Kessler received
the Iron Cross Second Class. After his recovery he attended officer's
school. Appointed a lieutenant on June 26, 1916, the news did not
reach Kessler before his death during the fighting near Mametz and
Montauban on July 1, 1916. Memorial services honored Wilhelm Kessler in Basel, Switzerland, on July 25, 1916, as well as five days later in
Salt Lake City.[16]

During the memorial service in the Salt Lake Assembly Hall, John
Dern, a German-born entrepreneur and a non-Mormon, expressed
regret over the loss of such a fine young man to both the church and
to Utah's German community. "Through his work and personal influence many were encouraged to nurture German customs, literature,

and culture," he said. But Dern's speech served primarily to bolster and legitimatize support of the German war effort by German Americans in Utah. Dern encouraged, "Let us not give up, but trust in God and the strength of German manhood that the outcome of the war will not be disappointing." He concluded with references to the oft-sung patriotic hymn, "Watch on the Rhein," and its applicability to Utah's German Americans: "Let us sing 'Dear Fatherland, you can be calm, strong and true stands the watch on the Rhein.' But not only do the guards stand watch on the Rhein, also far away in the enemy's land."[17]

Removed from the activities of larger German-American groups in the East and Midwest, Utah's German-American community sought ties to the national movement. In August 1915, Dr. Charles J. Hexamer, president of the German American National Alliance, made a twenty-four-hour stop in Salt Lake City while en route to San Francisco. Escorted on a tour of the city by John Dern and honored with a dinner at the Newhouse Hotel by leading German businessmen, Hexamer spoke about the immigration of Germans to America, the service they had given their new country, and the heritage of culture in the United States and the world as he declared, "No one will find us prepared to step down to a lesser Kultur; no, we have made it our aim to draw the other up to us."[18]

Earlier German Americans in Utah used this theme, though in a much less offensive manner, to try to counter the Utah anti-German press. Writing in late August 1914 to answer the question "Must we be ashamed of being German?" Fritz Boede expressed the frustration of many with American newspapers that for years had praised the industry, loyalty, piety, culture, and education of the German people but in less than three weeks forgot all the good Germany had created and fostered and now spoke only of Germany's arrogance, lust for conquest, and blind allegiance to their kaiser.[19]

The first great crisis for German Americans erupted with the sinking by a German submarine of the British ship *Lusitania* and the death of nearly 1,200 passengers, including 124 American citizens, off the coast of Ireland in May 1915. The *Salt Lake Herald Republican* reported in an interview with the director of the *Beobachter* that Utah Germans considered the attack a serious mistake in the conduct of the war. Arnold Schulthess claimed he was misquoted and that he found no fault with the German government, although he—as did all Germans—regretted the loss of so many lives and wished they could have been brought to safety before the ship sank. Such tragedies, however, could not be avoided when ships carried war materiel. Schulthess concluded, "The enemy had been given warning enough, more than is usually done, and the German submarine had done nothing more than what the enemy would have done under similar circumstances."[20] Later, in response to an article in the *Salt Lake Telegram* entitled "The German Spy System in the United States," Schulthess insisted that history demonstrated German Americans had always proven their loyalty to America, and it was "unjust to insinuate that every German in the United States goes to bed at night with his boots on so that he is ready at any time to spy for Germany."[21]

Other writers to the *Beobachter* found the other Salt Lake newspapers—the *Deseret News*, the *Salt Lake Tribune*, and the *Salt Lake Herald Republican*—to be pro-English and guilty of inflammatory writings against Germany based on fabricated reports from London, Paris, and Petersburg. Furthermore, Utah German Americans charged the Salt Lake papers with failing to support President Wilson's policy of strict neutrality.[22]

By early 1917 America stood on the brink of war with Germany. The infamous Zimmermann telegram, in which Germany secretly offered to restore to Mexico American territory (including all of the state of Utah) lost during the Mexican War of 1846 if Mexico joined in a military alliance against the United States, plus Germany's decision to resume unrestricted submarine warfare, indicated Germany already regarded America as an enemy. Following the sinking of several American ships by German submarines, Congress responded to Wilson's call for a declaration of war against Germany "to make the world safe for democracy" with an overwhelming vote of support on April 6, 1917—373 to 50 in the House and 82 to 6 in the Senate.

Utah's Germans became even more preoccupied with the war situation. A period of adjustment set in as the potential for divided loyalties became a reality. Indicative of the situation, during the first Salt Lake City German LDS Conference held after the declaration of war, President Carl F. Buehner welcomed the congregation and reminded them that they had come to hear the gospel and be strengthened in their belief. Therefore, he expected to hear no comments about the war.[23]

Still the problem persisted. Recruiting officers made their rounds and urged the sons of German immigrants to show their loyalty by joining the army to fight against Germany. As Elizabeth Hofer, a resident of Washington, Utah, expressed: "While I was in Switzerland, the Elders said to us, whoever does not want to raise a sword against his neighbor should come to Zion. But now our sons here must use weapons against their own relatives. That is, for me, very terrible."[24]

Concerned with the state of affairs, citizens of German and Swiss origin living in the Logan area had met the last week of March 1917, before America's declaration of war, to consider the political situation and their options. They found no reason for the United States to throw itself into the war and allow thousands of America's young men to be slaughtered. Reassuring doubters of their loyalty to America, they nevertheless expressed sympathy for Germany and its defense against a superior enemy force. However, if the United States did enter the war, they stood ready to offer their possessions and lives for their new homeland, maintaining that no reason existed to doubt the sincerity or loyalty of citizens of German or Swiss descent to America.[25]

Sensing the future course of events, the German-American community had held a mass meeting on March 29, 1917, more than a week before Congress declared war. At the meeting Gov. Simon Bamberger, a German-born Jew, justified concerns that the foreign born prove their loyalty by becoming American citizens. The Americans have the right to say "who is not for us, is against us," he said; furthermore, "you cannot expect the United States to allow foreigners to move freely among its citizens, if one does not know that they are in harmony with them." LDS apostle B. H. Roberts spoke to the young men in the audience, urging them to join the National Guard in case they were needed and promising he would accompany them to the trenches as a chaplain. The mass meeting concluded with those assembled unanimously passing a resolution declaring their allegiance to the United States.[26]

As spokesman for Utah's Germans, the *Salt Lake City Beobachter* made a conspicuous demonstration of loyalty. Upon the declaration of war, the American flag, "The symbol of Freedom," found a prominent place in the center of the front page. A later edition published all four verses of "The Star-Spangled Banner" in English and German. The newspaper's masthead announced the *Beobachter*'s role as the "Official German organ of the Church of Jesus Christ of Latter-day Saints—American in everything but language," and that "This paper has enlisted with the government in the cause of America for the period of the war."[27]

German Americans saw clearly that the impending conflict posed a greater threat to their status as American citizens than anything since their entry into the country. As one writer concluded, Americans saw everywhere spies ready to betray the United States to Germany even though the German born had taken an oath of allegiance upon becoming American citizens. Neighbors no longer trusted neighbors, and "if one is so uncautious as to suggest that . . . America had no reason to throw itself into the world conflict, that is enough to consider him a traitor to the country and have the police watch him carefully."[28]

The war soon touched the lives of all Utahns in a direct way. The Selective Service Act required the registration of all men between the ages of 18 and 45. In the first draft lottery in July 1917, 53 Germans were among the 1,050 men selected. In Washington County 60 young men drafted were identified as of German or Swiss descent.[29]

Utah's German born were encouraged to purchase liberty bonds. One ad in both English and German summed up the proper conduct for loyal Americans: obeying cheerfully the laws made necessary by the war; learning to speak English or teaching others to speak it;

preparing to become a citizen if not one already; and purchasing liberty bonds with every dollar that could be spared.[30]

German-American leaders prodded their countrymen who had not become U.S. citizens to obey the law and register as aliens. The *Beobachter* published the names of some of the 470 Salt Lake City Germans who complied with the law, noting that a number of the registrants were respectable businessmen who had already applied for citizenship. German citizens were encouraged to attend American citizenship and English language classes offered at West High School.[31]

Loyal German Americans were concerned about alien malcontents creating problems in the already tense situation. Information was provided on how aliens could leave the United States if they could not be good citizens. The *Beobachter* published accounts of how unpatriotic Germans were made patriotic, such as a Boise resident who spoke against the U.S. government and painted his hay barn with the German colors—red, white, and black. Angry neighbors went to his farm and forced the man to kiss the American flag and repaint his barn red, white, and blue.[32]

When German prisoners of war incarcerated at Fort Douglas attempted to escape by tunneling out of the prison, the *Beobachter* wondered why the prisoners were not happy to be in a camp where they were better cared for than any other prisoners in the world. The German prisoner of war camp was an enigma for the German-American community, a constant reminder to Utahns of the German enemy. Community leaders warned German Americans not to speak about the camp or attempt to visit the prisoners lest they arouse more suspicion. Yet leaders also asked German-speaking Mormons to donate church books printed in German for the prisoners. Issues of the *Beobachter* circulated among the prisoners and a few letters from prisoners appeared in it.[33]

The *Beobachter* dutifully published lengthy articles prepared by the Committee on Public Information in Washington, D.C., and distributed by the Utah Council of Defense. Thirteen months after America's entry into the war, a front-page article tried to explain again the reasons for America's declaration of war.[34] Reports of German Americans who served in the U.S. Army reflected the patriotism of the German-American community.

While most German Americans expressed loyalty to the United States, evidence for continued sympathy toward Germany can also be found. One speaker at the mass meeting held on the eve of America's declaration of war with Germany questioned the conspicuous absence of a number of prominent Salt Lake City German Americans. In November 1917, the Beobachter Publishing Company advertised for sale such German-language books as *Zeppelins over England* and *Die Fahrt der Deutschland*, an account by Capt. Paul Koenig of the travels of the German submarine *Deutschland.* In a later advertisement for German books by another dealer in Salt Lake City, the ad carried the poignant lead sentence: "German books of which even the greed of our enemies cannot rob us and wherein we can seek enjoyment and from which we can find the spiritual strength of which we are now in such great need."[35]

German Americans, embittered by the seemingly excessive anti-German hysteria that expanded with America's declaration of war, could do little. The non-German public demanded that Congress outlaw the publication of German newspapers and magazines and place other restrictions on the use of the German language. Utah German Americans resented that their own senator, William H. King, took the lead in attaching a rider to the Trading with the Enemy Act requiring German-language newspapers to supply English translations of "any comments respecting the Government, . . . its policies, international relations, the state or conduct of the war, or of any other matter relating thereto." Later King introduced a bill to revoke the charter of the National German-American Alliance and chaired a Senate investigation aimed at the organization's destruction.[36]

Recognizing the call for German customs, German names, German songs, and the German language to be suppressed, a *Beobachter* editorial reminded readers that German was spoken in America before the country was founded, that the first Bible printed in America was in German, and that during the war for independence the issue of freedom was promoted through leaflets and newspapers in the German language. The editorial maintained that in the seeming fight to destroy everything German (including the suppression of German-language newspapers) American citizens and their elected officials stood on the verge of attaining what no autocracy could accomplish or would even attempt without great harm to itself. The editorial warned that although it was hard to imagine America would deny its history, principles, and ideals by suppressing German-language newspapers, the danger was real and could only be thwarted by demonstrations of loyalty to America and support for everything the administration did or requested.[37]

Contradicting those who would suppress the German-language newspapers, German Americans argued that the newspapers helped America's war effort in a number of ways. First, they taught and explained why the United States was at war against Germany. Second, they demonstrated the loyalty and patriotism of the German Americans to their adopted country. Third, the newspapers could help allow German Americans to continue to live the kinds of lives they had before the war—as loyal, hardworking citizens who found meaning in their German religious services, songs, customs, and heritage.

The *Beobachter* did continue publication without restrictions during the war years, but not without difficulty. When war broke out in August 1914, Canadian subscribers stopped receiving it in a blanket prohibition of German-language publications. In 1915, long before America entered the war, anti-German sentiment made it impossible to offer the *Beobachter* for sale in Salt Lake City newspaper stands. When publication of the *Beobachter* was delayed for two weeks in a row because typesetter G. F. Buschmann was ill, rumor spread that the repression of German-language newspapers had at last become a reality. In a near-desperate move to maintain subscribers and advertising, the *Beobachter* staff printed a long explanation that concluded with a commitment to continue to publish until forced to stop by the government.[38]

Anti-German sentiment did not end with the campaign against German-language newspapers but broadened to include a call to boycott the teaching of the German language in American schools. Germans and others responded that such proposals were a misguided expression of patriotism, as "German was not taught and learned to serve the Kaiser and the German Reich, but for the same reason that one would learn any language or pursue useful knowledge."[39] Through a knowledge of German, scholars could read scientific works as well as literature in the original language so the full meaning of the author could be understood and not distorted through imprecise translations. In contrast to the United States, Germany emphasized the teaching of English while England and France stressed the teaching of German. Finally, those calling for an end to teaching German had a shortsighted view of the future. The fighting would not last much longer and there would be an even greater need for expertise with the German language when dealing with postwar issues and problems.

Despite all the arguments and logic against restrictions on teaching German, war hysteria prevailed in Utah. The State Textbook Commission and the Utah Council of Defense passed resolutions calling for an end to German instruction in all schools and colleges. Responding to government pressure "that the teaching of the language would be an aid to German propaganda in America, and the presentation of . . . everything unfavorable to the German nation . . . would tend to weaken the morale of the German Army," principals in the LDS Church's school system voted unanimously to eliminate the teaching of German for the duration of the war. This action came even though "a number of the school heads declared that they saw not the slightest relation between the teaching of the Teutonic language in the classroom and the successful waging of the big war."[40]

Anti-German sentiment took other forms of expression as well. At the Utah State Capitol, designed by German-born Richard K. A. Kletting, two German double eagles, which had been placed as decorative elements at the foot of the wide stairs when the capitol was constructed in 1915, became thorns in the eyes of certain patriots during the height of the anti-German hysteria and were replaced with "American eagles."[41] Other extremists accused Utah German Americans of harboring enemy aliens who poisoned the water used by cattle. In addition, German sympathizers reputedly tried to discourage loyal Americans from planting victory gardens with the argument that Salt Lake City did not have enough water to meet the demand.[42]

Critics also charged that the *Beobachter* was disloyal. In an article published in the *Salt Lake Tribune*, Gustav Buschmann claimed that all German-language newspapers, including the *Beobachter* with which he had been associated for fourteen years, were disloyal. Since he had recently left the *Beobachter*, his attack seemed personally motivated against the paper's editor Arnold Schulthess."[43]

A more serious attack on the newspaper came when Schulthess announced a one hundred dollar reward to anyone who could substantiate rumors circulated by several Utah papers about the relocation to Utah and Idaho of Belgian children whose hands, noses, or ears had been cut off by German soldiers. In justifying the reward, Schulthess said he considered it not a defense of the German cause but an attempt to learn the truth and defend German Americans when they were slandered. The *Logan Journal* saw the reward as evidence of pro-German sympathies; the editor charged that the reward portrayed a German soldier as honest, humane, and "incapable of committing an act so brutal as the cutting off the hands of a child; that he is in fact, a Christian soldier, even though he may be upholding a mistaken cause." According to the editor, it made no difference if the mutilated children could be found in Utah or not, because without question such atrocities had been committed. The German crimes, he declared, "would shame the lowest devils in hell and . . . make the name German a stench in the nostrils of civilized, Christian peoples, for generations to come . . . and the one who will either deny or defend will bear watching." Schulthess countered by refocusing the issue on false allegations of the mutilated Belgian children in Utah and insisting the reward had nothing to do with the question of a German soldier's humanity. He noted that contrary to the charge he was not German but a native of Switzerland, that he had lived in the United States for over forty years, and that he had become an American citizen as soon as he could.[44]

This and other problems had a devastating effect on Arnold Schulthess. Less than three weeks after his gallant defense of Utah's German born he suffered a severe stroke, and friends found him unconscious in the Sharon Building.[45] The forced retirement ended his twelve-and-a-half-year career as editor of the *Beobachter*.

By the time the war finally ended in November 1918, an obvious weariness was present within Utah's German-American community. Despite the purchase of liberty bonds, sending sons off to the American army, and other demonstrations of loyalty, a cloud of defeat and resignation covered the German Americans of Utah and would continue for the next several years. Instead of sounding the honor of Germany and the glories of her culture, the community saw only hunger and need in the homeland and the beginning of an unjust peace. A committee, armed with a letter of support signed by the LDS First Presidency, collected money, food, clothing, and shoes for several years after the war to send to Germany. Energy was also directed toward building up the German LDS organizations, but under a constant fear that church authorities would dissolve and withdraw support for the *Beobachter* in a dual attempt to bring greater uniformity to the Utah church and more quickly "Americanize" members from non-English-speaking lands.

Looking to Europe, Utah's German Americans were frustrated with a disappointing peace that brought increased problems with the Poles in the East and the occupation of the Rheinland, in part by black troops. The latter development scarred Salt Lake Germans and caused them to circulate petitions unashamedly through LDS church organizations as well as non-church groups calling for the withdrawal of the unwanted troops "to protect women and girls in the Rheinland from the black pest!"[46]

The 1920s saw discouragement prevail as hunger and want persisted in much of Germany and runaway inflation destroyed the savings and lives of thousands of Germans. America gave little thought to the plight of Germany, and for most Americans Germany in the 1920s was still the Germany of 1917. But in time evidence of a reconciliation appeared as ideals of equality and sympathy replaced the iron-hearted intolerance of an earlier day. Perhaps the first public demonstration that the healing was underway came from those who had suffered the most.[47] When American disabled veterans held their fourth annual national convention in Salt Lake City in June 1924, they enthusiastically recognized the noted German-born singer Ernestine Schumann-Heink as their "honorary mother." As Utah governor Charles Mabey proclaimed, "Hate is dead, long may love reign." The respect paid by the wounded veterans of World War I seemed most appropriate to a mother who had lost one son fighting under the stars and stripes as an American citizen and another fighting for the German cause.

NOTES

Originally published in the *Utah Historical Quarterly* 58 (Fall 1990): 371–87.

1. Between 1890 and 1910 the number of Utah residents from Germany, Austria, and Switzerland more than doubled from 3,574 to 7,524. As immigration continued, the number was well over 8,000 by 1914 and, according to one source, just under 10,000 in 1917. By comparison, the 1910 census disclosed that of a total U.S. population of just under 92 million, 2.5 million were born in Germany with another 5.8 million counted as second-generation German Americans. In 1910 German Americans were the most numerous immigrant group in the United States, representing 26 percent of the total foreign white stock in the country. Counting second-generation children, Utah's German-American community is estimated as slightly over 25,000—or about 6 percent of Utah's 400,000 residents—in 1914. On the eve of World War I the Utah German-American community was an obviously important but minority group in a state whose population was primarily British and Scandinavian. See Frederick C. Luebke, *Bonds of Loyalty: German Americans and World War I* (Dekalb: Northern Illinois University Press, 1974), 29–30, and Ronald K. Dewsnup, "The Waves of Immigration," *Utah Historical Quarterly* 54 (1984): 348. *Leslie's Weekly Newspaper* for March 8, 1917, listed the number

of German born in each of the forty-eight states. Utah, with 9,935, ranked thirty-fifth, well ahead of Wyoming with 6,500 and Arizona and Nevada with 4,000 each, but far behind Idaho with 14,000 and Colorado with 55,882. The heaviest concentrations of German-born residents were in New York, 1,234,584; Illinois, 1,014,408; Wisconsin, 794,943; Ohio, 673,795; Pennsylvania, 654,684; Michigan, 424,753; Minnesota, 396,859; Missouri, 367,511; and Iowa, 360,005.

2. John Higham, *Strangers in the Land: Patterns of American Nativism, 1860–1925* (New York: Atheneum, 1955), 206.

3. Nearly 25,000 Utahns served in the armed forces during the war and 665 died in service, including over 200 who fell on the battlefields in Europe. Thomas G. Alexander, "Political Patterns of Early Statehood, 1896–1918," in Richard D. Poll, et al., *Utah's History* (Provo: Brigham Young University Press, 1978), 424.

4. Thomas G. Alexander, *Mormonism in Transition: A History of the Latter-day Saints, 1890–1930* (Urbana and Chicago: University of Illinois Press, 1986), 46.

5. Thomas L. Broadbent, "The *Salt Lake City Beobachter*: Memoir of an Immigration," *Utah Historical Quarterly* 26 (1958): 329–50, and Gilbert Scharffs, *Mormonism in Germany* (Salt Lake City: Deseret Book, 1970), 46–47. Original copies of the *Beobachter* were preserved by LDS church historian Andrew Jenson. Microfilm copies of the newspaper are available at a number of locations, including the Utah State Historical Society Library in Salt Lake City.

6. *Beobachter*, December 31, 1913.

7. Ibid., August 12 and September 30, 1914.

8. Ibid., August 12, 1914.

9. Ibid., September 30, October 14, and November 18, 1914; June 14, 1916.

10. Ibid., September 9, 1914.

11. Ibid., December 30, 1914.

12. Ibid., March 17, 1915. The concern for safety was genuine; many missionaries had been expelled or imprisoned in peaceful times before the war.

13. Ibid., September 29, 1915.

14. Ibid., December 25, 1914.

15. Ibid., October 21, 1914.

16. *Der Stern*, September 15, 1916, 273–75.

17. *Beobachter*, August 16, 1916. Dern was born in Germany in 1850 and immigrated to America after the Civil War. A Utah mining magnate with a mansion on South Temple, he was the father of George Dern,

governor of Utah from 1924 to 1932. Margaret D. Lester, *Brigham Street* (Salt Lake City: Utah State Historical Society, 1979), 141–44.

18. *Beobachter*, August 4, 1915, and Luebke, *Bonds of Loyalty*, 100.
19. *Beobachter*, August 26, 1914.
20. Ibid., May 19, 1915.
21. Ibid., February 16 and May 24, 1914.
22. Ibid., September 30, 1914.
23. Ibid., July 18, 1917.
24. Ibid., April 18, 1918.
25. Ibid., April 4, 1917.
26. Ibid.
27. Ibid., March 22 and May 30, 1917; May 2, 1918.
28. Ibid., April 4, 1917.
29. Ibid., July 25 and August 1, 1917.
30. Ibid., August 1, 1917.
31. Ibid., July 18 and October 10, 1917; January 9, February 13, and March 27, 1918.
32. Ibid., May 2, 1917.
33. Ibid., October 10 and December 12, 1917; January 9 and September 19, 1918; June 19, 1919.
34. Ibid., December 29, 1917; January 9 and May 2, 1918.
35. Ibid., October 28, 1920.
36. Luebke, *Bonds of Loyalty*, 241, 269–70.
37. *Beobachter*, April 18, 1918.
38. Ibid., November 11, 1914; January 5, 1916; January 9, 1918.
39. Ibid., May 23, 1916.
40. *Salt Lake Tribune*, April 14, 1918; *Deseret News*, April 18, 1918.
41. *Beobachter*, February 27, 1918.
42. Ibid., April 4 and May 2, 1918. The editor of the *Beobachter* concluded that such rumors were completely false and were the fabrication of people who were too lazy to plant.
43. Ibid., February 12, 1918.
44. Ibid., February 6, 1918.
45. Ibid., February 27, 1918.
46. Ibid., December 25, 1918.
47. Ibid., June 25, 1924.

10

ENEMY ALIENS AND INTERNMENT IN WORLD WAR I

Alvo von Alvensleben in Fort Douglas, Utah: A Case Study

JOERG A. NAGLER

*For many Americans, spies and saboteurs were everywhere—
in unmarked airplanes, planting bombs near railroad tracks and
reservoir dams to destroy the nation's critical infrastructure, sending secret messages to offshore enemy submarines about ship sailings
and cargo, conspiring with our Mexican neighbors, and infiltrating
munitions plants and shipping facilities like the Black Tom facility
in New Jersey, near the Statue of Liberty, where on July 30, 1916,
explosions of suspicious origins destroyed millions of dollars worth of
munitions ready for shipment across the Atlantic for use against the
Germans on the western front in France and Belgium. Enemy aliens
were a threat to the United States; therefore, three internment camps
were established to incarcerate those guilty of violating laws against
sedition and support of the German enemy—two in Georgia at Fort
Oglethorpe and Fort McPherson and the other at Fort Douglas, Utah.
The Fort Douglas internment camp also housed naval prisoners of
war captured from German warships in Guam and Hawaii. Alvo
von Alvensleben—born on an estate near Magdeburg, Germany,*

a former officer in the German army, and, at the time of his arrest, a businessman in Seattle, Washington—was one of some eight hundred enemy aliens and anti-war activists sent to Fort Douglas during the war. He was released from Fort Douglas in 1919 and returned to Seattle, where he died in 1965. In this chapter, German historian Joerg Nagler describes the experience in Fort Douglas, highlights the anti-German sentiments that marked von Alvensleben's internment, and addresses the question of whether or not the controversial German American was an enemy who deserved internment for the duration of the war.

During World War I, especially after the American declaration of war against Germany on April 6, 1917, a wave of xenophobia engulfed everything endowed with a German name. Many individuals suffered tragic fates in the wake of this virtually hysterical atmosphere of persecution. Reports concerning pro-German activities and actions of the German *Geheimdienst* ("Secret Service") were already coming into the Justice Department during the neutrality period, which could only alarm the Wilson administration. According to the reports of the fledgling Bureau of Investigation, where J. Edgar Hoover was already serving as a "special agent,"[1] German spies and saboteurs were at work undermining the internal security of the United States, planning and carrying out bombings of strategically important bridges and munitions factories. The best known of these actions was the destruction of the Black Tom munitions depot on July 30, 1916, and the bombing of the assembly plant of the Canadian Car and Foundry Company in Kingsland, New Jersey, on January 11, 1917.[2] The Wilson administration saw itself confronted with a virtually insoluble task. How could a population so large as the quarter-million persons classified as "enemy aliens"—defined as males born in Germany over fourteen years of age and unnaturalized—be politically evaluated and controlled?[3] Following the American declaration of war against Austria-Hungary on December 11, 1917, another two million enemy aliens were added in, generally categorized as "Austrians" by authorities. In April 1918 Congress extended surveillance and registration to female enemy aliens. With that the number of persons classified as enemy aliens had grown to about four-and-a-half-million persons.

On the very day of the American declaration of war against Germany, President Wilson issued twelve "enemy alien regulations," adding eight more the following November. These twenty regulations defined the legal foundation for the registration, surveillance, and restriction of the rights of enemy aliens. They were not permitted, for example, to live in Washington, D.C., or to visit there; they were also not allowed to be found within a specific radius of canals, docks, railroad depots, and similar installations. Enemy aliens were also required to carry a registration card on their persons at all times. These regulations provided the legal foundation for officials to oversee and intern those who were believed to be potentially dangerous to the public.[4] The historic foundation for these regulations was the Alien and Sedition Acts of 1798, which declared that the president was authorized to restrict the rights of noncitizens by proclamation in times of war.

Both during and after World War I (1917–20) about 6,300 men and a few women were kept in four internment camps in the United States. The majority were crew members of German ships seized in areas under American sovereignty at the start of the war. They were classified by the Immigration and Naturalization Service as nonlegal immigrants and thus fell technically into the category of enemy aliens. About 2,300 of the prisoners, however, were civilian enemy aliens who had either been determined to be threats to internal security or had made themselves conspicuous through pro-German statements.

Internment camps in the United States during the First World War have yet to receive the attention they deserve from historians.[5] This is all the more unfortunate because this theme provides insight into the systematic violation of civil rights, the beginnings of the (Federal) Bureau of Investigation and the American Protective League, as well as military intelligence in the period.[6] During the Second World War, experiences with the treatment of enemy aliens from this time were often cited as precedents for administrative purposes.[7] As the example of the internment of Japanese Americans demonstrates, not a great deal was learned from the failures of the First World War. The wave of hatred against foreigners as well as the hysteria—which John Higham describes as a "Crusade for Americanization"[8]—about anything even distantly related to German culture that gripped the country after America's entry into the war was immense.[9]

According to the census of 1910, 8.3 million Americans out of a total population of almost 92 million regarded Germany as their land of origin; 2.5 million had been born there, 4 million were born in the United States to German parents, and the remnant had one German parent.[10] Of these, approximately 6,000 were arrested and of that number 2,300—predominantly of German origin—were interned during the war, a microscopically small percentage of the total number of potential internees, particularly when measured against the prevailing social climate of "100 percent Americanism."

Geography determined who was interned where: enemy aliens living east of the Mississippi were taken either to Fort Oglethorpe or to Fort McPherson in Georgia. Hot Springs, also located east of the Mississippi in North Carolina, housed only merchant officers and seamen. Enemy aliens living west of the Mississippi were interned at Fort Douglas, three miles east of downtown Salt Lake City at the foot of the Wasatch Mountains. At the height of its use 870 enemy aliens lived there.

One of them was Alvo von Alvensleben, whom I have chosen as the subject for a case study of the problems of the internment of German enemy aliens in the United States. Alvensleben was by no definition a typical internee; rather, he was a member of what could be called the "ethnic elite." These had made themselves conspicuous to surveillance through their education, their families, and often their wealth as well.

Alvo von Alvensleben—his complete name was Gustav Konstantin Alvo von Alvensleben—was born in 1879 in Neugattersleben, near Magdeburg. The estate of Alvensleben had been in the family's possession for several centuries, and the family had been closely tied with emperors and kings; the von Alvensleben house played a significant role in German history from the twelfth century on. At the age of twelve, Alvo attended the *Kadettenanstalt* ("cadet school"), leaving it at the age of nineteen to become a lieutenant in a rifle battalion stationed in Berlin. The many opportunities for diversion in this attractive metropolis along with Alvensleben's extravagant lifestyle soon landed him deeply in debt. His father, Werner Alvo von Alvensleben, gave him the choice of either being disgraced or resigning from the army. Alvo chose the latter, following his father's wish that he seek his fortune in the Americas. Alvo went in 1904 to El Salvador, where his brother owned a coffee plantation, but did not linger there long, traveling on to Vancouver, where he arrived later in 1904 almost penniless. For a short time he worked as a common laborer in Seattle, eventually becoming a fisherman with his own small boat. During the real estate boom then taking place in British Columbia and Washington State he became relatively prosperous through intelligent buying and selling. By means of newspaper advertisements in German papers he managed to attract German investors to the potential for profits in British Columbia. Alvensleben traveled to Germany several times to enlist investors—the largest flow of capital into British Columbia during that period—including such noted persons as Field Marshal von Mackensen, Reich Chancellor von Bethmann-Hollweg, Bertha Krupp, and even Kaiser Wilhelm II. Through his extraordinarily successful management, Alvo rapidly rose to the highest circles in Vancouver. He managed investments totaling $8 million in wood, coal, and land. He lived in one of the largest houses in the town with his Canadian wife, Edith May Westcott, whom he married in 1908, and their three children.[11]

The war broke out while Alvensleben was on a trip to Germany in 1914. Although he had been an officer in the German army from 1899 to 1904, he had been mustered out without taking the usual commission in the reserves because his residence overseas made it impossible for him to fulfill the duties. For this reason Alvensleben was not required to enter German military service at the outbreak of the war.

Ignorance of this fact later disturbed the Canadian as well as the American press. An officer who left his country at the start of a war, if not a spy, certainly seemed suspicious. So, in August 1914 Alvensleben left Germany to resume his business interests. At this time he was in correspondence with the Canadian prime minister, Sir Richard McBride, seeking a Canadian visa to allow him to settle his business investments there. Since his representative in Canada had been interned,[12] Alvensleben did not return there but remained near the border in Seattle, unsuccessfully attempting to prevent the collapse of his Canadian investments from there. In 1916 and 1917 he spent most of his time in Indianapolis and Chicago. When diplomatic relations between Germany and the United States were severed, Alvensleben went to the German embassy to ask Prince Hatzfeld,[13] a diplomat, to issue exit visas for himself and his family to return to Germany. Hatzfeld was unable to fulfill this request, so Alvensleben returned to Seattle.

At this point the American press began to become interested in Alvensleben's affairs, not least of all because of publicity he had received in the Canadian press before and especially after the outbreak of the war. These accounts speculated that he had taken on "other assignments" for the German government overseas, since he had been allowed to leave his country in wartime and had not been inducted as an officer. The American press repeated these and similar rumors. Despite the fact that Alvensleben had voluntary interviews with the district attorney and the Secret Service in Seattle in which he was assured that he had conducted himself properly, he was arrested on August 8, 1917, during a business trip to Portland, with the approval of the Justice Department. He was never informed of the reason for his arrest.[14]

What was the actual motivation for his arrest, and what evidence was there against him? Even before the American declaration of war against Germany, the Justice Department had received a notice that Alvo von Alvensleben should be classified as a dangerous German spy. This information had been provided to the Justice Department by British intelligence, together with reports on other Germans suspected of espionage in America. Alvensleben appeared, remarkably enough, at the top of the list.[15] Naturally he was predestined to be included in any surveillance operation of the Military Intelligence Division (MID), the Bureau of Investigation, and the American Protective League—an organization of 250,000 self-appointed volunteers doing surveillance for the Justice Department.[16] His ties to the German imperial house through his father, Werner Alvo von Alvensleben, awakened suspicions that his residence in the United States was a center of secret operations. The telephone conversations of Ernst Leybold, a business partner of Alvensleben, began to be tapped in May 1917.[17] Alvensleben's mail was under surveillance, and when he stayed in Chicago on a business trip his bags were taken to the Bureau of Investigation office there and searched. None of these investigations provided any evidence that he was involved in espionage.[18]

So clear evidence was lacking. Despite this, high officials were convinced that Alvensleben had to be interned. A statement by the U.S. attorney for the western district of Washington is particularly informative about the motivation behind Alvensleben's internment and the whole complex of problems about enemy aliens. In a message to the attorney general he recommended that Alvensleben and such acquaintances as Ernst Leybold be interned, even if no evidence against them emerged, since "the local atmosphere would be improved rather than hurt by the internment of these men."[19] When the U.S. marshal in Tacoma, Washington, hesitated to arrest a "man of family, with acquaintance and prominence" such as Alvensleben without direct proof, he still followed the recommendations of the MID and approved internment, even if only on the grounds that Alvensleben had not obtained the necessary permit to be in areas closed to enemy aliens.[20] A significant, but unstated, factor was that publicity about Alvensleben had forced the Justice Department to demonstrate to the public an official response in proportion to the individual's notoriety.

Following Alvensleben's arrest in Portland he spent two nights in the city jail and was escorted during the day by a marshal. Then he was taken back to Seattle, and from there he was brought to Fort Douglas on August 13.[21] In Portland, Alvensleben had attempted to inform dinner acquaintances about his internment. The waiter to whom he gave the names happened to be a member of the American Protective League and passed information at once to the district attorney.[22]

What was the appearance of the internment camp Alvensleben entered in August together with his business partners Hans Cron, Georg Schloetelberg, and Ernst Leybold? What internees were already there? Fort Douglas had been officially declared an internment camp on May 3, 1917, with Col. Arthur Williams named as camp commandant. The camp consisted of fifty buildings on an area of fifteen acres. The first internees arrived in June. The *Salt Lake Tribune* described the delivery of about three hundred "enemy German prisoners" on June 10, 1917, as a great spectacle without equal in Salt Lake City. The word of the day was "See the Germans!" and thousands of curious citizens ran to the streets to view "Teutons" in the flesh.[23] These men were the crew of the SMS *Cormoran*, which had been blown up by its captain to avoid impending seizure. Colonel Williams declared to the press on this occasion that he proposed "to make the Third War Prison barracks at Fort Douglas the cleanest, most sanitary and best regulated prison camp in the United States."[24]

Unfortunately, the last of Williams's proposals was not put into practice, since the camp more often resembled a combat zone than an internment camp. More prisoners soon arrived, including the balance of the *Cormoran*'s crew as well as the first true enemy aliens, including Baron von Elpons, who was supposedly a member of a pro-German organization on the Pacific coast.[25] At the start of August there were fourteen enemy aliens in the camp, including such later opponents of Alvensleben as Dr. William Othmer, a jurist and former "junior judge of the Prussian Supreme Court,"[26] and Julius Knispel, a respected attorney from the Portland area. At first both groups—prisoners of war and enemy aliens—were kept together on the grounds of the internment camp. The crew of the *Cormoran* had a status different from the civilian enemy aliens, and they claimed certain privileges; they received new clothing (uniforms), while the enemy aliens had to keep wearing what they had owned on their arrival in camp. The camp administration resolved these conflicts by dividing the two groups with barbed wire at the beginning of August. Henceforth the camp consisted of two separate units, with the military prisoners able to use the sports facilities on their side that were not available to the enemy aliens. This led to protests and tension between the enemy aliens and the guards, who obviously favored the military prisoners.[27] Cursing and humiliation by the guards were routine and helped to poison the atmosphere of the camp. This was the situation Alvensleben encountered on his arrival at Fort Douglas, where he was placed with about thirty other enemy aliens.

His arrival in the camp attracted considerable attention in the American press. In an article with the headline "German Lieutenant was Kaiser's Financial Agent" and decorated with a large picture of Alvensleben, the *Salt Lake Tribune* reported: "Von Alvensleben is a typical officer of the Prussian type, highly educated, polished in manner and with the upright carriage that denotes years of service in the army. . . . Canadian government officials declare they have positive information showing that German machinery was set to work before the war to make von Alvensleben governor of British Columbia."[28] It was true that Alvensleben corresponded at least in appearance with the stereotype of a Prussian officer. The last assertion concerning a role as governor in a German occupation of Canada—without any basis in fact—appeared frequently in the materials of the MID and the Bureau of Investigation.[29] On the German side, there had certainly been discussions about attacking Canadian territory from the state of Washington. The background of these plans was Berlin's fear that Japan could transport troops to Europe via Canada.[30] Alvensleben's involvement in or knowledge of such plans has never been proved.

Soon after his arrival in the internment camp, Alvensleben wrote the Swiss legation in Washington, which had taken over the representation of German affairs there since the American entry into the war. The Swiss legation would receive a flood of letters during Alvensleben's internment. His first message exemplified the concerns of many internees. How could the economic support of the families left behind be guaranteed once their chief supporter was interned? In the case of Alvensleben, his arrest left a family, consisting of a wife and three children in Seattle, without support.

Another interesting aspect of this letter is that Alvensleben claimed his rights under the Prussian-American treaty of 1785 (revised in 1799 and 1828). From the time of the ratification of the Treaty of Amity and Commerce between Prussia and the United States, still in effect at the outbreak of World War I, there existed special regulations in the event of a conflict between Prussia (or the German Empire, its legal successor) and the United States. The relevant passage on the treatment of foreign civilians (Article 23) provided that merchants should be permitted to remain for nine months in the enemy's country to finish up their remaining business. According to the agreement, the parties to the treaty had the right to name a representative in the other country who could concern himself with the well-being of all internees and who would have the right to visit them regularly and inspect the camps. After the American declaration of war this treaty was continually mentioned in the German-American press and became very familiar to Germans in the United States.[31] In his letter to the Swiss legation, Alvensleben also asked that his father be informed of his internment.[32] A few days later he made the same request of the attorney general in Washington, D.C., and included these interesting assertions: "If I do not clear myself entirely, I am entitled to be sentenced to something more severe than internment in a detention camp. If I *do* clear myself of every suspiscon [*sic*], internment singles me out necessary [*sic*] from thousands of Germans to whom the privileges as set out in the President's proclamation of April 6th, 1917, are freeley [*sic*] extended."[33] Alvensleben was justified in referring to a situation that applied to most of the other enemy aliens: they seldom were informed by the Justice Department of the reasons for their internment, which made defense and justification impossible.

Internment and the rumors that circulated on the grounds for imprisonment naturally had consequences for family members, and in the anti-German climate they often became as much the targets of suspicion as the internees. Alvensleben's Canadian wife reported to him the feelings in their neighborhood in Seattle after his internment: "Two fool women . . . seem to be making themselves busy during my absence in telling the neighborhood generally that in their opinion I am just as much a spy as you are supposed to be! Isn't it perfectly disgusting! There is no end to it"[34] She received both moral and financial support from her German neighbors, however, and German-born merchants extended her credit during this difficult time.[35]

In the middle of September 1917 almost two hundred crew members of the ships *Geier* and *Locksun* arrived at Fort Douglas,[36] and an increased number of German-speaking members of the leftist Industrial Workers of the World (called IWWs or Wobblies)[37] entered the camp. At this time the administration, now under its new commandant, Col. George Byram, learned of the first escape attempt.

By November 1917, the time of the first inspection by the Swiss embassy, eighty-seven enemy aliens were confined at Fort Douglas. Afterward, Theodor Stempfe, an acquaintance of Alvensleben who was also interned there, wrote with resignation: "The long-desired inspection by the Swiss embassy is over! The newspapers spat out all their poison yesterday morning to greet the commission, and they called us civilians the 'agents of the Kaiser,' the 'German Spys [*sic*]', pelted us with dirt . . . although the commission has nothing at all to do with the question of whether we have been rightfully interned or not. Today, to finish up, the same rude lies!" Afterward a critical memorandum was composed to be sent to the attorney general in Washington, D.C.[38]

The repeated attempts made to escape by digging tunnels were eloquent testimony that conditions in the camp did not invite people to linger. In December the first internees, two members of the IWW managed to escape through such tunnels.[39] There would be many more attempts to escape from this camp. The press was always interested in escapes. For example, the *Seattle Post-Intelligencer* reported in February 1918: "Col. George L. Byram, commandant at the war prison camp, announced today that the seventeenth tunnel which interned Germans had built as a road to liberty had been discovered."[40] On February 2, 1918, the Seattle newspaper reported that a certain Augusta Minnie Dechmann had worked with Alvensleben on plans for "conspiracies" and that Alvensleben had been interned in part to break this connection. The woman herself was arrested because of alleged evidence that she had been preparing for Alvensleben's escape from the internment camp.[41]

At the end of February 1918, Alvensleben was again in the center of camp events. A bomb, obviously made by an internee, was discovered by a guard on the camp grounds. The press, notified of this event with astonishing rapidity, reported it as a plot to kill the camp commandant and his aides.[42] Alvensleben and another internee went to the camp administration to discuss the affair. The commander confirmed that the bomb had presented a real danger and threatened to shoot every tenth internee if anything serious happened in the future.[43] This statement naturally produced a good deal of tension and excitement among the internees. A telegram to the Swiss embassy requesting an investigating committee was signed by a majority of the internees but was not permitted to be sent. A letter by Alvensleben to the embassy on the matter was not held back, but it was accompanied by a letter from Colonel Byram casting doubt on Alvensleben's truthfulness: "His record in both this country and in Germany, as given me by a party who knows it well, is not of such a nature as to justify one in giving much credence to anything he says."[44] It is probable that Byram received the information from Dr. William Othmer, who was serving as an informant and had previously offered his services to the Justice Department.[45] The fact that Othmer was living in a barracks apart from the other prisoners confirmed their suspicions that he was an agent of the camp leadership, creating irritation. Byram wrote: "His [Othmer's] segregation is apparently causing a great deal of uneasiness among certain other prisoners (notably Alvo von Alvensleben). Von Alvensleben is so anxious to see this man that he is going to all sorts of extremes to get himself confined in the building where he is. Both of the men apparently fear that something has come to our knowledge which endangers them."[46] As a result of this incident, as well as the increasing radicalization of internees and the fear of negative influences from the agitation of the IWWs in the camp, the War Department transferred all military prisoners to Fort McPherson.[47]

Alvensleben increasingly came to be seen by the administration as one of the biggest troublemakers in the camp. This evaluation often had serious consequences for him. He passed many days in the so-called "Hindenburg House," the euphemistic term for an isolation cell measuring a mere four by seven feet, in which the prisoner endured indecent hygienic conditions.[48] The names of barracks and "streets" reflected grotesque humor as well: the internees called the main road of the camp Unter den Linden after the main street of Berlin, and a small mustering field was known as Bolsheviki Plaza.[49]

In April 1918 a camp committee was established with Alvensleben as chairman, representing an overwhelming majority of the 335 enemy aliens then in the camp.[50] The creation of this committee must be seen as the internees' answer to two events in the camp. First, a general search of the camp had uncovered handmade weapons among the internees, and the camp leadership feared a violent attempt to escape. A second episode, in which an internee was fired on by a guard, actually precipitated the formation of the committee. The leadership of the camp refused to recognize any such committee, especially with Alvensleben as chairman. It was declared that every individual was responsible for himself and would be punished for giving false information, particularly to the Swiss embassy. Alvensleben was the first to be penalized by this regulation, having written to the embassy complaining of what he saw as the inadequately honorable burial of an internee. He was placed in the Hindenburg House for five days.

Alvensleben's leadership role is astonishing in view of the large number of IWWs in the camp, who could have been expected to choose someone else. There is no doubt, however, that they accepted him as the representative of the internees. Erich Brandeis, a member of the anti-Alvensleben minority and a self-proclaimed pro-American,[51] reported on this in an article in the *New York Sun* entitled "Birds in a Barbed-Wire Cage." It was widely publicized nationwide, and at the head of the article was a short introduction by Brig. Gen. Marlborough Churchill, chief officer of the MID, in which he expressed his belief that the article would "serve a useful purpose." Directly referring to Alvensleben, Brandeis wrote:

> The peer of the camp nobility is the worthless son of a well known family of counts in Prussia. He is looked up to by the other men, or at least most of the other men, with an awe that amounts almost to worship. . . . That this man is really a dangerous enemy is certain; that he had connections with the fatherland which he used against the welfare of the United States is also sure. This son of a count is the chief trouble maker in the camp, and many of the disturbances which occur can be traced directly to him.[52]
>
> . . . Although a typical German aristocrat, with all the arrogance, the snobbishness, the conceit of the breed, he allied himself soon after his arrival with the most turbulent element in the camp, the I.W.W. And, strangely enough, these men, who decry all rights of class and heritage, were glad enough to accept his leadership and under his guidance to be as obstreperous as possible.[53]

Internal social controls were partially suspended under the impact of the shared experience of imprisonment. The guards made it very clear to the prisoners what they thought of them. Curses were used as a matter of routine. Erich Brandeis's interesting comment that Alvo von Alvensleben was totally acceptable to the IWWs, who were radical workers, is another example of how internment relativized social contradictions. The minority in the camp was represented by Brandeis and Othmer, both of whom disliked Alvensleben intensely, not least because of his alleged pro-German orientation and his reputed support for the digging of tunnels.

A report on the camp, composed by intelligence officer Lorenzo D. Browning, reached the MID in Washington, D.C., in August 1918. At the head of the report was a general description of the camp and its 590 enemy aliens, which the author divided into two classes: "the I.W.W. and the Germans." According to this officer, at least some of these enemy aliens were agents of the German Empire. Prisoners were permitted to write four postcards and two letters a month, which were read by the censor before they could leave the camp. Relatives of an internee could visit him once a week for two hours under the control of a guard. The guard personnel had risen to 142. In the last paragraph of this report Browning dealt with the group of internees causing the camp leadership the most concern, to which Alvensleben of course belonged: "About fifty of the worst prisoners in the camp, agitators and trouble makers, have been organized in one company and are kept separate from other prisoners. . . . This does away with a great deal of trouble in the camp."[54] Once again internees "loyal to America" were mentioned, even if not by name, who provided the camp administration with information about other prisoners. Through these informants officials learned of conversations in which plans were laid for setting fire to the camp. Beginning August 1, 1918, all members of the internees' committee, including many IWWs, were placed in a single dormitory separated from the rest of the camp by a double barbed-wire fence and fed on bread and water. These conditions provoked a riot during which several internees were wounded by gunfire.[55]

The abrupt end of the war on November 11, 1918, brought no radical change for the internees. New enemy aliens actually continued to enter the camp, since Wilson's suspension of war regulations did not cover internment. Armistice did not alter the climate in the camp, but there was a change of administration: Col. Emory West was replaced by Lt. Col. Frank L. Graham. Alvensleben's relationship with the camp leadership changed dramatically, as a comment from a Justice Department official shows: "Following a change in the executive officers at Fort Douglas, Alvensleben's relations with the military authorities became much more *cordial*."[56]

In fact, Alvensleben's attitude altered considerably. His complaints lessened, but the intensive correspondence between him and the Justice Department did not decline. His letters to the attorney general contained some remarkable analyses of the times and an objective vision that extended far beyond his own fate. Questions covered included national loyalty, the international treatment of "enemy aliens," and the American press in time of war. Here is one example among many:

> It has served your purpose to use me—just as you have used thousands of my countrymen—as an apparent object-lesson of German intrigue. You arrested and gave no reasons, the press did the rest. It vilified, exaggerated, invented, insinuated, in short it did the dirty work and you remain "The Department of justice." Your part was to appear lenient, just, broadminded, liberal—the press was vindictive, unscrupulous, sensational, untrue and to use your own words: "Your department was not aware of any means at your disposal to control public opinion." The alien enemy was indeed between these two levers. If perfection per se is to be applauded; excellently done; if an excuse is wanted something along the lines of the old Jesuit motto: "Omnia in majorem Dei gloriam" might do. Possibly! But is the process to be continued?
>
> The period of general reconstruction is so vital and necessary for the whole world, [it] can spare the effort of no man; it demands bigger efforts by the individuals of every nation to co-operate and rebuild, than those which were ever put forward in the past years to dislocate and destroy.[57]

The camp continued operating until April 1920. The release of the internees proceeded very slowly, in part because of the requirement of the Justice Department that only those internees be released who had a job ready for them. This was, of course, extremely difficult in postwar conditions with an overcrowded labor market. Also, the "Red Scare," which began in 1919, did its bit to keep "dangerous radicals" in custody for as long as possible. This demonstrated clearly the connection between xenophobia and the fear of radicals, as the administration shifted its attacks against an "international German conspiracy" to an "international communist conspiracy."[58]

When Sen. Reed Smoot of Utah visited the camp in March 1919 his comments on the internees appeared the next day in the *Salt Lake Tribune*; he described them as "a bunch of criminals of the worst kind, men who would bring misery, disaster and trouble wherever they went."[59] Despite this extremely negative assessment and the efforts of Senator Smoot to convince the attorney general to deport as many of these "criminals" as possible, 200 internees were released in April 1919.[60] Of the 791 enemy aliens in Fort Douglas, more than half (412) were paroled, perhaps a third (271) were repatriated, and only 7 were deported, ignoring the recommendation of the attorney general that undesirable "enemy aliens" should be deported en masse.[61] The alien deportation bill passed by Congress in May 1920 came a month too late for the internees, some of whom would probably have been deported if it had been in force before their release.

It is remarkable that Alvensleben was not among those deported; rather he was released and permanently paroled in March 1920 after having spent two and a half years in the Fort Douglas camp. In July 1919 he said he intended to leave the United States immediately after release, perhaps to go to Mexico,[62] but in September 1919 the attorney general informed him that he had no hope for release except for the purpose of repatriation.[63] Then, in February 1920 he indicated that he wished to remain in the United States until his business affairs could be settled.[64] The fact that Alvensleben was not deported demonstrates that the Justice Department had no evidence for expulsion, and it also shows that Alvensleben, despite the length and harshness of his treatment during internment, did not wish to be repatriated. After his release the Canadian government rejected his request to return to Canada, since he had been declared an "enemy of the Dominion" after the peace treaty. His total property was confiscated without time limit by the Canadian government. He was only permitted to enter Canada nine years after the conclusion of peace. But by then he had determined to remain in the United States. In 1939 he became an American citizen. In the meantime he had made an attempt at launching an import business (with German wares), requiring several trips to Germany to restore his old financial situation. However, these attempts did not have the desired result.[65] Alvensleben saw the emergence of fascism in Germany as a misfortune, and he observed the acts of Adolf Hitler with horror. After the Second World War he invested for a time in a gold mine but without large-scale success. Alvo von Alvensleben died in Seattle in 1965.

Since the conviction of British intelligence that Alvo von Alensleben was a spy was probably wrong,[66] and since the authorities would have brought him to trial as a spy if there had been substantial evidence (as was the case with about 150 enemy aliens),[67] the actual grounds for his internment have to be seen in the overwhelmingly anti-German mentality of the time. Alvensleben's direct ties to the German imperial house had to provoke reaction from the public, since the newspapers had taken to portraying the lurid deeds of the child-murdering "Hun-Kaiser." The sabotage and spying of the German *Geheimdienst* contributed as well by enveloping all German-born, especially noncitizen enemy aliens, with grave distrust, since the concept itself suggested that individuals were enemies.

The press helped elevate anxiety through exaggerated accounts, which led to hysteria and finally a crusade against everything German. During the war the Justice Department was bombarded with proposals to intern all enemy aliens in the United States or to make them more visible, such as through the wearing of armbands.[68]

The xenophobia, which is always an aspect of the mobilization of patriotism, achieved a life of its own and threatened to get beyond the control of the authorities. Although Alvensleben continued to recall his time of internment for the rest of his life, he harbored no resentment toward the country whose citizen he had become. Instead, he rationalized his fate, insofar as he responded to his children in later years when they asked him about the reason for his internment and his unjust treatment during that time: "It was just the hysteria which emerges in every war and under which individuals must suffer."[69]

NOTES

Originally published in the *Utah Historical Quarterly* 58 (Fall 1990): 388–405.

1. From the end of 1917 Hoover worked in the Alien Enemy Bureau; see Richard Gid Powers, *Secrecy and Power: The Life of J. Edgar Hoover* (New York: The Free Press, 1987), 36–55.
2. See most recently Jules Witcover, *Sabotage at Black Tom: Imperial Germany's Secret War in America, 1914–1917* (Chapel Hill, NC: Algonquin Books, 1989); Reinhard R. Doerries, *Imperial Challenge: Ambassador Count Bernstorff and German-American Relations, 1908–1917* (Chapel Hill: The University of North Carolina Press, 1989), 188–89, 197; and Doerries, "The Politics of Irresponsibility: Imperial Germany's Defiance of United States Neutrality during World War I," in Hans L. Trefousse, ed., *Germany and America: Essays on Problems of International Relations and Immigration* (New York: Brooklyn College Press, 1980), 3–20.
3. Persons from Austria-Hungary were included in this definition following the United States' declaration of war against that state in December 1917, and women were included in early 1918.
4. For the first twelve enemy alien regulations, see *U.S. Attorney General: Annual Reports, 1917* (Washington, D.C.: Government Printing Office, 1917), 57–59; for the November regulations, see *New York Times*, November 20, 1917.
5. Exceptions are William Barnes Glidden, "Casualties of Caution: Alien Enemies in America" (PhD diss., University of Illinois at Urbana-Champaign, 1970), and Raymond Kelly Cunningham Jr., "Internment, 1917–1920: A History of the Prison Camp at Fort Douglas, Utah, and the Treatment of Enemy Aliens in the Western United States" (master's thesis, University of Utah, 1976).
6. On the Bureau of Investigation, see David Williams, "The Bureau of Investigation and Its Critics, 1919–1921: The Origins of Federal Political Surveillance," *Journal of American History* 68 (1981): 560–79. The "Old German Files," which are part of the "Investigative Case Files of the Bureau of Investigation (1908–22)," Record Group 65 in the National Archives, have been available to researchers for only a brief

time. They consist of almost six hundred microfilm rolls and are an extremely valuable source for researchers interested in the surveillance techniques of the period. On the American Protective League, see Joan M. Jensen, *The Price of Vigilance* (Chicago: Rand McNally, 1968).

7. See, for example, the memorandum to FBI Director Hoover, November 18, 1940, Justice Department, RG 60 (henceforth abbreviated as JD), 9-16-12, Section 20, National Archives.

8. John Higham, *Strangers in the Land* (New Jersey: Rutgers University Press, 1990), chap. 9, 234–63.

9. See what is still the standard treatment of German Americans during the First World War: Frederick C. Luebke, *Bonds of Loyalty: German-Americans and World War I* (De Kalb: Northern Illinois University Press, 1974); Carl Wittke, *German-Americans and the World War with Special Emphasis on Ohio's German-Language Press* (Columbus: Ohio State Archaeological and Historical Society, 1936); Ronald Fernandez, "Getting Germans to Fight Germans: The Americanizers of World War I," *Journal of Ethnic Studies* 9 (1981): 53–68; and most recently John Christine and Sister Wolkerstorfer, *Blanket of Suspicion: The Rejection of German-Americans during World War I* (New York: Associated Faculty Press, 1988). See also works that do not concentrate on German-Americans but portray the spirit of the home front as well as the official reaction to the aliens: Felice A. Bonadio, "The Failure of German Propaganda in the United States," *Mid-America* 41 (1959): 40–57; Paul L. Murphy, *World War I and the Origins of Civil Liberties* (New York, 1979); John D. Stevens, "When the Sedition Laws Were Enforced: Wisconsin in World War I," *WASAL* 58 (1978): 39–60; Steven Vaughn, *Holding Fast the Inner Lines: Democracy, Nationalism, and the Committee on Public Information* (Chapel Hill, NC, 1979).

10. U.S. Bureau of the Census, *Thirteenth Census of the United States: 1910 Population* (1913), 1: 875–79.

11. Telephone interview with Gero von Alvensleben, son of Alvo von Alvensleben, June 26, 1989; telephone interview with Margaret Newcomb, nee von Alvensleben, June 28, 1989; JD, 9-16-12 between 33 and 35, National Archives; Ingrid E. Laue, "Gustav Konstantin Alvo von Alvensleben (1879–1965) Ein Lebensbild," *German-Canadian Yearbook* 5 (1979): 162–63; Udo von Alvenseben-Wittenmoor, *Alvenslebensche Burgen und Landsitze* (Dortmund, Germany, 1960), 48.

12. For internment camps in Canada in the First World War, see Desmond Morton, "Sir Richard Otter and Internment Operations in

Canada during the First World War," *Canadian Historical Review* 55 (1974): 32–58.

13. Prince Hermann Trachtenberg-Hatzfeld, second counselor of the German Embassy.

14. Military Intelligence Division (War Department General Staff), Record Group 165 (henceforth abbreviated MID), 9140-1421-6, August 9, 1917, National Archives.

15. Investigative Case Files of the Bureau of Investigation, 1908-22 (henceforth abbreviated BI), British suspect list, reel 877, 9-19-1880-0, National Archives. The British consul in Chicago gave this list to the local chief of the Bureau of Investigation, who passed it several days later to the director of the Bureau of Investigation, A. Bruce Bielaski, in Washington, D.C.

16. On the ties of the American Protective League to the Justice Department, see Jensen, *The Price of Vigilance.* For a description of the holdings of the Justice Department and the Immigration and Naturalization Service concerning enemy aliens, see Mary Ronan, "Watching and Warning: Reactions of the Department of Justice and Immigration and Naturalization Service to World War I" (paper delivered at the eighty-second annual meeting of the Organization of American Historians, April 7, 1989).

17. August 11, 1917, MID, 9140-1421-7.

18. Office of U.S. Attorney for the Western District of Washington, Seattle, to the Attorney General, Washington, D.C., MID (RG 165), 9771-23-1103 and 9140-1421.

19. July 6, 1917, MID, 9140-1421-45, National Archives. In the attorney general's reply, which included the order for arrest, he confirmed this evaluation: "his [Alvensleben's] presence in our district at large is to the danger of the public peace and safety of the United States." Attorney General to U.S. Attorney, Western District, August 8, 1917, JD, 9-16-12-33-6.

20. U.S. Marshal, Western District of Washington, Tacoma, to the Attorney General, July 28, 1917, JD, 9-16-12-33-6.

21. *Salt Lake Tribune*, August 14, 1917. See Alvensleben to the Legation of Switzerland, September 11, 1917, MID, 9140-1421-48.

22. August 18, 1917, MID, 9140-1421-12.

23. *Salt Lake Tribune*, June 11, 1917, 14.

24. Ibid.

25. *Salt Lake Tribune*, June 21, 1917, 1, 14.

26. Memo for Colonel Van Deman referring to May 18, 1918, July 5, 1919, MID, 10972-5-24.

27. Glidden, "Casualties of Caution," 329–30.

28. *Salt Lake Tribune*, August 14, 1917, 16.

29. See, for example, the memorandum of the Attorney for the Western District of Washington, Seattle, to the Attorney General, MID, 9140-1421-45, National Archives: "Canadian authorities at Vancouver believe that von Alvensleben was already slated in German military circles as the governor of British Columbia when the time should come that that section fell under the control of the German government."

30. Doerries, *Imperial Challenge*, 205.

31. See, for example, the *New Yorker Staatszeitung*, May 9, 1917, 1. For the complete text of the treaty, see the trilingual edition. *The Treaty of Amity of 1785 between His Majesty the King of Prussia and the United States of America*, ed. Karl J. Arndt (Munich: Heinz Moos Verlag, 1977).

32. August 21, 1917, MID, 9140-1421-46.

33. August 24, 1917, MID, 9140-1421-47.

34. Edith von Alvensleben to Alvo von Alvensleben, April 1, 1918, in War Department, Records of the Adjutant General's Office, RG 407 (henceforth abbreviated as WD), Box 1, Alvensleben file.

35. Telephone interview with Margaret Newcomb, nee von Alvensleben, June 28, 1989.

36. *Salt Lake Tribune*, September 14, 1917, 16.

37. On the Industrial Workers of the World, see Melvyn Dubovsky, *We Shall Be All: A History of the Industrial Workers of the World* (Chicago: Quadrangle Books, 1969).

38. Theodor Stempfe to his wife, November 21, 1917, MID, 9140-1421-26, National Archives.

39. On Kurt G. Wilkens, one of the escapees, see David G. Wageman, "'Rausch Mit': The I. W. W. in Nebraska during World War I," in Joseph R. Conlin, ed., *At the Point of Production: The Local History of the I.W.W.* (Westport, CT: Greenwood Press, 1981), 124–25.

40. *Seattle Post-Intelligencer*, February 24, 1918, MID, 9771-23-1103.

41. Ibid.

42. *Salt Lake Tribune*, February 24, 1918, 1.

43. Cunningham, "Internment," 117.

44. Ibid, 120.

45. Colonel Byram to the Adjutant General, January 9, 1918, RG 165, MID, 10972-5-17, on Dr. William Othmer and his function as a spy, especially concerning Alvensleben.

46. Dr. Othmer: "I did my best to discover a bomb plot against his life (Col Byram) in the Camp," referring to September 1918, July 5, 1919, MID 10972-5-49.

47. Glidden, "Casualties of Caution," 330.
48. Alvesleben to Swiss Legation, June 1, 1919, RG 165, MID 10972-20, "I had to spend altogether eleven days in the guardhouse under humiliating conditions."
49. Erich Brandeis, "'Little Prussia' in an Internment Camp," *American Law Review* 53 (1919): 107–8.
50. WD, Box 184, Alvensleben file.
51. Erich Brandeis came to the United States in 1908 to avoid military service in Germany. After the First World War he went to New York and became a respected journalist there. Among other things, he published a biography of Roosevelt, *Franklin D. Roosevelt, the Man* (New York: American Offset Corporation, 1936).
52. Brandeis's article appeared in the *New York Sun*, then reprinted in the *American Law Review* 53 (1919): 107–14.
53. Ibid., 110. After reading this article, Alvensleben complained to the attorney general that his name had been injured by direct reference even without being given. He objected particularly to Churchill's comments; Alvensleben to Attorney General, March 27, 1919, JD, 9-16-12-33-28.
54. August 1, 1918, MID, 10972-7-2.
55. Cunningham, "Internment," 142–43.
56. December 20, 1918, JD, 9-16-12-33, emphasis in original.
57. Alvensleben to Attorney General, May 2, 1919, JD, 9-16-12-33-30.
58. Glidden, "Casualties of Caution," 390–91.
59. Cited in Alvensleben to Attorney General, April 10, 1919, JD, 9-16-12-33-29.
60. Cunningham, "Internment," 163.
61. List of internees with information on their release, repatriation, and deportation in WD, Box 184; on the attorney general's attitude, see Glidden, "Casualties of Caution," 369, 397.
62. Alvensleben to Attorney General, July 23, 1919, RG 407, Box 184, Alvensleben file.
63. Attorney General to Alvensleben, September 8, 1919, RG 407, Box 184, Alvensleben file.
64. Memorandum for Mr. Garvan, February 3, 1920, JD, 9-16-12-33-41.
65. Laue, "Alvo von Alvensleben," 170–71.
66. My research in the relevant archives of the German Foreign Office in Bonn (Politisches Archiv, Auswartiges Amt, Bonn) has discovered no information about any sort of official German activities by Alvensleben.
67. Jensen, *The Price of Vigilance*, 160–61.

68. See, for example, Edward Yates to Attorney General, November 14, 1917, JD, 9-16-12-814. An employee of the Macbeth Evans Glass Company made the following recommendation to the Attorney General: "make all alien enemies and those Americans upon whom justified suspicion of disloyalty rests wear on one or both arms of outer garment a distinctive arm band, say of white cloth. Failure to comply with order would, of course, carry with it the strictest sort of punishment, nothing less than internment at hard labor at any rate" (JD, 9-16-12-689).

69. Telephone interview with Gero von Alvensleben, June 26, 1989, and with Margaret Newcomb, nee von Alvensleben, June 28, 1989.

A crowd gathers at the Midvale train station for a patriotic rally. Used by permission, Utah State Historical Society, all rights reserved.

A crowd in Midvale listens to a speaker promote the sale of war bonds. Flags representing Midvale's ethnic communities can be seen alongside the American flag. Used by permission, Utah State Historical Society, all rights reserved.

This series of photographs show the Red Cross Fundraising Parade in Salt Lake City on May 21, 1918. Businesses and schools closed for the afternoon to allow all to participate in what the *Salt Lake Tribune* headlined as "Salt Lake's Red Cross Pageant Greatest in History of the City." Used by permission, Utah State Historical Society, all rights reserved.

Conserving, sharing, and rationing were important in the civilian war effort, as depicted by this poster. Used by permission, Utah State Historical Society, all rights reserved.

Patriotic posters were widely used to promote the purchase of government bonds. Used by permission, Utah State Historical Society, all rights reserved.

The German prisoner of war compound at Fort Douglas housed a maximum of 870 prisoners during the war. It was one of three camps in the United States—the only one west of the Mississippi River—in which military and civilian enemy prisoners were interred. Used by permission, Utah State Historical Society, all rights reserved.

German naval prisoners of war, captured in Pacific ports after the war began, were brought to Fort Douglas in 1917. Used by permission, Utah State Historical Society, all rights reserved.

The *Salt Lake Herald* announces the end of the Great War on November 11, 1918. Utah Digital Newspapers, Marriott Library, University of Utah.

The November 12, 1918, edition of the *Salt Lake Tribune* edition reports on the Armistice Day celebration in downtown Salt Lake City. Utah Digital Newspapers, Marriott Library, University of Utah.

The news of the Armistice brought thousands of Utahns to downtown Salt Lake City on November 11, 1918. Used by permission, Utah State Historical Society, all rights reserved.

Red Cross volunteers march along Vernal's Main Street during a patriotic parade in 1918. Uintah County Library, Regional History Center.

Utah veterans of the Great War ride aboard a tank during a welcome home parade in Ogden in 1919. Used by permission, Utah State Historical Society, all rights reserved.

The funeral march for James Foy, the first Moab casualty of World War I, proceeds down 400 East to the Moab cemetery. Foy died of pneumonia at a training camp in the East. Used by permission, Utah State Historical Society, all rights reserved.

General Jack Pershing, commander of the American forces in Europe during World War I, leaving Salt Lake City's Hotel Utah on January 16, 1920, for the University of Utah and Fort Douglas. Used by permission, Utah State Historical Society, all rights reserved.

The Doughboy Monument, erected in downtown Vernal in 1925, is now located on the grounds of the Uintah County Courthouse. Veterans from left to right: Isabrand Sander, 48th U.S. Artillery, World War I; Thomas W. O'Donnell, Teddy's Rough Riders, Spanish-American War; Dr. Harvey Coe Hullinger, age 101 years, member of the 1862 Lot Smith Company during the Civil War; Daniel H. Minick, age 85, member of the 134th Pennsylvania Volunteer Infantry, 1861; Charles W. Hanna, 12th U.S. Infantry, Spanish-American War; and George R. Goodrich, Machine Gun Company, 5th U.S. Marines, Second Division, World War I. Uintah County Library, Regional History Center.

Utahns participate in a memorial service for fallen Utah soldiers of World War I, held at Memory Grove Park, City Creek Canyon, Salt Lake City. Special Collections, J. Willard Marriott Library, University of Utah.

This monument, placed by Utah's German-American community in May 1933, commemorates the German prisoners of war who died while in captivity at Fort Douglas and who are buried in the fort's historic cemetery. Photo by Allan Kent Powell.

11

GOSIUTE-SHOSHONE DRAFT RESISTANCE, 1917–18

DAVID L. WOOD

The passage of the Selective Service Act of 1917 extended the reach of the federal government into every city, village, farmstead, and mining camp in the United States, and even to the remote Gosiute reservation in the Deep Creek Mountains of western Utah. Registration, induction, and fighting a foreign war far from their homeland were strange and unsettling concepts for many Americans. For a group of young Gosiutes and Shoshones—who had no knowledge of faraway Europe, the reasons for war, and the process of the draft—the idea of forced registration seemed to be just one more action against a people who had suffered decades of abuse and neglect at the hands of those now demanding their surrender to military service. Their resistance and the perceived threat to the war effort resulted in the sending of a detachment of soldiers from Fort Douglas to punish and arrest those who had violated the new federal law. The story of this challenge and encounter is recounted in the following chapter.

The desert of west-central Utah is a long way from the Meuse River and the Argonne Forest, yet, improbable as it may seem, it briefly became a theater of action during World War I. In this instance, however, there were no trenches or gas attacks, and American doughboys did not face the steel-helmeted troops of Kaiser Wilhelm II. Instead, in a unique wartime operation, khaki-clad soldiers marched against a small band of Gosiute Indian draft resisters whose recalcitrance was intimately linked with events among the Shoshone. This is not to say that these were the only Indians who opposed conscription. Utes, Navajos, and Mission Indians (to name a few) expressed similar sentiments. But though several agents threatened to call in troops, soldiers were actually employed only against the Gosiute—a people Mark Twain once called "the wretchedest type of mankind I have ever seen."[1]

The Selective Service Act of May 18, 1917, applied to Indians and non-Indians alike in that it required the registration of all male residents of the United States between the ages of twenty-one and thirty-one. (Later legislation extended the age limits to include men from eighteen to forty-five.) The provost marshal general assigned the states the responsibility for enrolling most eligibles, including Indians living on the public domain, but he gave the commissioner of Indian affairs the task of registering reservation Indians. The commissioner established a draft board at each agency. He instructed the superintendents to handle the enrollment "diplomatically but firmly"; they should explain the law to all men within the age limits, emphasizing that enrollment did not necessarily mean they would be conscripted since noncitizen Indians were exempt.[2]

Washington declared that Indians were citizens (1) if they had received a trust patent under the Dawes Act prior to May 8, 1906; (2) if they had received a fee patent for an allotment acquired subsequent to May 8, 1906; (3) if they "lived separate and apart from any tribe" and had "adopted the habits of civilized life"; (4) if they were minors at the time their parents became citizens or were born to citizen parents; or, (5) by special act of Congress (as in the case of the "Five Civilized Tribes" of Oklahoma).[3]

When the Shoshones at Fort Hall, Idaho, learned their sons must register, "a thousand or more" gathered in council. Garfield Pocatello and others advised the young men not to enroll. Later, the tribesmen reportedly bought "between thirty and forty rifles" and "a goodly quantity of ammunition." Then, some fifty of them fled to the hills. This potentially explosive situation was settled amicably. In another council, A. W. Fisher, "an old timer and great friend of the Indians," explained that registration was "more on the order of a census than anything" and informed the tribesmen of their noncitizen exemption. Reassured, the chiefs pledged their cooperation, requested a time extension, and reassembled their youth. One hundred and six eligibles registered on June 5; by the end of the month, twenty more had enrolled. Only fourteen remained unaccounted for.[4]

Meanwhile, two Fort Hall Indians had visited Box Elder County, Utah. About a dozen tribesmen living there refused to register. The local sheriff arrested them and all were enrolled.[5]

Events on the Gosiute reservation at Deep Creek were more complicated. Correspondence, described by Superintendent Amos R. Frank as "treasonable," passed between Annies Tommy, "reputed head of the Goshute Tribe"; Willie Ottogary, an "unusually intelligent and scheming Indian" from Box Elder County; Jacob Browning, the interpreter at Fort Hall; and Moody, a resident of Skull Valley. Their letters, said the superintendent, condemned President Woodrow Wilson for leading the nation into war and opposed Indian participation. Furthermore, Ottogary and Tommy traveled all over the region "spreading discontent wherever they went." Frank recommended that they be arrested. When nothing happened, he gathered the Gosiutes together and, with the help of his interpreter Jim Clover, explained the draft law to them. All the eligible men then left the reservation for Nevada "under the pretense to shear sheep," while Annies Tommy went in search of Willie Ottogary. No Gosiutes registered.[6]

G. J. Knapp, deputy special officer for the suppression of the liquor traffic, saw Tommy and Ottogary en route to Deep Creek the day after registration day.[7] Knowing Superintendent Frank anticipated trouble if Ottogary came to the reservation, Knapp followed the Indians. Should trouble arise he would be on hand to assist the superintendent. Along the way Knapp boasted openly that he was going to arrest some bad Gosiutes. Not surprisingly, Ottogary and Tommy, who had learned of his coming, stopped him at the reservation gate. The Indians were "very insulting," but "I laid the law down to them," the deputy reported. Before this exchange got out of control, Superintendent Frank invited Knapp into the agency office. Ottogary and Tommy protested. Frank said they were insolent and arrogant, insisting that the Gosiutes "would not register and could not be made to register."

Forty Gosiute men held a lengthy council. The superintendent and his wife were summoned, and the Indians reiterated their determination not to register. The tribesmen then sent for Knapp, allegedly threatening to "soon fix him."[8] According to the deputy, "Mrs. Frank came running out of the council place" and said the Indians had resolved to force him off the reservation. (The Indians later denied this.) Knapp, in turn, "decided that if there was to be violence, it might as well be had right then." He entered the room "with a rush," Frank recalled, "and immediately proceeded to place Ottogary and Tomy [*sic*] under arrest. . . . Certain of the Indians then seized, overpowered and disarmed him." Frank ordered the tribesmen to release Knapp. They did, but when he tried to leave in the agency wagon, Al Steel, an Indian judge, unhitched the horses and reportedly used "threatening language" in his efforts to prevent Knapp from going. Knapp claimed there was talk of holding him indefinitely and eventually trying him in the Indian court. After an hour of fruitless wrangling, however, he was released.

Before Knapp left Deep Creek he and Frank decided to wire Washington, requesting soldiers to enforce the draft law, but the nearest telephone was at Gold Hill, thirty-two miles away. Fearing the Indians might intercept a written message, Frank signed a blank telegram and gave it to Knapp, who left in the agency wagon with Pon Dugan, a "trustworthy" Indian. Mrs. Frank rode as far as Ibapah to do some "trading." When Dugan returned to the reservation, he was alone, and he bore startling news. Knapp refused to let Mrs. Frank come home as a posse was forming.

Knapp had told residents of Gold Hill that the Gosiutes had "hog-tied" the Franks and "were . . . liable to kill them and burn the buildings." His telegram to Washington contained a similar statement. When two Indians tried to wire their version of events, the deputy arrested them. At Deep Creek, meanwhile, great excitement prevailed. The Gosiutes armed themselves, stationed lookouts, and awaited battle. They also urged Superintendent Frank to turn the posse away.

An advance party arrived first: Mrs. Frank; Mr. and Mrs. George D. Felt of Ibapah; Joe Sims, who had "lived among the Indians most of his life"; F. W. Ferris, "a very diplomatic and able man"; and an unidentified person. They had preceded the posse, said Frank, to ascertain "the real situation and to get myself and family out before the posse entered." They said seventy-five armed citizens were just five miles away and would attack if the vanguard "failed to return by midnight." When Frank learned that Sims spoke Gosiute "fluently," he assembled the Indian leaders. Sims, however, was unable to calm them, and the tribesmen warned that if the imprisoned messengers were not released by the following evening, the Indian women would make "much trouble." Sims agreed to return the captives, being determined to secure their release "by force if necessary." When he and his companions departed, Frank and his family refused to go with them.

Sims reported the results of his mission to Knapp, urging that the posse not proceed further until the Indian prisoners were released and the Franks' safety assured. Knapp freed the captives. Sims returned them to Deep Creek and "received a most hearty appreciation" from the Gosiutes, who reputedly "agreed to register for the Selective Draft and go as soldiers if called." They also agreed to surrender Willie Ottogary but refused to give up Annies Tommy. Since Knapp seemed determined to arrest both Indians, Sims again tried unsuccessfully to persuade Frank to leave his post. His refusal averted a confrontation that almost certainly would have resulted in bloodshed. Knapp disbanded the posse "in the interest of peace," and left the region. Frank, presumably as a conciliatory gesture, gave certain "old and needy"

Gosiutes twenty-five dollars, but he refused to pay other tribesmen for roadwork, even when Ottogary allegedly threatened him.

Meanwhile, the commissioner of Indian affairs sent special agent L. A. Dorrington to investigate the Gosiute disturbance. Dorrington discovered Ottogary posting notices announcing that the tribesmen were not "on the warpath." Nevertheless, he found the Indian to be "insolent and grosely [*sic*] insulting . . . , disrespectful . . . , dictatorial and haughty," threatening "trouble and plenty of it."

The same day, Superintendent Frank sent a telegram to Washington warning that conditions among the Gosiutes had "assumed a serious aspect." Fifty Indians had come from Nevada and more were expected momentarily. With white citizens and tribesmen eyeing one another suspiciously, Frank questioned his ability to "prolong the situation very much longer." Ottogary, Tommy, and eighteen others must be arrested, he said, before another attempt was made to register the Gosiutes.[9]

Dorrington counseled with the Gosiutes. On the question of registration they remained adamant. The investigator warned them that their recalcitrance would lead to arrest, imprisonment, and a stint in the army. He informed them that the commissioner had extended their enrollment period ten days, and, he told them, as tribal Indians they would not be conscripted. Early in the afternoon of the second day of meetings, Jim Clover, the interpreter, offered to register in what Dorrington described as "a splendid and manly manner." The investigator excused himself and went to get Superintendent Frank.

When Dorrington returned, he found pandemonium: "everybody seemed to be talking." As Frank entered the room, Ottogary reportedly "pointed his finger at him, and . . . stated in a loud and most contemptible manner: 'There he is. We don't want Amos Frank here any longer. We want another superintendent.'" Dorrington claimed that he quickly stepped between Frank and Ottogary, thrust his face into the Indian's, and exclaimed: "Willie Ottogary, you have carried this too far. You cannot make threats of that nature and get away with it. Your bluff is called and from now on you will be treated accordingly."

Ottogary, the investigator remembered, "immediately wilted and his attitude changed at once." Jim Clover was registered and, urged by Tommy and Ottogary, four other youths complied.[10]

Having met defeat, Ottogary left for home, but not before asking Dorrington for a writ of safe passage. The investigator refused, ordering him never to return to Deep Creek. Dorrington opined that Tommy, Ottogary, and Al Steel were guilty of "treasonable conduct" and should be "prosecuted to the fullest extent."

Most of the Gosiute eligibles had registered by the end of June. In mid-July, however, newspapers declared that two Indian draft dodgers had stolen some horses and were menacing white ranchers near Baker, Nevada. After the sheriff of Millard County, Utah, visited the reservation the excitement again died down.[11]

Although the War Department had announced that noncitizen Indians would not be drafted, it had also cautioned that tribesmen must prove their status, and "unless an Indian specifically claimed exemption on the ground of non-citizenship . . . , he waived his right to such exemption." Although some Gosiute registrants explicitly relinquished immunity, others (apparently unwittingly) failed to declare their noncitizenship. After a few of them received orders to appear for physical examination, Annies Tommy rushed to Idaho, where an "Indian Grievance Committee" wired a protest to the Indian Rights Association. When Dr. Joseph H. Peck visited the reservation to examine the draftees, eighty-year-old Antelope Jake told him the boys were out herding sheep, "an activity," the doctor reflected, "that was foreign to a Gosiute's nature and not a very likely story." The old Indian told Peck that the Gosiutes did not understand the war, for they had never seen a German. Germans were a type of white man, the doctor explained, suggesting that Superintendent Frank was probably of that extraction. "Jake brightened up," Peck recalled, volunteering to kill Frank and any other Germans who appeared at Deep Creek. Otherwise white men should fight their own war.[12]

In January 1918 the Western Shoshone superintendent at Owyhee, Nevada, reported "a feeling of perturbation and excitement" among his charges. Inquiry, he said, had revealed that Garfield Pocatello and another man from Fort Hall, Idaho, were holding meetings on the reservation, endeavoring to turn the Indians against the government and the draft. Confronted with these accusations, Pocatello swore that he was merely visiting relatives. He admitted telling them of the Fort Hall "draft riot" but denied trying to incite a local rebellion. He did say, however, that Charles Damon Jr., a Western Shoshone, had visited Fort Hall announcing that Jack Wilson (Wovoka), the Paiute prophet, wanted to see a Shoshone delegation and that $150 had been raised at Fort Hall to pay for the journey (shades of the Ghost Dance and Wounded Knee!). Again, Pocatello denied that he and his companion were on such a mission. A meeting of the Western Shoshone reassured their superintendent; both older Indians and a number of "returned students" pledged to support the government.[13]

Although the Western Shoshone agent called Damon "a young, irresponsible Indian, without influence or following" and scoffed at his story about Wovoka, the agent's reports to Washington probably affected subsequent events among the Gosiute. Coincident with Garfield Pocatello's visit to Nevada, Annies Tommy allegedly urged Indians there not to enlist or answer draft calls, and the Gosiute tribal council sent a letter to Washington demanding that Superintendent Frank be replaced before the end of February.[14] Frank declared that he would leave only if the commissioner so ordered, and, "if necessary, he would arm himself" and face the Indians alone rather than "desert his post."

Again, special agent Dorrington investigated, reporting that the Indians were dead serious and would expel the superintendent with force if necessary. He said the Gosiutes were "absolutely against their men going to war . . . and would rather die on the spot . . . than enlist or submit to draft." Even tribesmen who had heretofore been cooperative, he wrote, were "disrespectful and defiant." The investigator tried to shame the Indians into registering by telling them they were almost alone in their resistance, but Al Steel and John Syme (members of the tribal council) angrily walked out of the meeting, and the entire gathering soon dispersed. Dorrington described the situation as "*bad and will probably not be any better until having been very much worse.*" He recommended that Annies Tommy and other members of the tribal council be arrested and held without bail until the draft question was settled. He further suggested that Superintendent Frank and his family be removed from danger.[15]

The situation soon became more urgent. On February 9 Frank reported that Indians from Nevada were gathering on the reservation. "To preserve order and enforce the selective draft" and "to avoid bloodshed," he believed he would need to call in the sheriff and the posse.[16] Frank, Dorrington, U.S. Attorney William W. Ray, and Marshal Aquila Nebeker met in Salt Lake City and concluded that the situation was "critical." Dorrington filed a complaint, and the marshal obtained a warrant for the arrest of Willie Ottogary, Annies Tommy, and three other Gosiutes.

Fearing the Indians might resist arrest, the officials recommended against sending a civilian posse for them. A posse lacked proper discipline; violence might occur unnecessarily. Instead, they requested fifteen soldiers from Fort Douglas. The army's presence, they reasoned, would prevent bloodshed, would leave no doubt that the United States was acting, and would have a "good effect" on all Indians "inclined to oppose authority."[17]

Superintendent Frank returned to Deep Creek and found that "at least twenty" more Indians had arrived from Nevada. "I do not think they intend to wait until the last of February," he telegraphed, urging that fifteen soldiers would not be enough.[18] Thus, fifty-four made up the expedition.

The soldiers left Salt Lake City on February 19 via special train; at Gold Hill they transferred to private vehicles. With headlamps ablaze, this strangely assorted convoy crossed Clifton Flats and snaked its way into the Deep Creek Mountains, the largest and most powerful car breaking a trail through more than a foot of new-fallen snow. The thermometer registered minus twenty degrees Fahrenheit. About 2:30 a.m., February 20, the expedition arrived at Sheridan's store near Ibapah. The surprised proprietor, when awakened, invited the men inside and built a fire so they could warm up. His wife and daughter prepared food for their unexpected guests. Then the troops awaited dawn.

Superintendent Frank rendezvoused with the expedition before daybreak, and at 6:00 a.m. the force descended upon the Indians. Annies Tommy and two other Gosiutes reputedly "showed fight and intended flight," but within thirty minutes the soldiers had rounded up, disarmed, and questioned about one hundred "restive bucks." Not a shot had been fired.[19]

Marshal Nebeker lectured the assembled captives about conscription. Comparing it to a game of chance, he illustrated the risk involved by flipping a coin and explaining, "heads, my boy go . . . ; tails your boy go." "If it had been explained to us this way at first," one of the Gosiutes remarked, "this trouble would not have come." The marshal detained three young draft evaders (two others had escaped) in addition to Annies Tommy, Al Steel, Jim Straight, and John Syme, who were charged with conspiracy. The rest of the Indians were set free.[20]

That evening, with the expedition safely back in Gold Hill and the prisoners "under heavy guard," citizens and soldiers celebrated. As the evening wore on even the sentries and the Indians joined the festivities. Soon, everyone was "well oiled" with bootleg liquor. Dr. Peck remembered seeing the guards "leaving the hall, their arms around each other's necks, singing 'K-K-K-Katy' at the top of their lungs while their prisoners trailed behind carrying the guns and ammunition belts belonging to their captors." The next day, army and Indians went to Salt Lake City. Simultaneous with events at Deep Creek, Deputy Marshal David Thomas had arrested Willie Ottogary in Tremonton.[21]

After the soldiers left Deep Creek, angry Gosiute women reportedly "made a raid" on the agent's house, "upset everything," threatened to burn the structure and kill Jim Clover (whom Frank had left in charge), and carried off some foodstuffs; the superintendent was cautioned against returning. News of these threats brought Dr. Peck to the agency with messages from the captives and a peace offering—a sack of dried apples for each of their wives. Another deterrent soon followed. The three youngest prisoners promised to register and Marshal Nebeker sent them home with a warning that further violence would bring the soldiers back.[22]

Superintendent Frank returned the "slackers" to the reservation and registered them. He reported that the Gosiutes had had "the scare of their lives," and all was now quiet because many of the men had "left for parts unknown." (According to Dr. Peck, some of the youths, impressed at seeing a Shoshone top sergeant "of the expeditionary force . . . bossing all those white soldiers around . . . , had sneaked over into Nevada and enlisted in the army.") However, Frank learned that prior to his return a council had been held, funds had been collected, and George Burt had left for Ruby Valley, Elko, Nevada, and Death Valley, California, allegedly to foment rebellion there and bring sympathizers back to Deep Creek. An all-points bulletin was issued for his arrest.[23]

The captives remaining in Salt Lake City were arraigned on February 23 and pled not guilty. Bond was set at $500 each. When white neighbors of the Gosiutes visited them and tried to get their bond reduced, Frank and Dorrington opposed the move, arguing this would defeat their cause by placing the Indians "under obligation to their bondsmen." The agents wanted to retain complete control of the situation and have the Gosiutes feel indebted to the government, not civilians. They recommended the tribesmen be released upon their own recognizance, provided the court identified the agents as their benefactors and provided, further, that the Indians agreed to obey the law and devote their energy to the proper improvement of their lands and the building up of homes on the reservation.

At the end of three weeks' "telling confinement," Annies Tommy and his companions seemed repentant and assured authorities that the draft trouble was over. Jim Straight said there were fifty Gosiutes who could plant "an average of at least twenty acres of wheat." If the government would build them a small flour mill they could not only feed themselves but could produce up to "sixty tons of flour . . . for use in the army." The captives were released after promising to behave properly and respect the superintendent's authority. (Federal officials had already decided that if the Indians "reasonably fulfilled their pledges" the charges against them would be dismissed.)[24]

Tommy and Straight did not remain on the reservation; perhaps they went to Nevada. Late in March a rancher reported that Indian Tom, who lived near Cleveland Ranch, said he had been visited by two tribesmen from Deep Creek. The sojourners were supposedly recruiting "1000 Indians" for a general uprising to occur when authorities tried to take the Gosiute "conspirators" back to Salt Lake City for trial. (There were no more than five hundred tribesmen in the entire region.) A white man had allegedly furnished twelve Kanosh Indians with "poison powders" that could "kill anything" and was supplying guns and ammunition for the rebellion. The plan was to kill Superintendent Frank, massacre all the whites at Deep Creek, sweep through the valleys of western Utah and eastern Nevada, and join Pioche Indians who would raid northward. Only Mormons would be spared. Indian Tom sold his equipment and moved to Deep Creek.

The sheriff of White Pine County, Nevada, scoured the country for eighty-five miles around Cleveland Ranch, locating only two Indians where there were normally fifteen or twenty. State and local law enforcement agencies were notified, Fort Douglas was alerted, settlers and ranchers were warned, and special agent Dorrington rushed to the scene. A visit to Deep Creek and a conversation with Indian Tom, who denied the stories and thought them a joke, led Dorrington to conclude that there was no need for apprehension.[25]

Unfortunately, Dorrington and Frank had already decided they had been wrong in recommending leniency for the Gosiute resistance leaders. A federal grand jury indicted the Indians for "unlawfully, wilfully, knowingly and feloniously" conspiring against the "peace and dignity of the United States of America" by advising "diverse other persons . . . that they should refuse to register, and if necessary use force to prevent themselves being made a part of the military forces." Trial was deferred.[26]

The September 1918 registration briefly rekindled Gosiute agitation and white fears. Annies Tommy, now in northern Utah, urged his fellow tribesmen to resist. None of them enrolled. Rumors circulated that the Indians had gone to "get ammunition cached in the mountains"; in reality, they left the reservation merely to gather pine nuts. Frank thought "the situation looked ugly" for a time, but with the aid of "the more conservative old Indians" and neighboring white ranchers he succeeded in completing registration by the end of October (total Gosiutes registered: 163). The indictment against Willie Ottogary, Annies Tommy, Al Steel, John Syme, and Jim Straight was dismissed for "lack of evidence."[27]

Why did the Indians oppose conscription? The Gosiutes blamed Superintendent Frank for their September 1918 failure to register, saying he gave the signal to assemble at the wrong hour; though they considered sending to him for instructions they decided against it. Frank, on the other hand, neither sought out nor sent for the tribesmen because he felt this would "show weakness." While investigator Dorrington found the Indians' excuse "absurd and wholly insufficient to warrant their actions," he also criticized Frank's unbending attitude, concluding that the Gosiutes and their superintendent were "completely out of touch with each other."

Jim Straight maintained that the Indians misunderstood the draft law. This explanation hardly seems adequate, given the fact that agents repeatedly told them what was required. Nor does cowardice explain their actions, for they readily prepared to fight Deputy Knapp's posse. The European war, however, was to them but a distant abstraction. Indian Tom said the Gosiutes were angry because an Indian woman had been arrested as a spy. Al Steel refused to register because he claimed to be over age, even though agency records showed him to be liable to draft under the extended age limits. Subsequent investigation revealed that Steel was too old. However, Dorrington said Steel's resistance had misled others. Additionally, both Gosiutes and Shoshones had signed treaties promising to lay down their arms and follow peaceful pursuits.[28]

Newspapers blamed "outside influences" for Indian resistance. The commissioner of Indian affairs flatly denied these stories, but Indian testimony indicates otherwise. Garfield Pocatello said during the first registration a white man called a meeting of prominent Shoshones. Jacob Browning, Pocatello, and others who attended went to "a very good house" in Pocatello, Idaho, entering through a back door. There a man seated in a darkened room told the tribesmen that the government wanted to take their boys and men overseas to be killed; none would return. (The recent leasing to sugar growers of twenty thousand acres of reservation land to boost the wartime food campaign, in the Indian mind, lent credence to this idea.) The man exhorted the Shoshones to warn other Indians, arm themselves, and resist. Jim Straight also complained of agitators, saying they were "worse than Germans, and delight in getting the Indians into trouble."[29]

Superintendent Frank wondered if Deputy Knapp was a spy. Had he been "up to more than the work assigned him" and "purposely arranged" the Gosiute "uprising"? Knapp's belligerence undoubtedly intensified Indian anxieties. Frank also speculated that "the Mormons" had "teased" the Indians, stirring them up in the hope that they "would lose their reserve." But, he cautioned, "I do not want it to go on record for the reason that it cannot be definite."[30] Charles Damon Jr. and Willie Ottogary were troublemakers of sorts. Who the other agitators were remains unclear.

Frank and the Gosiutes disagreed over the Indians' citizenship status. The Gosiutes believed they were noncitizens because they were not allowed to vote, but Superintendent Frank held otherwise, at least until the middle of 1918. Then uncertainty crept in: "At first," he wrote, "all [took] out Indian Homesteads [but] when the Goshute reservation was set aside, all . . . relinquished their homesteads and said lands were included in said reserve . . . would such Indians be considered citizens?" The Indians who flocked to Deep Creek in 1917–18 came to avoid being counted as citizens and thus subject to the draft. They argued that they had been living on the public domain through no fault of their own, since the government had never established a reservation for them at Ruby Valley, as promised in their 1863 treaty. Of these tribesmen Frank wrote: "Indians coming from Nevada and living on the Gosiute Indian reservation, Utah, have no rights here. As said Indians have no reservation and had been living either on the public domain or with white ranchers, they have had all the rights of citizenship."[31] Such differential treatment was bound to create problems.

Long-standing grievances underlay the immediate conflict. The Gosiutes believed the government was cheating them. Dorrington reported, "Willie Ottogary had considerable to say about certain money due the Indians for road work." However, after the investigator explained that the government did not pay Indians for maintaining reservation roads, Ottogary conceded: "I guess it is different on the reservation than up where I live." Annies Tommy complained about not being paid for his service as an Indian judge. The government said his position had never been officially sanctioned. The Indians demanded retribution for five Gosiute deaths, including that of Tommy's brother. They said white men were stealing their fish, water, timber, and minerals; Frank had closed their school and had tried to sell them the harnesses and wagons the treaty promised, and they had not received the proffered land and annuities.[32]

An examination of the Ruby Valley treaty reveals that it was misinterpreted by the Indians. The document explicitly authorized white developers to exploit both minerals and timber (Article 4). Annuities were to compensate the tribesmen for these concessions (Article 7). The treaty did not promise the establishment of a reservation in Ruby Valley but authorized the president of the United States to "make such reservations for their [the Indians'] use as he may deem necessary." Furthermore, the tribesmen agreed to "remove their camps to such reservations as he [the president] may indicate, and to reside and remain therein" (Article 6). Over five years had elapsed since the establishment of the Deep Creek reservation (1912), and the government assumed Indians living on the public domain were doing so by choice, thereby becoming citizens. Despite the Indians' righteous indignation over the government's failure to investigate the deaths of their tribesmen, they erred when they asserted that this, too, was a treaty violation. Although the treaty provided that "if depredations are at any time committed by bad men of their [the Indians'] nation, the offenders shall be immediately taken and delivered up to the proper officers of the United States, to be punished as their offences shall deserve," it made no provision for reciprocity (Article 2).[33] The justice of the entire agreement is questionable, but the fact remains that the Gosiutes misconstrued their rights.

Great enmity existed between Annies Tommy and Superintendent Frank. Tommy accused the agent of unlawfully opening private mail and using Indian money to purchase hay and grain, then withholding it from the tribesmen. The superintendent admitted opening one letter "by mistake" but maintained that neither he nor any of the agency employees had read it. Instead of explaining his alleged misuse of Indian monies, however, he attacked his accuser, saying Tommy did not belong on the reservation because he was "not one of the original Goshute band and is on the reservation only by reason of his mother (Annie) having married . . . Antelope Jake, a recognized head man." Frank called Tommy "the very worst Indian residing on the reservation," predicting, "There will be nothing but trouble as long as he remains." Dorrington exonerated Frank, and the superintendent succeeded in removing Annies Tommy from the reservation, reporting in May 1918: "Annies Tommy and family have left the reservation" because the other Indians have "had enough of him."[34]

Frank was not happy at Deep Creek and seems to have feared the Indians. He reminded special agent Dorrington that it was "just such doings" that had led to the death of a colleague in California. To avoid a repetition of that incident, he urged that the Gosiute "outlaws" be dealt with "in an energetic way . . . by those . . . in a position to do so." Furthermore, neither Frank nor his wife enjoyed complete health. Since the agency was located at nine thousand feet above sea level and quite isolated, he requested a transfer to a lower, more salubrious climate.[35]

Together, all these factors demonstrate that the Gosiutes were living in a volatile ambience long before 1917–18. The draft, with its attendant confusion over the citizenship of individual tribesmen, both magnified their discontent and unleashed the resentment of many years. Shoshone resistance seems to have been motivated by more immediate concerns. The white reaction is perhaps best explained by Frank's paranoia and by wartime hysteria fanned by journalistic sensationalism.

NOTES

Originally published in the *Utah Historical Quarterly* 49 (Spring 1981): 3173–88.

1. Mark Twain, "Roughing It," *The Works of Mark Twain*, vol. 2 (Berkeley: University of California, 1972), 144; Richard N. Ellis, "'Indians at Ibapah in Revolt': Goshutes, the Draft, and the Indian Bureau, 1917–1919," *Nevada Historical Society Quarterly* 19 (1976): 163–70; Jacob Browning to Commissioner, June 5, 1917, National Archives, National Resources Branch, Civil Archives Division, Record Group 75, Ft. Hall, file 737521-125 (hereafter NA, RG 75); E. E. McKean to Commissioner, August 22, 1918, NA, RG 75, Southern Ute, 71280-125; J. E. Jenkins to Commissioner, December 30, 1917, NA, RG 75, Malki, 1208–926.

2. U.S. Department of the Interior, Office of Indian Affairs, Circular no. 1305, May 15, 1917 (hereafter OIA); OIA, Circular no. 1305-N, August 15, 1918; Provost Marshal General to Commissioner, May 2, 1918, U.S. Department of the Interior Library, North American Indians in World War I, vol. 1; Commissioner to W. Runke, June 8, 1917, NA RG 75, Western Navajo, 55149-125.

3. OIA, Circular no. 1305-D, May 15, 1917; OIA, Circular no. 1305-H, April 27, 1918; OIA, Circular no. 1305-M, July 19, 1918.

4. *Pocatello Tribune*, June 1, June 5, June 30, 1917.

5. *Salt Lake Tribune*, June 7, 1917.

6. A. R. Frank to Commissioner, May 28, 1917, NA, Judicial and Fiscal Branch, Civil Archives Division, File 186233-281 (hereafter NA, JFB); Frank to L. A. Dorrington, June 12, 1917, ibid.; Annual Report, Goshute Indian School, 1917, National Archives, microfilm publication, M1011-57.

7. Unless otherwise noted, discussion of the 1917 draft resistance is based upon the following: G. J. Knapp to Barrington [*sic*], June 11,

1917, NA, JFB; Frank to Dorrington, June 12, 1917, ibid.; Dorrington to Commissioner, June 20, 1917, ibid.

8. Frank to Commissioner, June 9, 1917, ibid.

9. Ibid.

10. Dorrington to Commissioner, June 11, 1917, ibid.

11. *White Pine News*, July 15, 1917; *Millard County Progress*, July 20, 1917.

12. *Daily Oklahoman*, August 24, 1917; Commissioner to T. Sterling, June 7, 1918, NA, RG 75, Standing Rock, 101703-125; E. B. Meritt to Frank, August 21, 1918, NA, RG 75, Gosiute, 71476-125; Joseph H. Peck, *What Next, Doctor Peck?* (Englewood Cliffs, NJ: Prentice-Hall, 1959), 190–91.

13. H. D. Lawshe to Commissioner, February 18, 1918, Federal Archives and Records Center, San Bruno (hereafter FARC, SB), RG 75, Dorrington, Western Shoshone; Testimony of Garfield Pocatello, February 13, 1918, ibid.

14. Frank to Commissioner, January 15, 1918, ibid., Gosiute; Jim Straight et al. to Commissioner, January 21, 1918, NA, JFB.

15. Dorrington to Commissioner, February 6, 1918, NA, RG 75, Gosiute, 30951-125.

16. Frank to Commissioner, February 9, 1918, ibid.

17. Dorrington to Commissioner, February 13, 1918, March 26, 1918, ibid.; Secretary of Interior to Attorney General, February 15, 1918, ibid.

18. Dorrington to Commissioner, February 15, 1918, ibid.

19. *Deseret Evening News*, February 21, 1918; Dorrington to Commissioner, March 26, 1918, NA, RG 75, Gosiute, 30951-125; Peck, *What Next*, 193–97.

20. *Salt Lake Tribune*, February 23, 1918.

21. *Deseret Evening News*, February 21, 1918; Peck, *What Next*, 198.

22. Dorrington to Commissioner, February 24, 1918, NA, RG 75, Gosiute, 30951-125.

23. Frank to Dorrington, March 7, 1918, FARC, SB, Dorrington, Gosiute; Frank to Dorrington, February 26, 1918, NA, RG 75, Gosiute, 30951-125; Peck, *What Next*, 203; Frank to W. W. Ray, February 28, 1918, FARC, SB, Dorrington, Gosiute; Frank to Governors of Nevada and California, March 23, 1918, ibid.

24. *Salt Lake Tribune*, February 24, 1918; *Deseret Evening News*, March 14, 1918; Dorrington to Commissioner, February 24, March 16, March 26, 1918, NA, RG 75, Gosiute, 30951-125.

25. [Rogers] to McLeen, March 27, 1918, FARC, SB, Dorrington, Gosiute; undated newspaper clippings, ibid.; Allen to Dorrington, April 8, 1918, ibid.; Dorrington to Woodburn, April 15, 1918, ibid.

26. Frank to Dorrington, April 4, 1918, ibid.; Dorrington to Ray, April 8, 1918, ibid.; United States of America v. Al Steel et al., Federal Archives and Records Center, Denver, Colorado, File 76703 (hereafter FARC, Denver).
27. Frank to Sells, September 13, 1918, NA, RG 75, Gosiute, 71476-125; Frank to Dorrington, September 13, 1918, ibid.; Dorrington to Commissioner, September 21, 1918, ibid.; unsigned telegram, October 15, 1918, NA, RG 75, 83548-18; Frank to Commissioner, October 29, 1918, NA, RG 75, Gosiute, 71476-125; Frank to Dorrington, October 29, 1918, FARC, SB, Dorrington, Gosiute; U.S. v. Al Steel et al., FARC, Denver.
28. Dorrington to Sells, September 21, 1918, NA, RG 75, Gosiute, 71476-125. *Salt Lake Tribune*, February 24, 1918; [Rogers] to McLeen, March 27, 1918, FARC, SB, Dorrington, Gosiute; Browning to Commissioner, June 5, 1917, NA, RG 75, Ft. Hall, 737521-125; Dorrington to Commissioner, February 6, 1918, NA, RG 75, Gosiute, 30951-125.
29. Commissioner to J. J. Cotter, March 6, 1918, NA, RG 75, Gosiute, 30951-125; Testimony of Garfield Pocatello, February 13, 1918, FARC, SB, Western Shoshone; H. D. Lawshe to Commissioner, February 18, 1918, ibid.; *Salt Lake Tribune*, May 31, 1917; February 24, 1918.
30. Frank to Dorrington, August 13, 1917, FARC, SB, Dorrington, Gosiute; Frank to Commissioner, October 29, 1918, NA, RG 75, Gosiute, 71476-125.
31. Frank to Commissioner, June 9, 1917, NA, JFB; Frank to Commissioner, July 30, 1918, NA, RG 75, Gosiute, 71476-125; Jim Straight et al. to Commissioner, January 21, 1918, NA, JFB; Frank to Dorrington, May 3, 1918, FARC, SB, Dorrington, Gosiute; Frank to Commissioner, August 29, 1918, NA, RG 75, Gosiute, 71476-125.
32. Dorrington to Commissioner, June 20, 1917, NA, JFB; Tommy to Commissioner, November 1, 1917, FARC, SB, Dorrington, Gosiute; Frank to Commissioner, November 26, 1917, ibid.; Jim Straight et al. to Commissioner, January 21, 1918, NA, JFB; Frank to Commissioner, May 28, 1917, ibid.
33. Charles J. Kappler, *Laws and Treaties*, vol. 2 (Washington, D.C.: Government Printing Office, 1904), 851–53.
34. Dorrington to Commissioner, June 20, 1917, NA, JFB; Knapp to Barrington [*sic*], June 12, 1917, ibid.; Frank to Dorrington, May 17, 1918, FARC, SB, Dorrington, Gosiute.
35. Frank to Dorrington, June 17, 1917, FARC, SB, Dorrington, Gosiute; Frank to Commissioner, October 23, 1918, NA, RG 75, Gosiute, 71476-125.

12

A QUESTION OF CONSCIENCE

The Resignation of Bishop Paul Jones

JOHN R. SILLITO AND TIMOTHY S. HEARN

Perhaps the most controversial individual to emerge in Utah during the war was Paul Jones. He became the Episcopal bishop of Utah in 1914, and was an outspoken critic of the war and advocate for peace. Jones was motivated in his opposition to war by what he saw as his Christian duty and, as a Socialist, his political responsibility. His supreme loyalty was to Christ and his gospel and any activity—such as war, which was against the teachings of Christ—must be opposed. That opposition became known when in March 1917, on the eve of the United States' declaration of war, he spoke against an ecumenical "patriotic demonstration" staged before an overflowing crowd in the Salt Lake Tabernacle. Under extreme pressure from lay members and church leaders and following an investigation by fellow Episcopalian bishops, Paul Jones acted upon their request and submitted his resignation. As a matter of conscience, Bishop Jones could not support the war and his resignation demonstrated a measure of courage and commitment not unlike that of other Americans willing to sacrifice their all in the war.

"Only a handful of American churchmen stood against American participation in World War I," wrote historian Ralph Lord Roy.[1] Numbered among that group was Paul Jones, Episcopal bishop of Utah, an active Socialist who believed the American people were being swept into the war on a wave of hysteria. Jones's pacifist sentiments and, in particular, his opposition to the United States' participation in the war ultimately cost him his ecclesiastical position. Moreover, Jones's resignation precipitated a major crisis within the Episcopal Church, dividing both clergy and laity within the Episcopal Diocese of Utah and throughout the nation. Understanding this crisis and its resolution requires an examination of Paul Jones's early life, his succession to the episcopate, and the factors leading to his 1918 resignation as bishop of Utah.

Jones became bishop in 1914 after the accidental death of his friend and mentor, Franklin Spencer Spalding. For nearly a decade Spalding guided Episcopal affairs in Utah while at the same time actively participating in the movement for socialism developing in his church. In 1911 Spalding was one of the founders of the Church Socialist League and served as its first president. The league united Episcopal clergy and laity who were Socialists into an organization that called for the "collective ownership of all the means of production and distribution." Members dedicated themselves to a twofold goal of advancing socialism by "all just means" while promoting "a better understanding between church people who are not Socialists, and Socialists who are not church people."[2]

In his capacity as a missionary bishop, Spalding spent much of his time on speaking tours in the East, raising funds for the Episcopal Church's work among the Mormons and recruiting clergymen to assist him in Utah. One of those answering this call was Paul Jones, who arrived in Logan in 1906, fresh from the Episcopal Theological School in Cambridge, Massachusetts, to work with students at the Utah State Agricultural College.

During the next eight years Jones clearly became a protégé of Bishop Spalding and grew close to the senior cleric in his commitment to the Christian faith as well as in his belief in the relevance of

socialism. In 1914, after Spalding's death and before his own consecra-
tion as bishop, Jones joined the Socialist party (a step Spalding had
never taken) so there would be no misunderstanding concerning his
political views. In a later account, Jones explained his motivation:

> I joined the Socialist party . . . not only as a matter of conviction,
> although the Socialist program and point of view seemed to
> represent the most honest effort in sight to apply Christian prin-
> ciples to the social order, but it was to some degree the casting of
> an anchor windward. I did not want, in the position of bishop,
> to get swung, as so many have been, into the easy acceptance of
> things as they are.[3]

There is little in Paul Jones's early life to suggest that one day
socialism would become his anchor. He was born in Wilkes-Barre,
Pennsylvania, in 1881. His formative years were, in his own view, not
characterized by any tendency toward radicalism:

> I . . . grew up in association only with right-thinking people of
> the best type. Again my years at Yale did nothing to shake those
> sound conclusions which I had naturally accepted, for I recall
> that I had no hesitation in going in as a strike breaker in the
> anthracite strike of 1902. . . .
>
> The natural right of the best people to have the best things,
> wealth as evidence of individual probity, punishment as the only
> proper treatment for crime, the foreigner to be kept in his place
> and to be treated kindly, but firmly, the army and navy as the
> loyal defenders of the nation, the worship of the church as the
> proper expression of all decent and respectable people—all these
> conceptions were mine by ordinary training and association.[4]

Jones identified three factors that ultimately altered these inbred
concepts: first, a realization that the validity of the teachings of Jesus
Christ "rested upon their essential truth rather than upon some

outside or supernatural authority" and a conviction that these truths could be applied to the "ordinary relationships of life"; second, his experience in Logan, which gave him the chance to "spread the understanding and practice of Christian principles among all the people of the community, Mormon and non-Mormon alike," instead of trying to build up only his own church; and, third, the "sound thinking and personality" of Bishop Spalding, which convinced Jones that the principles taught by Jesus "not only could but should be applied to both industrial and international relationships."[5]

Jones's activities as a Socialist continued after he became bishop of Utah. He succeeded Spalding as president of the Church Socialist League and wrote and lectured in support of socialism. At the same time, he began to speak out against the war in Europe and the military preparedness movement sweeping the United States. At the Episcopal General Convention in 1916 Jones participated in a forum on "Christianity and Force" and took a militant pacifist position that war was always a rejection of Christian principles. During this period, Jones joined the Fellowship of Reconciliation, a nondenominational religious organization whose antiwar views he believed most closely resembled his own.[6]

In general, Jones's pacifist sentiments were based on a desire for moral consistency in all aspects of life, not just regarding war. In a pamphlet entitled *The Christian Soldier*, Jones attributed his stand not to traditional pacifism, which he regarded as too narrow and concerned with only one aspect of life, but rather to a "Christian attitude . . . concerned with the reclamation of the world from evil, and the development of perfection, tasks which in their very nature imply a continued struggle."[7]

Citing biblical sources in support of his views, Jones asserted that the "Christian Soldier" must attempt to "win to Christ those who are crucifying him afresh," not only by their attitudes toward war but also by their attitudes toward business, society, and the church itself. Moreover, Jones wrote, for the Christian "there is but one supreme loyalty and that is to Christ and His Gospel. Duties to country, to home, and to family must always give way to the larger loyalty which alone is capable of . . . giving them full significance."[8]

In another tract Jones outlined his concept of "Christian loyalty," which led him to oppose war as an inherently "un-Christian activity." Instead of war, mankind should pursue a policy of "active, aggressive, militant goodwill founded on the example and teachings of Christ." The day will come, Jones proclaimed, when "Christian men and women will be brave enough to stand openly for the full truth, [and] the terrible anachronism of war between Christian nations will be done away with."[9]

Consistently, Jones argued that opposition to war from a Christian perspective is not a passive approach but an active one. He also insisted that Christians must be consistent in their commitment to the teachings of Christ regardless of the outcome:

> To prosecute war means to kill men, bring sorrow upon women and children, and instill suspicion, fear and hatred into the hearts of the people on both sides. No matter what principles may appear to be at stake, to deliberately engage in such a course of action . . . is repugnant to the whole spirit of the Gospel.[10]

Jones's pacifist sentiments were well known to the residents of his own diocese. In November 1915 he preached at Saint Mark's Cathedral, telling the congregation that the calls "for this or any other nation to resort to force to resist an invasion of rights" would ultimately lead to war, and "plunge the world in an inferno of blood." The true safeguard for any nation, Jones believed, was "not to be found in the weapons of war, but in those eternal principles which make for righteousness and truth and brotherhood and peace."[11]

In March 1916 Jones published an article in the *Utah Survey*, a magazine sponsored by the Episcopal Church in the state, in which he decried the "agitation for preparedness" that he saw as sweeping the governmental, business, educational, and religious sectors of American life. Jones argued that preparedness in itself would never prevent war and maintained that the breakdown of the military alliances that characterized prewar Europe was evidence of that fact. Moreover, he asserted, American involvement in the war would put an end to the Progressive movement because it would divert funds from needed domestic social projects and threaten both public morality and civil liberties.[12]

Thus, by 1917 Jones's support of socialism and his commitment to pacifist sentiments were well known both in Utah as well as on the national level. Within a few months, Jones's identification with and support for these views became so controversial that he was forced to resign his position as bishop of Utah.

The chain of events that precipitated this crisis began in March 1917. At that time, a rally labeled as a "patriotic demonstration" in support of possible American involvement in the European war was held in the Salt Lake Tabernacle, attracting some ten thousand people. Included in the assemblage were representatives of government, business, and education, as well as several local clergymen and LDS general authorities.

A resolution passed at the rally asserted that the United States had been pushed to the brink of war and that it was necessary for this country to take action to "reassert its traditional principles" of freedom of commerce, respect for the sovereignty of all nations, and opposition to tyranny. The resolution, which was to be sent to Utah's congressional delegation for transmittal to President Woodrow Wilson, called for the "loyalty, unity and solidarity" of all Americans "in support of whatever course becomes necessary to preserve our honor as a nation and to protect the lives of our fellow citizens at home or abroad, on land or sea."[13]

In response to the actions taken at this rally, a meeting was held the following evening at Unity Hall, the headquarters of numerous radical and labor organizations, to protest American involvement in the war. Several Utah radicals spoke in opposition to Wilsonian policies toward the war. Paul Jones told these antiwar Utahns that the United States was being "swept on a war wave" and the American people were "no longer using their heads" when it came to the question of involvement in the European conflict. In assessing the situation, Jones said:

> The speakers at the Tabernacle . . . put democracy, loyalty and truth in terms of guns, fighting and bloodshed, terms that this new world, if not the old, has grown beyond. No adequate reasons were presented by any of the representatives of state or federal government for entering the war. There was nothing but an emotional appeal, and the people were carried off their feet. There was no appeal for democracy, or for suffering humanity in Europe.
>
> I believe we should stand by the President, but we should not forsake the high ideals we have always had. The President is still in a position to keep us out of war. There is still time to appeal to him with sentiments other than those fostered by hot-headed pseudo-patriots of today.[14]

Reaction from the local Episcopal community to their bishop's views was swift in coming. Hugh A. McMillin, a vestryman at Saint Mark's, ridiculed the notion that an Episcopal bishop could truly be a Socialist and further stated that it should be thoroughly understood by the people of Salt Lake that Jones was speaking "as an individual and not in any way as a bishop of the church." Subsequently, the entire vestry of Saint Mark's issued a statement expressing their "keen regret" over Jones's utterances because they believed many citizens might attribute his opinions to the church as a whole. The vestry urged Jones to make it clear that his opinions did not reflect, by virtue of his official position, "the Episcopal church or . . . any member thereof."[15]

Jones responded with a cordial, but nonetheless negative, answer. He told the vestry that because his stand opposing American involvement in the war was based upon what he believed to be "the clear teachings of the scriptures," he did not feel it necessary to make the disclaimer requested.[16] For a time the matter rested there, although other leaders in the Utah Episcopal community continued to seek, publicly and privately, to dissociate Bishop Jones's views from the church. Clearly these local critics were not as willing to tolerate Jones's pacifism at a time when American involvement in the war seemed imminent as they had when such action seemed remote or speculative.

As might be expected, Jones's attitudes were not altered, nor was his voice stilled, by the American declaration of war on the Central powers a week later. During the next few months his opposition intensified, though it was less visible and created less public attention. Jones did alienate local Episcopal critics further, however, when he affiliated with the People's Council for Democracy and Justice, a national organization that campaigned "for a quick peace on liberal terms, civil liberties, and repeal of conscription."[17] The council was regarded by many as extremely radical, and possibly seditious, and Jones's affiliation further supported the impression of many local Episcopalians that their bishop was following a traitorous path.

By fall 1917 Jones's opposition to the war was again attracting public attention. In October he attended a conference in Los Angeles sponsored by an interdenominational peace group known as the Christian Pacifists. His participation was relatively minor (he offered a prayer and made brief remarks), but because the meeting was broken up by the police he made headlines in Los Angeles and Salt Lake newspapers. The *Salt Lake Tribune*, for example, proclaimed in bold headlines, "Swarms of Police Chase Bishop Jones."[18]

This new publicity prompted the Utah Council of Advice, a body of local clergy and lay people appointed by the bishop to advise him on diocesan matters, to send a letter to Jones calling for his resignation due to the "loss of respect and confidence of loyal Americans not only within the church, but outside, without which no bishop can be acceptable or successful in the prosecution of his work."[19] Jones's response came in the form of a questionnaire to the council seeking a more specific rendering of the charges against him. Piqued by the bishop's attitude, the Council of Advice and the vestries of the two largest parishes in Utah appealed directly to a special meeting of the House of Bishops then being held in Chicago for the removal of

Bishop Jones. The groups stressed their belief that Jones's inability to support U.S. war policy had destroyed his credibility.

> Since the day when the United States accepted the challenge of war from Germany, the Bishop of Utah has persistently maintained an attitude of hostility to the United States government.
>
> On Sunday, April 29, 1917, while preaching in St Marks Cathedral . . . he asserted that the United States was preparing to send its young men forth for organized murder and butchery.
>
> From that day to the present time, he has not ceased to proclaim, in public utterances and in private conversations, antiwar doctrines which are held by the people of this state to be inimical to the best interest of the nation in this present crisis.[20]

After several unsatisfactory attempts to deal with the controversy over Jones in committee, the House of Bishops decided (apparently at Jones's suggestion), that the Utah bishop should request a leave of absence while a special commission of three bishops investigated the situation. The commission met twice, first on November 7 and again on December 12. It reviewed the facts of the case, received information and depositions, and interviewed two members of the Council of Advice as well as Jones himself. Soon after the December meeting the special commission recommended that Jones submit his resignation to the House of Bishops.

Jones complied with this request in late December. In his letter of resignation, addressed to Presiding Bishop Daniel S. Tuttle, himself a former bishop of Utah, Jones noted that he had hoped "that there might be room in the Church for a difference of opinion on the Christianity of warfare and the ways of attaining peace," but he now realized this was not the case:

> The commission, speaking I take it, for the House of Bishops, maintains, first that war is not an unChristian thing and that no Bishop may preach that this war is unChristian; and second

that a Bishop should not express the opinion that peace can be secured otherwise than by the prosecution of the war when the government and the preponderance of the membership of the Church believe otherwise.

Those conclusions I cannot accept; for I believe that the methods of modern international war are quite incompatible with the Christian principles of reconciliation and brotherhood, and that it is the duty of a Bishop of the Church, from his study of the word of God, to express himself on questions of righteousness, no matter what opinion may stand in the way.[21]

When the House of Bishops met in April it had trouble disposing of the case because of its inability to accept either the report of the special commission or Jones's letter of resignation, which seemed to imply that the House of Bishops supported restrictions on the freedom of expression of its members. Finally, the House of Bishops accepted a simple, one-sentence letter of resignation from Jones because they believed he had lost his usefulness and effectiveness as bishop. At the same time, however, they asserted the right of "every member of this House to freedom of speech in political and social matters, subject to the laws of the land," thus making the issue Jones's ability to function as bishop and not his opposition to the war.[22]

Shortly thereafter, Frank Hale Touret, bishop of western Colorado, was named acting bishop of Utah, and the Church Board of Missions assigned Jones to a position as a missionary in Maine. At that time, Benjamin Brewster, former dean of St. Mark's Cathedral and a colleague of Jones in the Church Socialist League, was bishop of that diocese. Thus, the brief and often controversial tenure of Paul Jones as bishop of Utah ended.

But several questions remain: What role did the secular and Episcopal press play in shaping public attention and sentiment against Jones? Did Jones's critics in Utah oppose him only because of his objections to American involvement in World War I? Or did other factors fuel the fire of anti-Jones sentiment, resulting in his removal from office?

During 1917 and 1918 Bishop Jones's activities and attitudes were frequently covered in the Utah press and, ultimately, in national publications. Much of the reporting tended to be both emotional and inflammatory. In Utah, the *Salt Lake Tribune* was particularly guilty of this type of coverage. In reporting the incident in Los Angeles, for example, the *Tribune* accused Jones of offering a prayer "for a German peace" and stated that the bishop and other leaders of the Christian Pacifists were "consciously or unconsciously . . . instruments of sinister German propaganda."[23]

Despite Jones's denial of these reports, which he labeled as completely inaccurate, they did severe damage to his credibility. This is particularly true in light of the intense anti-German and pro-American campaign then sweeping the country. These news accounts were picked up by other newspapers and fed the anti-Jones sentiment throughout the nation. Moreover, such accounts gave those members of the House of Bishops who disapproved of Jones even more justification in their own minds to seek an end to the public notoriety caused by the activities of their outspoken colleague.

The Episcopal press, sensitive to the delicate issue involved in infringing upon a bishop's freedom of conscience and expression, was not nearly as zealous in reporting the controversy surrounding Jones. Few of the major Episcopal publications agreed with Jones's attitudes on war, but most tended to be tolerant toward him. A moderate paper, the *Witness*, said it did not agree with much of Jones's views of the war but believed his attitudes should receive a hearing. On the other hand, the *Churchman*, while praising Jones in many respects, questioned not only his loyalty but his right to dissent: "What strikes us in the attitude of Bishop Jones and some other pacifists is their audacity. Liberty of speech is not an absolute right . . . in this critical hour."[24]

Despite the critical accounts in the press, it is unlikely that the House of Bishops would have taken action against Jones had not the impetus for his removal come from within Utah. Although Jones's opposition to American involvement in the war was the primary offense motivating calls for his resignation, at least three other factors contributed to the rise of sentiment against him: the desire of some Utah Episcopalians for an older, more prominent bishop; a fear on the part of some that their relations with the Mormon majority of Utah would be seriously disrupted by Jones's outspoken opinions; and opposition on the part of some to Jones's Socialist allegiance.

Two close associates of Jones provide the most direct evidence that animosity toward him was based to some degree on considerations of social status. In a letter to William Lawrence, bishop of Massachusetts, Marguerite Schneider, a friend and occasional secretary for Bishop Jones, emphasized this view:

> I feel very sure that the whole thing arises from the personal prejudices of the laymen. In fact, even before Bishop Jones was consecrated, the feeling among the laymen was that they wanted some "big" Eastern man to be their bishop. It was argued against Bishop Jones that he knew nothing, could not preach, had no experience and was unknown outside of Utah. I feel that the prejudice which existed then has persisted up to the present time and that is now seeking open expression under the cover of a lack of patriotism on his part in the call for [his] resignation.[25]

A similar letter was written to Arthur Selden Lloyd, president of the Church Board of Missions, by Francis B. Affleck, a pacifist, Socialist, and friend of Jones and his wife. Affleck offers additional evidence to support the assertion that some Utah communicants desired a more prestigious bishop. Affleck charged that J. Walcott Thompson, junior warden at St. Mark's and a member of the Council of Advice, repeatedly stated his belief that Jones was "a mere nobody" and that he felt the diocese needed a "bishop from the East with a big reputation." Affleck further asserted that from the day of Jones's election as bishop, a group within Utah had "been disloyal at heart, and often openly; they have slighted the Bishop and his wife socially—and have shown in every way that they did not intend to make them welcome among them."[26]

Naturally, some skepticism should be allowed in assessing the views of these individuals since both were close personal friends of the bishop. There is other evidence, however, that suggests opposition to Jones did have social connotations. In the first place, the agitation against Jones came overwhelmingly from the two largest parishes in Utah: St. Mark's with 385 communicants and St. Paul's with 300 communicants. Both were located in Salt Lake City. All of the vestry resolutions against Jones sent to the House of Bishops originated with the vestries of these two congregations. Moreover, of the six members of the Council of Advice, all but one attended one of these parishes, and, indeed, one member of the council was dean of St. Mark's. Furthermore, when Maxwell W. Rice, minister at All Soul's Church in Garfield, reported the results of a statewide survey he had taken to Presiding Bishop Tuttle, he noted: "except for the two [Salt Lake City] parishes of St. Mark's and St. Paul's, the district is loyal to our Bishop though most of us are against him on this question of war."[27] Thus, it appears that opposition to Jones was motivated, at least in part, by the desire of some members of the large and growing city congregations for a bishop who could fulfill a higher social function than that normally demanded of a missionary bishop.

In terms of the relationship between Utah Episcopalians and their Mormon neighbors, one commentator has suggested that the primary reason the House of Bishops accepted Jones's resignation was the threat his opinions posed to the Mormon people's "high respect for the Episcopal church and for its patriotic, as well as religious spirit."[28] Although this is probably an overstatement, the records of the House of Bishops reflect concern, both within and without Utah, that the pacifist activities of Paul Jones brought shame and embarrassment. Such sentiments are certainly found in the report to the House of Bishops from the Council of Advice:

> The Church has become an object of suspicion, and Church people throughout the state are covered with shame and confusion. The outlook for the future appears very dark . . . [and there

is] increasing criticism of the Church at large, that an ecclesiastical organization, which would maintain in a position of power a man who uses the weight of his high office to disseminate unpatriotic and dangerous doctrines, itself shares the implication of disloyalty.[29]

Despite these assertions, the attitude of the Mormon Church, at least as seen in the editorial pages of the *Deseret News*, reflected a somewhat different view. On March 29, 1917, the paper editorialized:

A disproportionate amount of importance seems to be attached to the remarks of the gentleman of the cloth at a Socialist-Pacifist protest meeting the other night. At the outset we can dismiss as wholly immaterial the fact the he was a clergyman. He was speaking not as a clergyman but as a Socialist.[30]

The *Deseret News* further commented that although it regarded the present crisis as one in which "there can be no neutrality," the question of the dissent of Bishop Jones was a matter "for the communicants of the church of which he is the head" to decide. Doubtless, the paper affirmed, they will take "whatever action is appropriate and the matter will be closed."[31]

On the other hand, Jones received intensive criticism from the non-Mormon press in Utah. The views of the *Salt Lake Tribune* have already been outlined. Another non-Mormon paper, *Goodwin's Weekly*, held similarly critical views of Jones's activities. In its March 31, 1917, issue the paper noted:

The patriotic demonstration at the Tabernacle . . . touched the very depths of the souls of the thousands who participated. . . .

Then what happened? The very next night a sorry bunch of Socialists led by the Rt. Rev. Paul Jones (what a travesty of the illustrious name of Paul Jones of old), got together and pulled off a "one-horse" opposition of their own.

After the simple minded bishop undertook to cite the charter of George Washington in justification of their cowardly action, they adopted a resolution aimed to belittle and offset the ringing resolutions of the night before. . . .

It was a shameful affair from start to finish and disgrace to the city.[32]

Thus, it is difficult to assess the source of the "shame and embarrassment" local Episcopalians felt over the actions of their bishop. The Council of Advice reported to the House of Bishops that Jones's activities had made the Episcopal Church an "object of suspicion," but local press accounts, both Mormon and Gentile, criticized Jones while making it clear that he was acting for himself and not his church.

In addition, no criticism was leveled at Bishop Jones during the April 1917 sessions of LDS General Conference. It seems probable that if the actions of Paul Jones had turned the Mormon hierarchy against Utah Episcopalians they would have expressed such views at this conference, held the same time that President Wilson was asking Congress for a declaration of war.

Finally, there is the question of Jones's Socialist allegiance and its significance. Assessing the impact of this particular factor presents considerable difficulty. Undoubtedly, many Utah Episcopalians must have shared the sentiments of one individual who characterized the "Socialist adventure of Bishop Spalding and Bishop Jones" as the "most lamentable episode" in Utah Episcopal history.[33] Yet, surprisingly, there is little mention of Jones's socialism in the deliberations of the House of Bishops or those of the Utah Council of Advice. Thus, the view of one historian that Jones was "hounded from his diocese . . . for his socialism as much as for his pacifism" seems an oversimplification.[34]

The possibility that Jones was driven out of Utah because of his Socialist affiliation also seems less likely due to the fact that one member of the Council of Advice—the Rev. William F. Bulkley—was himself a Socialist who had been, in fact, the nominee of the Utah Socialist Party for state treasurer in 1916. Little is known of Bulkley's Socialist commitment, and his particular attitudes at this time are unclear. It is possible, for example, that Bulkley was one of many American Socialists who broke with the party over American involvement in World War I. Nevertheless, the fact that Bulkley served on the council makes it seem less likely that Jones was forced out by a reactionary cabal.

Of course, there can be no question that Jones's Socialist views were a source of irritation to many and played a part in the creation of sentiment against him within Utah and throughout the nation. Certainly other antiwar Socialists were subjected to personal vilification and repression during those years. The difficulty lies in trying to separate criticism of socialism in general from opposition to the war effort in particular.

In the end, though all of these factors played a role, it was his opposition to the war that constituted the primary reason for Bishop Jones's loss of office at a time when pressure in America to enter the war reached unprecedented heights. Such sentiments were as much in evidence in Utah as elsewhere. Jones himself realized that his chance of surviving as bishop in such an atmosphere of intolerance was unlikely. Still, he refused to give the church an easy way out by resigning before they addressed his right to conscience and freedom of political expression. This issue was of far more importance to Jones than his own personal well-being or the retention of his office as bishop. At the same time, he realized his critics were genuine in their own convictions. In his address to the district convocation in 1917 he said:

> To try to harmonize these two points of view would probably be an impossible, or at any rate thankless, task. But the fact that sincere Christian people are represented on both sides, brings before us all the great necessity for tolerance in judgement, caution and consideration in expression and restraint in action.[35]

Jones continued to work for the causes he believed in. During the 1920s he served as secretary of the Fellowship of Reconciliation and on the boards of numerous leftist organizations. He also continued to be an active member of the Socialist Party, serving as a delegate to party conventions and as the nominee of the Socialist Party of Ohio for governor in 1940. In 1929 Jones joined the faculty of Antioch College as a professor and chaplain, remaining in that position until his death in 1941.

The former bishop of Utah lived long enough to see many in his church, along with others throughout the religious establishment in America, regret the role they had played in the war effort during 1917–18.[36] Such a view was expressed by the eminent American theologian Reinhold Niebuhr:

> Every soldier, fighting for his country in simplicity of heart without asking many questions, was superior to those of us who served no better purpose than to increase, or perpetuate, the moral obfuscation of nations. . . . The time of man's ignorance God may wink at, but now he calls us to repent. I am done with this business.[37]

In 1929 the Episcopal Church tacitly acknowledged its error of a decade before by appointing Paul Jones to serve for six months as acting bishop of southern Ohio. Although not a position of tremendous influence, the call represented a vindication for the Right Reverend Paul Jones and a confirmation of his belief that bishops of the Episcopal Church have the right of political expression and freedom of conscience.

NOTES

Originally published in the *Utah Historical Quarterly* 50 (Summer 1982): 209–24.

1. Ralph Lord Roy, *Communism and the Churches* (New York: Harcourt, Brace, 1960), 15. For information on the role of clergymen during World War I, see Ray H. Abrams, *Preachers Present Arms* (Scottsdale, PA: Herald Press, 1969). Abrams identifies some seventy individuals,

including Jones, who actively opposed the war. Nine different denominations were represented, with a few coming from the Unitarians, Congregationalists, Universalists, Baptists, and Episcopalians. Of these clergymen, fifty-nine were occupying pulpits during the war. Approximately half were able to remain at their posts; the other half were forced or chose to resign.

2. *The Social Preparation* 1 (January 1913). For a decade this magazine was the official publication of the Church Socialist League.

3. Paul Jones, "What the War Did to My Mind," *Christian Century*, March 8, 1928, 310–12.

4. Paul Jones, "The Philosophy of a Madman," *Christian Century*, September 13, 1923, 1164–66. In the Yale student annual the year he graduated, Jones noted his "highest ambition was to send a son to Yale."

5. Ibid.

6. John Howard Melish, *Paul Jones, Minister of Reconciliation* (New York: Fellowship of Reconciliation, 1942), 38. Jones's antiwar attitudes were strongly influenced by those of his wife, May, who was a pacifist and also a member of the Fellowship of Reconciliation.

7. Paul Jones, *The Christian Soldier* (n.p., n.d.). Jones differed from Spalding in that he frequently used militaristic metaphors and symbols when expressing his antiwar views. Spalding was so adamant against using military symbolism that at one point he wrote a set of new lyrics to the standard Protestant hymn "Onward Christian Soldiers," which he retitled "Onward Christian Workers."

8. Ibid.

9. Paul Jones, *Christian Loyalty* (n.p., n.d.). Copies of this pamphlet and *The Christian Soldier* are on file at the Utah State Historical Society Library, Salt Lake City.

10. Ibid.

11. *Deseret News*, December 22, 1915.

12. Paul Jones, "Armed or Unarmed," *Utah Survey* 3 (March 1916).

13. *Deseret News*, March 27, 1917.

14. *Deseret News*, March 28, 1917.

15. "Petition from the Council of Advice, Missionary District of Utah, to House of Bishops, Chicago, October 17, 1917," Records of the House of Bishops, Record Group 9, Episcopal Church Archives, Episcopal Theological Seminary of the Southwest, Austin, Texas (hereafter cited as Episcopal Church Archives).

16. Paul Jones to H. A. McMillin, March 30, 1917, Records of the Episcopal Diocese of Utah, Special Collections, Marriott Library, University of Utah, Salt Lake City.

17. Charles DeBenedetti, *The Peace Reform in American History* (Bloomington: Indiana University Press, 1980), 104. See also, *Salt Lake Tribune*, July 31, 1917.
18. *Salt Lake Tribune*, October 3, October 4, 1917; *Los Angeles Times*, October 3, October 4, 1917.
19. "Petition from the Council of Advice," Episcopal Church Archives.
20. Ibid.
21. Paul Jones to Daniel S. Tuttle, December 20, 1917, Episcopal Church Archives.
22. *Journal of the General Convention of the Episcopal Church, 1919* (New York, 1920), 497.
23. *Salt Lake Tribune*, October 3, 1917.
24. "Bishop Jones' Reply," *The Churchman* 116 (September 1917): 423.
25. Marguerite Schneider to William Lawrence, October 11, 1917, Episcopal Church Archives.
26. Francis B. Affleck to Arthur Selden Lloyd, October 11, 1917, ibid.
27. Maxwell W. Rice to Daniel S. Tuttle, October 10, 1917, ibid.
28. Chauncey P. Overfield, "The Church and the Mormons," *The Living Church*, April 6, 1935, 420.
29. "Petition from the Council of Advice," Episcopal Church Archives.
30. *Deseret News*, March 29, 1917.
31. Ibid.
32. *Goodwin's Weekly*, March 31, 1917.
33. Kenneth S. Guthrie to Thomas Gailor, March 22, 1918, Episcopal Church Archives.
34. Charles Chatfield, *For Peace and Justice: Pacifism in America, 1914–1941* (Knoxville: University of Tennessee Press, 1971), 43.
35. "Journal of the Proceedings of the Tenth Annual Convocation of the Protestant Episcopal Church of Utah, 1917," Episcopal Church Archives.
36. Clifton E. Olmstead, *History of Religion in America* (Englewood Cliffs, NJ: Prentice-Hall, 1960), 565. As Olmstead notes, "many Christian leaders [suffered] pangs of conscience for the part they played in World War I. Through the 1920s there was an increasing resolve on the part of large numbers of the clergy never again to bless another war." In 1931 the *World Tomorrow* polled nineteen thousand Protestant ministers on their attitude toward war and learned that twelve thousand would disapprove of any future war and more than ten thousand would decline to take part in a conflict. A second poll taken three years later reaffirmed this sentiment. The American religious community was divided on this question through the 1930s. The

debate ended with Pearl Harbor, but response to American involvement in World War II from the religious community was considerably less extreme and jingoistic than had been the case in 1917–18.

37. Quoted in Abrams, *Preachers Present Arms*, 235.

13

THE INFLUENZA EPIDEMIC OF 1918–19 IN UTAH

LEONARD J. ARRINGTON

One of the unforeseen consequences of war was the outbreak of a worldwide influenza epidemic that killed more than twenty-one million people. Utah was not spared as the first influenza cases were reported in the state in early October 1918. By 1921, when the epidemic had run its course, thousands of Utahns had been infected and more than thirty-five hundred were dead. The following article, focusing on Utah's urban cities, gives an overview of the epidemic in the state.

The influenza epidemic spread from U.S. army camps in the Midwest to ports and battlefields in France in the spring of 1918 and moved quickly around the world to China, Africa, Brazil, and the South Pacific, infecting millions of people. Because some eight million Spaniards came down with it, the disease came to be known as Spanish influenza. As the Allies neared victory over the Central powers in September 1918, the epidemic returned to the United States and spread rapidly from Boston, New York, and Philadelphia to the Midwest and the Pacific coast. Approximately a fifth of the world population endured the fever and aches of influenza during 1918–19, and more than twenty-one million died in just four months. In the space of one year, approximately six hundred and seventy-five thousand Americans died from the same disease—more than ten times as many as were killed during World War I—and approximately one-half of the soldiers who died in Europe were felled not by enemy firepower but by the influenza virus.[1]

People around the world have been familiar with influenza, perhaps for thousands of years. Almost everyone has had it several times. One goes to bed for three or four days, feels miserable, gets up feeling a little weak and shaky, and then goes about his or her business. One does not view it as a thing of terror, like AIDS or smallpox, typhoid fever or tuberculosis, perhaps because in most instances many have suffered but few have died. This was not true of the 1918–19 virus. Medical researchers have determined in recent years that the influenza virus, an infectious agent so small that thirty million would fit on the head of a pin, can reproduce only in living cells. Of the several influenza viruses, most of them without serious effect on the human body, one particular strain, perhaps working in combination with a swine virus, proved deadly, producing the 1918–19 epidemic, the worst humanity has undergone since the Black Death (bubonic plague) of the fourteenth century.[2]

Not only was the 1918 virus unprecedented for its ferocity, but it was also unique in killing a high proportion of those eighteen to forty-five years of age, the healthiest and most vigorous of its victims. Some 621,000 soldiers caught the flu in 1918, one-sixth of the total number of combatants in World War I, of whom 43,000 died of influenza or pneumonia.[3]

The first cases in Utah were noted in early October 1918, and by October 10 Utah state health officer Dr. T. B. Beatty was sufficiently concerned to issue a directive banning all public gatherings, including church meetings and theater performances. He warned school districts and universities that they should give serious consideration to closing schools and colleges. They did so two days later and most of them remained closed until early January 1919.[4]

Salt Lake City, as the "crossroads of the West," began to report an outbreak on October 3, and, because of the large number of visitors, the city felt the impact of the disease intensely. Within four weeks there were more than 1,500 cases of influenza and 117 deaths. On a single day, October 15, Salt Lake City officials reported 161 new cases and 6 deaths. Entire families were down in many instances. On that same day 65 other towns in Utah reported outbreaks of the disease.

Ogden, the leading railroad junction and principal destination for many returning servicemen and western travelers, was also an immediate target of the virus. From October 3 to October 26 there were 2,628 cases of flu, with 73 deaths. Because the Dee Hospital—owned at the time by the three Latter-day Saint (LDS) Weber stakes—was full, local officials equipped the Ogden LDS Third Ward amusement hall as a temporary hospital, with Myrtle Swainston, a recently graduated nurse from the LDS Hospital School of Nursing in Salt Lake City, in charge. Her salary and the costs of operating the emergency hospital were shared by the American Red Cross, the city of Ogden, and Weber County.[5] Ogden was fortunate to have "borrowed" one of the finest nurses in Salt Lake's LDS Hospital at the very time Salt Lake was experiencing its own critical shortage of nurses because of the virulence of the epidemic there.

The day after Swainston's arrival Ogden reported forty new cases of the flu. With the help of local authorities Swainston had acquired a few hospital beds from Fort Douglas and some sheets, blankets, and other equipment, and was prepared to treat the initial six patients. The *Ogden Standard* for October 16 reported the emergency hospital to be "splendidly equipped." The next day, October 17, arrangements were completed to move the emergency hospital out of its temporary quarters in the LDS Third Ward and into the basement of the First Congregational Church, where beds were prepared for twenty patients. Swainston appealed for donations of nightshirts, pneumonia jackets, flannel blankets, and screens. She was particularly appreciative of the willingness of Weber valley teachers, whose schools were closed, to serve in homes as volunteer nurses and in the hospitals as practical nurses. All were alarmed at the rapid velocity of the deadly disease. On the day the hospital was moved to the Congregational church, there were twenty-six influenza-related deaths in Salt Lake City and six in Ogden.

The flu continued its march across the nation. The Ogden city clerk reported 5 deaths and 175 new cases on October 19. Since October 3, when they experienced the first death, there had been 20 deaths in Ogden. Salt Lake City had had 1,179 cases of flu since October 10, with 40 deaths. The clerk reported 6 patients in the emergency hospital, with 7 others to join that day. Swainston was gratified to acknowledge the receipt of flowers, fresh vegetables, jams and jellies, flannel materials for making nightshirts and pneumonia jackets, bed screens and window curtains, and lamp shades. The hospital was now equipped with telephone connections.[6] Most of the staff, consisting of eleven persons, were from the Ogden city schools.[7]

As the epidemic continued, Ogden needed additional hospital facilities, and a temporary hospital annex was built on the north end of the Dee Hospital to provide for thirty patients. The regular hospital staff and nurses of Dee would serve it. The annex was ready none too soon, for eighty-two new cases of flu and five deaths were reported the next day. Meanwhile, the LDS Relief Society provided many women to help in afflicted homes.[8]

Influenza was rampant throughout Utah, as it was elsewhere in the nation. On October 30 Salt Lake City reported 2,300 cases, with a cumulative number of 117 deaths since the siege began. What alarmed everyone was that most of the deaths were young mothers and fathers, the most robust segment of the population. There were fewer deaths than usual among the very young and the very old. The city adopted stringent regulations. Homes where the flu appeared had to be quarantined and placarded with the word "INFLUENZA" in large letters. The order of the State Board of Health prohibiting public assemblages was rigidly enforced. To make the point clear, the police arrested the proprietor and seven card-playing customers of a soft drink establishment and card room at 547 West 2nd South. The city also reminded citizens of the requirement that gauze masks be worn in public places.[9] The schools, of course, remained closed.

With an average of fifty persons per day coming down with the flu in Ogden and almost double that number in Salt Lake City, the business of the state slowed to a standstill. The minister of the First Baptist Church in Ogden, the city editor of the *Ogden Standard*, and Albert Scowcroft, a leading Ogden merchant, all died. Store clerks, mechanics, salesmen, farmers, and stockmen—all were hit. In some districts as many as 90 percent of the schoolchildren were afflicted with the flu. So urgent was the need for nurses that the Red Cross, which had already put to work the unemployed schoolteachers and actors and actresses, persuaded employers to grant any of their employees who worked all night on a nursing assignment the next day off with pay. The women's page of the *Ogden Standard* for November 9 carried the names of forty-five schoolteachers, all women, who had volunteered to serve as nurses and helpers in homes, where they had to be housekeepers, cooks, and laundresses. In addition to Nurse Swainston and her two assistant nurses at the emergency hospital, another twenty women worked there regularly. The *Standard* praised them for their "heroic and self-sacrificing service." In the process, of course, some of them contracted the disease and at least three died.[10]

There was no medication for influenza at the time. The patient was put to bed, kept warm with blankets and quilts, and given plenty of liquids. The windows were kept open because of the insistence upon "fresh air." If pneumonia developed, something everyone dreaded because of the high mortality, the attendant would put a hot pack on the chest to loosen the infection and keep the lungs warm and would place the patient in an insulated jacket to keep the heat in. This would make it easier for the patient to breathe—to get oxygen.

Most doctors and nurses also administered "spirits"—the polite name for brandy or whiskey. Although Utah went dry on August 1, 1917, doctors, nurses, and pharmacists could administer alcohol to patients. Inevitably, some persons contracted the disease quite often or at least wanted a good preventive. A certain Ogden citizen was arrested late one evening for public intoxication. When the police dragged him to the municipal court, the man explained that he had merely drunk a bottle of whiskey he had bought two years before in Salt Lake City. He had drunk it, he explained, "to keep down an attack of influenzy." He told the judge that many doctors administered whiskey as "good for influenzy," and he hoped the court would be broadminded enough to agree with the doctors "once in a while." The judge's response: "Doctors don't order you to drink it in doses like those you had last night," whereupon "the horrid, narrow-minded judge"—to use the newspaper's language—sentenced the man to a fine of fifty dollars or thirty days in the city jail.[11]

If one were to judge by the newspapers, everyone was preoccupied, not with the deadly pestilence that was killing so many, but with the conclusion of the war in Europe. After several false alarms the armistice came on Monday, November 11. Should the authorities attempt to enforce the ban on public gatherings? They didn't dare! They agreed to bow to the will of the people "for play and jollification." And Salt Lake City, for one, "went mad," to use a journalist's phrase, and "Great joy reigned uncontrolled and uncontrollable." "It was," wrote the reporter, "a merger of the wildest New Year's Eve demonstration when John Barleycorn wielded the scepter, with the biggest Labor Day and Fourth of July manifestations and the greatest of all festivals and carnivals ever witnessed in Salt Lake all rolled into one." The merged events, he wrote, "would not outshine the spontaneous people's celebration which dominated the entire community from early day to late night." A condition of "happy chaos" prevailed—so much so that an immense parade planned to take place at 3 p.m. could not proceed. The scene was so hectic that Mayor W. Mont Ferry, Commissioner Karl A. Scheid, and Chief of Police J. Parley White decided it was futile.

Three bands that had expected to participate in the parade instead played for dances on Main Street between 1st and 2nd South. The bands alternated in three-hour shifts. In front of the Tribune building in the evening was a "dense human flood." As the reporter described it,

"Government of the streets was banished and a screaming multitude laughing and gay took possession, a riotous revel." Whistles shrieked, horns hooted, cans battered noisily, and taut drums boomed forth in concomitant cacophony. "Brass bells that once dangled from the neck of a lead cow were employed to swell the dinning chorus." While hands manipulated rattles and squawkers, kitchens were raided in search of something to substitute for cymbals. "Even rubbish dumps were denuded of tin and iron waste to add to the uproar." The brass bands tried manfully, in vain, "to drown the inharmonious but happy ruction, which swelled in impetuosity and volume as the day and night wore on." The Denver and Rio Grande Railroad contributed a steam locomotive that traversed the street along the rails of the streetcar company, emitting "an incessant shrieking scream." On its decks men, women, boys, and girls crowded, giving the appearance of a well-laden excursion steamer. Carried away himself, the reporter wrote: "From the high reaches of skyscrapers great showers of vari-colored papers fell upon the masses in the canyon below, forming a carpet on the street. 'Victory confetti' aided the carpeting process. Dignity was flung aside. William Hohenzollern [the kaiser of Germany] was hung in effigy."[12] Other Utah communities had their own celebrations—perhaps not so noisy or raucous but surely as heartfelt and joyous—with everyone in the streets.

The outcome was predictable; there was another outbreak of "influenzy." Seventy-one new cases were reported in Ogden alone on November 13, 153 on November 15, and 123 on November 16. The impact on Salt Lake City was proportionally greater. Clearly, health had not benefited from the celebration. As one official noted, "The epidemic is not under control." Once more health officials felt the need to insist on strict regulations: all patients must be isolated, each house with a sick patient must be placarded, masks must be worn in sick rooms and in other specified places, and conductors must prevent overcrowding on streetcars—no more than seventy-five passengers at any time on large streetcars and no more than fifty on smaller ones. Health officials also established business hours for grocery stores,

8 a.m. to 6:30 p.m.; department stores, 9:30 a.m. to 5:30 p.m.; and offices, 9:00 a.m. to 4:30 p.m. No social gatherings were to be held, and no stores were to hold special sales. Funeral services were limited to thirty minutes (later reduced to fifteen minutes) with no more than three vehicles besides the hearse in a cortege. No patient was to leave a quarantined house until ten days had elapsed. Enforcement of the emergency ordinance was facilitated by the employment of one hundred additional deputies. Within a day one person had been arrested for violation of the order and other arrests were pending. A barber who refused to wear a mask was fined ten dollars.[13]

One long-time employee of Hotel Utah recalled the enforcement period of wearing gauze masks. Once a few of the management people went into the board room and removed their masks to have a smoke. Suddenly, one of them spotted a policeman approaching. "Jiggers, a cop!" he exclaimed, whereupon all dropped their cigarettes and hurriedly replaced their masks. By the time the inspecting policeman arrived all were properly attired.[14]

Despite some merriment and ridicule, fear of the disease assured public support for the restrictions. A staff member of the *Salt Lake Tribune* recalled that in late November he checked out of the Fort Douglas Hospital and registered at the Hotel Utah. As O. N. Malmquist wrote, "About 10 p.m. he walked from the Hotel Utah to the Newhouse Hotel and back, a distance of eight blocks on Main Street, and saw one human being and two cats. The human being, wearing a ghostly white mask, was a night watchman checking shop doors. The cats were, appropriately, black."[15]

So many people required hospitalization that the Judge Memorial Hospital, which had closed its doors in 1915, was reopened under the management of the Red Cross in response to the emergency.

While the larger cities were regarded as more vulnerable, smaller towns in the state also wrestled with the disease. There was a rigid quarantine in Cedar City, where no person dared appear on the street without a mask. In Escalante there were two hundred cases of the flu. Panguitch, with no cases at all since the epidemic began, did not escape; on December 19 this last holdout in the state was heavily infected. Again, the onset was predictable. A soldier who returned home discovered later that he was infected, but in the meantime he had been entertained at a party at which many residents were present. The epidemic quickly spread through the town.[16]

An official of the U.S. Public Health Service visited Utah on November 25 to "inspect what you are doing" and to urge everyone to cooperate in stamping out the evil. By that time there had been 225 influenza deaths in Ogden and more than 500 in Salt Lake City, surely ample reason for distress if not panic. "If you could see the state of many homes where sufferers lie with none to help, you would agree that the situation is appalling," said Rev. John Edward Carver, the clergyman who made the rounds with him.[17] The very day the officer visited Salt Lake City there were 21 new cases in the German prisoner-of-war camp at Fort Douglas.[18]

Soon after Thanksgiving, with the number of new cases remaining large, Ogden decided to join some other local communities (e.g., Park City) in setting up a citywide quarantine to be enforced against communities whose health regulations were not as strict as those of Ogden; specifically, this meant Salt Lake City, which had just lifted its quarantine system. Any Ogdenite who shopped in or visited Salt Lake City had to present a health certificate before he or she could re-enter Ogden and must wear a mask or pay a fine of five dollars. The certificate had to be signed by a physician acting on behalf of the Salt Lake Board of Health. The certificate read: "This is to certify that the bearer (name) was on this date and at this hour seen and examined by me and shows no trace of any acute infectious disease." Officials of the Bamberger and Oregon Short Line Railroads were instructed that they must not accept passengers for Ogden unless they held a certificate of clearance.[19]

Salt Lake City did not take this calmly. The feisty director of the state health department, Dr. T. B. Beatty, entrained for Ogden and convened a meeting of local physicians, elected officials, businessmen, and civic leaders to make his protest.[20] Said Beatty, "I was the most damned man in Utah when we imposed the ban [on October 10], and now I am more heatedly damned as it is lifted." Beatty said that the wearing of masks had proven ineffective, that the city should quarantine sick persons instead of homes, and that the ban on travel from Salt Lake to Ogden was unfair. His Ogden hearers listened politely but skeptically and then applauded the response of the Ogden mayor. The only reason Dr. Beatty had lifted the ban in Salt Lake, he said, was because business interests had put pressure on him to allow people from Ogden and the smaller towns to go to Salt Lake City to buy Christmas presents. He knew this was true because the Salt Lake Board of Health and Salt Lake County Commission had issued a statement that they opposed the Utah Board of Health decision to lift the Salt Lake quarantine. Since the beginning of the epidemic on October 3 Ogden had reported 3,307 cases of flu, and 203 of these had been fatal. There was a slight decline from 457 cases during the last week of November to 305 cases the first week in December, but many new cases were still reported every day—30 cases that very day and 50 the day before. People were still dying from the disease. So Ogden continued the rigid enforcement of its regulations. However, the group agreed they might make wearing a mask voluntary.[21]

The usual frictions arose in enforcing the regulation. Highway patrolmen turned back a number of cars without certificates to the accompaniment of considerable profanity. One man was angered almost to the fighting stage, a patrolman reported, but no arrests were made. Passengers on the trains without certificates were told not to leave the platform in Ogden. Those driving or riding through Weber County to Idaho were, of course, permitted to pass.[22] Whatever the inconveniences to Salt Lake business interests, the Ogden decision was unquestionably popular in the Junction City. Letters to the editor and newspaper editorials supported continuation of the Ogden ban.[23]

The relentless continuation of the epidemic caused officials in several population centers to look to further expansion of their hospital facilities. Serious consideration was given to the construction of additional buildings in Salt Lake City, Ogden, Provo, and Logan. While those plans were being studied, Ogden officials announced that the temporary emergency hospital would be moved out of the basement of the First Congregational Church. On November 29 they announced their decision to set up an emergency hospital in the high school, where kitchen arrangements "are so perfect." A staff of nurses was ready and cots were to be sent from Fort Douglas."[24] At a hearing that night, however, strong objections to the plan were registered by Dr. Edward Rich, perhaps the most prominent physician in the county. He feared "permanent contamination [of the building] endangering the lives of the students returning to school." His objections, echoed by others, caused the emergency committee to investigate other options.[25] On December 2 the Elks Lodge, which had acquired the abandoned Central School in Ogden in 1911, proffered the club's building. By the next day Swainston and her staff were prepared to receive the thirty-five patients transferred from the First Congregational Church hospital; eventually they were able to handle as many as seventy-five patients. In addition to Swainston, three trained nurses were provided and two male nurses were requested, one for the daytime and one for the night.[26] A reporter for the *Ogden Standard* described the new facility:

> Large spacious rooms, well lighted, clean, and bright to look upon, nurses whose every movement said, "We are here to assist your speedy recovery." A . . . set of rooms for the convenience and welfare of the nursing staff, and in short, to use the phrase of the real estate advertisement, "every modern appliance that human nature may call for" during a time of sickness. . . . Above the door and beneath the insignia B P O E . . . there ought to be written, "Abound in hope all ye who enter here."[28]

The difficulty of finding nurses was made clear in a news release from Winnemucca, Nevada. A Basque sheepman living on a ranch near McDermott on the Oregon line said all the members of his family were down with the flu. They needed a nurse/housekeeper. He offered twenty dollars per day to anyone who would look after his family and found no takers; in Winnemucca he found a black woman who was available for thirty dollars per day. Seeing no alternative, he consented to what she asked. "I thought it was worth $30," the woman said.[27]

Early in December there were an average of fifty new cases per day and two or three deaths in Ogden, with approximately double that number in Salt Lake City. Ogden held to its regulations; on December 6 several retail store clerks failing to wear masks were taken into city court and fined.[29] On December 14 sixteen people were arrested for having a banquet at the Stimson Cafe to celebrate the departure of a friend. The police arrived at the conclusion of the meal, just before the celebrators were ready to begin a dance. Five participants escaped the police by darting out the back door.[30]

As the epidemic began to slow down in mid-December 1918 state health officials learned of the severity of the virus' impact on Indian reservations in Utah and Arizona, where an estimated two thousand Navajos had died. Several family groups or tribes were decimated. On the Uintah reservation sixty-two died before the end of the year, including Chief Atchee of the Ute Indians. Another twenty Uncompahgre Indians also died.[31] An Office of Indian Affairs report—covering influenza among American Indians from October 1, 1918, to March 31, 1919—indicates how severely the epidemic affected Native Americans:[32]

State	Native American Population	Number of Cases	Number of Deaths
Arizona	45,707	17,237	1,948
Colorado	1,222	399	59
New Mexico	22,005	10,550	1,214
Utah	1,704	448	72
Total	70,638	28,634	3,293

Even though many deaths were probably not reported, this summary shows a far higher morbidity and mortality rate among Indians in the Four Corners area than for the general population of the region or nation. Approximately 40 percent of the native population came down with the flu, and almost 12 percent of those infected died. These figures are approximately four times as high as those for large cities in the United States during the same epidemic period.

City and county officials in many Utah cities decided their quarantine had been effective in controlling the spread of influenza (invariably referred to, even at this date, as Spanish influenza), and with the diminution in new cases and deaths they set Thursday, December 19, as the last day of their ban. Beginning December 20 in many communities, theaters, churches, and poolrooms could reopen. All public assemblages except dances and funerals were free of restrictions. Because of the approach of Christmas, schools would not reopen until December 30.[33]

The ebb in new flu cases led Ogden to close down its emergency hospital after five weeks of healing ministry. On December 20 the four patients remaining at the Elks Lodge influenza unit were taken to the influenza ward of the Dee Hospital, and Nurse Swainston returned to Salt Lake City on December 22.[34]

After slowing down during the last two weeks of December, the epidemic suddenly sped up again in early January when, to everyone's consternation, 108 new cases of influenza were reported in Salt Lake City, 46 in Ogden, and disturbingly large numbers in communities around the state. Was it the result of people mixing during the Christmas vacation period? Was it the removal of the bans, quarantines, and strict regulations? Or was it a renewed effort of the destructive virus? Whatever the case or causes, a new wave of sickness continued for several weeks. Fortunately, it was not as virulent as the fall epidemic. Fewer people died, and those in the twenty- to forty-year age group were not as severely affected as earlier.

The new outbreak, however, caused officials to reinstitute the prohibitions against public gatherings. Most churches held no services, and many communities closed theaters, pool halls, and civic auditoriums once again. Cities were divided on the question of schools. Where they remained open, the principals and superintendents were instructed to take forceful action to keep down the epidemic by sending home students showing signs of the disease, requiring the teachers to give lessons on "what to do," insisting on immunization, and maintaining a staff doctor and/or nurse.[35]

Soon after the regulations were reinstated, three northern Utah cities faced the problem of what to do about a planned celebration for the returning 145th Field Artillery Regiment. Organized in June 1917 from units of the Utah National Guard, the group had trained at Fort Douglas until October 1917, when they were ordered to Camp Kearny, near San Diego, for further training. When they left Salt Lake City there was a mammoth parade downtown, where they were cheered by twenty thousand young people given a special dismissal from school. Finally, after chomping at the bit to get into "the thick of it," the unit crossed the Atlantic and landed in France on September 2, 1918.

Once in France, though not required to engage in offensive or defensive activity, the regiment was exposed to the Spanish flu. Some thirty thousand soldiers near Bordeaux were stricken and the death toll reached two hundred per day. Fourteen men of the 145th died. The regiment left France on December 23, landed in New York on January 4, and were shortly on their way to Utah.[36]

Though they had served sixteen months without action as a unit, members of the regiment were universally regarded as heroes. They deserved a parade and, according to later testimony, wanted a parade. They would be arriving at the Ogden depot in three trains at 8:00, 8:15, and 8:30 a.m. on January 17. On the one hand, everyone wanted to honor the returning men; on the other hand, officials and others wondered if this would be a prelude to another round of influenza. Agonizing decisions had to be made.

After an emotion-packed meeting on January 15, Ogden officials decided to abandon plans for a celebration.[37] A public outcry greeted this announcement. The Ogden mayor also received a telegram reply from Col. William C. Webb, who was accompanying the troops, saying how disappointed they all were. After all, he wrote, the men had been welcomed that morning (January 16) at Green River, Wyoming, where the citizens had turned out, given a band concert, and encouraged the men to roam the town. The men had not been under quarantine at any time during their journey west; they had mingled with residents of towns all along the route from New York, and not one case of flu had developed aboard the military specials.

This was enough to persuade Ogden officials, and they announced the parade would be held the next day as originally scheduled. There would be a three-mile march in formation; the men would not be dismissed. Everyone could cheer, but tight measures would be taken to patrol the entire route. There would be no speeches and no lunch except box lunches delivered to the railroad cars. There would be no mixing with the public. But the good intentions of both the regiment and the city were not enough.

The next morning shrieking whistles and sirens announced the special trains arriving at the Ogden depot. Relatives and close friends were allowed to pass through the gates to meet "their boys." (Who would deny them?) The 1,174 men and 43 officers, dressed in full battle gear, complete with a full pack and a steel helmet, lined up behind Gov. Simon Bamberger and the regimental band to stage the biggest parade in the history of Ogden. They marched from the depot up the flag-decorated 25th Street, along Washington Boulevard to 21st, back to 28th, and again down to 25th. Twenty thousand cheering Ogdenites joined in the welcome. The police prevented most of the crowd from gathering at the station. There was plenty of yelling at the troops, but no soldier was allowed to break ranks. All the schoolchildren were given a half-day holiday and were there to cheer. Four hundred women had worked into the night preparing 1,500 box lunches.[38]

The troops entrained for Logan at 10:35, 10:50, and 11:05, with a special car attached to the first train for the governor and his staff, the board of trustees of the college, state officials, officials of the LDS Church, the entire state legislature, and delegations from the Commercial Clubs (chambers of commerce) of Salt Lake, Ogden, and Provo—all told, some 350 persons in addition to the regiment. Everyone in Logan, all masked with "flu protectors," came to meet them. But, as the *Tribune* correspondent reported, "the arrival of Utah's own regiment made them remove their masks and smile and cheer." Just as the procession turned up Main Street a huge illuminated sign flashed "Welcome Home." In addition to box lunches, Cache County citizens gave them 200 dozen doughnuts, 10 bushels of apples, 6 cases of oranges, 115 pounds of candy, 2,000 pies, 1,200 cakes, 60 gallons of coffee, and assorted cigars, cigarettes, gum, and cookies.

As the returning troops went to their demobilizing bivouac they would have seen fifty-three flags flying from homes in which were resting seventy-eight cases of influenza under quarantine. Schools were still closed, and the troops were placed in quarantine until the mustering-out process was over. This did not prevent a welcoming assembly addressed by the governor, the chairman of the board of trustees, the president of the LDS Church, the mayor of Salt Lake City, Brig. Gen. Richard W. Young, and other dignitaries.[39] The process of demobilization required a week, after which the three companies (five hundred men) of northern and central Utah veterans left Logan by train to participate in a parade in their honor in Salt Lake City. Having been mustered out, they would parade without heavy packs and rifles.[40]

Salt Lake newspapers, fearful that the parade would be called off, announced no new flu cases, although, as readers learned later, the city had 124 new cases and 6 deaths on January 18. The Salt Lake Board of Health unalterably opposed the parade, as did the Utah Board of Health. Both announced as much publicly. But the night before the cancelled parade was originally scheduled to be held, Governor Bamberger, Mayor Mont Ferry, and Brigadier General Young held a conference and agreed to revoke the postponement and go ahead with the festive parade. A public reception, however, was called off. Once again, officials planned the kind of parade held in Ogden, strictly controlled to prevent any mixing of watchers and soldiers. The Oregon Short Line Depot (now the Union Pacific Depot) was nevertheless thronged with anxious relatives and sweethearts. Many of the khaki-clad lads wore steel helmets (which they had been permitted to keep after their discharge in Logan) and placed their gas masks at alert position as an added interest. The men had not marched as far as two blocks east on South Temple before the crowd, which had stood waiting for two hours, broke and rushed in to take a good look at the soldiers. Police were unable (or unwilling) to handle the crowd. The soldiers (actually they were now civilians) broke ranks, waved, shook hands, and mixed with everyone.[41]

The joy of reunion was soon dulled by grief and apprehension. Within a few days, as the alarmists had predicted, there was another outbreak of the dreaded flu, with multiplying misery and mourning.

In the meantime, however, the disease seemed to have run its course in several communities. The Utah State Agricultural College reopened on January 25, after three months of shutdown because of the flu. The Brigham Young College, also in Logan, opened a week later. At that time Logan gave up its requirement of wearing masks. The frustrated local health board declared: "The coming of the 145th regiment, the state legislature, and the sugar manufacturers convention so demoralized the discipline in mask wearing that the police department has been unable to enforce the ordinance for the last two weeks."[42]

The epidemic diminished in the spring of 1919, and there were virtually no cases during the summer. A few cases were reported in the fall and many hundreds during the winter. By the spring of 1920 the epidemic was over. Fortunately, the infections of 1919–20 were light and there were few deaths.

All in all, perhaps because of their large families, Utah suffered more severely from the influenza epidemic than any other state, with the possible exception of Colorado and Pennsylvania. If one takes the cases reported to the Utah Board of Health, which is certainly not complete but still suggests the extent of the affliction, the data from October 1, 1918, to February 1, 1920, are as follows:[43]

	1918–1919	1919–1920	Total
Total cases reported	72,573	19,226	91,799
Number of deaths reported	2,607	308	2,915

In making this report, state health commissioner T. B. Beatty expressed his belief that there had been no fewer than 130,000 Utah flu cases in 1918–19, and that the above figures, based on reported cases, grossly understated the true impact of the disease. Not quite 4 percent of those who came down with the disease in 1918–19 died. Not quite 2 percent died in 1919–20. In Salt Lake City the percentage of deaths was approximately 6 percent in 1918–19 and 4 percent in 1919–20.

The U.S. Public Health Service, to which Utah was one of thirty-four "registration states," gave the following summary of the cases and deaths from influenza and pneumonia by years as follows:[44]

Utah population, 1920	449,396
Deaths from Influenza and Pneumonia, October 1 to December 31, 1918	1,800
Deaths, January 1 to June 30, 1919	1,044
Deaths, July 1 to December 31, 1919	162
Deaths, 1920	574

The Utah Department of Health prepared a more accurate summary in 1941:[45]

Year	Cases of Influenza/Pneumonia	Deaths
1916	766	293
1917	834	257
1918	44,900	2,282
1919	30,352	Inc.
1920	33,361	1,170
1921	1,598	547

To this day medical historians are not certain why the epidemic of 1918–19 took place, why it was so deadly, why it ended, or where it went. But the lives of many Utahns were affected—many lost parents, brothers and sisters, uncles and aunts, etc. And some still alive—and I am one of them—just barely survived this viral holocaust.

NOTES

Originally published in the *Utah Historical Quarterly* 58 (Spring 1990): 165–82.

1. The best treatment of the influenza epidemic of 1918–20 is Alfred W.
    Crosby Jr., *Epidemic and Peace, 1918* (Westport, CT: Greenwood Press,
    1976). Other works on the subject include: A. A. Hoehling, *The
    Great Epidemic* (Boston: Little, Brown & Co., 1961); Richard Collier,
    The Plague of the Spanish Lady: The Influenza Pandemic of 1918–1919
    (New York: Atheneum, 1974); Edwin O. Jordan, *Epidemic Influenza,
    A Survey* (Chicago: American Medical Association, 1927); William Ian
    Beveridge, *Influenza: The Last Great Plague* (New York: Prodist, 1978).
        Published articles include: Irwin Ross, "The Great Plague of 1918,"
    American History Illustrated 3 (July 1968): 12–17; Joseph E. Persico,
    "The Great Swine Flu Epidemic of 1918," *American Heritage* 27 (June
    1976): 28–31, 80–86; and Francis Russell, "A Journal of the Plague:
    The 1918 Influenza," *Yale Review* 47 (December 1957): 219–35.
        Two excellent doctoral dissertations are William R. Noyes,
    "Influenza Epidemic, 1918–19: A Misplaced Chapter in U.S. Social
    and Institutions History" (PhD diss., University of California at Los
    Angeles, 1968); and Dorothy Ann Pettit, "A Cruel Wind: America
    Experiences the Pandemic Influenza, 1918–20" (PhD diss., University
    of New Hampshire, 1976).
        Model treatments of adjoining states are Richard Melzer, "A Dark
    and Terrible Moment: The Spanish Flu Epidemic of 1918 in New
    Mexico," *New Mexico Historical Review* 57 (July 1982): 213–36; and
    Bradford Luckingham, *Epidemic in the Southwest, 1918–1919* (El Paso:
    Texas Western Press, 1984).
2. K. David Patterson, *Pandemic Influenza, 1700–1900: A Study in Histor-
    ical Epidemiology* (Boston: Rowman & Littlefield, 1986); Alfred W.
    Crosby Jr., "The Influenza Pandemic of 1918," in June E. Osborn, ed.,
    Influenza in America, 1918–1976 (New York: Prodist, 1977), 5–13; and
    Giovanni Cavini, *L'influenza epidemica attraverso i secoti* (Rome: Possi,
    1959).
3. Crosby, *Epidemic and Peace*, 205–6, 216.
4. The *Salt Lake Tribune* and *Deseret News* for October 10, 1918, to May 1,
    1920, contain innumerable articles on what they usually referred
    to as Spanish influenza. There are also articles in Utah's small-
    town newspapers. For purposes of this study I have followed most
    carefully the day-by-day accounts in the *Ogden Standard*. Ogden's
    experience is representative of Utah's experience generally, and the
    coverage in the *Standard* is very good.
5. *Ogden Standard*, October 15, 1918. Citations to the *Standard* will be
    made only when the date of publication is not made clear in the text.
6. *Ogden Standard*, October 19, 1918.

7. Ibid., October 21, 1918.

8. Ibid., October 22, October 23, 1918.

9. Ibid., October 29, October 30, October 31, 1918.

10. Ibid., November 9, 1918.

11. Ibid., November 29, 1918.

12. "Salt Lake Goes Mad and Rejoices Over Peace," in *Ogden Standard*, November 12, 1918.

13. *Ogden Standard*, November 22, November 23, November 26, November 30, 1918. See also Thomas G. Alexander and James B. Allen, *Mormons and Gentiles: A History of Salt Lake City* (Boulder, CO: Pruett Publishing Co., 1984), 182.

14. The informant prefers to remain anonymous. See also Nancy Rockafellar, "'In Gauze We Trust:' Public Health and Spanish Influenza on the Home Front, Seattle, 1918–1919," *Pacific Northwest Quarterly* 11 (July 1986): 104–13.

15. See O. N. Malmquist, *The First 100 Years: A History of the Salt Lake Tribune, 1871–1971* (Salt Lake City: Utah State Historical Society, 1971), 293.

16. *Ogden Standard*, December 10, 1918.

17. Ibid., November 25, 1918.

18. A dispatch from Salt Lake City in the *Idaho Falls Daily Post*, November 27, 1918.

19. *Ogden Standard*, December 7, December 9, 1918.

20. Considerable treatment is given to Dr. Beatty in Ralph T. Richards, *Of Medicine, Hospitals, and Doctors* (Salt Lake City: University of Utah Press, 1953), 44–50; and Joseph R. Morrell, *Utah's Health and You: A History of Utah's Public Health* (Salt Lake City: Deseret Book Co., 1956), 88–151.

21. *Ogden Standard*, December 9, December 10, December 11, 1918.

22. Ibid., December 9, 1918.

23. See, for example, ibid., November 13, 1918.

24. Ibid., November 29, 1918.

25. Ibid., November 20, 1918.

26. Ibid., December 2, 1918.

27. Ibid., December 3, 1918.

28. Ibid., December 4, 1918.

29. Ibid., December 6, 1918.

30. Ibid., December 14, 1918.

31. Ibid., December 17, 1918, January 22, 1919; *Salt Lake Tribune*, January 21, January 30, 1919.

32. "Influenza among American Indians," *Public Health Reports* 34 (May 9, 1919): 1008–09.

33. *Ogden Standard*, December 18, 1918.
34. Ibid., December 21, 1918. Swainston served as a private nurse at a Nevada ranch for a few months, after which she went to Hawaii, where she served as superintendent of the Kapiolani Queens Maternity Hospital in Honolulu. She married Dr. Lyman Home, Utah's first trained obstetrician, in January 1923, and later served as president of the Utah Nurses Association.
35. Ibid., January 11, January 13, 1919.
36. The regiment consisted of 1,460 officers and enlisted men from around the state under the command of Col. Richard W. Young (later brigadier general), a grandson of Brigham Young, West Point graduate, and veteran of the Spanish-American War. The chaplain was the popular B. H. Roberts, LDS church leader, orator, and active Democrat. See Louis Paul Murray, "The Life of Brigadier General Richard W. Young" (master's thesis, University of Utah, 1959). See the account of Chaplain Roberts in Truman G. Madsen, *Defender of the Faith: The B. H. Roberts Story* (Salt Lake City: Bookcraft, 1980), 301–14. Also Noble Warrum, *Utah in the World War* (Salt Lake City: Utah State Council of Defense, 1924), 56–59; B. H. Roberts, *A Comprehensive History of the Church. . . .*, 6 vols. (Salt Lake City: LDS Church, 1930), 6: 457–64.
37. *Ogden Standard*, January 15, 1919.
38. Ibid., January 17, 1919; *Salt Lake Tribune*, January 17, 1919. See also Richard C. Roberts and Richard W. Sadler, *Ogden, Junction City* (Northridge, CA: Windsor Publications, 1985), 111.
39. *Salt Lake Tribune*, January 18, 1919.
40. *Logan Journal*, January 16–24, 1919.
41. *Salt Lake Tribune*, January 25, 1919.
42. *Logan Journal*, January 25, February 1, February 3, 1919.
43. *Salt Lake Herald*, February 22, 1920.
44. Bureau of Census, *Mortality Statistics, 1919* (Washington, D.C.: Government Printing Office, 1921), 28–31; and Bureau of Census, *Mortality Rates, 7970–7972* (Washington, D.C.: Government Printing Office, 1923), 63–68.
45. Utah State Department of Health, Division of Communicable Disease Control, *Morbidity and Mortality Report*, Communicable Diseases, 1941.

14

THE INFLUENZA EPIDEMIC OF 1918

A Cultural Response

ROBERT S. MCPHERSON

*As the flu epidemic spread throughout Utah, families and commu-
nities responded to the challenge with determination, hope, and,
at times, frustration and bewilderment. In the article that follows we
see how five different southeastern Utah communities and groups—
Moab, Monticello, Blanding, the Navajos, and the Utes—responded
in quite different ways to the causes and conditions of the epidemic.
We learn the responses were often based on cultural factors that were
unique to each group. Not only were responses different, but so too
were the explanations of the causes and meaning of the epidemic.*

As 1918 drew to a close, the bloody annals of World War I became a
part of history and a prelude to the hope for peace. Another enemy,
however, stalked the living, spreading death throughout the world.
Even in countries that were technologically advanced in health care,
such as the United States, the disease known as Spanish influenza
took its toll, killing over twenty-one thousand Americans in the last
week of October.[1]

Spread primarily through the respiratory system, the sickness leaped from person to person, from community to community, and from region to region, infecting the masses with an often nonlethal but invariably difficult illness that affected them for as long as a month. The purpose of this chapter is to compare reactions to the influenza epidemic of 1918–19 in a limited geographical area—southeastern Utah—and to show how differing cultural responses influenced the severity of the disease. This region is ideal for analysis because of its diversity, ranging from Euro-American to Native American and from scientific medicine to folk remedies, animistic divination, and ceremonial practices. What emerges is a better understanding of the cultural values that pervaded the societies in the Four Corners area at that time.

The origin of Spanish influenza is still not clear. Despite its name, this strain most likely started in the United States and spread to Europe. The first cases of sickness were reported at Fort Riley, Kansas, where dust and smoke from burning manure infected soldiers, over eleven hundred of whom became sick with forty-six actually dying.[2] Later, some of the troops training at Fort Riley deployed to Europe for service in the war and with them traveled the influenza virus.[3] It spread rapidly, first to the soldiers fighting on both sides of the war and then to the civilian masses who welcomed them home.

Rural as well as metropolitan areas suffered from the disease, and the West was no exception. Moab, Utah, first reported an outbreak of influenza on October 18, 1918, when three cases appeared in the J. P. Miller family.[4] The town reacted immediately. Fearing the effects of the disease then sweeping the nation, Dr. J. W. Williams, Moab's health officer, ordered the closing of schools, churches, and other public gathering places. The community fully supported his actions, especially the children, half of whom were withdrawn from school as soon as the disease's presence was reported.

The Utah Board of Health next went to work, outlining precautions to be taken and publishing them in the *Grand Valley Times* of Moab. Most of these instructions were common knowledge, such as having plenty of bed rest, eating healthy food, and seeking a doctor's care; other practices were more innovative. For instance, the Board of Health encouraged people to keep a bedroom window open at all times, to "take medicine to open the bowels freely," and to wear a gauze mask that covered the nose and mouth when entering a sickroom.[5] How many people complied with these instructions is not known. Within a week's time the ban on public gatherings in Moab was lifted because no more cases of influenza had appeared. In Monticello, however, fifty-five miles to the south, the first two incidents of the disease were reported.[6] Moab's respite from influenza was short-lived. By November 1 newspaper headlines splashed warnings of the "alarming" spread of the disease and reported two deaths from it in Moab and two in Monticello. The disease attacked sixty miners in Sego, a coal camp near Moab, while at least six new cases were reported within city limits.

Dr. Williams and the city council took prompt action again, posting guards on the outskirts of town to stop visitors and direct them to the local hotel, where they were quarantined for four days, examined by the doctor, and released if they showed no signs of illness. Failure to comply with these regulations could result in a misdemeanor charge and a fine of up to one hundred dollars. Williams and the city council prohibited all public gatherings in Moab and applauded the many citizens who wore gauze masks outside of their homes.[7]

Normal activities in rural Moab ceased. The election process in Grand County became more difficult as campaigning for political office stopped. The drafting of soldiers for the final phase of the war slowed down, and because the flu was raging in the cantonments in northern Utah, the seventeen men already qualified for service were held in Moab until the epidemic abated. When District Attorney Knox Patterson became ill, cases before the district court for San Juan and Grand counties were postponed.[8] Sheriff W. J. Bliss and Marshal Abe Day from Moab enforced the new local law on wearing masks and prevented attempts of people to gather in large numbers. Even funeral services were not held because of the quarantine.

Still the epidemic raged. Particularly hard hit were occupations that required people to work in large numbers at close quarters. Sego reported one hundred flu cases, while everyone was sick in bed at a uranium camp on Polar Mesa. In Monticello the Mexican population was the hardest hit, with forty cases of influenza.[9] A prominent livestock owner, Ed Taylor, who had accompanied his large herd of sheep to market "back East," apparently contracted the disease there. While returning home he stopped at Grand Junction, Colorado, where he sickened and died.[10] Thus, ordinary business practices also opened the doors to affliction.

Late in November the citizens of Moab started to congratulate themselves on beating the contagion. The disease appeared to have run its course with no new cases reported. The satellite mining communities seemed ready to start back into production. The doctor lifted the quarantine in Moab and school and public gatherings resumed. The control of visitors continued in effect, however. With the Christmas season, peace and goodwill replaced the fear of the previous month.

Yet it was during the Christmas gatherings that a new onslaught of influenza got its start. By January 3, 1919, banner headlines again proclaimed one hundred cases of influenza in Moab. A week later the number had jumped to two hundred and fifty. Cold, wet weather encouraged incubation of the disease, causing it to soar again to epidemic proportions.

Dr. Williams telegraphed for assistance, receiving another doctor from the Utah Board of Health and two nurses from Colorado. After again suspending any type of public meeting, Williams set about establishing a fifty-bed hospital in the high school for the seriously afflicted. Two nurses operated the facility, while the physicians handled the vaccinations. Although the doctors claimed the serum was "an almost infallible preventive," the various strains of influenza proved too versatile to be brought under control.[11] The type of vaccine used is not known; several varieties were available at the time, including a mixture of organisms from influenza patients, diphtheria antitoxins, and antitetanus and antimeningitis serums.[12] Immunity was seldom achieved. One report stated, "A number of people who had the disease a month ago are again stricken, indicating that no one is immune."[13]

During the first bout with influenza late in 1918 a strict external quarantine had sealed Moab off from the outside world. By early January the *Grand Valley Times* could report that "Travel to and from Moab is in no way restricted, so far as local authorities are concerned. People from the outside will be free to come here and transact their business. The neighboring towns, however, have indicated that they will establish stringent quarantine against people coming from or passing through Moab."[14] These changes were at least in part due to the large number of sick in Moab; Dr. Williams estimated that two-thirds of the town, or about five hundred people, were by then afflicted.[15]

Other interesting sidelights to the epidemic were the treatments—advertised and unadvertised—used to fight the malady. Whiskey was one of the most desirable, ten gallons of which Williams ordered from state sources. Because Utah was already dry and the Eighteenth Amendment, requiring national prohibition, was in the process of ratification, legal sources of alcohol were disappearing. The assistant physician, Dr. C. Clark, was supposed to bring ten gallons to Moab with him and deliver it to the sheriff, who would in turn dispense it under the doctor's orders, thus circumventing a state law forbidding shipment of alcohol. The whiskey was not released to Dr. Clark, however, prompting another flurry of letters from the concerned citizens of Moab. Statements such as "ship whiskey. Have eleven down with flu," and "Have two children and wife in bed. Come through if possible," were attached to a petition signed by "every businessman, county and town officers and the Baptist minister." Acting in Gov. Simon Bamberger's absence, Harden Bennion, the secretary of state, relented and sent a special courier to Moab with two gallons of the illegal brew.[16]

Commercial sales of medication skyrocketed. Advertisements warned: "Druggists!! Please Note Vick's VapoRub Oversold Due to

Present Epidemic . . . Last Week's Orders called for One and Three Quarter Million Jars—Today's Orders Alone Number 932,459 Jars."[17] The firm was stepping up production in an effort to meet the unprecedented demand. Another product, Dr. Kilmer's Swamp-Root, was "advertised as healing the kidneys after an attack of grip. . . . A Trial will convince anyone who may be in need of it." Eatonic, on the other hand, supposedly helped "Millions [who] are now suffering from the after effects of the deadly flu . . . by giving attention to the stomach— that is removing acidity and toxic poisons."[18]

The Moab Board of Health offered a different kind of advice by warning that "Two or three days lost from work or business has a distinct advantage over paying the undertaker." The health announcement concluded by stating, "The Creator provided all the oxygen necessary in the fresh air, therefore, don't shut this out of your home and then in case of sickness pay good money for a tank of oxygen."[19]

By January 17 the epidemic in Moab was starting to abate. Reports for that week indicated only five new flu cases, and many of those previously afflicted were on the mend. Dr. Williams estimated that a total of 250 people in the town had not contracted the disease, in comparison to "the great majority of the people of Moab [who] have already had the disease."[20] The townspeople heaped praise upon Doctors Williams and Clark for their round-the-clock efforts, while both doctors lauded the work of the nurses in the temporary high school hospital and the serum made available for vaccinations. The hospital proved to be the most expensive of the community's efforts, costing almost $1,700 for less than a month's operation, during which only ten very critical cases were handled.[21]

In summarizing the city of Moab's experience, one finds an organized, orderly approach to combating the effects of influenza. Two doctors, two nurses, and an active health board combined in an effective program of quarantine, vaccination, hospitalization, home health care, and informational services. Cooperation proved to be the rule and not the exception, with the end result being that fewer than a dozen people died during the combined November and January outbreaks. By January 31 the Moab Board of Health could lift its ban on public gatherings and allow normal town life to resume.

Smaller communities to the south, such as Monticello and Blanding, lacked the organization and medical care available in Moab. Nevertheless, their small size and overwhelmingly Mormon population fostered cooperation of a different nature and helped many to survive. For instance, when the owner of the Grayson Co-Op in Blanding became sick, customers stopped by his home, got the key, opened the store, and took what they needed with a promise to pay later.[22] Although most of the town was afflicted at one time or another with the disease, some men and women made a daily practice of helping their neighbors. The men hauled wood, fed livestock, and performed heavier chores, while the women—including knowledgeable midwives—cared for the sick and helped in the home.[23] Professional medical help was limited to infrequent visits from Dr. Williams in Moab. To speed his travel to Monticello town members met him approximately halfway with a fresh team of horses.[24] No doctor visited Blanding during the epidemic.

As in Moab, public meetings and schools came to a halt in many outlying areas, but some activities had to continue. One woman who lived in the community of Dove Creek, Colorado, just over the Utah border, ran a combination store and post office in 1918 while her husband was in the Cortez hospital with typhoid fever. She remembered how she "saw them bringing in[to the hospital] big, husky, young men. They were bringing them in delirious and maybe in an hour or two they'd be dead. . . . One fellow came and stayed overnight. The next day or two later, he was dead."[25]

For some of the sick, folk remedies served an important function in the healing process. Beyond bed rest and warm food, a common treatment was to apply mustard plasters to the patient's chest to provide heat.[26] Quinine helped break the fever, hot packs and warm olive oil relieved the pain of earaches, and wild sage boiled in water and sweetened with honey loosened a congested chest. One man, ill with the flu in a lonely campsite, doctored himself back to health by eating a big gob of pine pitch.[27] The folk repertoire also included preventive measures such as eating wild garlic and hanging a bag of asafetida around the neck. This latter substance is an offensive smelling, resinous material extracted from the roots of several kinds of plants. One survivor of the ordeal of wearing asafetida swore that "It's the stinkingest stuff. . . ever . . . but it makes a good coyote bait."[28]

Unfortunately, no statistics exist for the effects of influenza in these outlying areas since there was no newspaper, no doctor, and no official organization to record the number of patients. A general impression gathered from oral interviews is that most families in these communities were afflicted, some more seriously than others, and that the mortality rate was higher than in Moab.

Of all the peoples in the Four Corners area the Native Americans, especially the Navajos, seemed to suffer the most. Oral tradition has kept alive the trauma that accompanied the disease. Although much of what was done to prevent it may appear to an outsider as ineffective, the main response to the disease for Navajos was a religious one. To them much of life and its accompanying problems carry supernatural significance that must be dealt with in both the spiritual and the physical realms of this world. The result is a practical, logical approach to disease prevention and cure according to traditional beliefs.

Events do not just happen. Omens appear beforehand but may not be recognized as such until after the fact. So it was with the influenza epidemic. On June 8, 1918, a solar eclipse occurred, presaging misfortune. The sun, an important Navajo deity, hid his light from his people because of his anger and so warned that a catastrophe would soon take place.[29] During the summer and fall, dawns and sunsets had pronounced reddish hues that bathed the landscape in an ominous red. The tips of pinyon and juniper trees started to die, a sign indicating sickness was in the area and would be visiting humans. Some Navajos had bad dreams portending disaster. Some informants indicated that the "Holy Beings" (gods) sent the disease in order to make room for a growing population of young people; still others suggested that poison gas or the smoke and fumes from artillery rounds fired in World

War I somehow infected the people.[30] But whatever the reason for the epidemic, the Navajos were ill prepared for the ensuing sickness.

Because their reservation is spread over a large geographical area, with many access routes and a mobile population, it is difficult to identify the actual entry of the epidemic. For instance, Louisa Wetherill (Asdzaan Ts'osi or "Slim Woman"), the wife of John Wetherill, a trader in Kayenta, Arizona, told of visiting many Navajo homes in southern Utah and northern Arizona to solicit sheep for the war effort. As she traveled from hogan to hogan she became increasingly tired and suffered from severe headaches, which later proved to be symptoms of the flu. She noted that the first death from this disease was in the area of Black Mesa, not far from where she had been visiting. Within a week her Navajo host was also dead, and by the time she arrived back at her trading post her front yard was filled with stricken Navajos. The Indians reacted by destroying the dwelling where a death occurred, and "Soon all over the reservation, smoke was rising from the hogans of the dead."[31] Louisa Wetherill may not have been the first to introduce the disease, but she was most likely an unwitting transmitter of it.

Other examples indicate how the disease spread. A Yeibichai ceremony was held in late October in Blue Canyon, approximately eighteen miles east of Tuba City. Many of the people who gathered for the performance contracted the disease but showed no symptoms for a week or two after. Navajos in the Monument Valley area claimed to have contracted the disease from Paiutes and Utes as they moved from Navajo Mountain to Allen Canyon and the area around Blanding.[32] Navajo miners returning to the reservation from the Silverton and Durango, Colorado, areas were infected as they passed through various towns, unwittingly spreading the disease along the northeastern boundary of Navajo lands. The first reported case occurred at the Shiprock Boarding School during the week of October 6. A letter to the commissioner of Indian affairs noted, "About one week prior to its advent on the agency, the towns to the east, north, and south had . . . their first cases, and in varying degrees of intensity, but these are all located at such distances and with such slow means of communication, that the disease here spread as rapidly as the news."[33]

The effects of influenza among the Navajos were deadly. Some of the best eyewitness accounts come from traders living on or near the reservation. These men and women were known and trusted by their Indian clients, who came to them for assistance in this time of dire need. Ken and Hilda Faunce ran the Covered Water Trading Post in northern Arizona. Near their establishment large groves of pinyon trees bore a heavy crop of nuts, which attracted many Navajos to the harvest. Exposed to cold temperatures and driving rains, the unsuspecting infected victims attempted to collect nuts until they were quickly overcome by the disease. Whole families died by their wagons, vainly seeking shelter from the storms and relief from the flu.[34]

Even those who remained at home were often deprived of their warm winter hogans, abandoning them once a person had died inside. The belief that the spirit of the deceased remained in the vicinity where the death occurred in order to haunt the living because of loneliness created a fear that drove the survivors into temporary brush shelters that provided ineffective protection from the cold and rain.[35] The results were inevitable. Influenza raged across the landscape, destroying entire families at a time. One eyewitness reported that

> whole families were wiped out, leaving their flocks wandering over the hills at the mercy of the wolves. Several related families living together all died but one small boy who was found herding the combined flocks of sheep. . . . A Piute woman died on their reservation north of the San Juan River. Fleeing from the place of the dead, the husband and five children crossed the river into the Navajo country with their sheep where they died one by one along the trail. Only one little boy survived and he is so small that he is unable to give his parents' name.[36]

Louisa Wetherill reported a constant flow of Navajos at her trading post seeking help with burials. Although it took two weeks for her husband to recover from his bout with the flu, both she and John spent considerable time burying the dead and nursing the living. John estimated that by December 6, in Kayenta alone, he had interred over one hundred Navajos.[37]

Hilda Faunce helped a woman who requested a wooden box in which to bury her child. Although this was against traditional practices, the bereaved mother explained that her son had gone away to school in California and had watched the burial of some Navajos, after which no building was destroyed or deserted: "He had not noticed any ill luck had followed such burials; therefore, he thought . . . perhaps the box . . . kept the gods from being angry because the buildings were not burned."[38]

In most instances, white traders dug holes for a final resting place, burned the deserted hogan with the dead inside, or simply closed the doors after shoveling dirt on the deceased. One government stockman riding the range in April 1919 buried two influenza victims who had died in their hogan the previous fall. Another man remembered parties of white volunteers from Colorado, New Mexico, and Utah going into the remote canyons of the reservation to bury the dead.[39] Thus geographical isolation and traditional beliefs combined to make suffering and death a lonely experience for the afflicted.

The Navajo response to this catastrophe came in two forms—spiritual and physical. To them the roots of the epidemic lay in the spiritual realm, and so successful prevention and treatment would be found in religious practices. The Navajos used two types of ceremonies to cure patients: the Blessing Way (Hozhooji) and the Evil Way (Hochxoo'ji). The former is a ritual that encourages beauty, health, and harmony to surround a person, while the latter protects a patient by fending off evil in a variety of forms. The ultimate aim of both ceremonies is to protect a person from harm and provide prayers acceptable to the Holy Beings, who in turn give the necessary help.[40] Medicine men were kept busy traveling about to perform ceremonies for the sick; how many cases of the disease were spread through these unwitting vectors and the close contact required in the rituals will never be known, but in the minds of the Navajos these healers saved many lives and performed a valuable service comparable to the work of the doctors in Moab. Prayers, not vaccine, held the cure.

In the isolated northern part of the reservation some families improvised when they could not obtain the services of a medicine man. One Navajo man remembered:

In those first days when the rains were cold and the Deneh [Diné or "The People"] were sick and died everywhere, two of my boys had the very hot bodies and could not get up. I went for a medicine man, and another, and another, many of them, but they were sick themselves or were singing the chants for others who had the sickness. All of the two days I rode but could find no one to go to my hogan to save my boys. At home I found the women and all of the other children, nine altogether, were very, very sick too. . . . I rode away again, seeking a medicine man. Where the cedar trees grow thick on the hill that stops suddenly I got off my horse to pray. I prayed to several Deneh gods that know me; then I knew I must be the doctor for my family and I took berries from the cedar trees and gathered plants here and there. It was slow work in the rain, but there were those nine sick ones in my hogan.

The plants and the berries I boiled with water in the coffee-pots and gave each of my family a drink. I sang one of the songs for healing and gave another a drink. So I timed the doses until the medicine was gone, and I . . . got more plants and made medicine and the sick ones drank.

There were days when no one came to my hogan. I did not sleep but sang the prayers and gave the medicine until all . . . was well.[41]

Although there were a multitude of protective symbols invoked through formal ceremonies, two objects served as primary means to ward off the disease. Arrowheads and fire pokers embodied protective values that were repeated often in Navajo mythology and religious beliefs. The arrowheads, for instance, were first used long ago by the

Anasazi to kill enemies and protect their people; similar reasoning led the Navajos to use these projectile points in ceremonies as protective devices to ward off the disease that was killing them. The arrowheads served as "a shield to the patient and those who are involved in the ceremony . . . and the things that are not seen just go back where they come from."[42] The points were left in the hogan for up to four days following the ceremony.

The fire poker, another important symbol of protection, delineated a line across which evil and sickness could not pass. This concept harkens back to physical warfare, geographical boundaries, and sanctified territory, but during the flu epidemic the hogan was the major spiritual realm demanding protection. Used both in ceremonies and as a general talisman, the poker represented "Forked lightning, rain-streamer, and zigzag and straight lightning, symbols that prevent the enemy [evil] from crossing." One woman reported,

> At night my father would lean a wood fire poker against the north side of the hogan. He would sit up and tell us, "Sleep my children, but do not go on the north side of the hogan. If you want to go outside, go out on this side only." He would pray all through the night. What prayers he prayed I do not know. No illness came over us, not even a headache.[44]

The poker also had prayers said over it, adding to the already potent association of fire and its role in protecting and serving the home. At the conclusion of the Evil Way ceremony, the medicine man took four fire pokers from the ritual to the east and, with plants and other materials, placed them in a tree. If they remained secure for a month or two, then the participants knew the offering of prayers and chants was accepted by the Holy Beings.[45] So vital were these prayers and protective devices—some Navajos today believe—that those who did not have them were the ones who died."[46]

Dreams, as omens, continued to play an important role during the sickness. One Navajo thanked Louisa Wetherill for visiting him in his hogan while he was ill. After telling him she had not seen him, he assured her that she had come in a dream and said he must not die. The man firmly believed her spirit had made the visit. Another trader was told by a patron that he had almost died, but "When I got to the other side, I saw my brothers. They came to get me. They were all riding horses. But I had no horse, because there was no one left to kill my horse. I couldn't join them without a horse. So I came back."[47]

A similar problem occurred one early winter morning when a man appeared at the Wetherills' trading post, asking for a gun to kill a horse. He explained, "Two days ago my little boy was buried . . . but they killed no horse for him to ride. Already he has nearly completed the second circle on foot, and he is only seven years old. He will be tired now. Lend me a gun that I may kill a horse."[48] His request was granted.

Although the major emphasis in combatting the disease was religious, the Navajos also employed a number of physical cures. Sweat baths provided both physical cleansing and spiritual preparation for ceremonies. People crowded into a small, hogan-like structure and baked in the intense temperatures created by heated rocks. Because influenza is primarily a respiratory disease, the crowded sweat bath, like the ceremonies, encouraged its spread.

The Navajos also used bitter herbal remedies made from boiled sagebrush and juniper to wash the body and internally cleanse. Sagebrush tea helped sooth sore throats, while juniper pitch mixed with a special kind of sand and plastered on the outside of the throat forced pus from the infected areas.[49] Another medicine given to patients came from the juice of Arizona jimson (datura), which caused the pulse to quicken and the patient to be delirious. One person who took jimson as a cure had a recorded pulse of 240.[50]

Physical treatments also included either fasting for ceremonies or eating for satiety. Extremes in either case could prove fatal:

> At one place on the reservation, during the plague, meat balls the size of one's thumb were forced down the patients who were too weak and sick to eat until no more could be forced down

them. The stomach of an influenza victim at another place, who had been abandoned and partly eaten by the wolves, was seen to contain about a quart of corn which had probably been boiled before it was forced down him. Such patients usually . . . died.[51]

This report also mentioned that a massage and a series of contortions were part of some treatments: "As the disease usually terminated in pneumonia and consequently the lungs became 'tight,' the medicine man jumped on the chest to loosen up the lungs." Thus, in many instances, the "cure" was as painful as the affliction.

Utes and Paiutes living in the Four Corners region were also affected by the disease, but apparently not to the same extent as the Navajos. The Ute agent, headquartered at Towaoc outside Cortez, Colorado, reported a population of three hundred Indians on his reserve. Many of them traveled off their lands and so had ample opportunity to contract the disease. But by December 27 there had been only a few deaths because the Utes had "yielded readily to medical treatment [which was not nearly as available to the Navajos], and seemed to suffer much less than their Indian neighbors."[52] A possible explanation is that, in addition to medical help, the curing practices of the Utes did not stress congregating in order to perform ceremonies. In fact, "When the flu was bad, most of the Indians left the agency."[53]

The Utes did not escape the effects of influenza entirely, however. Like the Navajos, they fled from their tepees when someone died inside and thus fell prey to the elements and the disease. Many of them had trouble understanding how white men could get sick, take medicine, and get better, while the Indians took the same medicine and died. Apparently by the end of the epidemic, white doctors lacked easy access to the Utes, who suggested "maybes medicine given Indian was coyote bait [poison]."[54] Mistrustful, some Utes ran from their camps to hide when a white man approached, fearing he might be a doctor. By February 22, 1919, the epidemic had subsided.[55]

The end of the epidemic on the northern part of the Navajo reservation raised the question of how many deaths had occurred. Because of the lack of records, a definitive answer cannot be given and even an estimate is difficult to obtain. One trader, John L. Oliver of Mexican Hat, suggested at least 3,000 Indians had succumbed to the disease on the reservation.[56] The *Walketon Independent* and the *Indian School Journal* both reported that 2,000 Navajos in the southern part of the reservation had died, a figure considered too high by some, based on a total tribal population estimated at between 31,390 and 35,000.[57] The northern and western agencies, extending from Shiprock to Tuba City, had population estimates that ranged between 6,500 and 8,000, with a suspected 75 percent incidence of influenza and a death rate of between 8.75 and 15 percent. The overall tribal population showed a 5.5 percent decrease between the 1918 and 1919 agency figures.[58]

The agency schools provide a far more accurate picture of the effects of the disease on the children, but their living conditions and access to medical attention were far different from those found in the rough canyon country of southern Utah and northern New Mexico and Arizona. For instance, in the Shiprock Agency School 200 of the 225 pupils were sick and 18 died, giving a mortality rate of 9 percent. All 81 students at the Toadalena Boarding School contracted the disease and 10 died, for a mortality rate of 12 percent. At the Tuba City Boarding School 138 students were sick but only 2 died, for a mortality rate of 1.5 percent.[59] The higher death rates seemed to be in direct proportion to the amount and type of care rendered the sick. As an illustration, Toadalena had the highest mortality rate though it had the smallest student population. The principal neglected to meet the needs of the sick students and was chastised following a special investigation.[60] But deaths among the vast majority of Navajos living at large were never investigated.

In summarizing the effects of the influenza epidemic on the various populations in the Four Corners region, one sees the importance of cultural beliefs, social practices, and economic patterns. For instance, the people of Moab viewed the epidemic as a respiratory ailment that could be avoided by limiting contact with others, by following contemporary medical practices, and by leaving the major decisions to medical professionals. Newspapers advertised cures, the health board organized a hospital, and outside aid in the form of nurses, vaccines, and commercial products became part of the health care scheme. Even the legal system joined the fray by passing laws and requiring the sheriff, marshal, and volunteer citizens to enforce them. All of this was done in a rural town with a small population. The even smaller communities of Monticello and Blanding, on the other hand, had limited access to professional care. Their predominantly Mormon populations turned inward for succor. Cooperation and help were of greater necessity and the burden of healthcare and farming chores rested squarely on those men and women who felt compassion and were not afflicted. Home remedies and self-doctoring eased the suffering of many and were generally aligned (though not in every case) with an understanding of the physical disease and how it was spread. There is no indication that religious practices intensified; indeed, organized religious services came to a halt.

For the Navajos an entirely different response was necessary because the epidemic lay in the realm of religion and spirituality. Forewarned by omens, the Navajo reaction was immediate, intense, and culturally defined. The disease, like other illnesses, was personified and attacked on a spiritual level, with familiar objects connoting intense symbolic meanings as part of the preventive and curative practices. From the Euro-American point of view, many of the ceremonies derived from the "darkest superstition," as the newspapers of the day proclaimed, but to the Navajos they were the first line of defense, comparable to the doctors in Moab and the home remedies in Blanding and Monticello. Superstition is always the other man's religion, and so it was for the outsider viewing Navajo practices.

Influenza appears to have been far more traumatic for the Navajo population than the white population for a number of reasons. First, the isolation of Navajo dwellings, because of a dependence on a livestock economy, did not afford the same type of community support found in Moab, Monticello, and Blanding, or even in the boarding schools. Often the sick had no choice but to perform their necessary labors, often in bad weather, which weakened their resistance to the disease. Second, the means of transmittal was not understood, and so the disease spread rapidly and was actually encouraged by ceremonial practices. The Utes, on the other hand, seemed not to have suffered as much as the Navajos because their general reaction was to get away from others, decreasing chances for infection. Once a death occurred, however, both the Utes and Navajos compounded the problem by leaving their secure winter homes and exposing themselves to the elements. Third, the physical remedies were, by white standards, only marginally successful in alleviating the victim's suffering. Many of the practices were based on the principles of "like begets like," "opposites cure," and "the bitterer the better." All of these concepts are common in the religious magic and shamanism of many non-industrialized cultures. To the Navajos, they were effective cures and, when coupled with the ceremonies, completed a logical system of defense. In fact, those who lacked prayers, chants, and herbal remedies were the ones most often believed to have died.

By March 1919 the number of Americans killed by influenza exceeded half a million.[61] The trauma of this catastrophe took years to get over; for Navajos the event also became a landmark in the tribal memory. Yet, at a time when much of humanity suffered, the experiences of individual men and women offered the greatest understanding beyond cold statistics; the responses of each individual to the epidemic were tied to the culture within which they were made.

NOTES

Originally published in the *Utah Historical Quarterly* 58 (Spring 1990): 183–200.

1. Joseph E. Persico, "The Great Swine Flu Epidemic of 1918," *American Heritage* 27 (June 1976): 28.
2. Ibid.
3. William H. NcNeil, *Plagues and People* (Garden City, NY: Doubleday Press, 1976), 289.

4. "Influenza Breaks Out in Moab," *Grand Valley Times*, October 18, 1918.
5. Ibid.
6. "No Further Cases of Influenza Make Appearance in Moab," *Grand Valley Times*, October 25, 1918.
7. "Influenza Spreading at Alarming Rate," *Grand Valley Times*, November 1, 1918.
8. Ibid.; "Court Postponed on Account of Influenza," *Grand Valley Times*, November 1, 1918.
9. "The Flu Epidemic on Decline" *Grand Valley Times*, November 8, 1918.
10. "Influenza Claims Prominent Stockman," *Grand Valley Times*, November 22, 1918.
11. "Influenza Raging in Moab," *Grand Valley Times*, January 3, 1919.
12. Persico, "The Great Swine Flu Epidemic," 82.
13. "Influenza Raging in Moab."
14. Ibid.
15. "250 Cases of Influenza Develop during Week," *Grand Valley Times*, January 10, 1919.
16. "Influenza Raging in Moab"; "Troubles Had in Getting Whiskey for Influenza," *Grand Valley Times*, January 10, 1919.
17. Advertisement, *Grand Valley Times*, November 15, 1918.
18. Advertisement, *Grand Valley Times*, January 21, 1919.
19. "Influenza–Play Safe," *Grand Valley Times*, January 10, 1919.
20. "Flu Situation Much Improved," *Grand Valley Times*, January 17, 1919; "Epidemic Has Been Stamped Out in Moab," *Grand Valley Times*, January 24, 1919.
21. Ibid; "Flu Hospital Expense Totals Nearly $1700," *Grand Valley Times*, January 31, 1919.
22. Margie Lyman, interviewed by Helen Shumway on April 11, 1986, tape in possession of Shumway.
23. Ibid. Mae Black, interviewed by Janet Wilcox on July 15, 1987, San Juan County Historical Society, 3–4; Ray Redd, interviewed by Jody Bailey on July 16, 1987, San Juan County Historical Society, 5–6.
24. Redd, interview, 6.
25. Pearl Butt, interviewed by Jody Bailey on July 2, 1987, San Juan County Historical Society, 1–2.
26. Ibid., 9.
27. Lyman, interview, 4; Black, interview, 7; Seraphine Frost, interviewed by Deniane Gutke on July 6, 1987, San Juan County Historical Society, 2; Rusty Musselman, interviewed by Robert S. McPherson on July 6, 1987, San Juan County Historical Society, 2.
28. Ibid.

29. Gladys A. Reichard, *Navaho Religion, A Study of Symbolism* (Princeton, NJ: Princeton University Press, 1963), 19; Ada Black, interviewed by Bertha Parrish on June 18, 1987, San Juan County Historical Society, 1–2.

30. Black, interview, 1–2; Rose Begay, interviewed by Bertha Parrish on June 17, 1987, San Juan County Historical Society, 3; Tallis Holliday, interviewed by author, November 3, 1987, tape in possession of author; Fred Yazzie, interviewed by author on November 5, 1987, tape in possession of author.

31. Frances Gillmor and Louisa Wade Wetherill, *Traders to the Navahos* (Albuquerque: University of New Mexico Press, 1953), 222–24.

32. Scott C. Russell, "The Navajo and the 1918 Pandemic," *Health and Disease in the Prehistoric Southwest* (Tempe: Arizona State University, 1985), 385; Yazzie, interview.

33. L. L. Gulp to Commissioner of Indian Affairs, "Report on the Influenza Epidemic at the San Juan Indian Agency," March 1, 1919, 2; Letters Received by Office of Indian Affairs, New Mexico, 1919, National Archives, Washington, D.C.

34. Hilda Faunce, *Desert Wife* (Lincoln: University of Nebraska Press, 1928), 296–97; Albert B. Reagan, "The Influenza and the Navajo," *Proceedings of the Indian Academy of Science* 29 (Fort Wayne, IN, 1921), 246; Gillmor and Wetherill, *Traders to the Navahos*, 227.

35. Faunce, *Desert Wife*, 297; Gillmor and Wetherill, *Traders to the Navahos*, 226–28; Reagan, "The Influenza and the Navajo," 246–47.

36. Reagan, "The Influenza and the Navajo," 246.

37. "Navajo Indians Are Dying by Hundreds," *Grand Valley Times*, December 6, 1918.

38. Faunce, *Desert Wife*, 299–300.

39. Reagan, "The Influenza and the Navajo," 274; Ray Hunt, interviewed by Janet Wilcox on July 20, 1987, San Juan County Historical Society, 15.

40. Yazzie, interview; Holliday, interview.

41. Faunce, *Desert Wife*, 301–2.

42. Yazzie, interview.

43. Reichard, *Navaho Religion*, 545–46, 581.

44. Pearl Phillips, interviewed by Bertha Parrish on June 17, 1987, San Juan County Historical Society, 3; also Begay, interview, 2.

45. Yazzie, interview.

46. Ibid.; Holliday, interview; Begay, interview, 3.

47. Gillmor and Wetherill, 226–27; Willow Roberts, *Stokes Carson: Twentieth Century Trading on the Navajo Reservation* (Albuquerque: University of New Mexico Press, 1987), 26.

48. Gillmor and Wetherill, *Traders to the Navahos*, 225–26.
49. Holliday, interview; Yazzie, interview; Begay, interview, 4.
50. Reagan, "The Influenza and the Navajo," 247.
51. Ibid.
52. "The Influenza among the Utes," *Mancos Times Tribune*, December 27, 1918.
53. "Superstitious Utes," *Mancos Times Tribune*, December 13, 1918.
54. Ibid.; "Influenza Very Bad among Indians," *Mancos Times Tribune*, December 13, 1918.
55. "Hearings on Indian Estates," *Mancos Times Tribune*, February 21, 1919.
56. "3,000 Navajos Succumb to Flu, Says Indian Trader," *Grand Valley Times*, January 3, 1919.
57. "Russell, "The Navajo," 382; Reagan, "The Influenza and the Navajo," 243.
58. Russell, "The Navajo," 382; Gulp to Commissioner, 2.
59. Ibid.; Reagan, "The Influenza and the Navajo," 245.
60. Gulp to Commissioner, 7–9.
61. Persico, "The Great Swine Flu Epidemic," 84.

15

BEYOND THE SPOTLIGHT

The Red Scare in Utah

ANDREW HUNT

For post-World War I America the threat of Bolshevism was real. If spies and saboteurs had worked to weaken America during the war, the same kind of un-Americans now threatened to destroy basic freedoms, the government, and the American way of life through actions whose ultimate end was to foment a revolution like the one that brought communism to Russia. Fear of a Bolshevik revolution, the alien ideology of communism, and the threat of violence posed by some radical individuals fostered a response known as the Red Scare. Other factors contributed to the Red Scare, especially the nativism and isolationism that held sway during the postwar decade. Utah was not immune, and the nature of the Red Scare in Utah is the subject of the following chapter.

As the United States began to heal from the excesses of the McCarthy era during the mid-1950s, a handful of historians turned their attention to the Red Scare of 1919. In studying this turbulent period, they sought to identify parallels between the post–World War I Red Scare and the anticommunism of the Cold War era. Their works chronicled the significant events—the flash points—that occurred. They focused on the thirty bombs sent to leaders and prominent citizens during the spring of 1919, general strikes in Seattle and Winnipeg, May Day riots in New York and Cleveland, the formation of domestic Communist parties, and the rise of nativist beliefs that swept much of the nation. Finally, researchers traced these events to the climax of the Red Scare: the Justice Department raids directed against thousands of suspected radicals in cities across the country in January 1920.[1]

Despite the dearth of secondary sources on the subject prior to the 1950s, two historians produced notable works about the Red Scare within a few years of each other. The first was Robert K. Murray's *The Red Scare: A Study of National Hysteria, 1919–1920* (1955), which historians have traditionally regarded as the premier general history on the subject. The second book, Stanley Coben's biography, *A. Mitchell Palmer: Politician* (1963), appeared eight years later.

While the two books represented significant, exhaustively researched contributions, the extent of the Red Scare has not yet been fully explored. Both Murray and Coben present the Red Scare as being broad in scope and creating an atmosphere of "intense public suspicion and fear."[2] For Murray this was a period when "the national mind ultimately succumbed to hysteria," characterized by "restrictive legislation . . . [and] mob violence."[3] Although Coben is less dramatic than Murray, he raises the theme of nationwide hysteria throughout his work. He writes that during the Red Scare there existed a "deeply rooted fear . . . that America stood on the brink of catastrophe."[4] According to Coben, "the xenophobia common in America before the war was greatly exacerbated," resulting in "widespread popular hostility toward radicals" and "a nativistic hostility that swept the land."[5]

Historians such as Murray and Coben are, to some extent, guilty of analyzing and describing abstract wholes based on selectively chosen accounts of significant events, individuals, and pieces of legislation. They assume a unity of society based on a cluster of specific instances. In doing so they run the risk of exaggerating the magnitude of the 1919 Red Scare.

What was the scope of the Red Scare outside of Murray's or Coben's spotlight? To what degree did authorities persecute radicals in areas where fears of revolution were less dramatic? As both authors point out, nativism played a big role in the virulent anticommunism of the era. How widespread was nativism in regions with more homogeneous populations? To answer these questions, this chapter will focus on Utah, particularly Salt Lake City. Does Utah fit within the standard framework? Were the men and women of Salt Lake City caught up in the hysteria? What light do local moods, perceptions, and behaviors shed upon the Red Scare of 1919?

By 1919 nearly half of Utah's 450,000 residents lived in the state's burgeoning cities. Nestled in fertile valleys west of the Wasatch Mountains in northern Utah, the two largest cities in the state, Salt Lake City and Ogden, had populations of 118,110 and 32,804 respectively.[6] With its rising skyline, growing population, and expanding neighborhoods, Salt Lake City was beginning to resemble a bustling urban center rather than a Mormon frontier settlement. The largest church in Utah was the Church of Jesus Christ of Latter-day Saints, with approximately 60 percent of the state's inhabitants as members. Nevertheless, the non-Mormon population in the state had grown dramatically since the 1870s.[7] In 1916 Utahns elected the state's first non-Mormon governor, Simon Bamberger, a Jew and a staunch progressive. During World War I there were intense displays of patriotic fervor throughout Utah, with victory gardens springing up across the state and liberty bond drives raising large contributions from Utahns. When the war was over, Utah's veterans returned to crowded celebrations in Salt Lake City.[8]

Yet, within months after the armistice of November 1918, the postwar economic recession that ravaged the United States began to take a heavy toll on Utah. The recession hit the state's farms the hardest, with prices of wheat declining after the war from $3.50 a bushel to $0.98 in 1921. The state's large mineral industry did not fare much better. In 1919 Utah's total production of lead, zinc, silver, copper, and gold plummeted 54 percent below the previous year's level. The

Utah Copper Company closed its mills, the Bingham Copper Mine laid off thousands of workers, and populations decreased dramatically in the neighboring towns of Magna and Garfield.[9] Throughout 1919 economic hardships led to strikes and labor demonstrations across the state. At the end of the year the Utah Industrial Commission estimated the fourteen labor disputes that occurred in Utah had cost the state an estimated $900,000 in lost production.[10]

According to historian Robert K. Murray, the economic hardships of 1919 coupled with postwar demobilization led to widespread "psychological torment and confusion." He argues that, faced with the example of the 1917 Bolshevik Revolution in Russia and widespread postwar political unrest throughout Europe, most Americans rallied behind the "prevailing drive for normalcy" that fostered a "confusing, intolerant, and irresponsible atmosphere."[11] For Murray, the quest for an illusory "normalcy" created tension in the minds of Americans. He contends that much of the confusion plaguing Americans was channeled into attacks against nonconformists, pacifists, and Communists.[12]

To a visitor to Salt Lake City in the early months of 1919 it would have appeared that Murray's thesis was manifesting itself in the corridors of the state's legislature. In February state representatives introduced two bills intended to curb radical activities in Utah. The first, House Bill 28, known as the Red Flag Bill, was a broadly worded piece of legislation that prohibited the "disloyal display of the red flag or any other emblem of anarchy" in Utah. J. E. Cardon, a businessman who introduced the bill the day after a massive general strike began in Seattle, Washington, referred to the law as "a warning to agitators that there is no place for them in this state." The Red Flag Bill passed by a healthy majority of two-to-one, with only ten representatives voting against it.[13]

The following day saw the introduction of a second piece of restrictive legislation, the Sabotage Bill, on the floor of the House. The purpose of the bill was to establish a "strong anti-syndicalism and sabotage law prohibiting the advocacy, teaching, or suggestion of same" and "prohibiting assemblages for such teachings or suggestions, and prohibiting the use of any building for such assemblages."[14] As was the case with the Red Flag Bill, prolabor representatives like Fred Morris and Robert Currie—both union members—as well as representatives from the Salt Lake Federation of Labor offered rousing condemnations of the Sabotage Bill. Morris, a member of the Typographical Union, Local 115, charged that such bills "emanate from a class who fear that the despotism which they are about to impose upon laboring people will cause a revolt." Currie, a leader in Salt Lake's carpenters union, took a more moderate approach, arguing against the bill from a civil libertarian perspective. In spite of their pleas, representatives overwhelmingly supported the Sabotage Bill, with twenty-four voting for the measure and five opposing it.[15]

Making it a felony to advocate sabotage or syndicalism was clearly aimed at the militant Industrial Workers of the World. Founded in 1905, the IWW, a radical labor union led by native Utahn William D. Haywood, maintained offices in Salt Lake City. The organization enjoyed some success in Utah's mining industry, especially after 1910, attracting members from the state's numerous squalid mining camps. Arguing that the "working class and the employing class have nothing in common," the IWW leadership advocated syndicalism—the theory that through the use of general strikes and force, workers would be able to overthrow capitalism and introduce an economic system in which trade unions would control the means of production. Moreover, following the teachings of French syndicalist Emile Pouget, the IWW advocated the use of sabotage. The organization never offered a precise definition of the term, yet IWW newspapers trumpeted sabotage and frequently published cartoons of its symbols—the wooden shoe and the black cat. For the IWW the word carried broad connotations. Some members of the organization defined sabotage as acts of passive resistance, including "the conscious withdrawal of efficiency," jamming machines, or sending railroad freight in the wrong direction. Others viewed sabotage as "striking on the job," while a handful of members included violent resistance in their definition. Yet, for opponents of the IWW, sabotage carried one simple definition: the violent destruction of private property.[16]

While legislators intended the Sabotage Bill to undermine the IWW, they aimed the Red Flag Bill at a newly formed organization called the Workers', Soldiers', and Sailors' Council, which met for the first time in Salt Lake City in February 1919. The purpose of the council was to act as an umbrella organization embracing representatives from various local unions and political clubs. In addition to endorsing the infant Soviet republic, the organization called for "mass action to build up a real democratic government, a government of the workers, for the workers and by the workers, to take the control of politics and industry out of the hands of big business." The council sent letters to labor unions throughout the state inviting them to join.[17]

With the passage of the Red Flag and Sabotage bills, conservative legislators sought to suppress organizations like the IWW and the Workers', Soldiers', and Sailors' Council. Yet once the laws were passed, they were never stringently enforced. Under the sabotage law, there were but two known arrests. Police jailed two immigrants in Carbon County on October 31, charging them with "distributing IWW literature and making anarchistic threats." Officials from the Justice Department interrogated the two men, then turned them over to the Department of Immigration for deportation.[18] Salt Lake City mayor W. Mont Ferry used the sabotage law to prohibit the IWW from holding its annual national convention in the city on June 25. Ferry consulted with city, county, state, and federal officials and then announced: "I am determined to enforce this law to the utmost limit and protect our community from anarchistic and revolutionary teachings."[19] Ferry and his advisors ultimately persuaded IWW leaders to select another site for their convention. Curiously, authorities made no attempt to use the sabotage law to repress or shut down the state IWW offices in downtown Salt Lake City.[20] When Ralph Chaplin, editor of the IWW newspaper *Solidarity*, came to Salt Lake City in November, he spoke to an audience of two hundred people with no interference from the police.[21]

The police enforced the red flag law even less rigorously than its anti-sabotage counterpart. No known arrests were made under the law, in spite of the efforts of law enforcement officials to scrutinize local radical organizations. Beginning in February, plainclothes officers from the Salt Lake City Police Department began attending the weekly meetings of the Workers', Soldiers', and Sailors' Council to monitor the group's activities. Police Chief J. Parley White called the council a "strictly bolshevist organization" and advised officers investigating the organization "to guard against an emergency in the present state of social unrest." Police officers maintained a close watch over the council until November 1919, but a frustrated Chief White eventually conceded that all meetings were "held in an orderly manner."[22]

That did not deter law enforcement officials from looking for other reasons to arrest council members under the red flag law. In April a flyer appeared in the streets of Salt Lake City announcing a council-sponsored May Day celebration. The flyer, printed in red ink, announced, "Grand International May Day Mass Meeting under the auspices of the Workers', Soldiers', and Sailors' Council. Subject of Speakers to be 'The Class Struggle.'" An alarmed Chief White charged that because they were printed in red ink, the circulars violated the state's red flag law. He urged authorities to treat the distribution of the flyers as a criminal act. But state officials were reluctant to accept Chief White's broad interpretation of the red flag law, and the police made no arrests.[23]

Thus, the months leading up to April 1919 saw little hysteria in the state. Utahns from Logan to St. George seemed absorbed in affairs of immediate local interest rather than the "specter of international bolshevism." Events like the Russian Revolution or the general strike in Seattle were too distant and seemed to have no impact on their lives. Yet the shattering events of May 1 would temporarily interrupt the stillness.

On the morning of May 1 postal carrier Fred Libby delivered a small package to the Judge Building in downtown Salt Lake City. He handled the package in the same manner he dealt with the rest of his mail, calmly delivering it to the sixth-floor offices of attorney Frank K. Nebeker. It was an eight-inch-long narrow box weighing eleven ounces, wrapped in manila paper, with a label pasted to it bearing the address of Gimbel Brothers, a department store in New York City. Stamped on one side of the package were the words "Sample— Novelty," directly above a figure of an old man carrying a pack and holding a staff in his left hand. The unsuspecting postal carrier had no idea the contents of the box consisted of a wooden tube filled with an acid detonator and a high explosive.[24] Two days earlier Nebeker had left for Chicago on a business trip. When his stenographer, Norma Best, signed for the package she was "on her guard" as a result of reading front-page newspaper accounts of prominent officials in New York City and Washington, D.C., receiving similar packages. In fact, Best later expressed surprise that Nebeker had not received any bomb threats before. This particular package piqued her attention because the illustration of the man on the box reminded her of an IWW poem titled "Wail of the Bindle Stiff."[25]

A year earlier, as assistant attorney general of the United States, Frank Nebeker had gained fame as the zealous prosecutor in the case of *U.S. v. William D. Haywood, et al.* In that case he had successfully prosecuted a hundred members of the IWW who were accused of violating a number of laws, including the Espionage Act of 1917. Nebeker argued the case before a federal judge, Kenesaw Mountain Landis, and ultimately convinced the jury that IWW leaders had participated in a conspiracy to sabotage the war effort. The jury deliberated for less than an hour before handing down a blanket guilty verdict, giving prison sentences to all of the defendants. One year later, when Nebeker was notified in Chicago that a bomb had been sent to his Salt Lake City office, his only reply was a brief telegram: "If I was selected to receive one of the bombs, then the IWW organization is behind it."[26]

Frank Nebeker was not the only prominent Utahn to receive a bomb in the mail on May 1. Later that day postal authorities in Ogden, acting on orders from the U.S. postmaster, intercepted a bomb en route to the Salt Lake City offices of Sen. William H. King. A Democrat, King was one of the most virulently antilabor and anti-Communist politicians in Congress. He advocated the passage of local restrictive laws as a means of stifling dissent, and his speeches often emphasized the threat of radicalism emanating from the remnants of the Seattle general strike. King also received attention in the national press as a member of a Senate committee investigating methods of curbing radical propaganda. Like the bomb sent to Nebeker, the device intended for King was wrapped in Gimbels' paper. Within days after postal clerks announced the discovery of the bomb, King prepared a bill making it illegal to transport bombs in interstate commerce and a capital offense to belong to an organization advocating the violent overthrow of the U.S. government.[27]

Authorities discovered a third bomb mailed to Sen. Reed Smoot. A conservative Republican and apostle in the Church of Jesus Christ of Latter-day Saints, Smoot was a puzzling choice to receive a bomb. He had never been as outspoken as King or Nebeker, and he showed very little concern about the Russian Revolution or the Seattle general strike. Nevertheless, postal inspectors notified Ogden postmaster W. W. Browning to watch for suspicious packages addressed to Smoot. The following day authorities discovered that the bomb intended for Smoot had never reached Salt Lake City. It was returned to Gimbels department store in New York City for additional postage, where it was confiscated by Justice Department agents. Authorities never apprehended the culprit or culprits responsible for the mail bombs.[28]

Nebeker, King, and Smoot were among thirty-six recipients of May Day bombs across the country. Other prominent bomb recipients included Oliver Wendell Holmes Jr., associate justice of the Supreme Court; Postmaster General Albert S. Burleson; Judge Landis; Attorney General A. Mitchell Palmer; John D. Rockefeller; J. P. Morgan; and Secretary of Labor William B. Wilson. Bomb blasts injured only two people, the wife and maid of former Georgia senator Thomas Hardwick. Yet the bomb scare created blazing headlines in newspapers across the country.[29]

The local press echoed the anti-Bolshevik sentiments of the rest of the mainstream media in the United States. "Death to the Terrorists" screamed bold, block letters above an editorial in the May 1 *Deseret News*. "The country's history records no similar instance of widespread diabolism," the editorial began. "It is almost unbelievable that the human mind can descend to the depravity that this wretched plot bespeaks." The *Salt Lake Tribune* used the incident to call for more legislation to curb bolshevism, referring to the bombs as the product of the "unrestrained menace" of free speech. Perhaps the most succinct response came from the editor of the *Ogden Examiner*, who stated that "red-blooded Americans have no use for the 'Red,' whether it is a red flag, a red badge, a red poem, or any other insignia which is anti-American." Ironically, the *Salt Lake Herald*, an otherwise conservative publication, was the only daily newspaper to suggest that the packages were likely the creation of a lone maniac.[30]

The May Day bomb scare also stirred conservative groups in Utah. A month after the incident the Elks Lodge held its annual state convention in Ogden, with its theme "The Elks vs. Anarchy." Elks president A. R. Diblee began the meeting by praising the record attendance of members from every chapter in Utah, then announced that the organization "is determined to fight against anarchy and bolshevism, while counter-battling for true-blue Americanism." The Utah Kiwanis Club followed the Elks' example by featuring bomb recipient Frank Nebeker as the keynote speaker at its July 3 gathering. Nebeker told the Kiwanis Club that "radicalism is not confined to the longhaired soap-box orator" and warned that "the spread of the doctrine demanding industrial revolution is far more serious than has been admitted." Salt Lake Rotary Club president James W. Collins, speaking before a club luncheon at Hotel Utah in November, expressed concern about what he perceived to be a growing IWW threat in the mining districts of eastern Utah. He called on state and federal authorities to rid Utah of the "cancerous infection" of the IWW. Eventually, the Utah American Legion joined the crusade. Commander Hamilton Gardiner, writing in the legion's December 1919 bulletin, called on the 101 posts in

Utah to campaign for "Americanism." Gardiner urged officials to pass legislation banning radical meetings and encouraged legion posts to appoint officers from each chapter to monitor local radicals.[31]

Yet, the overall calm that prevailed in Salt Lake City on May 1, 1919, contrasts with Robert K. Murray's assertion that it was a day when "American radicals put on a colossal show" and "numerous riots arising from radical May Day celebrations" erupted. No sizable riots or demonstrations occurred in Salt Lake City, Ogden, or Provo on May 1. Because most accounts of the local bomb scare (with the exception of the *Deseret News*) appeared on May 2, residents of cities such as Provo, Ogden, and Salt Lake City had not yet reacted to the delivery of the "infernal machines" to Nebeker, King, and Smoot.[32]

This is not to suggest that Salt Lake City was completely insulated from momentous events in Cleveland, Boston, New York City, Seattle, and other cities where May Day riots did occur. On May 1, Police Chief J. Parley White assured the public that the local police would "take precaution to suppress all bolshevist and anarchistic sentiment in Salt Lake City." White also indicated that federal authorities were monitoring the activities of local radical organizations.[33]

When the Workers', Soldiers', and Sailors' Council held its May Day celebration at the downtown musicians' hall, Chief White personally attended the festivities, accompanied by six plainclothes police officers. Before a crowd of four hundred people, council member Bertha Bennett encouraged members of "the Soviet of Salt Lake" to donate money to the Bolshevik cause. She was followed by speaker R. E. Richardson, a self-proclaimed "poor tramp wobbly," who called the nationwide bomb scares "the bunk." Neither Chief White nor his colleagues attempted to halt the festivities, and no arrests were made.[34]

In other parts of the state clusters of radicals met without interference from police. At a Socialist party forum in Ogden a "few dozen people" listened as local party secretary O. A. Kennedy declared, "The working class of the world is awakening." Kennedy read a statement prepared by the Ogden chapter expressing solidarity with Socialists around the world. Unlike the council celebration in Salt Lake City, there is no evidence that police agents attended the Ogden gathering. Although the meeting was by no means a "colossal show," it serves as evidence of reluctance on the part of police to obstruct the activities of left-wing groups in Utah in 1919.[35]

Almost a month after the May Day bomb scares, a series of mysterious explosions occurred in eight cities in other states, destroying a handful of buildings and killing two individuals. Yet the June 2 bombings failed to arouse the same enthusiasm in Utah's newspapers as the May Day scare. A headline in the *Deseret News* announced "Anarchists in Nationwide Bomb Plot," while the *Ogden Examiner* carried an editorial arguing that foreign-born radicals should be "show[n] the way to their homeland" to test their ideas. Other newspapers, such as the *Salt Lake Tribune*, devoted little attention to the explosions.[36]

The traditional interpretation of the Red Scare maintains that labor unions, like the highly publicized May 1 mail bombs, played a crucial role in provoking hysteria. Coben wrote that 1919 was a "vintage year for strikes" and labor conflicts aggravated "public fear of revolution or economic disaster." Murray regarded organized labor as a "trigger mechanism" that produced "the ultimate manifestation ... of national psychoneurosis."[37]

The activities of organized labor in Utah are inconsistent with Coben's and Murray's statements. There were strikes, demonstrations, and displays of union militancy in Utah in 1919; nevertheless, the number of strikes in Utah ranked low when compared with national figures during the period. Fourteen major labor disputes occurred in the state throughout the year, some of which, such as the Park City mining strike, lasted no longer than one or two months. Nationally, there were more than 3,600 strikes involving 4 million workers. Utah's contribution to the number of strikes in 1919 was therefore relatively minor. Toward the end of the year the Utah Industrial Commission released a report praising the state's labor leaders for their conservatism. The report concluded, "employers and employees generally in this state are making an honest effort to adjudicate their differences without resorting to the lockout or strike."[38]

Nevertheless, there were examples of redbaiting directed against some labor unions. A mining strike that erupted in Park City on May 6 and involved nearly one thousand miners made headlines in local newspapers because of IWW participation. The strikers demanded a six-hour workday, a daily salary of $5.50, and an end to discrimination based on union membership. Two federal investigators and a commissioner from the Department of Labor traveled to Park City to investigate "agitation on the part of active IWW members." The Department of Justice also conducted an investigation of IWW business agent Albert W. Wells for his alleged role in instigating the strike. However, the ill-fated strike lasted only a month and a half. With their modified demands for an eight-hour workday and a daily wage of $5.15 rejected by mine owners, the Park City miners went back to work on June 21.[39]

The Park City strike proved to be the only major IWW-led strike in Utah in 1919. For the most part labor unions in Utah moved to distance themselves from Syndicalist or Communist ideas. The one exception occurred in September at the annual convention of the Utah Federation of Labor, the central body of the majority of Utah's labor unions. At the convention, UFL members voted by a three-to-one majority to endorse the newly formed Soviet government in Russia. The federation released an official resolution declaring the Soviet government to be "controlled by workers . . . in the interest of the working class," and they demanded the withdrawal of U.S. troops occupying the Soviet Union. Federation leaders stated their hostility toward the resolution, yet it passed by a vote of forty-nine to thirteen.[40]

Conservative labor spokesmen such as state representative Robert Currie feared the federation's Soviet resolution would cause a backlash in the Utah legislature against labor unions. Their concerns appeared to be justified. At the beginning of the month the Utah Associated Industries, the state's largest businessmen's association, requested that Governor Bamberger repeal a 1917 law introduced by Currie that gave unions the right to organize and picket peacefully. Bamberger immediately called for a special session of the legislature, and a group of

Utah senators drafted a bill to overturn the 1917 law. When the special session convened on October 4, labor unions organized effective protests against the bill. Before the bill was even introduced 2,500 workers marched to the Utah State Capitol to rally against its passage. One thousand shopmen from the Denver & Rio Grande and the Oregon Short Line railroads jammed the galleries of the capitol to capacity. Both unions had declared October 4 a holiday in order to be present for the debate. Eventually, the bill was killed in the Senate by a 10 to 9 vote. Labor was victorious.[41]

The defeat of the antipicketing law undermines the thesis that by the end of 1919 antiunion groups had successfully challenged organized labor and its public support. Few labor unions in Utah lost members in 1919. A number of labor organizations, such as the Amalgamated Carpenters, the United Mine Workers, the Street and Electric Railway Employees, and the Brotherhood of Railway Carmen, flourished in 1919.[42]

According to the traditional interpretation of the Red Scare, nationwide hysteria reached a climax between November 1919 and January 1920 with the infamous Palmer Raids. Attorney General A. Mitchell Palmer organized the Justice Department sweep of foreign-born radicals. An estimated three thousand anarchists and Communists were arrested in cities such as New York, Chicago, Detroit, Boston, Kansas City, Portland, and Denver. In his biography of Palmer, Stanley Coben wrote that once the Palmer Raids ended "the American public was ready for a reconsideration of the Red Menace" and "the popular anxiety of 1919 and early 1920 evaporated." Similarly, Murray argued that following the Palmer Raids "anti-Red hysteria subsided almost as quickly as it had developed and . . . the nation rather rapidly regained its composure." To his credit, Murray conceded: "In the west and far west, while raids were conducted, they were not especially significant."[43]

When the sweeps and arrests began on January 2, 1920, the Justice Department ignored Utah entirely. With the exception of a few headlines and newspaper editorials, the Palmer Raids had no impact on the state. Outside of Coben's and Murray's spotlights, Salt Lake City and its neighbors followed a dramatically different pattern from New York City, Boston, Seattle, and even Denver. It is possible to liken the Red Scare in Utah to a defective stick of dynamite. With Fourth of July speeches warning about the spread of IWW-ism, the passage of laws designed to suppress radicals, police surveillance of the Workers', Soldiers', and Sailors' Council, and a variety of other actions, conservatives attempted to light the fuse of the dynamite. It never exploded.

Clearly, federal, state, and local authorities did not see a need to crack down on Utah dissenters in 1919 and 1920. William J. Flynn, head of the U.S. Bureau of Investigation (later the FBI), visited Salt Lake City on February 27, 1920, and explained that radicals had a much weaker presence in the western states than in the East. "This is due," he explained, "to the fact that the 'reds' and 'the communists' have not found their way, to any great extent, west of the Mississippi river." Yet the feebleness of radicals in Utah during the Red Scare had little to do with their inability to find their way to Utah. Rather, it had a great deal to do with a series of events that began nearly a decade before 1919.[44]

After World War I, Justice Department agents, state legislators, and law enforcement officials saw no reason to devote their time and resources to the repression of dissenters in Utah. This was not because leaders in the state were more tolerant than their counterparts in New York City or Seattle. Sen. William King, Mayor Mont Ferry, Police Chief J. Parley White, and several members of the legislature were rabidly anti-Communist. The Church of Jesus Christ of Latter-day Saints remained neutral on the issue of the Red Scare, but the church-owned newspaper, the *Deseret News*, frequently expressed antipathy toward Communists, Socialists, and anarchists. Nevertheless, authorities were not threatened sufficiently to take drastic action. By 1919 radicals and militant labor organizers in Utah were too few to be regarded as a menace by authorities. However, this had not always been the case. Leftists had obtained a foothold in Utah before World War I, and although their numbers were always relatively small they had some influence on local politics. But the gradual repression of dissenters that began in 1910 and lasted until the war slowly eroded the remaining leadership within Utah.

Before World War I the two major radical organizations in Utah were the Socialist Party and the IWW. The Socialist Party first appeared in Utah in 1901 and reached its peak between 1905 and 1912. Historian John McCormick, who has exhaustively researched the Socialist Party in early twentieth-century Utah, points out that, at its height in 1911, thirty-three party members were elected in ten communities, including city councilmen, mayors, and city treasurers in such towns as Bingham, Fillmore, Salt Lake City, Cedar City, Eureka, and Mammoth. According to McCormick, many party members were so-called gas and water Socialists—progressive reformists who emphasized electoral politics and sought to work within the system. The party was especially powerful in mining areas.[45]

The IWW first made its presence in Utah known at a mining convention in Eureka in April 1910. The Western Federation of Miners, which allied itself with the IWW, organized the event. The IWW, like the Socialist Party, found much of its support in Utah's mining towns. Two months after the Eureka convention, the WFM attracted 2,000 miners to its annual outing at Lagoon amusement park. The union boasted 2,500 members in Utah during the summer of 1912, largely as a result of a huge miners' strike in Bingham Canyon. The Bingham strike of 1912 ultimately ended in failure for the miners, but the IWW played a key role in instigating smaller labor disputes that year, such as a smelter workers' strike in Murray and a construction workers' strike in the central Utah town of Tucker.[46]

Despite the organizations' shared radicalism, the IWW and the Socialist Party in Utah were not always on good terms. The two organizations made their ambivalence toward one another known as early as 1910. Both groups frequently conducted outdoor street meetings in Salt Lake City and Ogden, a popular method of drawing sizable crowds. The large meetings prompted the Salt Lake City Police Department to ban Socialist Party meetings during the summer of 1910. The Wobblies (or IWW members) responded to the ban by organizing "free speech" fights in which radical street-corner orators denounced efforts to curb free speech. One of the soapbox speeches, delivered in Liberty Park by W. J. Kerns, was broken up by soldiers under the orders of the police. The Socialist Party hastily announced that Kerns was not affiliated with their organization, and party officials emphatically stated they had nothing to do with authorizing the meeting. The party went to great lengths on a number of other occasions to dissociate itself from the IWW. Prominent Socialist William Knerr, who later became chairman of the Utah Industrial Commission, often emphasized that he had nothing to do with the union. When Knerr gave a speech during the Park City strike of 1919, he criticized miners who held IWW cards and the audience replied with boos and catcalls.[47]

Local No. 69 of the IWW in Salt Lake City retaliated against the Socialist Party's criticisms by attacking the efforts of Socialists. Wobblies often referred to those party reformists who believed that gradual change could be achieved in the ballot box as "slow-cialists." For Wobblies, the solution to the ills of society was simple: direct action through strikes, demonstrations, and sabotage. They believed political action was ineffectual. "Let the workers as a class fight the bosses as a class," demanded Lee Pratt, a Salt Lake City Wobbly.[48]

After 1912 the Socialist Party began to wane in Utah. McCormick partially attributed its decline to the suppression of the party by law enforcement during free speech fights in 1910 and 1912. The party also lost much of its labor support at that time. Before 1911 the Salt Lake Federation of Labor and the Utah Federation of Labor had endorsed the Socialist Party on many occasions. In September 1911 the latter organization enthusiastically embraced the Socialist Party and encouraged all workers to join, referring to it as "the party of the working class." However, after 1911 an increasingly conservative leadership steered the two groups away from the party. As a result, most Socialist political candidates suffered.[49]

The IWW faced harsher repression in Utah than did the Socialists. Arrests of IWW members in Utah before World War I were common.

On June 14, 1912, police arrested and jailed five Wobblies involved in organizing the Tucker strike. A couple months later, on August 12, a strikebreaker named Axel Steele and a group of hired "deputies" interrupted Wobbly leader James Morgan in the middle of a speech in downtown Salt Lake City. Steele and his strikebreakers severely beat Morgan and several audience members. When the skirmish ended, police arrested Wobbly Thomas Murphy, who had shot and injured four of his assailants, charging him with intent to commit murder. Police also arrested Morgan and fined him $1,000. Charges were never filed against Steele or his hired deputies. Law enforcement officials stepped up their efforts to repress IWW activities in Utah when they arrested twenty-one Wobblies, charging them with trespassing on an Oregon Short Line railroad car on their way to an IWW meeting in Salt Lake City. Two years later, on October 30, 1915, Maj. H. P. Myton, a city police officer, shot and killed IWW member R.J. Horton during an argument. Judge L. R. Martineau charged Myton with voluntary manslaughter and released him on $3,500 bail.[50]

The now-legendary trial of Joe Hill, the famed Wobbly songwriter and poet, accelerated the IWW's decline in Utah. Police arrested Hill on January 13, 1914, charging him with the murder of grocer J. G. Morrison and his son. The so-called "Wobbly bard" was executed on November 19, 1915.

Hill's trial is significant inasmuch as it further undermined the IWW's presence in Utah. Most city, rural, and mining town newspapers viciously attacked Hill and applauded his execution. The Utah Federation of Labor angrily denounced the American Federation of Labor when its leader, Samuel Gompers, appealed to President Woodrow Wilson to intercede on Hill's behalf. Following Hill's execution, the Utah Bar Association disbarred Hill's attorney, O. N. Hilton, for critical comments he made during a funeral oration. The *Park Record* in Park City vilified Hilton: "His looks alone should debar him from the practice in the courts of Utah—to say nothing of . . . the vile epithets hurled at the state officials in his funeral oration of the murderer, Hillstrom, in Chicago recently." In retaliation, Hilton devoted most of his Hill eulogy to attacking Gov. William Spry, the Utah Supreme Court, and the "humanity of Salt Lake City in this enlightened age."[51]

The trial and execution of Joe Hill disillusioned many IWW activists. Virginia Snow Stephen, an instructor of art at the University of Utah and daughter of former Mormon Church president Lorenzo Snow, devoted much of her energy to the Joe Hill defense committee. After Hill's execution the university fired Stephen, disclosing that the cause for her dismissal was her involvement in the Hill case. Stephen left Salt Lake City, married a former member of the IWW, and settled in California. Nationally, the IWW denounced Utah, and its songs, poems, and articles about Hill emphasized their belief that the state was a lost cause. Hill's last words to IWW leader Bill Haywood, "I don't want to be found dead in Utah," were made legendary in the Wobbly press. Ralph Chaplin, another IWW poet, declared that Hill was "murdered by authorities of the state of Utah." IWW leaders placed Hill's ashes in envelopes and sent them to locals in every state but Utah.[52]

Ultimately, the Joe Hill trial weakened the IWW in Utah. When Governor Spry threatened to "bring to bear a force" that would stop inflammatory street speaking after Hill was executed, prominent Salt Lake attorney Harper J. Dininny advised that there was no need for such drastic measures. Dininny estimated that only thirty Wobblies remained in the city, and the sheriff could "handle them with ease."[53]

The final blow to the IWW occurred during World War I. When the federal government rounded up antiwar activists for violating the Espionage Act, the IWW in Salt Lake City was a prime target. On September 6, 1917, federal authorities raided the IWW's Radical Bookstore downtown and its state headquarters in the Boyd Park Building. The government confiscated all IWW property in Salt Lake City, including the organization's records. Between 1917 and the end of the war authorities arrested nine IWW leaders in Utah, most for their involvement in antiwar activities. On September 28, 1918, police arrested Joe Roger, secretary of the local IWW group and manager of the Radical Bookstore, for circulating a pamphlet calling for a general strike. They also jailed Alex Zennikos for translating Roger's pamphlet into Greek. Carl Larson, a Swedish member, was arrested in May 1918 and charged with "making seditious utterances" against the war. Finally, federal agents subpoenaed local IWW leader G. H. Perry to stand trial in Chicago with one hundred other Wobblies.[54]

So devastated was the Utah IWW in 1919 that the organization's only show of strength was the poorly organized Park City strike in May, which lasted but a month and a half. The IWW also suffered at the hands of Utah's conservative labor unions, which often attacked the Wobblies. On August 24, 1918, during the height of wartime repression, unions organized an anti-IWW gathering in Bingham. Representatives from the Salt Lake Federation of Labor, the Utah War Labor Bureau, and the International Union of Mine, Mill, and Smelter Workers delivered impassioned speeches against the IWW.[55]

In 1919 the most visible left-wing organization in Utah, the Workers', Soldiers', and Sailors' Council, could not attract significant numbers. The council's letter-writing campaign urging Utah's labor unions to affiliate with it was, at best, unproductive. The "Soviet of Salt Lake" merely stirred paranoia in Salt Lake City's police force and the press. The council faded into obscurity after 1920.

The state's labor unions were another factor decreasing the potency of Utah's Red Scare. Internal conflicts plagued unions and depleted them of resources in 1919. Conservatives clearly had the upper hand in most unions, but they still faced contentious radical elements within. When the Utah Federation of Labor endorsed the Soviet Union at its September convention, it also rejected—by a vote of thirty-two to eighteen—a resolution calling for radical unionism along IWW lines. Similar splits between radicals and conservatives occurred in the Salt Lake Federation of Labor. In the middle of May 1919 a powerful faction of radicals in the SLFL drafted a resolution supporting the Park City strike and calling for affiliation with the Workers', Soldiers', and Sailors' Council. Conservatives steadfastly opposed the Park City strike and wanted nothing to do with the council. Ultimately, conservatives triumphed on both issues. SLFL president Otto Ashbridge had the last word when he announced, "no union as a union had become affiliated with the Council in any manner." The cost for that victory was internal division in Utah's unions.[56]

The lack of militancy on the part of unions enabled the Utah Associated Industries, an organization whose goal was "to put an end to industrial disturbances," to implement its "American Plan" (or the open-shop movement) with virtually no resistance. The American Plan was the product of industrialists and businessmen following World War I. Its purpose was to "combat union tyranny" by "putting an end to industrial disturbances." The open-shop movement proved to be an effective strategy in restructuring work relations by opening up unionized businesses and industries to nonunion members, thereby weakening labor's grip on the workplace. In 1919 labor's only resistance to the open-shop movement occurred when Salt Lake City's cooks and waiters joined a Culinary Alliance strike in May. After a yearlong walkout the strikers ultimately succeeded in maintaining a closed shop. But in the years that followed, the open-shop movement had a crippling effect on Utah's railroad shopmen, building trade unions, and the typographical union.[57]

One final aspect of the Red Scare that must be explored is nativism. The foreign connections of so many radicals in the United States strengthened widespread suspicion that sedition was chiefly foreign-made. Murray summed up the nativist tone of the Red Scare: "The belief was perpetuated that most aliens were susceptible to radical philosophies and therefore represented an element which particularly endangered the nation." According to Coben, a "fanatical 100-percent Americanism . . . pervaded a large part of our society between early 1919 and mid-1920," resulting in a "popular clamor for deportation of allegedly subversive aliens." Anti-immigrant animosity was, in most cases, directed against the large influx of immigrants sweeping into the country between 1910 and 1919. Many of those immigrants were from southern and eastern European nations—Greece, Italy, Russia, and so forth. Nativism was often rabidly anti-Semitic, anti-Catholic, and chauvinistic toward people with different customs, beliefs, and ethnic origins.[58]

ANDREW HUNT

How widespread was nativism in Utah? One possible clue to this question is found in U.S. census records. In 1919 the proportion of foreign-born people living in Utah was comparatively small. Between 1910 and 1919 Utah's population jumped from 373,351 to 449,369. However, in this ten-year span the number of foreign-born residents in the state actually dropped from roughly 63,000 (or 16.9 percent) in 1910 to 56,455 (or about 12.6 percent) in 1919. Thus, Utah had a relatively small foreign-born population during the Red Scare.[59]

The Palmer Raids and the deportations of alleged radicals in January 1920 were directed primarily against large pockets of southern and eastern European immigrants living in cities. At that time Utah had a much more homogeneous population than Massachusetts, New York, or Pennsylvania. More than 25 percent of Utah's foreign-born population came from Great Britain. Nearly 25 percent more were born in Sweden and Denmark. In contrast, the number of Russian-born residents was about 684, or 0.15 percent, while only 240 Polish-born residents lived in the state. The number of people who immigrated to Utah from southern European countries was higher. Of the state's foreign-born residents, 3,225 were from Italy, followed closely by Greece with 3,029. In total, immigrants from southern and eastern European countries comprised about 14.5 percent of foreign-born people in Utah.[60]

These figures mean nothing unless placed in a demographic perspective. More than twice the number of Italians lived in the mining areas of Carbon County (1,215) than in Salt Lake City (496). Only 548 Greeks lived in Salt Lake City, as opposed to nearly 900 in Carbon County. More Yugoslavians lived in Tooele, Summit, and Carbon counties than in Salt Lake County. In total, according to the U.S. census, fewer than 25 percent of Utah immigrants from southern and eastern Europe lived in Salt Lake City.[61]

The figures for 1920 indicate that the immigrants—who were usually the victims of nativist, anti-alien hostility in other states—were small in number in Utah and most lived away from the lawmakers, police officers, and newspaper editors in Salt Lake City and Ogden.

It is not surprising that A. Mitchell Palmer, William J. Flynn, J. Edgar Hoover, and the Justice Department ignored Utah entirely during the Palmer Raids.

The state's homogeneous population was reflected within the membership of the Socialist Party between 1900 and 1923. According to John McCormick's findings, 90 percent of its 1,423 members were men, 90 percent were married, two-thirds were born in the United States, and 70 percent were native Utahns. Half of the foreign-born members were from the British Isles, and the majority of the rest had been born in northern and western European countries. Nearly 42 percent were Mormons. It was not the sort of organization that inspired nativist animosity or even fear in the hearts of Utahns.[62]

The Red Scare manifested itself in different ways in Salt Lake City than it did in New York City, Chicago, or Cleveland. Outside of the historians' spotlight Utah followed a separate pattern and responded to events differently. The region felt the ripples of the Red Scare, but it was distant enough from the nation's centers of conflict that the ripples had little impact. Newspapers devoted more columns to local news and social events than to strikes in Seattle or revolutions in faraway lands.

Nevertheless, a disturbing precedent was set in 1919. Legislators passed laws that blatantly violated civil liberties and, though seldom enforced, evoked little public outcry. With no resistance, the Salt Lake City Police Department openly spied on dissenters. Groups of businessmen systematically stripped labor unions of their power. And even though reports of anti-immigrant hostility were rare, ideas and beliefs considered threatening to the status quo were regarded as un-American. During the Palmer Raids a frustrated *Deseret News* editorial lamented:

> Surely if we have laws by which we can rid ourselves of foreign hyenas and jackals, we must have laws to enable us to sterilize domestic snakes and vipers. . . . Their deeds are of that black type that is properly known as treason, against which, by every

consideration of sense and self-protection, the government must move promptly, firmly and mercilessly.[63]

Was Utah representative of other areas outside of the lens of historians? How did events in Utah differ from Red Scares in other areas out of the historical focus, especially states with relatively homogeneous populations? Was the national "hysteria" that Robert K. Murray and Stanley Coben wrote about confined to a handful of cities? Were these scholars guilty of overstating or exaggerating their cases? How much wind was removed from the sails of the Red Scare by the repression of radicals in the United States between 1910 and 1918? Such questions beg for further research.

NOTES

Originally published in the *Utah Historical Quarterly* 61 (Fall 1993): 357–80.

1. For example, earlier works include Louis F. Post, *The Deportations Delirium of 1920* (Chicago: Charles H. Kerr and Company, 1923); Frederick Lewis Allen, *Only Yesterday: An Informal History of the 1920s* (New York: Harper and Brothers, 1931); Robert Dunn, ed., *The Palmer Raids* (New York: International Publishers, 1948); and Max Lowenthal, *The Federal Bureau of Investigation* (New York: William Sloane Associates, 1950). The most notable later works are Robert K. Murray, *The Red Scare: A Study of National Hysteria, 1919–1920* (New York: McGraw-Hill, 1955); and Stanley Coben, *A. Mitchell Palmer: Politician* (New York: Columbia University Press, 1963).
2. Murray, *The Red Scare*, 18.
3. Ibid., 280.
4. Coben, *A. Mitchell Palmer*, 212.
5. Ibid., 198, 203, 245.
6. U.S. Bureau of Census, "Fourteenth Census of the United States: 1920, Population: Utah" (Bulletin), 1.
7. Dean L. May, *Utah: A People's History* (Salt Lake City: University of Utah Press, 1987), 170–71.
8. Ibid.
9. Ibid., 173.

10. Karl Alwin Elling, "The History of Organized Labor in Utah" (master's thesis, University of Utah, 1962), 103.

11. Murray, *The Red Scare*, 3–17.

12. Ibid., 14.

13. *Deseret News*, February 8, 1919.

14. This description of the Sabotage Bill is contained in *Deseret News*, April 23, 1919.

15. For the Red Flag Bill see *Deseret News*, February 8, 1919. On Sabotage Bill see *Salt Lake Tribune*, February 9, 1919. For Currie and Morris, see Elling, "The History of Organized Labor," 12, 89, 112.

16. For a good discussion of the IWW's definition of sabotage, see Peter Carlson, *Roughneck: The Life and Times of Big Bill Haywood* (New York: W. W. Norton & Co., 1983), 196–97.

17. The "Preamble, Resolutions, and Plan of Action" of the Workers', Soldiers', and Sailors' Council is contained in the records of the Utah Federation of Labor and Utah Industrial Union Council at Western Americana, Marriott Library, University of Utah, Salt Lake City.

18. *Deseret News*, November 1, 1919.

19. *Deseret News*, April 23, 1919.

20. *Deseret News*, November 19, 1919.

21. Elling, "The History of Organized Labor," 55.

22. *Deseret News*, November 1, 1919. Although police records pertaining to this matter no longer exist, throughout 1919 there are newspaper accounts of plainclothes police officers attending meetings of the Workers', Soldiers', and Sailors' Council. Other accounts will be noted later.

23. *Deseret News*, April 29, 1919.

24. For descriptions of the so-called infernal machines, see *Salt Lake Tribune*, May 2, 1919, and Murray, *The Red Scare*, 70–71.

25. *Salt Lake Tribune*, May 2, 1919.

26. For the best account of Frank Nebeker's role in *U.S. v. William D. Haywood, et al.*, see Carlson, *Roughneck*, 265–82. For Nebeker's comments on the bomb, see *Salt Lake Tribune*, May 2, 1919.

27. Murray, *The Red Scare*, 65, 71, 80, 83, 95, 232; *Salt Lake Tribune*, May 2, 1919.

28. *Deseret News*, May 1, 1919.

29. Murray, *The Red Scare*, 70–71.

30. See *Deseret News*, May 1, 1919; *Salt Lake Tribune*, May 3, 1919; *Ogden Examiner*, May 3, 1919; *Salt Lake Herald*, May 2, 1919.

31. *Ogden Examiner*, June 7, 1919; *Deseret News*, July 4, November 19, and December 6, 1919.

32. Murray, *The Red Scare*, 73–74.
33. *Deseret News*, May 1, 1919,
34. *Salt Lake Herald*, May 2, 1919.
35. *Ogden Examiner*, May 2, 1919.
36. *Deseret News*, June 3, 1919; *Ogden Examiner*, June 5, 1919.
37. Coben, *A. Mitchell Palmer*, 173–74; Murray, *The Red Scare*, 105.
38. Elling, "The History of Organized Labor," 103; Coben, *A. Mitchell Palmer*, 173; *Deseret News*, December 11, 1919.
39. Elling, "The History of Organized Labor," 33–35; *Deseret News*, May 9 and June 6, 1919.
40. *Deseret News*, September 11, 1919.
41. Elling, "The History of Organized Labor," 114–15; *Deseret News*, October 4, 1919.
42. Dee Scorup, "The History of Organized Labor in Utah," (master's thesis, University of Utah, 1935), 70–158.
43. Murray, *The Red Scare*, 217, 239; Coben, *A. Mitchell Palmer*, 236.
44. *Deseret News*, February 28, 1920.
45. John S. McCormick, "Hornets in the Hive: Socialists in Early Twentieth-century Utah," *Utah Historical Quarterly* 50 (1982): 226–27.
46. Gibbs M. Smith, *Joe Hill* (Salt Lake City: University of Utah Press, 1969), 115–19; Elling, "The History of Organized Labor," 29–32.
47. Elling, "The History of Organized Labor," 36–37, 42; *Deseret News*, May 8, 1919.
48. Smith, *Joe Hill*, 117.
49. McCormick, "Hornets in the Hive," 226–27; Elling, "The History of Organized Labor," 109–11.
50. Smith, *Joe Hill*, 115–28; Elling, "The History of Organized Labor," 35–43; *Salt Lake Tribune*, October 24, 1913.
51. Smith, *Joe Hill*, 179–80, 185–86.
52. Ibid., 90, 172, 179.
53. Ibid., 179.
54. *Deseret News*, February 11, 1919; Elling, "The History of Organized Labor," 53–55.
55. Elling, "The History of Organized Labor," 32–33.
56. *Deseret News*, April 29 and May 24, 1919; Elling, "The History of Organized Labor," 93–94.
57. Elling, "The History of Organized Labor," 28–42.
58. Murray, *The Red Scare*, 265; Coben, *A. Mitchell Palmer*, 196–97.
59. Comparing 1910 population figures, see May's *A People's History of Utah*, 136. For all figures from 1920, see *The Fourteenth Census* (1920), 1040.

60. *The Fourteenth Census* (1920), 1040.
61. Ibid.
62. McCormick, "Hornets in the Hive," 231–32.
63. *Deseret News*, January 5, 1920.

16

SOME TIMELY OBSERVATIONS ON THE LEAGUE OF NATIONS CONTROVERSY IN UTAH

JAMES B. ALLEN

Throughout the war and in its immediate aftermath during the Paris treaty negotiations, of primary importance was what nations could do to prevent such a world calamity from occurring once again. For Woodrow Wilson, the answer lay in his "Fourteen Points," which called for self-determination, open treaties, freedom of the seas, and, most important to Wilson, the establishment of a world organization where nations could come together in the cause of peace. The League of Nations was the answer. Wilson and other supporters of the league feared if leaders failed to implement the league then there was no means to prevent future wars and the millions of soldiers and civilians who had lost their lives would have died in vain. But the League of Nations had its skeptics, if not opponents, who feared the United States would surrender its sovereignty by joining. Ratification of the Treaty of Versailles in the Senate hinged on acceptance of the league. Friends, families, communities, even religious institutions divided over the issue. In Utah, Mormon general authorities were divided over the question, which effectively ended the myth that ecclesiastical leaders were united in all things. As the following chapter finds, individuality, free agency, and disagreement were paramount to conformity and compromise even among individuals united by religious tradition and beliefs.

For nearly twenty years as a teacher either in the seminaries and institutes of the Church of Jesus Christ of Latter-day Saints or at Brigham Young University, I have frequently been called upon to counsel with young students as well as adults on various matters. For many the problem of making political decisions is one that seems to cause a great deal of frustration. Constantly I have been asked the question, where does the church stand on this or that political issue? Repeatedly I have been confronted with statements to the effect that this or that person has said Latter-day Saints must, if they understand the gospel, take such and such a stand on such and such an issue. I have been touched by students who are confused and frustrated when they hear leaders and teachers whom they respect cite the scriptures and quote the prophets on opposite sides of the same questions. What role, they seem to be asking, does my faith have in helping me make political decisions? Is it a sign that I don't understand the gospel if my attitude on some public policy is different from that of a church leader, or leaders? For most of us, such questions are probably elementary, for we have solved them long ago. For me, the constant contact with students who still have such questions has led me to search the history of the church for precedents and insights that, in proper perspective, can help young people achieve a personal balance in their quest for a solution to the problem of personal faith and public policy.[1]

The League of Nations controversy in Utah presents just such an opportunity. All the questions are raised: American isolationism or world cooperation? Should the LDS Church take a stand on political issues? Should a church official speak to problems of national policy? Can he turn to the scriptures for support of his position? Where does the lay member find himself when he disagrees with his ecclesiastical leaders on political issues?

Actually a study of this old controversy does not answer any of these questions. But it does demonstrate with one intensely moving incident that men of devout loyalty to the church, who understand and live the basic principles of the gospel and have sincere goodwill toward each other, can and often do disagree on public policy, even to the extent of relating their views on that policy to their religious views. And yet, at the same time, they display no public animosity, hostility, or lack of genuine respect toward those with whom they disagree, and they see no reason to question the faith or integrity of their opponents.

Let's review the political drama of 1919, letting the chips fall where they may as I try to tell, as accurately as possible, what happened as LDS Church members at all levels wrestled with the perplexities of relating personal faith to public policy.

The drama of that year included many subplots and characters, all tightly interwoven. Yet we must at the outset separate at least some of them in order to fully appreciate the complexity of the story and the impact one element could have had upon the other.

In the background, but nevertheless clearly visible throughout the controversy, was Woodrow Wilson, Democratic president of the United States, whose idealistic plans for permanent world peace actually set the stage for the impending drama in Utah. At the end of the Great War, Wilson went personally to the peace conference in Paris and was able, through much persuasion and compromise, to make his proposed League of Nations an integral part of the peace treaty. At home, however, the battle for ratification of the treaty in the Senate became intensely partisan. Most Republican senators tended to favor American entry into the league only if certain reservations or amendments were agreed to, which they believed were necessary to protect American sovereignty. The leader of this group was Henry Cabot Lodge of Massachusetts. Other Republicans were known as "irreconcilables" because they refused to endorse the league under any circumstances whatsoever. The Democrats, on the other hand, generally supported Wilson, although some of them would have agreed to Lodge's reservations if it were necessary to save the league at all. Wilson became irreconcilable in his own way by refusing to accept any major reservations, and—in a direct challenge to the powerful Republican leadership in the Senate—he took his case directly to the American people. The controversy set off a series of debates throughout the country, but hardly any of them were more intense, partisan, or emotional than that which took place in Utah. In the end, Wilson's own followers defeated the league when, after the Senate accepted Lodge's reservations, Wilson instructed them to vote against it.[2]

The main events in the present plot took place among the Latter-day Saints in Utah, with a few dramatic scenes in Washington, D.C. There were many characters in the drama; the lineup was indeed impressive. Some who played the most active roles were these:

Senator Reed Smoot, the Mormon apostle who had won nationwide publicity in 1904–1906 when a long and bitter investigation was carried out by the Senate before it would accept him as a colleague, but who was now gaining wide respect not only within the Republican Party but among all his Senate colleagues. A man of unquestioned integrity, he displayed an intense nationalism that led him to question anything, including the League of Nations, that would undermine the total independence of America.[3] From the tone of some of his statements, it appears that Smoot was almost irreconcilable, but after much soul searching he joined forces with Senator Lodge as a "reservationist," and refused to endorse the League of Nations without the proposed amendments.

Although Smoot made no speeches in the Senate on the League of Nations and was not known in public as a leader of the reservationists, he often met privately with Lodge and others to help plan strategy to be followed by the reservationist Senators. As a confidante of Lodge, he even acted on one occasion as a go-between when Lodge wanted someone to attempt to persuade former president William Howard Taft that the league, which Taft supported, would never be ratified without the reservations.[4] Smoot's intense concern with the league is seen in the fact that throughout the debates of 1919 and early 1920 he regularly recorded in his diary candid comments on what was happening. In addition, he assiduously collected all the speeches made in the Senate on the treaty and the league and had them bound into a book that "contained over 3000 pages, about 2100 words to the page making a book of about 6,300,000 words."[5]

Complicating Smoot's role was the fact that he would stand for reelection in 1920 and he realized that generally the people of Utah supported the League of Nations. After repeated warnings from friend and foe alike as to the political implications of his stand, he boldly made his feelings known in the faith that by election time either the people of Utah would have been persuaded to his view or the issue would no longer be important. In this he was correct.

Charles W. Nibley, presiding bishop of the Mormon Church. Nibley was a close friend of Smoot and was even more intensely opposed to the league than was the senator. He was, in fact, an "irreconcilable" in attitude. He corresponded frequently with Smoot, met with him in Washington to plan anti-league strategy, and generally became one of the most outspoken voices in Utah against the league. In addition, Bishop Nibley was avidly working for the reelection of Smoot, and used the means at his disposal to achieve that end.[6]

B. H. Roberts, a member of the First Quorum of the Seventy, and a member of the Democratic Party. He was as much convinced that the Democratic Party came closest to reflecting the will of God as Smoot was that Republicanism, Americanism, and Mormonism were almost inseparable. Roberts had not been as fortunate as Smoot in his quest for a seat in Congress. After being elected to the House of Representatives in 1898, he was refused his seat by that body because he had been a practicing polygamist. In 1919 Roberts became the most active proponent of the League of Nations among the leadership of the church.

Joseph Fielding Smith, son of the late president of the church, Joseph F. Smith, and himself a member of the Quorum of the Twelve, who would become the president of the church in 1970. Other than Reed Smoot, Elder Smith and David O. McKay were the only apostles who stood in opposition to the league.[7] Elder Smith apparently drew especially close to Smoot during this emotional controversy as he encouraged Smoot through mail, kept him informed of what was going on among the leadership of the church, and warned him of possible consequences of a strong, unwavering stand.[8]

George F. Richards, member of the Quorum of the Twelve Apostles who, at the time of the debate, returned from England, where he had been presiding over the European mission. Probably as a result of that mission he was especially conscious of the ravages of war and sympathetic to the yearnings of the European people for the final end of such destruction. Equally convinced with Smoot that God guided the destiny of America, he nevertheless interpreted the direction of that guidance differently. He declared on July 27 at a quarterly conference of the Pioneer Stake:

> You know something of the history of our forefathers, how they fought for their liberty, and how the constitution of the United States was framed. The Lord has told us by direct revelation that He had a hand in the matter; that He raised up the men who framed the constitution of the United States; that He inspired them; and we believe firmly that the Lord led the Pilgrim fathers to this land.
>
> I believe that the president of the United States was raised up of the Lord. I believe that the Lord has been with him. He is regarded in Europe as one of the greatest men—a man with one of the greatest minds in the world—Woodrow Wilson. . . . It may be possible that amendments [to the league covenants] may be necessary. Scarcely any great movement has been so perfect in its inception that no amendments were necessary later, and I believe that the league of nations is inspired of God.[9]

Reed Smoot, it is safe to say, had a hard time believing that Woodrow Wilson was inspired to do anything. In fact, as the controversy heated up in November, and as more was said about the league being the product of inspiration, he wrote in an impassioned letter to George H. Brimhall:

> I cannot help feeling that we have made a mistake in thinking that President Wilson has been directed and inspired of God. . . . I think that if the Lord had anything to do with the League of Nations, it was during the last election, when the Senate of the United States was changed from Democratic to Republican.[10]

Heber J. Grant, who became president of the church in 1918, served the Democratic Party faithfully in all his early political activities and in this debate was fully and openly on the side of Wilson and the League of Nations.

J. Reuben Clark Jr., a prominent international lawyer, former member of the judge advocate general's office in the U.S. Army, and author of an important reference work on the German peace treaty that was being used by the U.S. Senate. As B. H. Roberts became a sort of traveling spokesman in favor of the league, Clark played the same role in opposition. Highly respected as a scholar, Clark was probably better informed on all matters related to the League, as well as the history of American international relations, than any of the other characters in the drama of 1919.[11]

C. N. Lund Jr., faithful Mormon, editor of a newspaper in Mt. Pleasant, Utah, and emotionally committed to the League of Nations. He set off a chain reaction of letters and discussions when he wrote to Senator Smoot not only complaining of his stand on the League of Nations, but also questioning how Smoot could refuse to believe that the league was inspired. Reflecting the spirit of what was going on throughout Utah, Lund wrote:

> Last Sunday evening I attended a meeting, one of many Church meetings that I have attended where the league has been favorably discussed. The elder who prayed asked God to give the

president and the senators sufficient wisdom to adopt this plan as one of the greatest steps forward in the great upward march of mankind, and as a literal carrying out of the doctrines of the Savior of the world. . . . Similar prayers and sermons have been spoken in many a church throughout the length and breadth of the whole United States. I feel justified that the head of our own church, the apostles and leaders and the lay members, almost as a unit, are for this great proposition.

Lund reminded the senator that, as a high churchman, he believed God had inspired Christopher Columbus, the *Mayflower* pilgrims, the writers of the Declaration of Independence, the framers of the Constitution, and Abraham Lincoln. He then went on to inquire:

Now, let me ask, believing so, why you do not see the hand of Providence in this mighty effort in our own day and time, to bring about peace to a war-weary world? Why can you not see that the same God who inspired Washington and Jefferson and Lincoln does also inspire Woodrow Wilson . . . in this the greatest step ever contemplated by the human race?[12]

Smoot sent a long reply to Lund in which some of the overriding themes of our plot were beautifully developed. Smoot's letter, though obviously filled with an emotional attachment to his principles, was exemplary in its lack of emotional wandering, in its solid reasoning, and in the spirit of goodwill with which the senator replied to his critic. Smoot wrote in part:

Dear Friend Lund:

. . . I want you to know that I appreciate your letter, as I do letters from any of my constituents, expressing their views on public questions.

I think I understand the spirit and meaning of your letter, and why it was written. Your surroundings, and no doubt your first impression that the League of Nations would insure the future peace of the world, have convinced you that the League is all that was first claimed for it, and as a friend, you concluded that I was letting political bias warp my better judgment. I hope to be able to convince you otherwise.

Then, after a long explanation of the problems in the league covenant, Smoot came to the question about the church and inspiration:

You ask me if I want to disappoint the Church and the State in my stand on this question. Certainly, I do not, but I have taken an oath of office to defend the Constitution of the United States. I have prayed as much over this question as any member of the Church, and I think I have studied it with more care than any member of the Church. The responsibility of my vote is upon me. If my vote is cast wrongly, I am the one that in the future will be condemned, not the members of the Church at home.

Yes, I do believe that the framers of the Constitution were inspired of God. I do believe that America, this land of ours, was reserved by God for the establishment of truth and liberty thereon, but I am not prepared to admit that President Wilson has been inspired of God in effecting the Covenant of the League of Nations, either in its original or its present form.

And after another long section on the implications of the league, he continued:

You testify to me that, if my stand on the league is not all that it should be before God and man, I will be badly repudiated at the polls. I want you to know that I am doing what I believe is my duty to my Church, to my Country, and to my God. I would not do otherwise if it cost me every vote in the State of Utah.

I am just as sure as I live that, when the present form of the Covenant is explained to the people, they will support me in standing for and demanding the reservations as I have already outlined. I believe in the Americanism of the Utah people, and will be content to abide by their decision in this matter.

I appreciate your friendship, your good will and your counsel, but in this matter, I am following the dictates of my conscience and the best inspiration I can get from my Heavenly Father.

Do not hesitate to write me upon any public question, for I am always glad to hear the views of my constituents, and I am never afraid to let them know where I stand.[13]

The faculty of Brigham Young University, of which there were fewer than sixty that year. Most of them, as well as several faculty wives, signed petitions asking Senator Smoot to change his position on the league.

The student body of Brigham Young University, especially the young editor of the student yearbook, Nels Anderson (later a distinguished sociologist), who stood squarely for the league without reservations.

George H. Brimhall, president of Brigham Young University and a close personal friend of Reed Smoot. Brimhall favored the League of Nations, and was frank to admit to the senator that he had told a newsman, "I am for the league of nations, first, last, and all the time, and I have implicit confidence in the United States Senate."[14] But in the controversy he turned out to be a sort of middleman between the university community on one hand and Smoot on the other. It was a frustrating position to be in, but he played his role well.

On October 15, 1919, the student body of Brigham Young University sent a resolution to the Senate urging immediate ratification of the League of Nations, without reservation or amendments. Smoot, an alumnus of BYU and now a member of its board of trustees, quickly acknowledged the resolution, but took the occasion to write a lengthy letter expressing to the students his reasons for opposing the league in its present form. Said he, in the spirit of goodwill in which he conducted nearly all his replies to such petitions,

> You must know that it would give me great pleasure to comply with the first request ever made of me as a United States Senator by the studentbody of my Alma Mater, but I am compelled, under my oath of office, and as one who is jealous of America's nationality and who fears the future of our Government in that internationality which is the League's highest aim, to advise you that, unless reservations are made to the League of Nations Covenant that will preserve to the American people the Independence and sovereignty of their Government, I will be compelled to vote against the Treaty. I am a nationalist, not an internationalist, and I cannot vote to submerge our nationality with a supernationality, which would be the result if the League of Nations in its present form were ratified.[15]

The students at BYU were not reluctant to debate the issue,[16] even though it meant arguing with an apostle of the church. Smoot had not attempted to use his apostleship to promote his political ends, but the fact remained that he was a church leader as well as a member of the board of trustees, and some people might have felt that students should be highly circumspect in the nature of their opposition to him. Student reaction, while not by any means disrespectful, was pointed. On November 11 an editorial appeared in the student newspaper that expressed disappointment in the nature of Senator Smoot's reply, especially in his personal criticism of Wilson. To be more precise, the editorial accused Smoot of distorting the facts, although the students tended toward a little historical distortion themselves when they said, "We are inclined to accept Oscar Strauss' [a Republican, by the way] prophetic picture of the progress of the ages. A few days ago in New York he declared, 'There are and have been four great land marks in human history, The Ten Commandments, Magna Carta, the

Constitution of the United States and the League of Nations.'" The editorial ended with a heartfelt plea on behalf of student veterans:

> Let us say that many of us who are supporting the resolution are not mere idealists; some of us have been in the camps and "over there" in the thickest of the fight. We felt ourselves fighting to end the war and to help secure the ultimate peace of the world. Nor did we feel less loyal to our country because of this larger vision.[17]

At the same time, the BYU faculty expressed similar concerns, and likewise petitioned Senator Smoot to support the league. It was an overwhelming show of solidarity on the issue when over fifty of them signed a letter on October 30, which declared "We feel that objections raised against the League of Nations furnish no substantial reasons for amendment or qualifications requiring reconsideration by the peace conference or any of its associated members."[18] Such a statement was a direct challenge to Smoot's oft-stated position that he would endorse the league only with the major reservations being proposed.

At least two members of the faculty wrote in support of Smoot's position, but the overwhelming opposition of the faculty, their wives, and the student body—together with the fact that the chairman of the board (President Heber J. Grant) shared their views—led the harassed senator to confide in his diary that if his position brought any embarrassment to the president of the university he would resign as a member of the board of trustees.[19]

In this troubled spirit the senator wrote a magnanimous letter to President Brimhall:

> I have received petitions from the faculty of the University, from the studentbody of the University, and from the wives of the teachers of the University, asking me to vote for the League of Nations without amendments or reservations. This I cannot do,

and I have thought that perhaps my position in this regard is very embarrassing to you and may be resented by the school.

It might be that it will be best for me, under the circumstances, to resign as one of the Directors of the University. I assure you that I will gladly do so if it will advance the interests of the University in any way. I never want it said that my position on any question reflects in any way upon that great institution of learning. Kindly let me know your views on this matter, as I will withhold action until I hear from you.

I want you to know that to do so would cause me regret, but I love the institution well enough to make almost any sacrifice for its betterment.[20]

Such an offer could only have been a bombshell to Brimhall, who was struggling valiantly to keep the debate above personalities, and who, in spite of their political differences, maintained a very close relationship with Senator Smoot. In one of the most touching letters written throughout our drama, Brimhall wrote his good friend as follows:

I am well and regretfully aware of the undue pressure that has been put upon you, and have been severely criticized and soundly abused for not "doing my bit" to bend you into a reversal of your convictions as to what is best for our country and the cause of human "life, liberty, and the pursuit of happiness."

Our petitioners do not know you as I do; for if they ever did know it, they have forgotten that you faced a world with a few friends and won out; and when I say a few friends, I mean that in comparison with your enemies your friends in number were few indeed,[21] but among friends was He, who with one man is always a majority. The trial of today is just another test of Faith, Hope and Charity which belong on both sides of every issue, and those to whom much of these three qualities has been given, from them much is expected.

One of the weaknesses of a democracy is the imperialism of the majority. This was exemplified in the cry at the court of Pilate, and yet democracy, the youngest of earth governments, will grow, make its own mistakes, learn by what it suffers, and wield the scepter of power as a gift from God.

I cannot entertain the thought of you resigning from the Board of Trustees of our beloved Alma Mater. The institution cannot afford it. Your head, and your heart, and your hand have guided, comforted, and carried the school in days of almost helplessness. . . .

If standing up for you, or refusing to ask you to reverse yourself works against me I shall enjoy the working. . . .

I am quite sure that both faculty and studentbody would register a vote against your severing your official connection with the school; and you could not get a single vote from either the Presidency of the school or the Board to sanction your retirement, and the secretary of both of these organizations, granted the opportunity, would register a No.[22]

Needless to say, Smoot did not resign,[23] and the general goodwill between himself and the student body remained, in spite of a few embarrassing incidents connected with the exuberance of the youthful editors of the school publications.[24] These, then, were some of the major characters in the drama taking place within the church in 1919. There were also several themes that made up the complicated plot, three of which I should like to mention. One was the deep reverence for America and its institutions that was felt among both factions in the controversy. The belief that God had inspired the founding fathers and was guiding the destiny of the country was a basic assumption on both sides. They only disagreed on whether an institution such as the league could also be inspired. Next, and certainly a more complex problem, was the ideal of unity in the faith and, in connection with it, the question of whether or not the scriptures and the teachings of the prophets could form a doctrinal basis for opposition to or support of such political issues. Finally, the spirit of goodwill in political debate, as opposed to bitter personal attacks on one's opponent, forms a conflict theme that is just as important as the issue of the league itself.

But time flies and we have hardly finished the prologue to our drama. This has been deliberate, for the real value of studying such an incident in history is not always in recounting the sequence of events. The value might lie, rather, as in this case, with the insight into what these events meant, and could still mean, in the lives of people, and I hope that some positive thoughts on this will be stimulated by what I have said and will yet say in this discussion.

Briefly, the major plot would run something like this:

Latter part of 1918 and early 1919: Woodrow Wilson goes to Europe, returns with the treaty. The League of Nations is discussed widely throughout the nation. Smoot, from the beginning, mistrusts Wilson, his motives, and his plans.[25]

February 22 and 23, 1919: As part of the effort to promote the league, the Mountain Congress of the League to Enforce Peace holds a convention in Salt Lake City. Former U.S. president William Howard Taft attends, as does President Heber J. Grant and other prominent church leaders. A resolution is passed by the nine thousand delegates from Utah, Idaho, and Wyoming, with only one dissenting vote, declaring the League of Nations is the means of guaranteeing that peace, liberty, and justice will be established and maintained. Among the members of the platform committee that drew up the resolution is George Albert Smith, a member of the Quorum of the Twelve. President Heber J. Grant conducts some of the activities of the convention.[26]

March 4, 1919: Reed Smoot makes his first public stand on the league by signing the so-called "Round Robin" sponsored by Senator Lodge. Three days later he dictates a form letter to send to those whom he knew would deluge him with mail criticizing Lodge's resolution. By the end of the month debates are being carried on regularly throughout Utah, and B. H. Roberts is becoming a major spokesman in favor of the league.

April 10, 1919: A *Deseret News* editorial signed by the First Presidency calls for the support of "peace day" and wide discussion of the League of Nations.

April–May 1919: Discussions held widely in Utah. Some bitterness is evoked as religion gets involved in the discussions. Both sides seem to feel the doctrines of the church support their own points of view.

July 15, 1919: C. N. Lund writes his significant letter to Reed Smoot. Result: The Lund letter and Smoot's reply are both eventually published and become the basis for further discussion in Utah.

July 20, 1919: The religious implications of the debate over the league become even more pointed as Apostle Anthony W. Ivins speaks out in favor of the league at the Weber Stake Conference in Ogden. "Those of you," he proclaims, "who do not want any more war, and any more bloodshed, any more destruction, any more devastation in the world make that fact known to your representatives in Congress, that they will not dare to oppose the League or the covenant." At the close of his address, the eighty-four-year-old president of the stake, L. W. Shurtliff, declares himself in hearty accord with all Elder Ivins has said, and calls for a sustaining vote for peace. All hands are raised. When he offers a chance for a vote in opposition to the league, no hands are raised. After the conference, the anti-league *Salt Lake Herald* attacks Ivins for his stand, which occasions a defense of Elder Ivins by the *Salt Lake Tribune* on August 16.[27]

July 27, 1919: George F. Richards, member of the Quorum of the Twelve, addresses the quarterly conference of the Pioneer Stake and declares his belief that President Woodrow Wilson was "raised up of the Lord" and that the League of Nations was inspired.

August 11, 1919: As the tempo of the debate increases in Utah, Senator Smoot sends his twenty-page reply to Lund.

August 24, 1919: The *Salt Lake Tribune* publishes the Lund-Smoot correspondence. On the same day, a reporter visits Reed Smoot in Washington, D.C., and Smoot amplifies his references to the scriptures in the Lund letter. Mormon scripture, he argues, shows that world peace is impossible, and this is evidence that the League of Nations will fail. In addition, he says,

> I believe this land, now called America, was held in reserve by God for ages, with a view of establishing upon it truth and liberty, and from this land truth and liberty would be carried to the farther ends of the world.
>
> As I have said before, I prefer that America should Americanize Europe and not that Europe should Europeanize America.
>
> If this country enters the League of Nations and mixes up with other nations, they will control and America will not be able to carry out its destiny.[28]

These arguments reflect the general religious arguments used by Mormon opponents to the league.

August 26, 1919: Presiding Bishop Charles W. Nibley expresses alarm to Smoot that other church leaders are active in stake conferences urging support of the league.[29]

August 27, 1919: Smoot records in his diary that the church newspaper, the *Deseret News*, has refused to print his reply to Lund, even after Bishop Nibley offered to pay for it as an advertisement.

August 28, 1919: After considerable prayer and agonizing soul searching, Joseph Fielding Smith writes a twelve-page letter to President Grant about his deep concern over the issue. Two major problems trouble him: (1) that the brethren are in disagreement, which he feels they should not be, and (2) that it would be wrong for America to join the League of Nations. In a touching and eloquent plea he says, in part:

> It appears that I am not in full harmony with the majority of my brethren. This is a solemn matter with me for I do not want to be out of harmony. I have but one desire and that is to support my brethren in defense of the truth and live in such a manner that I am at all times be in possession of the Spirit of the Lord. I have

prayed about this matter and have lain awake nights thinking about it, and the more I reflect the more the position which I have taken appears to me to be correct. Under such conditions I know of no one to whom I can go, only to you, and I do so in the hope, and I believe the confidence, that I will not be misunderstood and that you will appreciate the position I am in.

Smith then argues, on the basis of scripture as well as the utterances of former church leaders, that peace is impossible in the last days, thus making membership in the league really "not a matter of politics, nor party affiliation, but of crying 'Peace, peace, when there is not peace.'"[30]

September 1, 1919: By this time there is widespread national publicity on the fact that Senator Smoot has used Mormon scripture to oppose the League of Nations.[31]

September 2, 1919: J. Reuben Clark Jr. speaks to a capacity crowd in the Salt Lake Tabernacle and gives an eloquent, well-studied argument against the League of Nations. In addition to the regular political arguments used by so many national speakers, he declares:

> I belong to that great class of American citizens who see in the present situation such a departure from the traditional attitude of our government toward other nations and toward world politics as to constitute this one of the most critical moments in our history.
>
> Taught from my infancy that this constitution of ours was inspired; that the free institutions which it created and perpetuated were God given, I am one of those who scan every prospect to change or alter either with a critical eye.[32]

B. H. Roberts attends this meeting and announces he will reply next week.

September 6, 1919: The *Deseret News* endorses the League of Nations and criticizes those who say it is impossible to avoid war. We have an obligation at least to try, reasons the *News*.

September 8, 1919: B. H. Roberts speaks in the Salt Lake Tabernacle, replying one by one to Clark's arguments. In addition, Roberts uses Mormon scripture in support of the league.[33]

September 13, 1919: Joseph Fielding Smith writes to Smoot warning him that some of the brethren are unhappy with his continued public stance against the league, and have even suggested some form of censure. He says only he and Elder McKay are with Smoot, and suggests that Smoot be more guarded in his actions. Nearly all agree, he writes, that "the standard works of the Church in no wise should be used in opposition to the proposed League, such a statement not to be a reflection on you if it can be made without."[34]

September 21, 1919: A severe blow to Smoot comes when President Heber J. Grant delivers the nearest thing to an official public rebuke. Speaking in a quarterly conference of the Salt Lake Stake, President Grant declares in unequivocal terms: "An illustrated hand-bill has been circulated and has been widely republished in newspapers under the heading: 'Mormon Bible Prophecies Become Issue in Opposition to the League of Nations.' The position of the Church of Jesus Christ of Latter-day Saints is that the standard works of the Church are not opposed to the League of Nations." Grant also endorses, in the strongest terms, the League of Nations, although he makes it clear that it is on the basis of his own opinion rather than scripture. Later, Grant considers his address important enough that he has it bound with the official report of the following October conference of the church.[35]

September 23, 1919: President Woodrow Wilson receives a tumultuous welcome in Salt Lake City as he arrives to speak for the league. President Heber J. Grant is on the reception committee. A few days later, Wilson is stricken ill, returns to Washington, and spends the rest of his days as an invalid.

September 29, 1919: Bishop Nibley is in Washington, D.C., discussing politics with Smoot. The two decide that Smoot should write President Grant in reply to his conference address, and that Nibley will deliver the reply personally to the president of the church.[36]

October 3–5, 1919: The LDS General Conference in Salt Lake City turns into a veritable flood of endorsements of the League of Nations, from Orson F. Whitney's opening prayer onward. Smoot, still in Washington, anticipates such a meeting and writes in his diary: "October Conference opened today in Salt Lake. I expect we will have more League of Nations propaganda."[37]

October 4, 1919: An interesting entry in Smoot's diary reveals both his loyalty to the president of the church and his dismay at the church leader's support of the league:

> I received a telegram from Pres. H. J. Grant in which he quotes a statement made by him at the morning session referring to the sickness of Pres. Wilson as well as the prayer offered by Elder Orson F. Whitney and requesting that I with Senator King convey same to President Wilson. I immediately dictated a letter to the President conveying the information contained in Grant's telegram. Went to King's office, read it to him and we both signed it and I had a messenger deliver it to the White House. Sen. King and I both thought it was not in very good taste. It was a great endorsement of the League of Nations.

October–November 1919: Although they have been active in the drama to this point, the BYU faculty and student body now play more prominent roles and find themselves in conflict with a man who is not only an apostle and senator but also on their board of trustees.

November 1919: The U.S. Senate votes on the League of Nations and rejects it.

November 1919 to early 1920: Attitudes in Utah begin to change, partly as expected by Smoot, and there is no longer so much concern over the league.

March 1920: In another vote on the League of Nations, the reservations sought by Smoot and the Republicans pass. The treaty with reservations is then voted on and defeated by the Democrats who, under Wilson's instructions, are demanding all or nothing. Smoot votes for the league with reservations, and the *Deseret News*, which earlier endorsed the league without reservations, commends him for his vote and criticizes Wilson's unbending stance. Writes the rather bemused Smoot in his diary: "a new thing for the *News*."

The debate over the League of Nations was now all but finished, even though as much as eight years later both B. H. Roberts and Reed Smoot were giving further speeches suggesting the same things they had espoused in the hectic year covered in our play. But the real story lies elsewhere. There was never an official statement regarding the question of whether or not the church should take a stand, although Grant's instructions that Mormon scriptures should not be used to oppose the league must also have implied that neither could they be used in its support. Throughout the controversy, when bitterness seemed to be raging in the newspaper comments—and sources suggest some Mormons at lower levels were allowing the issue to embitter them, questioning each other's faith, tearing down each other, and using scriptures to put down their brothers in argument—the spirits of most church leaders were far above such attacks on personality. In the 1920 October General Conference, President Grant recalled what had happened the year before and expressed regret at the bitterness the league controversy had caused. Much of his sermon was devoted to a plea for the spirit of forgiveness to characterize the Latter-day Saints. While he was not speaking directly of the league controversy, the principle certainly applied in context. He referred to the advice that, as a young apostle, he had received from President John Taylor:

> My boy, never forget that when you are in the line of your duty your heart will be full of love and forgiveness, even for the repentant sinner, and that when you get out of that straight line of duty and have the determination that what *you* think is justice and what *you* think is equity and right should prevail, you ofttimes are anything but happy. You can know the difference between the Spirit of the Lord and the spirit of the adversary,

when you find that you are happy and contented, that you love your fellows, that you are anxious for their welfare; and you can tell that you *do not* have that spirit when you are full of animosity and feel that you would like to mow somebody down.[38]

And so the church went on. Perhaps at no time in its history had there been such divergence of opinion among its leaders, but it seemed to have had little effect upon their working together in harmony to build the kingdom. Does this answer the question as to whether they *should* have been unified? Perhaps not, but at least it demonstrates that, in this instance, those who really wanted to follow the example of their leaders would not avoid debate or the expression of personal opinion, but would refuse to let that opinion stand in the way of goodwill based on genuine respect for the right and responsibility of each man to think and speak for himself on such issues. For those who still doubt that such conciliation is possible, let it be remembered that President Grant soon found himself to be a great admirer and friend of Reed Smoot; that Bishop Charles W. Nibley was called to be his second counselor in the First Presidency in 1925; that a third opponent, J. Reuben Clark, became a counselor in 1933; and that still another opponent, David O. McKay, became a counselor in 1934. In this case there *is* a moral in history.

NOTES

Originally published in the *Brigham Young University Studies* 14 (Autumn 1973): 77–98.

1. Similar concerns led me to write an earlier article on Mormon attitudes toward presidential elections. See "The American Presidency and the Mormons," *The Ensign* (October 1962).
2. For more on the League of Nations controversy, see Thomas A. Bailey, *Woodrow Wilson and the Great Betrayal* (New York: The Macmillan Company, 1945).
3. For the best political analysis of Reed Smoot, see Milton R. Merrill, "Reed Smoot, Apostle in Politics," (PhD diss., Columbia University,

1950). See especially the sections on "Reed Smoot—American," and "The League of Nations." Unfortunately, at the time Merrill wrote his dissertation the Smoot diaries were not available to him. Additional insight into Smoot's role in the league controversy has been gained as a result of examining the diaries.

4. Reed Smoot Diaries, handwritten manuscript, Brigham Young University Library, October 1, 1919. See also entries for August 6, August 31, November 6, and November 18.

5. Ibid., February 3, 1920. On this date "movie men" (apparently newsmen) took pictures of Smoot with the book.

6. Ibid., September 28, 1919.

7. Joseph Fielding Smith Jr. to Reed Smoot, September 13, 1919, as quoted in Merrill, "Reed Smoot," 321.

8. Smith even warned Smoot that many of the brethren were inclined to censure him for his use of Mormon scriptures in opposition to the league.

9. *Salt Lake Tribune*, July 28, 1919. A major portion of Richards's address was devoted to the league.

10. Reed Smoot to George H. Brimhall, November 17, 1919. George H. Brimhall papers, Brigham Young University Library.

11. For a detailed discussion of J. Reuben Clark's lifetime attitude toward American involvement in international organization, see James B. Allen, "J. Reuben Clark, Jr., on American Sovereignty and International Organization," *BYU Studies* 13 (Spring 1972): 347–72.

12. This letter was originally written on July 15, 1919, but apparently Lund misplaced his copy. He rewrote it for the sake of publication on August 22, and it appeared in the *Salt Lake Tribune* on August 24, 1919.

13. Reed Smoot to C. N. Lund Jr., August 11, 1919. Copy filed with Brimhall papers.

14. George H. Brimhall to Reed Smoot, November 7, 1919, Brimhall papers.

15. Reed Smoot to BYU student body, October 22, 1919, in *White and Blue*, November 5, 1919.

16. One student who participated actively in public debates and favored the league, Ernest L. Wilkinson, later became president of the university and was well known for his political conservatism.

17. *White and Blue*, November 1, 1919.

18. *Provo Post*, November 7, 1919.

19. Smoot diaries, November 12, 1919.

20. Reed Smoot to George H. Brimhall, November 12, 1919, Brimhall papers.

21. Brimhall is obviously referring to the controversy in the Senate over the seating of Reed Smoot.

22. George H. Brimhall to Reed Smoot, November 20, 1919, Brimhall papers.

23. In reply to Brimhall's touching letter, Smoot wrote, in part: "At the time I wrote you in relation to my resignation as one of the trustees of the Brigham Young University, I had no resentment in my heart. I did it because I thought that it was better for the institution to have the faculty a unit with the teachers of the institution and the studentbody itself. Before taking any steps, however, I felt that it was my duty to write to the man who had given the best that was in him, and nearly his life besides, endeavoring to make the institution what I believe God intended it to be. I shall take no further action in the matter, but hope to have a heart-to-heart talk with you about the future of the institution as soon as I return to Utah." Smoot to Brimhall, November 28, 1919, Brimhall papers.

24. On one occasion a rather snide remark was included in the joke column, for which the student editor quickly apologized (*White and Blue*, November 19 and November 26, 1919). On another occasion Nels Anderson, editor of the yearbook, was giving a lantern-slide lecture. After showing a slide of Smoot and Senator Lodge, he said these were not the only opponents of the League of Nations, and flashed on the screen a picture of some monkeys. This brought a flurry of giggles from the audience and was eventually reported, probably with some distortion, to Senator Smoot. Brimhall was dismayed at what he considered an inappropriate embarrassment to a member of the board of trustees. The incident soon brought an exchange of letters between Smoot, Anderson, and Brimhall that are themselves an interesting study in differing human perspectives. Anderson understood that he was being asked to apologize to Smoot. He wrote to Smoot expressing dismay at such a prospect, for he felt he had nothing to apologize for. This was, to him, only in the category of the same kind of political joke that Smoot himself would laugh at, and he claimed nothing but respect toward the senator. Smoot replied that he was not seeking an apology, but he hoped Anderson would see there was a difference between a political joke against an individual and something that would seem to be pointed toward an officer of the institution. In a letter to Brimhall, Smoot declared, "Poor Brother Anderson cannot see the difference between ridiculing an individual as such and doing so before the studentbody of an institution in which the person ridiculed is an officer.

I hope someday that he may." See Brimhall to Smoot, December 11, 1919; Smoot to Brimhall, January 29, 1920; Smoot to Anderson, January 29, 1920, Brimhall papers. Some of these letters contain copies of still other letters.

25. As noted earlier, Smoot made constant reference in his diary to the league controversy. The following is representative of his attitude. December 21, 1918: "Lodge made a great speech on the present world situation and terms of peace. It no doubt will have weight with members of the Peace Conference of foreign countries. It punctured some of Wilson's idealisms." March 1, 1919: "Senate took recess to allow the Republicans to hold a conference to agree upon a legislative program. At the conference it was decided by a vote of 15 to 14 not to prevent the passage of the Bond Bill. Some very pointed remarks against Wilson were made and the 14 in favor of preventing any further legislation with a view of forcing an extra session of Congress charged (and it was well understood by all) that Wilson's statement that he would not call an extra session until he returned from the Peace Conference was in order that the people should not be informed of what was going on at the Conference. The Senate is the only place left that information can be gotten to the people and for this reason Wilson does not intend to call an extra session of Congress if he can help it." August 7, 1919, after noting the president's call for a joint session of Congress to discuss the high cost of living: "This is a clever political move and done to draw attention from the growing opposition to the League of Nations."

26. *Salt Lake Tribune*, February 22 and February 23, 1919.

27. *Salt Lake Tribune*, July 22 and August 16, 1919; *Deseret News*, July 22, 1919. There are many exchanges of letters that may be followed in the *Salt Lake Tribune, Deseret News,* and *Salt Lake Herald* showing the bitter intensity of the fight.

28. *Salt Lake Tribune*, August 25, 1919.

29. Charles W. Nibley to Reed Smoot, August 26, 1919, in Merrill, "Reed Smoot," 315.

30. Joseph Fielding Smith to Heber J. Grant, August 28, 1919, Joseph Fielding Smith papers, LDS Church Archives.

31. A copy of a national news service broadside, apparently distributed throughout the country, is on file in the Reed Smoot papers, LDS Church Archives. It is dated September 1, 1919, San Francisco. The scriptures quoted include 1 Nephi 13:19; 2 Nephi 10:11–12; Ether 1:22; Ether 2:12 and Doctrine and Covenants 87:1–6.

32. Complete text of this address is found in the *Deseret News*, September 6, 1919.

33. *Deseret News*, September 13, 1919. Roberts quoted, among other scriptures, 2 Nephi 12 as a chapter forgotten by the opponents of the league.

34. Joseph F. Smith to Reed Smoot, September 13, 1919, in Merrill, "Reed Smoot," 321.

35. *Conference Report*, October 1919.

36. Smoot diaries, September 29, 1919. It is interesting that in his reply Smoot extensively used the same language as Joseph Fielding Smith in his earlier letter to Heber J. Grant. Long passages are verbatim. Why is difficult to ascertain, but it is interesting to note that Smith wrote to Smoot about the same time he wrote to President Grant. Perhaps he included a copy of his letter to Grant, and since Smoot accepted it so wholeheartedly he saw nothing wrong with reinforcing the argument verbatim.

37. Orson F. Whitney prayed for Woodrow Wilson, "Thy servant who so recently addressed us from this stand with whose remarks and sentiments and the truths that he uttered our hearts so powerfully impressed and illuminated." George F. Richards again declared his belief in the inspiration of the league, and Richard R. Lyman even identified Reed Smoot by name, saying, "I have hesitated to do this because my views do not agree with those of my life long friend, the Honorable Reed Smoot, whom I have admired since childhood. But I know this broad-minded statesman well enough to realize that he will have greater respect for me if I speak than he could have if, with my convictions, I were to remain silent." Other leaders also endorsed the league. When Smoot heard of the prayer, in particular, he was dismayed and wrote in his diary: "Eastern papers reported the action of the Conference at Salt Lake in praying for the President. I know the statement of Pres. Grant and prayer by Elder Whitney will have a great effect upon the people attending conference. I had no objection to a prayer being offered for Wilson but I thought it very unwise to endorse his views on the League of Nations in the prayer or President Grant's statement." Smoot diaries, October 6, 1919.

38. *Conference Report*, October 1920, 7, emphasis in original.

17

A HISTORY OF MEMORY GROVE

WILLIAM G. LOVE

How do we remember and honor those who have made the ultimate sacrifice? Partial answers came with the construction of memorials in many Utah towns listing the names of those from the area who had served and those who had lost their lives. A statewide memorial was established in Memory Grove at the mouth of City Creek Canyon, just below the Utah State Capitol in Salt Lake City. The idea for the commemorative park was announced in April 1920 and by early summer 1924 Memory Grove, with its bronze tablet listing the names of the 665 Utah servicemen who died during the war, had become a reality. Subsequently, two World War I artifacts were placed in Memory Grove—a captured German artillery piece by the Disabled American Veterans in 1926, and, in 1949, one of forty-nine railroad boxcars known as a "40 & 8" because of their use during World War I to transport either forty men or eight horses. The railroad car, an expression of gratitude by France, is now preserved in the Ogden Railroad Museum. In 1948 a meditation chapel was completed in Memory Grove as a World War II memorial. Our concluding chapter recounts the efforts of mothers, veterans, and other Utah citizens to create Memory Grove on a site where Mormon pioneers camped following their arrival in the Salt Lake Valley in 1847.

Parks are volatile places. They tend to run to extremes of popularity and unpopularity. Their behavior is far from simple. They can be delightful features of city districts, and economic assets to their surroundings as well, but pitifully few are. They can grow more beloved and valuable with the years, but pitifully few show this staying power.[1]

As one of Utah's most enduring city parks, Salt Lake City's Memory Grove has never strayed far from urban planner and activist Jane Jacobs's ideals. Its 1924 inception as a war memorial spawned a long tradition of support and involvement by private, civil, fraternal, military, and political organizations, and its evolution over the span of five generations reflects Utah's changing values along with her participation in world events. After eight decades as a city landmark, the park's continued success begs analogies to nature versus nurture. Should a period tribute expect perpetual reverence? Can a labor of love remain viable after its founders pass from living memory, or must changes in theme follow changes in stewardship? What, if any, is the community's stake in its survival? Complex questions, to be sure, but the answers to these and others may be found by examining the park's diverse history along with the motivations of its many supporters.

Memory Grove sits at the mouth of City Creek Canyon, which has long played a role in Salt Lake City's history. When the Mormon pioneers reached the Salt Lake Valley in 1847, they camped within the park's current boundaries, and for the remainder of the century the canyon's resources proved crucial to the establishment of a permanent community. Those early settlers, and the many who came after, used the canyon's timber and stone to build homes and businesses and harnessed the creek for culinary and irrigation use. The upper part of the canyon also hosted various water-powered endeavors between 1850 and 1880, including Utah's first flour and saw mills, an experimental silk mill, and a road construction company.[2] In early 1884, Scottish immigrant Robert R. Anderson built one of Utah's earliest for-profit tourist attractions, the Anderson Tower, on the canyon's southeast rim. However, as the valley view was not appreciably better from the top than the base it fell into disuse and disrepair and was ultimately demolished in 1932.[3]

As the Salt Lake settlement became a bona fide city, its residents found less and less use for City Creek Canyon, and by the time the city incorporated the land in 1902, most of the industries had either relocated to the valley or closed down altogether. Over the next eighteen years, the canyon saw use as a rock climbing area, an informal Avenues neighborhood garbage dump, and even a landfill for some of the dirt displaced during construction of the capitol building, but despite a 1914 city funding allocation for a proposed "City Creek Park," the canyon remained undeveloped as America entered the First World War in 1917.[4]

During the war, a number of organizations provided for the welfare of millions of Allied and American servicemen. The American Red Cross and the American Field Service shipped supplies, vehicles, and personnel to France both before and during direct U.S. involvement, while other local and national concerns served stateside in various veteran support positions. One of the latter groups, the War Mothers, designed the service star flag for display in homes so entitled, with a red border, a white background, and a single star for each son in service. A blue star indicated military membership, a silver star signified a wound or wounds suffered in combat, and a gold star represented the ultimate sacrifice. Four stars were the maximum number that would fit on each flag; if a fifth son served, a second flag would be added. After the war, the logistical and political need for a unified lobbying and support system drove the various entities to form the Service Star Legion and its ancillary, the American Gold Star Mothers. The legion received congressional recognition in 1919, and the War Mothers' service star flag became the official legion symbol.[5]

After the armistice, the United States faced the grim aftermath of an unprecedented event: never before had so many U.S. troops fought on foreign soil, and their high casualty rate coupled with the era's lengthy transportation times necessitated overseas burial in most cases. Congress established the American Battle Monuments Commission (ABMC) to construct and oversee American cemeteries in Europe, and the Service Star Legion responded in similar fashion by creating the National Memorial Grove in Baltimore, Maryland.[6] This park, which was the first of its kind, featured forty-eight trees with bronze markers to represent the forty-eight states, five to symbolize our wartime allies, and one each to honor President Woodrow Wilson and the American Expeditionary Forces commander, General John J. Pershing. These efforts inspired monument initiatives across the country and became the catalysts for the creation of Memory Grove.[7]

The idea for Memory Grove, or Memory Park as it was initially known, first appeared in official records on April 11, 1920, when the Service Star Legion's Utah chapter met to discuss the establishment of a local war memorial. The legion formed the Memory Grove Committee to petition the mayor for thirty acres of City Creek Canyon land, and after several weeks of discussions with city officials the southernmost twenty acres were ultimately reserved and marked out for development. Boy scouts, students, and adult volunteers began removing weeds, stones, and garbage, and by the May 20 committee meeting three hundred small trees had been purchased for planting. This occasion also marked the introduction of Ethel Howard, whose son, army captain James F. Austin, was one of only three Utah officers lost in the war. Howard had recently returned from Europe and gave a short presentation describing her tour of the American cemeteries in France; afterward, she received an invitation to join the Gold Star Mothers and later assumed the post of Memory Grove Committee treasurer.[8]

During 1922 and 1923, the committee forged ahead with its plans for the park. The group raised additional funds for landscaping and further tree planting, and in February 1924 it appointed Howard permanent chair. Utah's 665 lost servicemen were memorialized on a large bronze plaque affixed to a stone wall on the canyon's east side, and several Gold Star Mothers erected personal tributes to their sons in the forms of modest granite markers, trees, and, in Howard's case, a terraced area with a plaque-bearing stone wall and a built-in bench. On June 27, 1924, Memory Grove began its mission as "A lasting memorial to the hero dead of Utah."[9]

With the park now established, the Service Star Legion next addressed the need for some form of chapter headquarters. The city offered the use of the 1890s-era P. J. Moran stable, which sat inside Memory Grove's western boundary. The following year, the legion remodeled the structure into a meeting and event hall with a second floor to accommodate offices and a caretaker's apartment. A lease arrangement authorized chapter occupancy for an annual one-dollar fee, and the building's rededication as Memorial House took place on June 13, 1926.[10]

The next six years saw the involvement of numerous veterans organizations in Memory Park's development. Many former servicemen belonged to local unit groups as well as such national associations as the American Legion, Disabled American Veterans (DAV), and Veterans of Foreign Wars. These entities held commemoration ceremonies in the park on national holidays and also added monuments of their own: on November 1, 1926, the DAV's Argonne Chapter No. 2 placed a captured German cannon near the inaugural bronze plaque, and in 1927 the Utah National Guard installed the 145th Field Artillery Memorial directly east of Memorial House.[11]

Even as Memory Grove's monuments were taking shape, civic groups were addressing the issues of aesthetics and accessibility. While the park proper was now landscaped and planted and the eastside steps connecting it with the Avenues were complete, the west face of the canyon still lacked development as well as an access route to and from Capitol Hill. The Memory Grove Committee still held funds received from the 1925 Utah legislature, and part of this appropriation ultimately paid for brush removal and landscape work. The construction of the Capitol Hill steps, which consisted of two zigzagging ascensions of concrete and asphalt, also began as a cooperative effort involving the Rotary Club, who provided the funding and design fees; local businesses, who provided the materials; and inmates from the

Utah State Prison in Sugar House, who provided the labor. Both this project and the Kiwanis Club's City Creek Bridge, which spanned City Creek between the 145th Field Artillery monument and Memorial House, were completed in 1927.[12]

During the first half of the 1930s, Memory Grove finally received its finishing touches. On May 30, 1930, city crews installed twin concrete and bronze columns at the park's southern convergence with Canyon Road, and two years later a bronze-paneled, bowl-topped column and pergola replaced the original memorial plaque. The last dedication of the decade, Gold Star Hill, took place in 1934. Unique among the monuments to honor Utah's fallen soldiers, this assemblage of modest bronze markers honored the group whose efforts had brought the park into existence.[13] Memory Grove was now ostensibly complete and would stand for the next seven years as a reminder of what was then known as the "war to end all wars."

NOTES

Originally published in the *Utah Historical Quarterly* 76 (Spring 2008): 148–67.

1. Jane Jacobs, *The Death and Life of Great American Cities* (New York: Random House, 1961), 89.
2. Utah American Revolution Bicentennial Commission, "The Early History of City Creek Canyon," 1976.
3. Jack Goodman, *As You Pass By: Architectural Musings on Salt Lake City* (Salt Lake City: University of Utah Press, 1995), 80–82.
4. Lisa Thompson, "Renovating Memorial House: The Power of Partnerships," *Utah Preservation* 3 (1999): 45.
5. Service Star Legion, *The Story of the Service Star Legion* (Salt Lake City: Utah Chapter, Service Star Legion, 1932).
6. American Battle Monuments Commission, *American Armies and Battlefields in Europe* (Washington, D.C.: U.S. Government Printing Office, 1938), 473.
7. Service Star Legion, *The Story of the Service Star Legion*.
8. Service Star Legion, *Memory Park 1920–1932* (Salt Lake City: Utah Chapter, Service Star Legion, 1932).

9. *Salt Lake Tribune*, June 13, 1926.

10. Utah American Revolution Bicentennial Commission, "The Early History of City Creek Canyon."

11. William Love, *Points of Interest in Memory Grove Park* (Salt Lake City: Memory Grove Foundation, November 1996); and Josef Muench, *Salt Lake City: A Pictorial Study* (New York: Hastings House, 1947), 32.

12. *Salt Lake Tribune*, June 13, 1927.

13. Service Star Legion, *The Story of Service Star Legion: Past, Present and Future* (Salt Lake City: Utah Chapter, Service Star Legion, 1951), 23. The whereabouts of the original World War I memorial marker as well as the circumstances surrounding its replacement are unfortunately lost to history.

CONTRIBUTORS

James B. Allen taught at Brigham Young University from 1963 until his retirement in 1992. He was also assistant church historian (half-time) from 1972–1979, chair of the BYU Department of History from 1980–1986, and Lemuel H. Redd, Jr. Professor of Western American History from 1986–1992.

Leonard J. Arrington (1917–1999) is best known for his seminal work on Mormons and Utah, *Great Basin Kingdom: An Economic History of the Latter-day Saints, 1830–1900,* published in 1958. He helped organize the Mormon History Association and served as its first president from 1966–1967. He taught at Utah State University and Brigham Young University and served as LDS church historian from 1972–1982.

Kerry William Bate is the author of *The Women*, published by University of Utah Press in 2016, which traces four generations of Mormon women in southern Utah.

Marcia Black helped research and write "Soldiers, Savers, Slackers, and Spies: Southeastern Utah's Response to World War I" while attending the College of Eastern Utah. She received her bachelor's degree in education from Southern Utah University. She currently teaches in Logan, Utah, and has three children.

Timothy Hearn is a partner and general counsel with the law firm of Dorsey & Whitney LLP in Minneapolis, Minnesota. Mr. Hearn, who has a BA in history from Brown University and a JD from Harvard Law

School, is a lifelong student of history and had the good fortune to co-author the article on Bishop Paul Jones while studying for the bar.

Andrew Hunt is a professor of history at the University of Waterloo in Ontario, Canada, and director of the Tri-University Graduate Program in History. He received his PhD in history from the University of Utah and has authored several books, including the historical mystery novel *City of Saints.*

Brandon Johnson earned his PhD in history from the University of Chicago. He lives in Virginia, where he is researching the emotional effects of war on American soldiers in the twentieth century.

William G. Love is a graduate of Weber State University, where he worked as an assistant processor in Special Collections. He has also worked for the Aerospace Heritage Foundation of Utah, at the Hill Aerospace Museum, as an archival technician.

Robert S. McPherson is a professor of history at Utah State University Eastern–Blanding Campus and has written extensively about the people and cultures of the Four Corners region. He has served on the Utah State Board of History for eight years and the Board of Editors for the *Utah Historical Quarterly* for twenty years.

Miriam B. Murphy (1933–2013) graduated from the University of Utah with a degree in English literature and worked at the Utah State Historical Society as associate editor of the *Utah Historical Quarterly* from 1970 to 1997. She authored many articles on Utah history and the book, *A History of Wayne County* for the Utah Centennial County History Series.

Joerg A. Nagler is a professor of history at Friedrich Schiller University in Jena, Germany. He served as a cultural adviser at the U.S. Embassy in Bonn, as a researcher at the German Historical Institute in

Washington, D.C., and as a visiting professor at both the University of Maryland and Simon Fraser University in Vancouver, B.C. His books include *National Minorities in the War: "Enemy Aliens" and the American Home Front during the First World War,* published in 2000.

Helen Z. Papanikolas (1917–2004) was a daughter of Greek immigrants to Utah. Ms. Papanikolas devoted her life to documenting, writing, and promoting the study of the immigrant experience in Utah and the American West. Her 1954 article, "The Greeks of Carbon County," pioneered the study of ethnic history in Utah and led to her books, *Toil and Rage in a New Land: The Greek Immigrants of Utah* and *The Peoples of Utah*, published in 1976.

Allan Kent Powell received his PhD in history from the University of Utah and was employed for forty-four years at the Utah State Historical Society, where he served as senior state historian and managing editor of the *Utah Historical Quarterly* from 2002 to 2013.

Richard C. Roberts is professor emeritus at Weber State University. He is the author of *Legacy History of the Utah National Guard from the Nauvoo Legion Era to Enduring Freedom*, published in 2003, and co-author, with Richard W. Sadler, of *A History of Weber County*, published in 1997 as part of the Utah Centennial County History Series.

John Sillito is professor emeritus at Weber State University. He is a longtime student of the Left in Utah and co-author, with John S. McCormick, of *A History of Utah Radicalism: "Startling, Socialistic, and Decidedly Revolutionary"* (Utah State University Press, 2011), which received the Utah State Historical Society's Frances A. Madsen Best Book Award in 2012.

David L. Wood lives in South Jordan, Utah, and is professor emeritus of history at California State University Northridge, where he was coordinator of the American Indian Studies program.

INDEX

Numbers in *italics* refer to illustrations and tables.

American Plan, 361
American Red Cross. *See* Red Cross
Anderson, Nels, 377, 391–92
Anderson Tower, 395–96
anti-German-American sentiment:
    German language and, 220;
    L. H. Farnsworth and, 109–11;
    in southeastern Utah, 144–46;
    Utah government and, 220–21;
    Utah newspapers and, 213–14
anti-German sentiment, 144–46,
    226–28, 243, 249
anti-picketing bill, 353–54
anti-Semitism, 157
antiwar Utahns, 284–85
Arivaca, Arizona, 15
Armistice Day celebration in Utah,
    255, 304–5
Army, U. S.: African American
    recruitment by, 195–96;
    criticism of, 19–20; Gosiute
    uprising and, 268–69; Utah
    recruiting for, 11
Arns, Lieutenant Carl H., 15
arrowheads and influenza, 331–32
artillery battery makeup, 45–46
Ashton, Wilford P., 66
Asian immigrants in Utah, 187, 197.
    See also Japanese immigrants;
    Japanese immigrants in Utah
auto mechanics, female, 75
Avgikos, Tom, 194, 202
Axelson, Sheldon, 66

Baker, Newton C., 20
Balkan immigrants in Utah, 187
balloon observation, 60, 63, 64–65
Balser, Claud, 163, 167–68
Balser, Leo, 163, 167–68, 183
Bamberger, Simon (gover-
    nor): election of, 3, 157, 343;

German-American com-
    munity and, 215; governing
    years of, 128; in his office, *128*;
    National Guard recruitment
    and, 26, 97–98, 120–21; in San
    Juan County, 142; unions
    and, 353; Utah Committee on
    Woman's Work in the World
    War and, 94; Utah Council
    of Defense and, 93, 115, *128*;
    welcome home speech of, 43;
    women's contributions and,
    142; women volunteer com-
    mittee and, 74
Barnes, Frank, 147, 149
Bassett, Freeman, 15
Battery A, 1st Utah Field Artillery,
    9–10
Battle of Casa Piedra, 15–16
Battle of the Bulge, 52–53
Battle of the Cow, 15–16
Beatty, T. B., 300, 307–8
Beobachter (Salt Lake City German-
    language newspaper): attack
    on, 221–22; call for suppression
    of, 218–19; demonstration of
    loyalty in, 216; German patrio-
    tism in, 207–9, 218–19; history
    of, 207; struggles to publish,
    111, 219; Utah German life
    reported in, 207–25; warning
    against, 110–11; war specula-
    tion in, 207
Bettilyon, Mabel, 82, 89
"big push" by United States, 59–60
"Birds in a Barbed-Wire Cage"
    (article), 239
Black 10th Cavalry, 8
Black Tom explosion, 226, 227
Bourne, E. LeRoy, 40–41
Brandeis, Erich, 238–39, 248

of, 356; at Fort Douglas internment camp, 236, 238–40; free speech fights and, 356–57; labor unions against, 360; national convention of, 346; Park City strike and, 353; prosecution of, 348; Socialist party in Utah and, 356–57; tactics of, 345, 356–57

Japanese immigrants: citizenship of, 201–2; citizenship denied veterans, 199
Japanese immigrants in Utah: American Legion and, 200; prejudice against, 200–201; war experiences of, 193; war fundraising by, 191
Jenkins, Colonel John M., 18
Jensen, W. F., 102–3
Jones, Paul (Episcopal bishop): arrival in Utah by, 280; call for resignation of, 286–87; call for tolerance by, 294; early life of, 281; Episcopal laymen and, 290–91; motivations for resignation, 289–90; pacifism of, 282–84, 286; resignation of, 287–88; response to call for resignation, 287–88; socialism and, 280–82, 294; Socialist party and, 294–95; vindication of, 295; wife's influence on, 296
Jorgensen, Fred, 46–47
Jouflas, T. H., 189–90

Kanarraites' personal experiences: Balser, Claud, 163, 167–68; Balser, Leo, 163, 167–68, 183; Davies, Bessie, 162–63; Davies, Elmer, 162–63, 174, 182; Davies,

Phebe Reeves, 162; Davis, James Lorenzo "Rens," 160, 161; Davis, Leon, 160–61, 165–67, 178, 180; Davis, Lorenzo Wendell "Wennie," 162; Davis, Wallace, 160, 161; Piatt, Grant, 168, 180; Roundy, George E., 159, 178; Roundy, James Lorenzo, 168, 182; Roundy, Jesse, 159; Roundy, Jesse C., 159, 167, 176; Roundy, Joel. J. "Dode," 167, 176; Roundy, Marion, 162, 183; Roundy, Sarah Catherine "Kate," 169–70, 176; Stapley, Elizabeth, 176; Stapley, Harriet Berry "Hattie," 163, 169; Stapley, Leland C., 56–57, 63, 159, 163–65, 178–79; Stapley, Lenna, 160, 162, 171; Stapley, William B., 162, 175; Williams, Kumen B., 161, 178; Williams, Wells, 159, 165, 168, 178–79; Wilson, Maryanne Campbell, 157, 177; Wood, Jewett, 161; Woodbury, Gene, 159
Kanarraville: civil liberties in, 173–74; demographics of, 156; disillusionment with U.S. in, 174–77; first war fatalities from, 163; LDS Church in, 167–73, 176, 180; liberty Loans in, 159–61, 179; men of in WWI, 181–82; military draft in, 56, 158–63, 177–78; volunteerism in, 159
Karous, Rose, 84–85
Kelley, Hugh, 67–68
Kelley, Jim, 68
Kennedy, O. A., 351–52
Kessler, Wilhelm, 211–12
Kim, Kil Seurk, 190
Kindsvatter, Peter S., 53